W9-BGT-097

TARGET TEHRAN

How Israel Is Using Sabotage, Cyberwarfare, Assassination—and Secret Diplomacy—to Stop a Nuclear Iran and Create a New Middle East

YONAH JEREMY BOB

AND

ILAN EVYATAR

Simon & Schuster

NEW YORK LONDON TORONTO
SYDNEY NEW DELHI

Simon & Schuster
1230 Avenue of the Americas
New York, NY 10020

First Simon & Schuster hardcover edition September 2023

Manufactured in the United States of America

1 3 5 7 9 10 8 6 4 2

Library of Congress Cataloging-in-Publication Data

Names: Bob, Yonah Jeremy, author. | Evyatar, Ilan, author.
Title: Target Tehran : how Israel is using sabotage, cyberwarfare, assassination—and secret diplomacy—to stop a nuclear Iran and create a new Middle East / Yonah Jeremy Bob and Ilan Evyatar.
Other titles: How Israel is using sabotage, cyberwarfare, assassination—and secret diplomacy - to stop a nuclear Iran and create a new Middle East
Description: First Simon & Schuster hardcover edition. | New York : Simon & Schuster, 2023. | Includes bibliographical references and index. |
Summary: "Drawing on confidential sources in Mossad, Israel's equivalent to our CIA, Bob and Evyatar, reporters for The Jerusalem Post, tell the remarkable story behind the most stunning development in the Middle East in recent years: the Abraham Accords that normalized relations between Israel and the UAE, Bahrain, Morocco, and Sudan. They show how Israel used sabotage, assassination, cyberwar—and diplomacy—to forge a new Middle East, uniting Israel with Sunni Arab nations in a determined, and so far successful, effort to delay Iran's development of a nuclear weapon"—Provided by publisher.
Identifiers: LCCN 2023020974 | ISBN 9781668014561 | ISBN 9781668014578 (trade paperback) | ISBN 9781668014585 (ebook)
Subjects: LCSH: Israel. Mosad le-modiʻin ṿe-tafḳidim meyuḥadim. | Espionage, Israeli. | Nuclear weapons—ran. | Israel—Foreign relations—Middle East. | Middle East—Foreign relations—Israel.
Classification: LCC UB251.I78 B63 2023 | DDC 327.125694056--dc23/eng/20230616
LC record available at https://lccn.loc.gov/2023020974

ISBN 978-1-6680-1456-1
ISBN 978-1-6680-1458-5 (ebook)

For want of strategy an army falls,
but victory comes with much planning.

BOOK OF PROVERBS 11:14
MOSSAD'S MOTTO

CONTENTS

PRIMARY CAST OF CHARACTERS

ISRAEL

Yossi Cohen Mossad chief from 2016 to 2021; a transformative figure in Israel and possible future candidate as prime minister, he was the architect of Israel's covert war against Iran and a key player in the negotiations leading to the Abraham Accords.

Meir Dagan Mossad director from 2002 to 2011, known for a doctrine of "divine intervention" aimed at continuously pushing back Iranian progress toward a nuclear bomb and made some preliminary breakthroughs which later served as an early foundation for the Abraham Accords.

Tamir Pardo Mossad director from 2011 to 2016, focused primarily on intelligence collection and assessment, though there were still attack operations during his era.

David Barnea Mossad director from June 2021 to the present, a protégé of Cohen and architect of the campaign in 2022 to assassinate Iranian IRGC officials and nuclear scientists.

Benjamin Netanyahu Israeli prime minister from 1996 to 1999, 2009 to June 2021, and again from December 2022 to the present, appointed Cohen his national security adviser and then Mossad chief.

Naftali Bennett Israeli prime minister from June 13, 2021, to June 30, 2022, continued assassination operations and expanded the Abraham Accords to include regional missile defense.

Ehud Olmert Israeli prime minister from 2006 to 2009, authorized Dagan's anti-Iranian campaign and initiated some early contacts with Sunni Arab countries.

Yair Lapid Israeli prime minister from June 30, 2022, to December 2022 as well as foreign minister from June 13, 2021, to June 30, 2022; expanded the Abraham Accords.

Ron Dermer close personal adviser to Benjamin Netanyahu and, as Israel's ambassador to the United States from 2013 to 2021, one of the architects of the Abraham Accords.

David Meidan former senior Mossad official.

Sima Shine former Mossad Iran analysis desk chief.

Meir Ben Shabbat Benjamin Netanyahu's National Security Council chief from 2017 to 2021.

Ronen Levy (code name: "Maoz") former Israeli intelligence agent who worked for Meir Ben Shabbat on the Sudan and Morocco negotiations and whose identity was only unmasked in December 2022 when he became Israel's Foreign Ministry director-general.

Yarden Vatikai senior public relations aide to Benjamin Netanyahu in designing the "reveal" of the theft of Iran's nuclear archives.

IRAN

Ayatollah Ali Khamenei Supreme Leader of Iran since 1989.

Mohsen Fakhrizadeh the father of Iran's nuclear program from the 1990s to his assassination in 2020.

Qasem Soleimani chief of the Quds Force of Iran's Islamic Revolutionary Guard Corps and Iran's second most powerful man, assassinated in January 2020. The IRGC is the regime's elite 190,000-member military and security force. The Quds Force is responsible for overseas operations.

Hassan Rouhani pragmatist Iranian president from 2013 to August 2021 and key supporter of the nuclear accord.

Ebrahim Raisi hard-line Iranian president from August 2021 to present, critic of the nuclear accord as too generous to the West.

Mohammad Javad Zarif Iranian foreign minister from 2013 to August 2021 and chief negotiator of the nuclear accords under Hassan Rouhani.

Hossein Dehghani Iranian defense minister from 2013 to 2017, a key figure in moving the secret nuclear archives and planning the security measures to keep them secure.

THE INTERNATIONAL ATOMIC ENERGY AGENCY

Rafael Grossi nuclear inspector chief from 2019 to the present.

U.S. OFFICIALS

The authors interviewed dozens of top current or former U.S. cabinet officials, negotiators, CIA chiefs, and advisers from the Biden and Trump administrations as well as others for this book. Some appear in a list before the Notes, while some appear in the text or the Notes.

SUNNI RULERS/OFFICIALS

Crown Prince Mohammed Bin Salman (MBS) de facto ruler of Saudi Arabia since June 2017.

Crown Prince Mohammed Bin Zayed (MBZ) de facto ruler of the United Arab Emirates since 2014, and since May 2022 the president of the Emirates.

Yousef Al Otaiba UAE ambassador to the United States and chief UAE negotiator of the Abraham Accords.

Omar al-Bashir ruler of Sudan from 1989 to 2019, maintained close relations with Iran, deposed in a coup in 2019.

Abdel Fattah al-Burhan de facto ruler of Sudan since 2019, who shifted away from relations with Iran toward normalization with Israel in October 2020.

Mohamed Hamdan Dagalo Sudanese warlord considered to be the military power behind Burhan.

TARGET TEHRAN

INTRODUCTION

A team of agents under the command of the Mossad, Israel's famed intelligence service, pulled off one of the most spectacular exploits in the entire history of espionage on the eve of January 31, 2018. After months of meticulous planning, endless hours of sophisticated electronic surveillance, and the risky infiltration of Israeli agents into Iran, the Mossad team broke into the secret warehouse where Iran's nuclear archive, containing the full record of its efforts to become a nuclear weapons power, was kept. Working through the night, the Mossad team loaded the archive onto trucks and, avoiding the watchful eyes of the Islamic Republic's security apparatus, smuggled it across one of Iran's porous borders and eventually to Israel.

The heist was one of the most sensational of many Israeli operations against Iran, a country that since its Islamic Revolution of 1979 has been Israel's most powerful and dreaded enemy. Paradoxically, Iran under its former leader, Shah Mohammad Reza Pahlavi, had for years been a rare friend of Israel in the otherwise almost entirely unfriendly Middle East. But following the revolution that deposed the Shah, the country's new Supreme Leader, the Ayatollah Ruhollah Khomeini, declared the annihilation of what he called "the Zionist entity" to be a goal of the new Islamic state. In the mid- to late 1990s, Iran began a concerted effort to develop nuclear weapons, a move seen by Israel as an existential threat. Since then, successive Israeli governments and successive chiefs of the Mossad have made foiling Iran's nuclear program a priority, one that has involved an array of measures—sabotage operations against its various nuclear installations, assassinations of its scientists and important personnel, diplomatic overtures to nations in the region, as well as the spectacular theft of its nuclear archive in 2018.

The 2018 operation provided vital intelligence for the Mossad in planning future strikes at the heart of Tehran's nuclear program. In addition, there were its diplomatic consequences, which went well beyond the collection of new information. The revelation of the archive's contents showed that Iran had been lying for years to the international community about its nuclear program, falsely claiming that it was only for civilian use. This disclosure led the International Atomic Energy Agency, the Vienna-based U.N. group charged with inspecting and reporting on Iran's nuclear program, to step up its demands for its inspectors to have greater access to Iranian facilities. Most important perhaps, it gave then president Donald Trump, informed by a delighted Israeli prime minister Benjamin Netanyahu of the information derived from the archive, the justification he needed to withdraw from the nuclear accords with Iran signed by the Barack Obama administration in 2015. According to that deal, Iran agreed to stop its nuclear development and the U.S. agreed to drop economic sanctions it had placed on the regime.

This book tells what until now has been a secret story—the decades-long effort led by the Mossad, Israel's intelligence agency, to prevent Iran from becoming a nuclear power. It will start with a daring theft of the entire record of Iran's nuclear weapons program, carried out in Tehran in 2018 under the very noses of Iran's security services, a remarkable exploit that exposed Iranian cheating for the entire world to see. The story will then flash back to the beginnings of Iran's concerted effort to make a nuclear bomb and to the multifaceted actions taken by Israel to stymie that effort. Along the way, we'll tell the full and closely related story of the Abraham Accords, the landmark set of agreements signed in 2020 by which Israel established diplomatic relations with several Muslim countries, forming a new alliance aimed at combating the Iranian threat. The Accords have continued to reap new fruit even as Saudi Arabia appears to be enhancing its dialogue with both Israel and Iran.

It is a story of espionage, sabotage, assassinations, and secret diplomacy every bit as exciting as such television thrillers as *Homeland, Fauda,* and *The Black List.* But this is not a work of fiction. It is the true story of the Mossad, formally the Institute for Intelligence and Special Operations, and its behind-the-scenes programs. It is based on numerous sources available to the two of us, Yonah Jeremy Bob and Ilan Evyatar, investigative reporters who have covered national security issues in Israel and the country's relations with its neighbors for many years. We had extensive access to Yossi Cohen, the head of the Mossad from 2016 to 2021, who planned and directed many of the operations that are the focus of this book, including much of the secret diplomacy that led to the Abraham Accords. We also had access to former Mossad directors Meir Dagan and Tamir Pardo, Israeli prime ministers, to many other Israeli intelligence operatives past and present, as well as to many American officials from the administrations of Donald Trump and Joe Biden who played key roles in the story.

The events recounted in *Target Tehran* were truly historic in their scope and impact, and the book provides the fullest and most richly detailed account of those events available in any other reporting. With Cohen at the center of the narrative, it describes the hybrid operations by which the Mossad waged its anti-Iranian war, including targeted assassinations of Iranian nuclear scientists, infiltrations into Iranian territory, the use of cutting-edge technologies, cyberattacks and drones to sabotage Iran's nuclear sites, as well as cooperation with the United States in the killing of Iranian military commanders.

The narrative also keeps the bigger picture in view, a picture involving not only Israel's goal of stopping Iran from getting nuclear weapons, but also the broader mission of preventing it from providing sophisticated weaponry to other countries and groups in the region. These include militias in Syria, Iraq, and Yemen as well as Hezbollah in Lebanon and Hamas and Islamic Jihad in Gaza, the Iranian-supported proxies who share Tehran's ultimate, oft stated goal of annihilating the Jewish state. Part of that bigger picture from Israel's point of view has always been its effort to win over other countries in the region and across the world to its side in its confrontation with Iran, and especially to maintain and nurture a special relationship with the United States, a relationship that at times was strained by differences over how best to deal with the Iranian nuclear challenge. This was especially true during the Obama administration and is true now with the new Netanyahu government which has attracted negative global attention for attempts to overhaul the Israeli judiciary and includes a cast of ministers making provocative statements on Palestinian issues.

The account includes the Iranian side of the ongoing war, in particular how Iran's rulers advanced their goal of building their nuclear technology and how they responded to Israel's deadly efforts to set that goal back. The book describes Iran's reactions and tactics, its factional disputes, the operations of its tentacular security services, and the methods it used to hit back against Israel, including terrorist attacks on Israeli targets, cyber strikes, and the use of its proxies. The Iranian strategy has been to surround Israel with a "ring of fire"; Israel's goal has been to prevent that ring from closing around it. Iran arms Hezbollah with precision-guided missiles. In retaliation, the Israeli Air Force carries out strikes against Iranian shipments of missiles in Lebanon, Syria, and sometimes western Iraq.

Target Tehran focuses on the Mossad and Iran, but there is a backstory to Israel's efforts to defend itself against nuclear threats in the hands of its enemies. That story begins on June 7, 1981, when two quartets of Israeli F-16A fighter-bombers left the Etzion Air Base in the Sinai Peninsula, then occupied by Israel, on their way to strike and destroy the Osirak nuclear reactor southeast of Baghdad, Iraq.

In a statement the following day, the Israeli government enunciated the policy that it has followed ever since when it has faced what it deems to be a nuclear threat. Israel, the statement read, had been persuaded by "sources of unquestioned reliability," that the Osirak reactor was intended, despite statements to the contrary, for the production of atomic bombs. The "goal for these bombs was Israel," the statement continued, and then concluded with this warning:

> On no account shall we permit an enemy to develop weapons of mass destruction against the people of Israel. We shall defend the citizens of Israel in good time and with all the means at our disposal.

In an interview a few days later, Israeli prime minister Menachem Begin said, "This attack will be a precedent for every future government in Israel . . . every future Israeli prime minister will act, in similar circumstances, in the same way."

And so was born what came to be known as the Begin Doctrine, which has ever since guided Israel's policy on weapons of mass destruction in the hands of enemy states. It was tested once more in 2007 when Israeli jets bombed and destroyed a North Korean–built, Iranian-financed nuclear reactor in Deir a-Zor, Syria.

But while the doctrine is certainly Israeli, Israel's actions against other countries' nuclear installations is neither unique nor unprecedented. In the Second World War, British Special Forces and Norwegian resistance fighters conducted ground raids against a heavy water plant operated in Norway by Nazi Germany as part of a potential nuclear weapons program. The same installation was also bombed on at least two occasions by the American air force. In early 1945, American bombers targeted a Japanese nuclear weapons research facility. In 1964, during the administration of Lyndon Johnson, the U.S. considered both covert action and bombing attacks against China to prevent it from becoming a nuclear power, though the Americans eventually resigned themselves to the People's Republic obtaining atomic weapons and no attack was carried out. Iraq and Iran bombed each other's nuclear research facilities during the eight-year war between the two countries.

No country, however, has undertaken as sustained an effort as Israel, an effort that has focused almost entirely on Iran for the past twenty years and has been the Mossad's most important preoccupation. So far Israel's reported actions have delayed an Iranian breakout to an actual atomic bomb, but if Israel obtains intelligence to the effect that Iran is about to produce such a weapon, the Begin Doctrine will surely be invoked again, and Israel could well launch a massive military raid against the Islamic Republic, no matter the cost.

While Israel has been outspoken about Iran's nuclear program, it has maintained a policy of ambiguity about its own nuclear capabilities. It has never denied or admitted possessing nuclear weapons, saying only that it will not be the first to introduce them into the Middle East. Nevertheless, it has refused to sign the Treaty on the Non-Proliferation of Nuclear Weapons, to which Iran is a signatory, and it has also opposed efforts to create a WMD Free Zone in the Middle East. It has faced sustained criticism on this issue from the U.N., including in a General Assembly vote in October 2022.

Estimates of Israel's nuclear arsenal range from eighty to two hundred weapons that it can reportedly deliver via various land, air, and sea-based systems, including submarine-launched cruise missiles that give it a second-strike capability.

Because Israel lacks any significant landmass, nuclear weapons, according to foreign sources, are considered the centerpiece of its strategic deterrence, since it signals to adversaries that it would be willing to cross the nuclear threshold in the event of an existential threat. This policy has been called the Samson Option after the biblical figure who killed himself and thousands of Israel's enemies by bringing down the pillars of the Gazan temple where he was held captive.

According to foreign sources, the country's nuclear program was begun in the late 1950s at the instigation of Prime Minister David Ben-Gurion, who believed Israel needed an insurance policy in the event of a disastrous military setback. Israel managed to complete its program around 1967 with French assistance, despite the opposition at that time of the United States.

Some observers, including some Israelis, argue that Israel's war against Iran is both counterproductive and, in the end, bound to fail. They posit that if a tiny country like Israel could develop a nuclear weapon despite the opposition of the U.S., then an enormous country like Iran, with a population of over 80 million, will surely be able to do so as well. Others express the view that even if Israel's nuclear program deters potential invaders, paradoxically it also gives an incentive to countries like Iran to develop nuclear weapons of their own.

The Israeli counter to these arguments has been a diplomatic initiative, in which Cohen as head of the Mossad played a key role. It has been to build on a fear of Iran shared by Israel and several Arab countries to refigure the entire Middle Eastern balance of power. The crowning achievement of this long, painstaking effort was the highly publicized Abraham Accords signed at the end of the Trump presidency, and which the Biden administration supports and is trying to expand. Through the

Accords, Israel established diplomatic relations with countries that had blacklisted it, first with the United Arab Emirates, then with Bahrain and Morocco, and finally with Sudan, a country that had been close to Iran and unremittingly hostile to Israel. Ties have also been built up with the most important of the Gulf states, Saudi Arabia, although it has not gotten to the point of formal relations with Israel. Even as they dialogue with Iran, the Saudis continue to be motivated by the same fear of radical Shiite Iran and its allies that motivated the signatories to the Accords.

But while the Abraham Accords are hardly secret, much of the story of the Mossad's role in how they were achieved has not been told. It was the fear of a nuclear-armed Iran that led the Arab states to stop insisting that Israel solve the Palestinian problem as a condition of normal relations. That alone is a major shift, though the absence of peace with the Palestinians creates many other issues not covered in depth in this book. In addition, the moderate Arab countries have come to see Israel as key to their economic vision for the future—a future in which technology eventually will replace oil as the most important ingredient for success. The key, and perhaps surprising, role that Cohen and the Mossad played in this set of remarkable changes is recounted in *Target Tehran*. It involved traditional intelligence gathering and analysis combined with ongoing secret contacts arranged by the Mossad and involving many clandestine trips and meetings carried out by Cohen himself.

The book describes all of the elements, large and small, open and secret, audacious and routine, by which Israel has dealt with a situation faced by only a very small number of other countries in today's world: the determination of a much larger nearby country to destroy it. It provides the fullest account to date of the covert operations carried out by the Mossad, the analysis behind them, and the means used. The account here does not shy away from hard and profound questions about all of this, particularly whether the Mossad's tactical successes have achieved a strategic victory, or whether, at least at times, they've led to strategic setbacks. The idea is to recount the Mossad's exploits in all of their riveting detail, but also to reveal both the moral and the practical uncertainties that surround the clandestine operations of countries at war.

Chapter 1

THE HEIST

ON THE NIGHT OF JANUARY 31, 2018, THE SPIES, THE ANAlysts, the technicians, and the operations chiefs of the Mossad, the State of Israel's fabled intelligence arm, were gathered inside the agency's state-of-the-art situation room on the outskirts of Tel Aviv to oversee an operation that they all knew could turn out to be momentous for their country—or, if things went awry, disastrous. Yossi Cohen, the dapper chief of the agency, dressed in his usual crisply ironed white shirt, sat at a desk, keeping his eye on the time, while the whole room was in a state of tense expectation, waiting for him to give the order for one of the Mossad's most audacious operations to begin. On the surrounding walls, an array of plasma screens glimmered, as if waiting for the satellite video feed of the operation to appear on them, providing a real-time view of what was taking place on the ground hundreds of miles away. Cohen and dozens of Mossad agents had been working for days, almost without sleep. The moment had arrived.

At exactly 10:31 p.m., Cohen said, "Execute," carefully enunciating each of the syllables of the command, which set in motion a Mossad team poised for action in Iran, specifically in the Shirobad industrial neighborhood on the southern outskirts of Iran's capital, Tehran. Shirobad wasn't the kind of place you would imagine as the scene of a spy drama with international consequences. It was just a drab zone of corrugated-iron-roofed warehouses stretching as far as the eye could see. But on that night, two dozen selected Mossad operatives—most likely a mix of Israeli agents and Iranians opposed to the Islamic Republic's theocratic regime—were propelled into a swift, well-rehearsed motion. While Cohen watched the clock back in Israel, they broke into one of the warehouses, used high-temperature blow torches to penetrate a series of steel vaults, and began to remove files, physical and electronic, that contained the entire record of Iran's strenuous effort to become a nuclear-armed power going back to its beginnings nearly thirty years before.

Cohen watched the clock because time was of the essence. The team in Iran had exactly six and a half hours to find the vast amount of material they needed, load it onto trucks, and make their escape, or they would be discovered, and the mission, with all its months of meticulous planning—data analysis, risky intelligence gathering by agents infiltrated into Iran, and more—would come to naught, and two dozen lives could be lost to the tender mercies of Iranian justice.

It was a long night stretching into morning, but as the Mossad's top people watched on their screens in Israel, the team in Shirobad walked out of the warehouse with half a ton of hard files and compact discs—perhaps the largest physical heist of intelligence materials from an enemy capital in the history of espionage. Within hours, they were racing toward Iran's border, their movements camouflaged by empty trucks, decoys being driven on fake routes in several fake directions. Back in the situation room outside Tel Aviv, a sense of triumph mingled with a sense of relief. All that planning, money spent, and months of surveillance were paying off.

Back in Tehran, Supreme Leader Ayatollah Ali Khamenei and Mohsen Fakhrizadeh, who had served for decades as his nuclear weapons chief, hadn't a clue about what was going on in Shirobad, where they had secretly moved the archive precisely to keep it out of the hands of the Zionist enemy, the U.S., and the IAEA.

The Mossad's decision to go after Iran's nuclear archives had been made two years earlier, in January 2016. Cohen, newly appointed as the Mossad's chief, was summoned to the office of Prime Minister Benjamin Netanyahu, in the glass-paned inner sanctum known as the "aquarium" on one of the lower floors of a drab 1950s-era building in Jerusalem. The setting was not new to Cohen. He had been the prime minister's national security adviser since 2013. But now things were different. He was no longer just an adviser. He was now running one of the world's most powerful intelligence agencies.

"We need not only to convince the world that Iran lied about its nuclear weapons program—we need to *show* the world," Netanyahu told Cohen. The Mossad director understood exactly what his prime minister meant. The year before, in 2015, the United States and five other major world powers had, after a long and difficult negotiation, signed what its proponents believed to be a historic agreement with Iran by which Tehran agreed to limit its efforts to enrich uranium and give up its efforts to make a nuclear bomb, in exchange for a relaxation of the sanctions that had been imposed on the country by the U.N., led by the Europeans and the U.S.

Netanyahu, whether rightly or wrongly, thought the deal was a disaster. Among other things, he objected to an expiration date that was built into the agreement, such that in just ten years, some of the restrictions on Iran's nuclear enrichment program would be relaxed and they would end entirely by 2030, just fifteen years later, after which Iran would be legally entitled to fully resume its nuclear development program. Aside from that specific issue, Netanyahu simply didn't trust the Iranians to live up to their obligations. In addition to that, the signing of the deal had an immediate, very undesirable practical consequence for Israel. Its nonstop, aggressive, no-holds-barred program of sabotage, assassinations, and cyberattacks that it had been conducting against Iran's nuclear program for years would have to be severely toned down, or risk angering the country's indispensable ally, the United States. For all those reasons, Netanyahu and Cohen wanted evidence that would undermine the agreement and enable them to resume covert actions. That's why they wanted the archive. They believed it would demonstrate beyond any doubt that Iran had lied outrageously in the past about its nuclear activities—saying, for example, that they were only for civilian uses while concealing the military dimension from U.N. inspectors—and couldn't be trusted not to lie in the future.

Immediately after the meeting with Netanyahu, Cohen met with his top spymasters to begin planning to steal the archive. Among them was his deputy, Ehud Lavi, who had previously led the Mossad's Caesarea unit, which operates agents in enemy territory and runs a squad known as Kidon that carries out targeted killings. Also involved were David "Dadi" Barnea, a graduate of the Israel Defense Forces' elite special forces' General Staff Reconnaissance Regiment, Sayeret Matkal, and head of the Tzomet division, which recruits and handles sources; and Dr. Eyal Hulata, a PhD physicist who was head of the Mossad's technology division.

Following these meetings, Cohen returned to Netanyahu to present the plan to infiltrate a Mossad team into Iran and to steal the archive.

"Do they have a copy?" Netanyahu asked. The question had to do with the risk of the operation versus the benefit. If there was no electronic backup, Israel would both expose Iran's lies and deprive it of documents critical to its nuclear program, a double win, and therefore more justification for the risk.

"I don't know," Cohen replied, "but they are so sure that nobody knows about this archive that they may not have made a copy."

"You think they didn't put all this information on computerized files?" the prime minister continued.

Cohen responded, "Not if they believed that we could get at such computer files [using hacking capabilities]. Maybe they thought that hiding [only] the original paper files is the best defense."

The prime minister was pleased with what he heard.

He approved the mission.

The Mossad usually appoints a project manager for each special operation, but Cohen decided the archive project was so important that he would manage the operation personally. He ordered his analysts to redouble their efforts to find the location of the archives. "Just make sure you bring that material home," Cohen told them.

Every resource was mobilized for the effort, including military intelligence, which operates one of the world's largest listening stations. Iran is a big country, larger than France, Spain, and Germany together, and its nuclear installations are spread over numerous distant locations. "It would be easier to find a needle in a haystack," a former Mossad source said. "At least there you know where to start looking."

But the truth is that the Mossad wasn't really searching from scratch. The agency and allied intelligence agencies had penetrated deep into the Iranian establishment. Numerous Iranian agents had been recruited, including "Nasiri," the top deputy to Iran's nuclear chief, and many others. These resources had enabled the Mossad to acquire recordings from the highest echelons of the Iranian government; it had also hacked into the Islamic Republic's communications and computer networks. Starting in the early 2000s, the Mossad together with Military Intelligence had perfected a synthesis of human spying and signals intelligence, which they called HUGINT. One of the architects of this synthesis was Cohen, who had been given the Iran file from the then Mossad director Meir Dagan in 2004.

Mossad's penetration of Iran was so deep that Iran's former intelligence minister Ali Yunesi warned: "The Mossad's influence in many parts of the country is so vast that every member of the Iranian leadership should be worried for their lives."

Cohen's immediate predecessor, Tamir Pardo, told us that while he was aware of the existence of the archives, he did not know where they were when he left office in January 2016. By a month or so later, the Mossad's agents had discovered their location.

Meanwhile, there was another issue that Israel and the Mossad needed to take into account: the Israelis were well aware that the Obama administration had been the prime mover behind the 2015 nuclear deal, which it had defended against fierce criticism both in the U.S. and Israel. Given that, Israel had to ask how the administration and President Obama himself would react to an operation aimed at discrediting what the Americans had fought so hard to obtain. Though close allies who shared intelligence about terrorist threats, the U.S. and Israel were already at loggerheads over other issues, especially the continuing Israeli settlement of the disputed West Bank and the failure of Netanyahu to make progress in talks with the Palestinians. The Israelis didn't want to add another area of disagreement to the list.

Indeed, for Obama, the issue was personal and had been made all the more so when Netanyahu addressed a joint session of Congress a few months before the nuclear accords—formally known as the Joint Comprehensive Plan of Action (JCPOA)—were signed. Without coordinating his address with the White House, Netanyahu lambasted the agreement as a "very bad deal." The speech further exacerbated the bad blood between the two leaders. Many Israelis also felt that Netanyahu's unprecedented move was likely to cause long-term damage between Israel and portions of the Democratic Party.

Even at this writing in April 2023, after extensive efforts by the Biden administration to return to the 2015 nuclear deal (from which President Trump withdrew), it is an open question whether the Netanyahu-Cohen Iran gambles paid off. But brilliant or foolhardy, the daring scheme Cohen and Netanyahu hatched in 2016 was an astonishing covert achievement that decisively altered both the balance of forces in the Middle East and U.S. policy.

Whatever worries Cohen and Netanyahu might have had about the possible opposition by the Obama administration, preparations for the nuclear archive theft continued, secretly. The U.S. was kept out of the loop. Then, everything changed in November 2016 when, contrary to almost everybody's expectations, Donald Trump beat Hillary Clinton in the American presidential election. Many in the U.S. and around the world were alarmed and horrified by Trump's isolationist "America First" rhetoric and his hostility toward traditional U.S. allies in Europe. But Trump had campaigned against the nuclear accord. Whatever Israelis thought of Trump himself, the majority of Israelis from the political right to even the vast majority of the political left were thrilled that he would take a tougher tone with the Iranian regime. And not only them. The Sunni Arab states in the region, also rivals of Iran, were happy to have an American president ready to take their side in the conflict.

Israel's military intelligence chief from 2018 to 2021, Tamir Hayman, has told us that the Sunni Arab states are even more terrified of Iran than Israel is because, sitting just across the Persian Gulf, they basically border it, which Israel does not. Analysts and academics consider the sectarian rivalry between Persian Shiite Iran and the Arab Sunni Gulf states as deeper than that between Israel and the Islamic Republic. "The conflict today between Israel and Iran is in many ways 'artificial' and would end with the collapse of the clerical regime in Iran," one senior Mossad source told us. That, he said, would not be the case with the antagonisms between Shiites and Sunnis, which have existed for most of the history of Islam.

Netanyahu and Trump had known each other before, but their first official meeting as heads of state took place on January 22, 2017, only two days after Trump was sworn into office. The conversation was warm. Iran topped the agenda. The two made it clear to their respective intelligence chiefs—Cohen and CIA director Mike Pompeo—that they wanted unparalleled intelligence sharing between the two countries. They also agreed to coordinate operations against Iran.

In February, Pompeo met Cohen at the King David Hotel in Jerusalem with his wife, Susan, and at some point also visited Mossad headquarters outside of Tel Aviv. His first words to Cohen, with whom he had instant chemistry, were "you're even better looking than in our surveillance photos of you." (Multiple American officials have jokingly warned spouses not to be overly taken with the dapper Mossad director.) When Cohen introduced Pompeo to the Mossad's Iran team, Pompeo said that Cohen threatened to fire anyone who did not rapidly work well and share intelligence with Pompeo's CIA people.

A few weeks later, Cohen visited Pompeo at "the Farm," the nine-thousand-acre base in Virginia where the CIA trains its operatives in spycraft. Shortly after, Pompeo and his wife paid a reciprocal visit to Cohen at Mossad headquarters outside of Tel Aviv. From that point on, Cohen and Pompeo operated very much as a team professionally and personally. In one instance which Pompeo has revealed, he received an urgent call from Cohen, which he took on the tarmac of an airport in an unnamed European capital after going back to his plane which was equipped with "communications equipment suitable for a classified conversation with the leader of Israel's intelligence agency.

"The voice on the other end was calm but serious: 'Mike, we just had a team complete a very important mission, and now I'm having a bit of trouble extracting some of them. Can I get your help?' "

Pompeo recounted, "Whenever Yossi called, I took it. He did the same for me. . . . I was there to help our friends, no questions asked, no matter the risks. My people swung into action across the world. We connected with his team, and within twenty-four hours we had guided them to safe houses. Within the next two days, they were back in their home countries without the world ever knowing that one of the most significant clandestine operations ever conducted was now complete."

The relationship between the two was so close that when Cohen retired from the Mossad in June 2021, it was Pompeo, not the serving CIA director, who attended the secret farewell ceremony, even though Pompeo had been out of government for six months and had not been CIA director since April 2018 when he was nominated secretary of state.

While planning for seizing the nuclear archive took place in Israel, in Tehran, Ayatollah Ali Khamenei was confronted by a troubling situation, also having to do with Iran's nuclear program. Khamenei lived in the Beit Rahbar, the House of Leadership, on Palestine Street in the center of Tehran, where he followed a predictable routine. He started his workday at five with morning prayers. At the end of the day, before heading to bed, the tireless ruler of the Islamic Republic—at that point approaching his eighties—would take a stroll in the extended gardens around the residence, usually with one of 170 antique walking sticks from his collection, often to find a short stretch of peace to think through the issues of the day. Sometimes he would find some temporary relief smoking one of his favored pipes or tasting some of the caviar that he kept around in ample quantities.

Other than these indulgences, Khamenei had few comforts or riches on display in the House of Leadership compared to his counterpart Arab monarchs and other dictatorial heads of state. He was a deeply religious man who had only taken power after a public display of uncertainty about whether he deserved it or not, worried that he wasn't qualified to be the supreme leader of the Iranian theocracy. He was selected for that honor, first by Iran's Assembly of Leadership of Experts and then in a nationwide referendum in June and July 1989 following the death of Ayatollah Ruhollah Khomeini, the founder of the Islamic Republic. Among his first acts was an extraordinary self-effacing speech acknowledging that he had not reached the highest levels of religious scholarship expected of the Islamic Republic's Supreme Leader. "I always considered my level too low for this highly significant and crucial post," he said. But, he added, "They voted for me. There I tried, debated and reasoned to prevent the vote, but they voted."

He told the Assembly initially he would only take on the role of Supreme Leader on a temporary basis, but then, perhaps belying his display of modesty, he moved carefully and meticulously in his early years to form his own new bases of power. It took him years, before he was able to rule Iran with an iron fist. There are even rumors circulating to this day that six years into his rule, Khamenei had Ahmad Khomeini, the son and right-hand man of Supreme Leader Khomeini, killed by poisoning. He was ruthless, but never rash. He believed he was a rational, stable man; certainly, his gradual ousting of religious rivals and his fostering of a succession of Iranian presidents to head the country's secular government showed him to be patient and calculating.

The Israeli raid of some of Iran's most closely held secrets would take priority over all his other problems. But in the weeks and months before that, Khamenei had been thinking more generally about a new challenge his country was facing. In 2015, after much deliberation, he had signed the JCPOA with the United States and five other nations—China, Russia, France, the United Kingdom, and Germany. Now, he must have been wondering if it had been a mistake to sign the nuclear deal in the first place.

When he'd done so, he'd known that there were risks. Among them was that there were only eighteen months to go in the presidential administration of Barack Obama, which had pressed hard for the JCPOA and was strongly committed to it. As a result, Khamenei knew there was a possibility that a more hard-line, anti-Iran leader could soon take power in the U.S.

And now that is exactly what happened with the election of Donald

Trump. Khamenei's worst nightmare about the deal had become reality, though he was as angry with himself about this turn of events as he was with Hassan Rouhani, Iran's president, and its foreign minister, Mohammad Javad Zarif. Both were Western-educated moderates who had persuaded Khamenei to "drink from the poison chalice"—a phrase coined by Ayatollah Ruhollah Khomeini after he signed a peace treaty to end Iran's eight-year war with Iraq without having achieved victory—and to sign off on the accord.

The immediate benefit, Rouhani and Zarif had argued, would be to free Iran's sinking economy from biting economic sanctions imposed by the U.S. and Europe. Khamenei did agree, but he did so not only with misgivings of his own over the concessions his country had made, but also against the advice of his top advisers from the Islamic Revolutionary Guard Corps and, most important, from Qasem Soleimani, the powerful and influential commander of its elite Quds [Jerusalem] Force, the branch of the IRGC in charge of overseas operations and proxy forces advancing the Islamic Revolution.

But the man Khamenei relied on most to make his decision was Mohsen Fakhrizadeh, the father of Iran's military nuclear program and Khamenei's closest adviser. Fakhrizadeh had headed the AMAD Project, Iran's first attempt to acquire nuclear weapons, supposedly suspended in 2003 when, having seen the United States invade Iraq on the pretext that it was in possession of weapons of mass destruction, the Iranians feared they could be next. The Mossad had maintained surveillance on Fakhrizadeh for decades and once had him in its crosshairs in an assassination attempt, only for the operation to be called off at the last minute. Fakhrizadeh had assured the Supreme Leader that all the concessions made under the JCPOA could be reversed within months or even weeks—as easy as reattaching the centrifuges Iran was putting into temporary storage. These assurances helped persuade Khamenei to side with Rouhani and Zarif and to sign the deal.

But now Iran faced an American president who harbored a deep distrust of the Iranian regime, was contemptuous of the deal struck by his predecessor, and was threatening to wreck it. For the first time since the U.S. invasion of Iraq, Khamenei felt that the full fury of America could be unleashed on his regime. At that time, Fakhrizadeh had masterminded a brilliant program of concealment and deception. At a series of secret intensive meetings over eight days in August and September 2003, Fakhrizadeh and four key lieutenants gave orders to downsize AMAD's assets, but to preserve them at the same time. In a very real sense, it was these eight days which led to the birth of the Iranian nuclear archives which the Mossad would steal fifteen years later. But at the time, Fakhrizadeh's plan to hide the archives played out flawlessly.

He kept significant portions of Iran's operations frozen, but ready to be thawed out at a "safer" moment when the world would be less focused on Iran. Some operations that would have been too hard to conceal were stopped completely or were given a lower priority. Some elements of the military nuclear program were embedded into the civilian program, where their purpose could be obscured. Other parts of the program continued clandestinely at reduced levels so as to hide their footprint from the International Atomic Energy Agency (IAEA) and key intelligence agencies. In subsequent years, Fakhrizadeh continued to outwit the West, managing, for example, to conceal the major Fordow nuclear site until 2009.

In other words, Fakhrizadeh had been fooling and misdirecting the IAEA and many Western intelligence agencies for around fourteen years. When Trump was elected, Khamenei ordered that Iran's nuclear program should go even further underground, and Fakhrizadeh played from the same playbook as before, moving, relabeling, and selectively splitting publicized items from items that remained concealed. One of the steps he took, in conjunction with Khamenei and Iranian defense minister Hossein Dehghani, was to move the archives. The 2015 nuclear accord required Iran to give the IAEA full access to the record of its past nuclear activities, but they'd managed to conceal it. They were deeply worried that these documents, which told the entire history of Iran's nuclear program, were too exposed in their existing location and potentially accessible to IAEA inspectors and Western intelligence agents.

The defense minister and the nuclear chief selected Shirobad from a menu of potential locations, figuring that a dilapidated abandoned warehouse would stay below the radar of the Mossad and anybody else tracking the nuclear program. Fakhrizadeh oversaw which files needed to be moved, and how both the physical and electronic files should be stored. Dehghani, an Islamic radical with a long résumé of accomplishments—he had been among the hostage takers at the American embassy in Tehran in 1979 and later helped to found Hezbollah in Lebanon—provided security for the operation.

The plan was carefully crafted, such that when he took his evening strolls on the House of Leadership grounds, the security of the archive was one issue that most likely did not cross Khamenei's mind. It was, or so he thought, safe in the inconspicuous neighborhood of Shirobad, well protected, out of danger.

Except that what Khamenei, and apparently nobody else in Iran's leadership, knew was that the Mossad was tracking the movements of the key personnel in Iran's nuclear program, and was able to follow the transfer of the archive to Shirobad with little difficulty.

Still, the relocation of the archive in early 2017 posed a serious problem for the Mossad. They knew where it was, but they now needed to figure out everything else. Where in the vast collection of records—much too big for it all to be hauled away—would they find the materials that would expose Iran's past lies? How would they break into the warehouse where the archive was now kept without being noticed? How was the archive guarded? How would the Israeli team avoid detection? How would they disable the warehouse's security alarm? And how would they manage to escape undetected?

One key element in the picture that wouldn't change, however, was who was going to carry out the action in Iran. It was way too dangerous to try to infiltrate Israeli commandos. They would be far too conspicuous, and if they were captured they would likely be the objects of a horrible show trial and probably a public execution. Precisely because of that terrible risk, the Mossad had for years been cultivating relations with a wide range of local Iranian dissidents and minority ethnic groups. These have reportedly included the Mujahedin-e-Khalq, the People's Mujahedin of Iran, known by its acronym MEK. The MEK was a Marxist Islamic group that participated in the 1979 Revolution that toppled the Shah and brought the ayatollahs to power, but then went into virulent opposition, accusing the new government of establishing a dictatorship. The regime responded by arresting and executing an untold number of MEK's members.

At one point, the United States and the European Union both designated the group a terrorist organization, but nevertheless it reportedly received Special Forces training in the United States. In 2012, NBC News, quoting two senior Obama administration officials, reported that the MEK had played a role in the Mossad's assassination of at least five Iranian nuclear scientists. According to the report, the MEK units were financed and trained by the Mossad. Contacts with the group would have been maintained by Mossad's Tevel division. Tevel is in charge of liaising with foreign agencies and countries with which Israel has no diplomatic relations.

But first some critical information was needed, and, despite months of surveillance by the team inside Iran, the Mossad didn't have it. Cohen and his colleagues met to talk about their options. Cohen was coming to the conclusion that an Israeli agent would have to be infiltrated into Tehran, but he was well aware of the terrible risks that that entailed, for the agent first of all, but for future operations as well. If he, or she, were caught, torture and execution would be the inevitable result, and, of course, the operation would be blown. The discussion was long and heated. But finally, they decided: the operation couldn't go ahead with the information the Mossad had gathered to that point. An Israeli agent would have some of the technical know-how that the Mossad team in place simply didn't possess.

Who to send? The choice that was made remains a closely guarded state secret, but the decision was made for it to be a woman, on the grounds that a female roaming a quarter containing a top secret nuclear archive might attract less attention than a man. Cohen had a candidate in mind, a female Mossad agent who spoke fluent Farsi and had an engineering degree. How she was slipped into Iran cannot be disclosed for obvious security reasons. However, she was there for several days, looking like an ordinary local. She was always accompanied by a man, sent into Iran for the sole purpose of forming a couple, since in any conservative Islamic society a woman walking around by herself would attract attention. The couple made several visits to the area of the warehouse, each time with the woman dressed slightly differently, again so as not to become an object of curiosity on the part of local people, or, more important, the security guards who were posted at the warehouse during the day. While the woman was in Tehran, Cohen and the very few aides who knew what was taking place lived in nervous anxiety, worried almost sick that the agent would be discovered. And then, they were able to breathe a sigh of relief when she and her companion returned safe and sound. They carried with them intelligence that enabled the Mossad to proceed with the rest of the operation.

Getting new intelligence wasn't the only problem the Mossad faced. In its first years in office, despite its opposition to the nuclear pact, the Trump administration actually made a diplomatic effort to close what it regarded as the deal's loopholes. These included: extending the nuclear limitations imposed on Iran beyond 2030, adding limits to the ballistic missile program, putting restrictions on Iran's destabilizing adventurism in the region, and broadening the powers of IAEA inspectors to go "anytime, anywhere." With those negotiations ongoing, it would have been awkward for Israel to get into a major flare-up with Tehran over stealing its nuclear archives, or worse, having some of its agents caught. So, the final stage of intelligence collection at the new site continued, but the operation itself was frozen, to take place at some unspecified time when the conditions permitted it.

The necessary change came in the beginning of 2018 when Trump's position on Iran had finally evolved to being ready for a broader confrontation. A number of events led to that moment. Back in April and July 2017, pressured by his top cabinet secretaries and security advisers, Trump had certified Iran as being in compliance with the nuclear deal, a necessary formality that allowed the United States not to reimpose sanctions against Iran. But on October 13, 2017, the president, in an effort to create a paper trail for the eventual withdrawal he wanted, declined the certification formality. This did not restore the full sanctions regime on Iran, but from that point on, the drumbeat calling for withdrawal from the accord was constant and loud. CIA director Pompeo made clear the administration's intentions in his continuing communications with Cohen. There were no signs, Pompeo said, that the Islamic Republic would agree to extend the nuclear limits beyond 2030. The ayatollahs, he continued, had not changed their basic anti-American, anti-Western, and anti-Israeli posture, and under those circumstances, Trump did not want to be seen granting Iran a pathway to a nuclear bomb with only thirteen years left before the deal expired.

Then, on the sidelines of the World Economic Forum in Davos, Switzerland, in late January, Netanyahu revealed to Trump that the Mossad was about to launch an operation in Iran that would expose the depths of its nuclear mendacity.

"Is it dangerous?" the president asked Netanyahu.

The Israeli prime minister replied, "The danger is not negligible, but the outcome justifies the risk."

The stage was now set for the heist.

It was the culmination of more than two years of work in which hundreds of Mossad personnel—intelligence officers, decipherers, hackers, cyber experts, linguists, technology personnel across a wide range of operational disciplines—had been involved. They all worked, Cohen would later say in a rare public speech, "with resolve, determination, creativity and courage to get their hands on the truth about Iran's military atomic plans and the depth of the lies of Iran's leaders."

And so, on that night in the Mossad situation room, Cohen enunciated the three fateful syllables—"Execute." In Iran, the longest total lunar eclipse of the century was taking place, making for an unusually dark night. As it happened, a fog had fortuitously rolled into Tehran providing an additional shield for the operation. The fog was at its thickest at precisely the times the team moved in and then in the early hours of the morning when they were to make their escape.

It was cold, 24 degrees Fahrenheit. The team members wore dark thermals that kept them warm, but gave them the flexibility to move easily and quickly. They wore night vision goggles and were armed with pistols equipped with silencers in the event they met with resistance inside, or in case the operation was busted. The actual theft took place in the cramped confines of the warehouse. There, mounted on flatbed trailers that could be hauled by a truck and moved at short notice, were two shipping containers. Inside were the nuclear files stored in two rows of eight two-meter-high steel vaults facing each other with barely a meter in between them. The vaults had to be cut open and only the high-value contents removed, otherwise the haul would be too big to remove in the time the team had, and too large to fit into the trucks waiting to haul it away.

The operations team had rehearsed the heist countless times on a one-on-one model in a foreign country, whose identity is still classified. They had practiced every aspect of the operation from breaking into the warehouse to timing how long it took to cut through the vaults. In fact, the Mossad had procured the same model of Iranian-made safes used to store the nuclear archives, brought them to Israel, and then figured out the best way to break into them. And thanks in large part to the female engineer agent, as well as some other operatives whose work is still classified, they knew everything down to the last inch, including exactly where to look for the specific files they wanted. They knew where the alarms and security cameras were and how to disable them.

Exactly how the Mossad team pulled off some aspects of the break-in is still classified, but Cohen has described the theft as an *Ocean's Eleven*–style operation, after the Hollywood movie in which a gang of thieves steals $163 million from a Las Vegas casino vault. In the movie, the thieves splice into an ethernet cable to substitute a fake video for the live feed the security men think they're watching on their monitors. A similar tactic may have been used in the warehouse break-in, so that any remote surveillance would fail to detect that the warehouse had been penetrated. How did the Mossad team know exactly where everything was in the warehouse? Again, that is a closely guarded state secret, but intelligence experts surmise that the Israelis must have slipped a disk on a key, cable, or some other device on the inside to facilitate the hack. The alarm systems would also have been hacked using similar tactics. Some of the measures would have been prepared in advance, but some of them had to have been implemented by the team in place, presumably the first crew to move into the warehouse, specially trained to take on electronic defenses.

A break-in is usually an in-and-out job with just minutes to seize the target before security arrives. But in this instance, the Shirobad warehouse was only very lightly guarded, probably because the regime wanted to make the facility appear nondescript, of no interest, and a heavy security detail would have given it all away. The two security guards on duty would leave around 10:00 p.m. and not show up again until 7:00 the following morning. This meant that the Mossad's team had precisely six hours and twenty-nine minutes, from 10:31 p.m. to 5:00 a.m., to get into the warehouse, seize the archive, and get out in time to have a head start for the getaway.

At precisely 10:31, the electronics team took out the alarm system. Almost simultaneously, the break-in team then forced open the heavy iron doors of the warehouse and moved inside undisturbed. Other members of the team took up positions outside to make sure no one had spotted the break-in, while another crew got to work inside the warehouse. While the break-in went smoothly, there was a hitch. Within the past twenty-four hours, it turned out, things had been moved around. Months and years of intelligence collection and preparation, no matter how perfect, can be thrown off in an instant by a quirk of fate. The operation could have been called off like so many other still classified operations that almost happened but were canceled at the last minute. There was a flurry of tense consultations among Cohen, Lavi, and others, and then Cohen rolled the dice and gave the go-ahead.

The team's knowledge of the facility was so intimate that despite the changes, they were able to find what they were looking for without any significant delay. Using special blowtorches, heated to 3,600 degrees Fahrenheit, one of the crews burned through six of the thirty-two Iranian-made two-meter-high vaults, enabling another crew to begin extracting the files they needed, leaving the vaults containing less-important material untouched.

The main target was a collection of black binders that contained the designs of the bomb Iran wanted to build, but as they went through the vaults, the Mossad agents found a bonus: over a hundred CDs with 55,000 files and videos documenting the nuclear program, and a further treasure trove of photographs of secret experiments. All of this was loaded onto two trucks that left the scene at exactly 5:00 a.m. and headed on separate predetermined routes toward different points on Iran's four-hundred-mile-or-so border (it's in dispute) with Azerbaijan in Iran's west. Even as the trucks careened toward the border, agents riding in them began to take digital photos of some of the findings, sending them to Israel so that even if the team was captured, some of the intelligence would have reached its intended destination.

Back at the situation room, Cohen watched as the images were livestreamed onto the plasma screens, feeling as if he could almost touch the long-sought documents. A team of the Mossad's Farsi-speaking analysts and nuclear experts confirmed that the agents had found what the Mossad was looking for. Iran's military nuclear secrets were already in its hands.

But the operation wasn't over yet. The team still had to get out of Iran with half a ton of documents and compact discs.

Contrary to reports in 2018, after news of the raid broke, there was no cinematic pursuit of the team by the Iranian security police or the army. It was only after the break-in was discovered at 7:00 a.m., two hours after the trucks had left the warehouse, that a massive nationwide manhunt commenced. Khamenei, Defense Minister Amir Hatami, and Qasem Soleimani ordered Iran's land, sea, and air borders to be sealed, and thousands of secret agents inside and outside of the country were put on alert. The police and the army also began to search for the thieves who took the archive and of course for the archive itself. It was a nail-biting wait for the agents to exit Iran safely, with Cohen keeping the prime minister updated on an hourly basis.

The Israeli government has censored information about how the Mossad smuggled the documents out of Iran to Israel, after Israel revealed the archive theft to the world, but, nevertheless, some basic aspects were leaked by Israeli intelligence. The leaks showed, most importantly, that the Mossad was well prepared for the expected all-points Iranian manhunt. It orchestrated a complex decoy scheme to lead the

Iranians onto a series of wrong trails. Some of the team quickly dispersed to different locations throughout Iran. Other agents who had nothing to do with the theft were activated to draw attention to themselves while the real team got away. This put the decoy teams at significant risk.

According to intelligence sources whom we interviewed it is thanks to the substantial drug trade going over the Iran-Azerbaijan border that the operation succeeded. Azerbaijan lies on one of the major drug trade routes from Afghanistan—which produces 90 percent of the world's opium—through Iran and on to Europe. In addition to heroin processed from Afghan opium, the drugs smuggled across the border with Azerbaijan include *shisheh,* high-purity crystal meth produced in the Islamic Republic, which has a major drug problem of its own.

According to our intelligence sources, only two Mossad agents on each truck were reported to have remained from the original team when the trucks arrived at the Azerbaijan border. The necessary payments made to smugglers, the Mossad agents would have taken possession of the document trove, which arrived in Israel soon thereafter. Although the borders were on high alert for several hours between the time the Mossad agents left Shirobad and the time they got to the border, the porous nature of the Iran-Azeri frontier and, apparently, the drug traders' ability to compromise Iran's border security would have enabled Israel's agents to get through.

If Cohen were American, this might have been when he spiked the football in the end zone or at least high-fived the others in the situation room that morning. Instead, being moderately religious, he chanted a prayer of thanks and upon his return home kissed the Mezuzah (Jewish ritual item placed on doorposts as a symbol of a Jewish home and spiritual protection), and went into his house.

All the agents managed to get out of Iran safely, though Israeli military and intelligence sources confirmed exclusively to us that some had to be extracted, requiring the involvement of IDF intelligence, Special Forces, and aerial assistance, which suggests that Israel had to dispatch planes or helicopters to preassigned destinations in Iran where they picked up some members of the team and flew them to safety. Details of the rescues beyond these few facts remain classified.

Back in Israel, Netanyahu met with members of the team to thank them for their daring operation. "You have performed a magnificent service to Israel and the world," he told them.

Soleimani, Fakhrizadeh, and Hatami, the minister of defense, did not often get emergency calls around 7:00 a.m. They had lieutenants to whom they delegated the job of putting out the usual fires. But when the call came in that morning reporting on the theft—discovered by the Iranian personnel showing up for work at the Shirobad warehouse—it was clear right away that this was different. This was Iran's nuclear crown jewels falling into the hands of Iran's worst enemy. Fakhrizadeh immediately conducted an assessment of the Shirobad site to identify exactly what was stolen and what the impact would be. He also advised Khamenei and Iran's Foreign Ministry about how they might respond to the revelations contained in the files, besides, of course, issuing a generic blanket denial (which no one took seriously) about the files' authenticity.

The idea that truckloads of secret nuclear files had been driven out of Tehran under the nose of Iran's domestic security services and its feared Revolutionary Guards left even the cynical Khamenei astonished. Normally, Iran's Supreme Leader prided himself on knowing what to expect. Even when the enemy hurt him or Iran, the damage was usually temporary, because he ordinarily would have taken into account potential setbacks and made contingency plans for every eventuality. This was a rare moment where not even he had dreamed that a setback could occur.

Over the first few days and weeks, Iran kept the heist secret, though on February 10, Iran made an attempt to launch an attack against Israel from Syria, possibly in retaliation for the archive theft just eleven days earlier. An Iranian drone packed with explosives crossed the border into Israel before being shot down by an Apache helicopter gunship over the northern town of Beit She'an. In response, two quartets of F-16 fighter jets fired missiles at Iranian positions at the Tiyas Military Airbase from where Iran had launched the drone. It was, the Israeli military said, "the most significant strike" on Syrian soil since the 1982 Lebanon War. It was also the first time in nearly forty years that Israel lost a fighter jet in combat, when one of the returning F-16s crashed on the Israeli side of the border after coming under heavy Syrian antiaircraft fire. After decades of proxy conflict, and even though Israelis and Iranians were fighting in a third country (Syria) and not on each other's sovereign territory, this was the first-ever direct military clash between Israeli and Iranian forces.

Despite this encounter, Israel also kept quiet about the theft, though it did secretly provide some information obtained from the archive to the Americans.

In Iran, for Khamenei and his advisers, the main goal was to prevent Israel from being able to act on the intelligence it had seized. They hoped they could avoid any permanent strategic damage.

It would take a few months, but on April 30, 2018, the Iranians would find out just how futile that hope would turn out to be.

Chapter 2

DIVINE INTERVENTION

"KHOMEINI! ARAFAT!" AND THEN AGAIN AND AGAIN, "KHOmeini! Arafat!" bayed the crowd. It was February 1979, the Islamic Revolution had just toppled the regime of Mohammed Reza Pahlavi, the Shah of Iran, thereby radically changing the balance of forces in the Middle East. Yasir Arafat, the leader of the Palestine Liberation Organization, was the first foreign leader to be there, and took full advantage of his presence to make a show of triumphant solidarity with the new regime.

Wearing his customary checkered black-and-white keffiyeh and khaki battle jacket, Arafat stood on a balcony overlooking a leafy street in central Tehran. Next to him was the Palestinian flag; the words "Viva PLO" were daubed in red graffiti on the walls of the building, which, until just a few days before, had been the embassy of the State of Israel in the now defunct Imperial State of Iran. "Today Iran, tomorrow, Palestine," Arafat pledged as the crowd below chanted its support.

It's hard to overestimate the significance for Israel of this event. Iran, which had been a reliable ally of the United States and Israel, had now become the Islamic Republic of Iran, ruled by Ayatollah Ruhollah Khomeini, an austere cleric with a virulently anti-Western and anti-Israel ideology. Suddenly, this country of 80 million people with vast natural resources was proclaiming the U.S. "the Great Satan" and Israel "the Little Satan," a "nucleus of evil" marked for destruction. There couldn't have been a clearer symbol of the new regime's hostility to Israel than Arafat's receiving the acclamation of the crowd at what had been Israel's embassy. But to make the message even clearer, Khomeini himself publicly promised the leader of the Palestinian cause that after consolidating its strength, the Islamic Republic would "turn to the issue of victory over Israel."

And with that, a war that has now lasted more than four decades began.

Iran would go on over that long stretch of time to fund terrorist attacks against Israel, use its agents to attack Israeli assets overseas, and provide arms and money to proxy groups on Israel's borders, namely Hezbollah in Lebanon and Hamas and Islamic Jihad in Gaza. In the wake of the Syrian civil war, it would establish a military presence there as well. All of this was threatening to Israel, but the most existentially worrisome of all of Iran's actions came after Khomeini's death in 1989, when Iran began its enormous investment aimed at building nuclear weapons, as it said, "to erase Israel from the passage of time."

Ironically perhaps, as long as Khomeini was alive, Iran resisted the temptation to go nuclear, largely out of the Supreme Leader's belief, as he told his followers, that weapons of mass destruction were "inconsistent with Islam." From 1980 to 1988, Iran fought a brutal war against Iraq, whose leader, Saddam Hussein, did use such weapons. During that conflict, Mohsen Rafigdhoost, the minister in charge of Iran's Islamic Revolutionary Guard Corps and the official who initiated both Iran's ballistic missile program and the creation of Hezbollah, reportedly told Khomeini that he had plans to develop nuclear weapons. Khomeini was opposed. When Rafigdhoost made another attempt to persuade Khomeini to allow weapons of mass destruction after an Iraqi chemical attack, he was told, again, that such weapons were *haram,* forbidden.

Rafigdhoost interpreted this as a *fatwa*—a religious decree—against weapons of mass destruction. But while Khomeini's restraint has often been viewed as a sign of moderation on his part, it was in fact a tactical consideration. Khomeini wanted first, as he'd told Arafat, to consolidate the Islamic regime's grip on power and only later to create the means to export the revolution and project power beyond Iran. He feared that developing nuclear weapons too soon would endanger Iran at a time when it was vulnerable to attack and already embroiled in its war with Iraq.

Khomeini's successor, Ayatollah Ali Khamenei, had no such compunctions. During the time that Iran was ruled by the now deposed Shah, it had begun a civil nuclear program that had Israel's tacit support. Now, Khamenei ordered work to begin on upgrading that program into one aimed at a military nuclear capability. It's confusing that Khamenei also issued a *fatwa* against the production or use of any weapons of mass destruction. But Harold Rhode, a former American intelligence analyst and Middle East specialist who spent many years in Iran, explained the apparent discrepancy. Even more than some other cultures, the Persian culture, he said, has "perfected the art of deception"; an ancient Persian term *ketman*, or dissimulation, translates roughly as concealing and camouflaging one's true thoughts. The Iranians, he said, attach little meaning to words, and should be judged on actions, something that was, he added, often misunderstood by Western negotiators.

The Islamic Republic acquiring nuclear weapons was a nightmare possibility that Israel could not allow, and by the mid-1990s its leaders were warning that military action would be taken if the Iranian program was not stopped. They and Western intelligence services knew Iran was buying nuclear knowledge from the father of Pakistan's nuclear weapons program, A. Q. Khan, who ran an illegal side business selling technology and know-how to other countries. North Korea and Iran were paying him tens of millions of dollars for that knowledge. The Mossad's director at the time, Shabtai Shavit, would later admit that the agency had failed to correctly interpret Khan's actions and that, had it known what Khan was up to, the Mossad would have killed him.

Later, Israeli intelligence also found out that the Iranians were setting up a nuclear enrichment facility in Natanz—a site deep in the heart of the desert in Isfahan province that Israel would go on to target repeatedly. In 1996, two Mossad agents entered Iran as tourists and managed to bring back soil samples that revealed traces of nuclear activity.

On August 14, 2002, the National Council of Resistance of Iran (NCRI)—the diplomatic wing of the MEK—publicly revealed two important developments: one, that a heavy water plant was in operation in Arak in northeastern Iran, and two, that at Natanz, the Islamic Republic had built a plant eight meters underground with a two-and-a-half-meter-thick concrete roof to protect it from any possible military strike. It was there that arrays of centrifuges were in the process of producing low-enriched uranium, an early step in the process of producing the fuel needed for a bomb.

The discovery prompted Israel into a new, more intense phase in its efforts to sabotage the Iranian nuclear program. Just two weeks before the NCRI's disclosure, Prime Minister Ariel Sharon, the legendary military commander who, among other things, founded Israel's Special Forces and commando units, had appointed Meir Dagan as the head of the Mossad.

Sharon had come to power around eighteen months earlier amid the bloody turmoil of a Palestinian uprising known as the Second Intifada, and he believed that Israel had been too cautious in its response to the threats that faced it. Specifically on Iran, he wanted more than just intelligence on its nuclear program; he wanted action. At the time, the Mossad was headed by Efraim Halevy, whom Sharon considered too cerebral, more of a diplomat than an operations man.

Not that Halevy had taken no actions, though it's true that at the time he was more concerned about Iranian-backed terrorism against Israel than he was about the nuclear issue. Also, his strategy, to use a common metaphor in Israel, was to cut off the octopus's tentacles rather than to go for the head. Still, he did take steps aimed at countering Iran's nuclear weapons program. In 2002, under Halevy's leadership, the Mossad sent a letter to a German national, Gotthard Lerch, who was working for the Khan network supplying centrifuge blueprints to Iran. The letter warned Lerch of "grave consequences" if he delivered the blueprints to the Iranians. The blueprints weren't delivered. In another instance on Halevy's watch, an Iranian colonel, Ali Mahmoudi Mimand, a senior missile program engineer on Iran's ballistic missile program, was found dead in his office from a single gunshot to the head. No details were ever published, and no government or group ever took responsibility. But the operation has long been assumed to be an early targeted assassination carried out by the Mossad, to be followed by many others.

Still, Sharon wanted a Mossad leader more in his image, someone who carried a "dagger between his teeth," and like Sharon himself was daring in his thinking and eager to use the Mossad for actual operations, not just for gathering intelligence. Dagan was his man. Born in 1945 in the Soviet Union where his parents had gone from Poland to flee the Nazis, Dagan came to Israel as a five-year-old. He served in the IDF's paratroop brigade. In 1970, Sharon, at the time the head of the Southern Command, recruited him to head a new counterterrorism unit, Sayeret Rimon, tasked with breaking the Palestinian terror infrastructure in the Gaza Strip. Dagan soon became known for his unorthodox methods and his bravery—he was awarded a medal of valor for disarming a terrorist holding a live grenade. "Dagan's specialty is separating an Arab from his head," Sharon, not one to mince words, said.

Dagan would remain in the army for thirty-two years, rising to the rank of major general, before retiring in 1995. He took some time off to make a round-the-world jeep tour with his longtime friend Yossi Ben Hanan, another storied graduate of the paratroop brigade. Then, he served as a counterterrorism adviser to Benjamin Netanyahu, before heading Sharon's victorious election campaign and serving as his national security adviser. Finally, Sharon made him the Mossad's director in 2002.

Dagan was a man of contrasts: He was both a fighter and an intellectual. He could quote French poetry, loved to listen to Bach, and was a talented painter whose brightly colored subjects often came from the field—an Arab and his horse, an olive tree, an old man stringing worry beads, a horse and cart. The pictures borrowed heavily from the Land of Israel style of painters like Reuven Rubin and Nachum Gutman. But he was also a gruff and brazen officer, and in many ways, despite not being born in Israel, he was the quintessential *sabra* or native Israeli—a prickly pear, tough on the outside like the thorny shell of the fruit and soft on the inside like its sweet flesh.

Former CIA deputy director Michael Morell described Dagan as "someone you wouldn't want to get into a street fight with, but somebody you also wouldn't want to play a chess match against."

Leon Panetta, the CIA director during the last two years of Dagan's term as head of the Mossad, recalled in his memoirs the chilling advice he received from Dagan on a visit to Tel Aviv: "We're dealing every day with Al Qaeda," Panetta told him and then asked, "What would you do?" Dagan didn't hesitate.

"I'd kill them," he said. "And then I'd kill their families."

Preventing Iran from obtaining nuclear weapons capability quickly topped Dagan's agenda. He came up with a five-pillar strategy: political pressure, covert measures, counterproliferation of technological know-how, financial sanctions, and regime change. But that wasn't all. His "five pillars" also were grounded in the understanding that Israel couldn't go it alone and had to increase cooperation on the Iran file with the CIA and other Western intelligence agencies to keep Iranian nuclear ambitions in check. Dagan worked studiously on fostering such relations. Those efforts would culminate in a sophisticated cyberattack on Iran in a joint operation with the CIA and others that was discovered in 2010.

Dagan went far afield. He cultivated relations with Azerbaijan, a Turkic-speaking country that, as we've seen, shares a long border with Iran, whose population is about one-quarter Azeri. Sending Israeli agents into Iran is complex and dangerous, but an Azeri in Iran is never out of place. Israel sold the oil-rich Azeris billions of dollars in advanced military equipment, which earned it pretty much a free hand to do as it pleased along the border. Why did the Azeris, who are also Shiites and see themselves as the original Persians, cut such a deal? Rhode, the former intelligence analyst, explained: the Azeris are afraid that the Iranians want to sow discontent in Azerbaijan as a way of getting them to leave Iran alone. "Everything in Iran," he said, "is a game of three-dimensional chess."

Early on in Dagan's tenure, as he built up his staff, chose his people, and prepared the intelligence and technological capabilities to be able to penetrate Iran, the Mossad focused on supply chain attacks, meaning sabotaging or booby-trapping materials destined for its nuclear installations. The Iranians, for reasons of pride or security, often didn't announce or even admit to such incidents of sabotage, and Dagan made sure nothing leaked from Israel's side. But in the words of a top former military officer, "From 2003, they had a lot of cases where things blew up."

The Mossad's tactics were based on the Iranians' need to keep their nuclear program a secret, which often forced them to buy parts and equipment on the black market. This gave the Israelis a singular opportunity to sabotage the supply chains. The Mossad and other Western intelligence agencies set up a network of companies designed to sell defective or infected parts to the Iranians, and thereby to "poison" its atomic networks.

We were told by senior sources that the Mossad worked on a global scale, wherever the Iranians were looking for resources and technologies not available in Iran. "We followed where they were buying and looked at how to sabotage what they were buying without them even being able to know they had been hit when their equipment didn't work. We attacked their supply chain throughout the world," Ehud Olmert, then a senior member of Sharon's cabinet and later prime minister, told us. "Israeli agents were everywhere including in Iran to learn what the Iranians were doing," he continued. "If they were building a plant, [the Mossad] would learn how it was being built, how to identify its weak points and where it could be hit. We did a lot of operations like that and we reached a very detailed level of knowledge."

Following the 2002 exposure of the Natanz nuclear site and years of preparation, the first known sabotage attack on Iranian soil happened in April 2006 during Iran's initial attempt to enrich uranium at Natanz. Two electric transformers, which Iranian authorities said later had been manipulated, blew up, wrecking some fifty centrifuges. The centrifuges are believed to have been supplied by three Swiss engineers, part of A. Q. Khan's nuclear smuggling ring—but had been recruited by the CIA. The attack pushed back the opening of the Natanz plant by several months.

The covert side of Dagan's strategy was, in the spirit of his "five pillars" approach, highly multifaceted, including both large-scale attacks aimed at destroying equipment, but also narrowly focused on key Iranians and other individuals, who were killed in a series of targeted assassinations. The logic behind these controversial operations was twofold: one, to create a situation where Iran would lose the nuclear knowledge that, as Dagan put it in our later interview with him, "resides in the brains of people," and two, to deter scientists from participating in the nuclear program in the first place.

"Hit the operation of a centrifuge, and they'll soon find other centrifuges," Dagan told us. "But target a nuclear expert—and you've destroyed vast knowledge acquired through hard work, time, and money. That will take a long time to rebuild."

Dagan's deputy, the silver-haired, chain-smoking former commando Tamir Pardo, who would go on to be his successor, formulated the operational plan to target Iran's nuclear scientists. But while the international media pointed the finger at the Mossad for the several killings, the Mossad under Dagan's leadership never once admitted to any of the attacks attributed to it.

Instead, Dagan would tell confidants with a wink that the assassinations and other covert operations were "divine intervention," which he was sure would continuously delay the mullahs' plans to develop a nuclear bomb.

The first "divine intervention" occurred in mid-January 2007. Dr. Ardeshir Hosseinpour was a specialist in electromagnetics who worked on uranium enrichment. He also reportedly had been personally enlisted by Ayatollah Khamenei, until he was found dead in his apartment on the third floor of a building on Saheli Street in Shiraz in northwestern Iran. News of his passing was only released several days after his body was found. Though officially Hosseinpour's death was attributed to asphyxiation from a gas leak, Western intelligence sources pointed a finger at Mossad. The Stratfor private intelligence group said he had died of radiation poisoning and that the Mossad was responsible.

Next in line was Masoud Ali Mohammadi, a fifty-year-old professor of neutron physics at Tehran University, who worked with Mohsen Fakhrizadeh. On January 12, 2010, shortly after 7:00 a.m., he was killed when a booby-trapped motorcycle blew up as he opened the garage door under his house in the Qetariyah district of north Tehran. He had been about to leave for the university to give a lecture, as he did every Tuesday at the same time.

The blast was so powerful that it shattered windows in nearby buildings and led neighbors to assume at first that there had been an earthquake.

Iran denied, as it often did, that the targeted scientist had anything to do with its nuclear program, saying that he was an ordinary academic.

Nevertheless, Iran later arrested, charged, and hanged an Iranian citizen, Majid Jamali Fashi, a twenty-four-year-old former international kickboxer, supposedly for carrying out the assassination on behalf of the Mossad. In a televised confession, Jamali Fashi said he had been recruited in Istanbul, equipped with an encrypted laptop to transmit information about Iranian military sites on which he had gathered intelligence, and that later he flew to Azerbaijan from where he was taken to Tel Aviv for weapons training.

"They gave me some training during that trip such as chase and counter chase, chasing cars, getting information on a particular place, and sticking bombs under cars," Jamali Fashi said in his confession. He also claimed that it was on that visit that his handlers had given him the mission to target Mohammadi and that he had trained for the task on a model of the professor's house.

Later that year, on November 29—incidentally the same day that Pardo was announced as Dagan's successor—Professor Majid Shahriari, an elementary particle physicist and a member of the nuclear engineering faculty at Shahid Beheshti University in Tehran, was killed in a blast as he drove through heavy traffic along the Imam Ali freeway on his way to work. His wife and driver were wounded in the attack carried out by a team of motorcycle assassins who attached a magnetic bomb to his Peugeot 206. Shahriari had reportedly worked closely with the IRGC-run weapons group on the development of a nuclear warhead. Iran this time, acknowledging the death of a nuclear scientist, accused the Mossad of carrying out the attack together with the United States.

Another attack, this one unsuccessful, was attempted about twenty minutes later, using exactly the same method. The target was also a member of the faculty at Beheshti University, Dr. Fereydoun Abbasi-Davani, an assistant professor of nuclear engineering, who had been part of the same team as Fakhrizadeh and Mohammadi. The attempted hit took place in a square near the university in Tehran's affluent Velenjak district in the north of the city. Eyewitnesses said Abbasi-Davani had pulled the car to a stop and, along with his wife, scrambled out of it seconds before it blew up. They were both lightly wounded.

Abbasi-Davani, a member of the Revolutionary Guards who had served in the Iran-Iraq War, was sanctioned in 2007 by U.N. Security Council Resolution 1747 as a person "involved in nuclear or ballistic missile activities." He would continue to be a major force within Iran's nuclear program. Iran accused the Mossad and the U.S. of the attempted assassination.

Then there were a variety of other explosions and mysterious "accidents."

Some of these incidents involved Israel acting against a volatile mix of Iranian–Syrian–North Korean cooperation. Dating back to 2007, there was the disappearance of Iranian IRGC General Ali-Reza Asgari, who went missing during a stay in Istanbul, Turkey. Iran accused Israel of "disappearing" Asgari, but, in fact, he was a defector taken to the United States, where he was debriefed by the CIA and given a new identity. He revealed critical information about Iran's nuclear program that was relayed to the Mossad, which had been following him for years and had played a role in his defection.

Among Asgari's revelations was that Iran was funding the construction of a secret nuclear reactor being built at Al-Kibar in northeast Syria with North Korean know-how. The reactor, a copy of the Yongbyon facility in North Korea, was intended as a backup for Iran's heavy water reactor under construction at the time in Arak. Heavy water reactors produce plutonium, which is an alternative material for a nuclear bomb, which Iran wanted to have if it failed to make a bomb with enriched uranium. The Syrians hoped to receive a bomb in exchange for their participation in the program.

Asgari's knowledge of the facility was limited, but the Mossad followed up on what he had provided and proved that the heavy water reaction indeed was in operation and that it was about to go "hot."

That proof was obtained, according to *The New Yorker*, when a team of agents broke into the Vienna hotel room of the head of Syria's Atomic Energy Committee, Ibrahim Othman, and downloaded the contents of his laptop while he was at a meeting at the International Atomic Energy Agency.

"We had been following him for years," Pardo would say later. "He was never interesting, but then he made a mistake and had something interesting."

On September 6, 2007, an Israeli air raid destroyed the Al-Kibar reactor. That the raid was an Israeli operation was pretty much an open secret for years. But on March 21, 2018—just three weeks before it would go public with the nuclear archives heist—Israel finally publicly admitted that it had been behind the strike. The military declassified top secret intelligence reports and described in detail how eight warplanes had flown 270 miles to Deir a-Zor in eastern Syria on the banks of the Euphrates River and dropped eighteen tons of munitions on the site. It was an open threat to Iran, which had invested around a billion dollars in the facility. "The [2007] operation and its success made clear that Israel will never allow nuclear weaponry to be in the hands of those who threaten its existence—Syria then, and Iran today," tweeted Intelligence Minister Israel Katz.

The following year in Damascus, Syria, the Mossad, together with the CIA, according to *The Washington Post*, pulled off another daring hit that took out Hezbollah's military chief, Imad Mughniyeh, an archenemy of both Israel and the United States whose assassination was a major triumph for both countries. Among the many attacks he had orchestrated were the 1983 bombing of the U.S. embassy in Beirut that had wiped out the CIA station there, killing eight agency personnel, including its Near East director Robert Ames. Later that year, there was also the bombing of the U.S. Marines barracks in Beirut. In total, over three hundred people were killed in the two attacks, 258 of them Americans. Later in 1984, Hezbollah kidnapped the CIA's new station chief in Beirut, William Buckley. He was tortured and his body dumped in an unmarked grave.

Mughniyeh was also the mastermind of numerous terrorist attacks against Israeli and Jewish targets, among them the 1992 bombing of the Israeli embassy in Buenos Aires, and two years later the bombing of the AMIA Jewish community center in that city in which eighty-five people were killed.

The overall Israeli record under Dagan was impressive enough, but perhaps the most devastating, certainly the most technically sophisticated, of Dagan's "five pillars" strategy was the use of a type of weapon that had never been deployed before. This was the cyberweapon, which essentially involves installing software into an enemy country's computer networks either to steal information or, in its most devastating form, to cause malfunctions leading to physical damage, often severe. Previously, most of the sabotage in Iran's enrichment installations had come from supply chain infiltration. But in June 2010, the Iranians detected a computer worm called Stuxnet that had spread throughout its nuclear facilities and destroyed over one thousand uranium-enriching centrifuges at the Natanz plant. A Dutch intelligence agency mole had placed the worm in Iranian computers three years earlier, using a USB flash drive. In 2011 and 2012, two new types of malware were detected by the Iranians. One was Duqu, which gathers information from industrial control systems, the other Flame, which steals data from infected computers.

The Stuxnet cyber operation was code-named "Olympic Games," after the five-ring Olympic symbol, representing the five countries involved—the United States and Israel, along with Germany, France, and the Netherlands. The Dutch had been brought in because Iran's centrifuges were based on designs that A. Q. Khan had stolen from a Dutch company.

Stuxnet was the first known example of a virus being used to attack industrial machinery. It worked by targeting a device known as a programmable logic controller (PLC), produced by the German manufacturer Siemens, which regulated industrial machinery. The Stuxnet worm overrode the normal controls, causing centrifuges to spin too quickly or for too long, destroying or damaging them. At the same time, it induced the PLC to trick computers into thinking systems were functioning normally, preventing them from shutting down until it was too late.

No country ever admitted responsibility for creating the Stuxnet worm, which not only destroyed as many as one thousand Iranian centrifuges out of five thousand operating at the time, but also infected twenty thousand devices at over a dozen other nuclear facilities in the country. It caused severe damage to the Iranian nuclear program and according to some assessments set it back by as much as two years. There was no immediate response by Iran, but it began to pour massive resources into developing its own cyberwarfare capabilities, and by 2012 had begun launching strikes of its own, hitting Saudi state oil company Aramco as well as several U.S. banks.

It's hard to overstate the importance of Dagan's tenure at the Mossad. When he took up the position in 2002, Israeli and Western intelligence services expected Iran to become a nuclear power within two years. But "divine intervention" had done its job. When Dagan stepped down in January 2011, after nine years in office, he predicted that Iran would not be able to pass the nuclear threshold before 2015, if that. And as of 2023, it still hasn't.

Dagan had not only bought time on the Iranian nuclear project. He had also hit arms shipments to Hamas and Hezbollah, had destroyed Syria's Iranian-funded nuclear program, and perhaps most importantly had taken the Mossad's capabilities to a new level, restoring its reputation as an uncompromising and intrepid organization for which anything is possible.

Chapter 3

TELL YOUR FRIENDS YOU CAN USE OUR AIRSPACE

ISRAEL WASN'T THE ONLY COUNTRY IN THE MIDDLE EAST worried about Iran's nuclear ambitions. The Sunni Gulf states, led by Saudi Arabia and the United Arab Emirates, adversaries of Shiite Iran, also felt threatened by their powerful neighbor. In fact, while Iran's public threats were directed against Israel, in many ways the ayatollahs saw the Sunni Arabs as near equal enemies. Iran wants to dominate the Muslim world and believes its Persian-Aryan culture to be far superior to that of the Arabs, for whom the Persian language has an almost infinite vocabulary of derogatory slurs.

Sharon understood this.

So, while he instructed Dagan to penetrate Iran's nuclear program, he also ordered him to strengthen ties with the Arab Gulf nations, building on their mutual fear of Tehran. In 2004, that task was given to David Meidan, who was moved from Tzomet, the Mossad division in charge of recruiting and handling foreign agents, to head Mossad's Tevel division, in charge of dealings with foreign intelligence organizations and with countries with which Israel has no formal ties. Meidan and his analysts got to work, making secret contacts, looking for mutual interests. In the UAE, Bahrain, Saudi Arabia, and elsewhere in the Gulf, they found a receptive audience.

Ties between Israel and the United Arab Emirates stretched as far back as the early 1990s after the Oslo Accords, by which Israel agreed to a degree of Palestinian self-government in the West Bank. The Emiratis, already fearful of Iran, wanted to buy F-16 fighter jets from the administration of President Bill Clinton and needed the Israeli government of Prime Minister Yitzhak Rabin to lift its objections to the sale of such advanced planes to a supposed Middle East adversary. Using connections they had with the Mossad, the Emiratis initiated a meeting in Geneva between Rabin's bureau chief Shimon Sheves, and Mohammed Bin Zayed, known by his initials MBZ, who would later become Crown Prince and ruler of the Emirates. Rabin agreed to okay the Emiratis' request for the F-16s, which helped to establish a foundation of mutual trust between the states.

Meidan and his staff set out to build on that slender thread of a relationship, seeing in the UAE the best chance to forge a new situation between Israel and the Sunni Arab world in general. "Once we found a connection in the UAE," Meidan recalled, "we started communicating, but everything was clandestine and each side made sure nothing leaked to the press." Early on, those ties were just between the intelligence agencies of the two countries. But gradually, a direct channel was established between Israel and the UAE with the goal of establishing a continuous working relationship. "Of all the Gulf states, they had the most guts," Meidan said. "They are a very daring nation. Their leaders are talented and seasoned, way ahead of everyone else in the region. Of course, everything was done secretly. But they were not afraid."

After his appointment to head Tevel in 2005, Meidan held a number of meetings in Europe with Sheikh Hazza Bin Zayed, the UAE national security adviser and a younger brother to MBZ. Later that year, he was invited to meet with Sheikh Hazza and MBZ, now the Emirati Crown Prince, at the royal palace in Abu Dhabi. Then in early 2006, accompanied by Dagan, Meidan returned to the UAE. The two took a private jet, stopping off in Jordan for a few minutes so that there would be no record of a direct flight from Israel. When they arrived in Abu Dhabi, the UAE capital, MBZ was waiting for them at the palace along with other influential members of the royal family. It was, says Meidan, "a launch party" for an Israeli-UAE relationship. Following the kickoff meeting,

Meidan brought a former Mossad agent out of retirement to be stationed in the Emirates and to take charge of ties with the UAE.

Meidan went on to hold a series of meetings with MBZ during which they conversed in Arabic, which Meidan spoke fluently. Although born in Egypt, he had come to Israel when he was a year old. He grew up speaking French at home but learned Arabic at school and went on to serve in the IDF's Unit 504, which was charged with recruiting agents from Arab countries. On the occasions that Dagan, who tried but never managed to pick up more than a rudimentary command of Arabic, would join in, the meetings would switch to English. Meidan and the Mossad director were on one side of a table and Bin Zayed and his closest aide on the other. Those meetings, however, were few and far between. Mostly, Meidan would meet solo with senior officials building up relationships and opening up possibilities for future business and defense industry ties.

But a foundation had been laid and that led, however gradually, to an increase in contacts that in turn paved the way for top-level but still veiled meetings. Diplomatic cables revealed by WikiLeaks showed that Tzipi Livni, Israel's foreign minister in the Olmert government, and herself a former Mossad agent, had formed close ties with UAE foreign minister Abdullah Bin Zayed, another MBZ brother. (MBZ is the lead figure of the "Bani Fatima Six"—the six sons of Sheikh Zayed Bin Sultan Al Nahyan, the founding father of the Emirates, and his third wife, Sheikha Fatima. Others in this group, considered to be at the nexus of the power structure in the UAE, include Sheikh Abdullah and Sheikh Hazza, as well as Sheikh Tahnoon, the minister of intelligence.) Marc Sievers, the political adviser of the U.S. embassy in Tel Aviv, described in one cable how, despite the good relationship, the Emiratis would not "do in public what they say behind closed doors."

In 2010, Israel's minister of infrastructure, Uzi Landau, a man known for his hard-line and uncompromising views, attended a conference of the International Renewable Energy Agency in Abu Dhabi. It was the first visit to the country by a sitting Israeli minister and paved the way for a permanent Israeli presence at IRENA.

Meanwhile, under the radar, business and defense ties between the

Emirates and Israel flourished. One of the first Israelis to conclude a major business deal was Mati Kochavi, who in 2008 signed an $800 million contract, agreeing to supply security surveillance equipment to the UAE through a Swiss holding company. According to a later Bloomberg report, "Twice a week at the height of the project, a chartered Boeing 737, painted all white, took off from Tel Aviv's Ben Gurion International Airport, touched down briefly in Cyprus or Jordan for political cover, and landed about three hours later in Abu Dhabi with dozens of Israeli engineers on board, many of whom used to work for Israeli intelligence services." Rumors spread that Mossad officials were also hitching a lift on the Kochavi charter in order to expand ties with the Emirates.

There were also official trade ties with Qatar and Bahrain in the post-Oslo period, but these soon collapsed as the Israeli-Palestinian relationship deteriorated. The bloody violence of the Second Intifada that erupted in September 2000 dealt them a final blow, but the private relationships continued.

Israel's history with Saudi Arabia was more complex. While the smaller Gulf monarchies had never fought in any of the Arab wars against Israel, the Saudis had sent a small force to fight under Egyptian command in the 1948 War of Independence and were openly hostile to the Jewish state. Saudi leaders often made statements that were outright anti-Semitic, and besides, the Saudis were a leading player in the Arab oil embargo following the 1973 Yom Kippur War.

Nevertheless, the maxim that the enemy of my enemy is my friend did encourage Israel and Saudi Arabia to see that they shared some mutual interests. In the 1960s, during the North Yemen civil war, Israel and Saudi Arabia had both supported the Royalists against the Republicans, backed by Gamal Abdel Nasser's Egypt. Then, following the 1967 Six Day War during which Israel took control of the West Bank, the Gaza Strip, the Golan Heights, and the Sinai Peninsula, the Saudis made several behind-the-scenes overtures to Israel. The Saudis broke ties with Egypt after Egyptian president Anwar Sadat made peace with Israel in 1979, in exchange for a return of the Sinai. But they had also come to terms with Israel's existence and were willing to recognize it within its pre-1967 borders. The catalyst for deeper engagement was the 1979 Islamic Revolution in Iran, which pushed the Saudis to a realization that they had an overriding interest in common with Israel, to stop the ayatollahs from expanding Shiite power through the Sunni world. During the 1980s and 1990s, informal ties between the Mossad and Saudi Intelligence continued to develop, which may be the reason that when Ehud Olmert became prime minister of Israel in 2006, Dagan, the intelligence chief, was among the first in the Israeli leadership to recognize the shifting dynamics in the region. During the Second Lebanon War that year, Saudi Arabia took a vehement stance against Israel's rival, the Iranian proxy Hezbollah, which it had come to see as a threat to its interests. The Saudis blamed Hezbollah for instigating the war, as did several other Arab countries, including Egypt. In the aftermath of the war, Israel, Saudi Arabia, Egypt, and Turkey decided to "accelerate intelligence exchanges" to counter Iran. Soon thereafter, Dagan met in Amman with his Jordanian counterpart and with Prince Bandar Bin Sultan, the head of Saudi Intelligence and a former ambassador to the United States.

At first, the Saudis had only a limited objective: they wanted Israel not to stand in the way of an arms deal with the U.S. But from Dagan's perspective, the meeting in Amman was the point when the ball started rolling on the formation of an axis between Israel and moderate Sunni states fearful of the designs of Shiite Iran. The U.S. secretary of state at the time, Condoleezza Rice, wrote in her memoirs that when she met with the leaders of the Gulf Cooperation Council, they told her that Iran "is number one, two, three and four" on their agenda.

Dagan had also created his own direct channels to Arab leaders, largely through his special relationship with King Abdullah II of Jordan, who had ascended to the throne a couple of years before Dagan was appointed head of the Mossad. As director, Dagan became close friends with King Abdullah. They shared the same birthday and would always call each other and sometimes celebrate together with a festive meal, sometimes at the king's palace and other times on neutral ground. Those special ties, together with American introductions, would open the door for Dagan to meet with other Arab leaders in the region.

While over the years Israel's overall relations with Jordan experienced many ups and downs—the worst moment coming after the Mossad's failed assassination attempt on Hamas leader Khaled Mashal in the Jordanian capital, Amman, in 1997—ties between the Mossad and its Jordanian counterpart, the General Intelligence Directorate, generally remained close and cordial.

Still, while the Gulf states were "scared" of a nuclear Iran, as Dagan told President Obama's counterterrorism adviser, Frances Fragos Townsend, they wanted "someone else to do the job for them." The job was to take concrete measures to sabotage the Iranian nuclear program, and Israel was ready to take on that task.

One of the pillars of Dagan's Iran policy was pressuring Iran in order to create the conditions for regime change. Part of that was financial sanctions, among them the U.N. Security Council Resolutions 1737 and 1747, which imposed sanctions in 2006 and 2007 against Iran because of its nuclear program. In Dagan's assessment these had been costly to Iran because they pushed European businesses out of the country. His analysis, according to a 2007 classified cable from the American embassy in Tel Aviv—part of the WikiLeaks haul—was also that Iran was paying a heavy price for something it had yet to achieve. Dagan told Townsend that the Iranians were making a "false presentation" of their capabilities and had not yet mastered the uranium enrichment process.

In an August 2007 meeting with U.S. under secretary of state Robert Burns, Dagan urged that more be done to foment unrest in the country, and he identified what he felt were weak spots in Iran that he thought could be exploited. Among the measures he suggested was supporting student democracy movements and ethnic minorities—Azeris, Kurds, and Baluchs—who make up 40 percent of the country's population and who don't like the regime. More could be done to develop their independent identities, he told Burns. He pointed out that unemployment exceeded 30 percent nationwide, inflation was over 40 percent, and people were criticizing the government for funding overseas groups such as Hamas and Hezbollah rather than attempting to relieve Iran of its own misery. "The economy is hurting and this is provoking a real crisis among Iran's leaders," he told Burns.

At the time, American and European officials were arguing that there was a moderate faction inside Iran's leadership that, if given support, might change the country's aggressive postures. But Dagan wasn't buying that analysis. He didn't believe that the reformist camp was any more ideologically moderate toward Israel than the hard-liners. Both, he felt, wanted to see the destruction of the Jewish state. But he recognized that the reformist camp had a worldview that was more tempered by reality and that there was a growing division in Iran when it came to tactics. Some supported a more belligerent policy vis-à-vis the West in general, while others favored a more realpolitik-based approach.

Dagan's analysis of the internal situation in Iran turned out to be correct. In the summer of 2009, protests erupted on the streets of Tehran, Shiraz, and all of the big cities. The immediate spark was President Mahmoud Ahmadinejad's reelection by a suspiciously massive margin ahead of the reformist Mir Hossein Mousavi. Three million people marched in the streets of Tehran, shouting "Where is my vote?" The protests, which became known as the Green Movement—the color green was the symbol of Mousavi's campaign—lasted for several months before the Basij, a volunteer paramilitary organization operating under the umbrella of the IRGC, brutally crushed it. Dozens of people were known to have been killed—though according to some reports, the death toll was as high as 1,500. Thousands were arrested and tortured.

One of the slogans adopted by the protesters was "Neither Gaza, nor Lebanon. My soul is for Iran," a reference to the billions the Islamic regime was spending on its foreign adventures, rather than addressing the needs of the Iranian people. But if the Green Movement presented an opportunity for Israel and, indeed, the West, they failed to exploit it. "We had a great chance to assist the opposition there, but we missed it," Pardo said. Western intelligence agencies, he believed, hadn't understood just how vulnerable the regime was. He declined to specify measures that could have been taken to take advantage of the protests, but he seems to have felt that the CIA and other Western intelligence agencies essentially just observed the movement and undertook none of the covert actions they've used at other times in other countries to undermine unfriendly governments. He believed they wanted to avoid a replay of the CIA's support of the 1953 coup against Iran's elected prime minister, the reformist Mohammad Mossadegh. Over sixty years on, the coup remains a source of Iranian animosity toward the West.

Olmert, who had been prime minister until about four months earlier, told us, "If the U.S. and others had taken action to undermine the regime together with other actions, some of them violent perhaps, [regime change] could have been achieved." But at the time, President Obama was trying to avoid foreign involvements, like the costly and frustrating interventions of the Iraq and Afghanistan Wars, and he wasn't willing to take on the risk of an intervention in Iran. And, absent a broad international agreement to create conditions to topple the Tehran regime, the Mossad itself did not feel able to take actions of its own.

Meanwhile there were also changes in Israel. In 2009, Olmert was forced to resign in the wake of corruption allegations, and in new elections, the right-wing Benjamin Netanyahu came to power for the second time, having served as prime minister from 1996 to 1999.

Dagan had enjoyed a strong professional and personal relationship with Olmert, as well as with his predecessor, Ariel Sharon. Both Sharon and Olmert had bought into Dagan's "five pillars" strategy. But it became clear soon after his return as prime minister that Netanyahu had a different view. He was skeptical that sabotage and subterfuge alone would be enough to stop Iran. His defense minister, the former IDF chief of staff Ehud Barak, harbored similar feelings. As early as 2007 when Olmert was still in office, Barak had instructed the IDF to "prepare operative plans to hurt the Iranian effort to achieve nuclear capabilities," and this included direct attacks on Iran by the Israeli Air Force.

But Barak's ardor to use Israel's military against Iran had led to a run-in with President George W. Bush. In 2008, when President Bush was visiting Israel, he held a one-on-one meeting with Olmert at the prime minister's residence in Jerusalem. Barak asked to be allowed in on the meeting to present the case for Israel to launch a preemptive military strike and why the United States should greenlight it. "You know

I'm against it," Bush told Olmert when he passed on Barak's request. "General Barak was IDF chief of staff; he was prime minister, I think it would only be fair for you to hear him out," Olmert replied.

Bush conceded, Barak made his presentation, and the U.S. president told him, "No way."

Barak persisted and Bush's patience wore thin.

"General, do you understand what no means?" the president asked Barak. Then, banging his fist on the table, he growled, "No means no."

At the time, Olmert had yielded to Bush and no direct Israeli military operations against Iran were undertaken. But now back in power, Netanyahu and Barak allocated billions of shekels to the Israeli Air Force with the aim of building capabilities to bomb Iran's nuclear facilities.

But these moves provoked some strenuous opposition elsewhere among senior officials who, in the end, stopped Netanyahu and Barak from being able to initiate direct military operations against Iran. Among these officials was Dagan himself, who, after retiring, said of the kind of strike Netanyahu and Barak were advocating that it was "the stupidest idea I ever heard." Later, in an interview with us, Dagan allowed that his statement had been made "in the heat of the moment." Even then, when speaking in private, he would say, "Give me another two billion and I'll make sure we continue to benefit from 'divine intervention,'" meaning that Israel's clandestine services, namely the Mossad, would have greater effect than open military operations. In his view, Israel should only resort to military action when all other options had been exhausted and "if the sword was at our necks." He thought that an undisguised strike by the IDF would only strengthen the resolve of the mullahs to acquire nuclear weapons and unite the Iranian people behind them. In any event, it would only manage to knock back the Iranian program by a couple of years. Some Israeli pilots, he argued, might be shot down and if that happened, they would be hanged in the Tehran town square. There would be terror attacks against Israeli and Jewish targets, if not all-out war with Iran, Hezbollah, Hamas, and Islamic Jihad all raining down missiles on Israel. Not only that, Dagan also feared that a military strike would leave Israel out in the cold by itself, without American support for its actions.

Netanyahu, however, was coming to see the Iranian threat in increasingly apocalyptic terms. "It's 1938 and Iran is Germany," he warned on several occasions. "It is racing to arm itself with atomic bombs. Iran's nuclear ambitions must be stopped. They have to be stopped. We all have to stop it now." His rhetoric met with a warm response in the Gulf where fears of what King Abdullah of Jordan called the rising Shiite Crescent were rapidly growing.

Part of what triggered the intensifying sense of alarm in Israel, the Gulf, and the U.S. was new intelligence gathered by Western spy agencies in September 2009: Iran, the intelligence said, was constructing a new nuclear enrichment facility buried deep underground in a reinforced concrete bunker on a mountainside near the Shiite holy city of Qom, where it could produce weapons-grade uranium. This Fordow Fuel Enrichment Plant (FEP) was known as Project Al-Ghadir. After the plant's existence was revealed, Iran reported it to the IAEA, but said it had no military purpose. This claim was later disproved by evidence seized in the 2018 archive heist, which showed that Fordow could be used as a secret weapons-grade uranium enrichment backup in case the enrichment plant at Natanz was bombed.

But while Israel and the U.S. agreed in their assessments of the progress of Iran's nuclear drive, their views on what to do about it were completely different. Netanyahu was by now pushing for an American green light for an Israeli strike. The Obama administration, while stating that "all options were on the table," believed that it could engage Iran diplomatically, and it tried to broker a deal by which Iran would remove most of its low-enriched uranium stockpile to another country. The idea was that the uranium could be converted to fuel rods useless for military applications. They would then be returned to Iran and used in medical research. Israel, believing that the American approach amounted to wishful thinking, demanded something else—that the U.S. impose crippling sanctions on Tehran.

While all this was playing out, the Israeli and Gulf intelligence officials intensified their contacts with each other. In the summer of 2010, according to reports from Arab sources (that were accurate, though denied by all sides), Dagan paid a visit to Saudi Arabia. It was one of several meetings he would hold with senior intelligence officials there to discuss the Iranian threat.

Other, unconfirmed reports claimed that Saudi Arabia had proposed allowing Israeli fighter jets to pass over the kingdom on their way to striking Iran's nuclear facilities. Obama's ambassador to Israel, Dan Shapiro, said that U.S. intelligence had confirmed the contacts between the sides on this issue. Some said that the Saudis had even expressed a willingness to allow Israel to land and refuel its jets in the Saudi desert, solving one of the major logistical problems involved in a potential strike against Iran, though some Israeli sources deny this.

But there is other persuasive evidence that the Saudis were trying to make it possible for Israel to hit Iran with a military strike. A few months before Dagan's trip to Saudi Arabia, the country's foreign minister, Saud Al-Faisal, approached a Spanish-Israeli journalist at a U.N. conference in Rio de Janeiro and gave him a message: "Tell your friends you can use our airspace."

Certainly, some of these "friends" were eager to do just that. In September, at the end of a meeting in the prime minister's office held to discuss the threat of rocket attacks by Hamas in southern Israel, Netanyahu and Barak instructed IDF chief of staff Gabi Ashkenazi and Dagan to prepare a thirty-day countdown for a strike on Iran.

But again, this order prompted opposition from Israel's military-security establishment. Both Ashkenazi and Dagan were shocked. Dagan even believed the order to be illegal, since a strike on Iran was tantamount to war, and war had to be approved by the cabinet. Ashkenazi agreed. "We will do everything we are instructed to, but only through a legal process," he said. Barak would later claim that Ashkenazi had said he wasn't confident that Israel's air force could demolish Iran's heavily fortified underground nuclear facilities, a claim the IDF chief of staff categorically denied. "I was confident in the IDF's operational capabilities and its ability to use its long arm, but I wasn't happy with the way Netanyahu was rolling out plans for an attack," Ashkenazi said. He was also worried that the mobilization of reserves and other unusual activity could tip off Iran and lose the crucial element of surprise. This caution infuriated Barak. "With a Chief of Staff like that, we wouldn't have won the Six-Day War," he is reported to have said of Ashkenazi.

A few weeks after this acrimonious exchange between the two generals, Netanyahu and Barak met again with Ashkenazi and Dagan, ordering them to concentrate on building operational capabilities, and to leave it to the civilian leadership to deal with the consequences.

But Dagan and Ashkenazi weren't the only ones opposed to a strike on Iran. Yuval Diskin, chief of Shin Bet, Israel's "unseen shield," its internal security service, and others inside the security establishment also argued against it. More importantly, the U.S. was opposed. The chairman of the Joint Chiefs of Staff, Admiral Mike Mullen, reportedly called Ashkenazi and asked him straight out. "Have you gone mad? Are you planning to surprise us?"

The plan was dropped—for the moment.

Chapter 4

CHANGING CIRCUMSTANCES

IN JANUARY 2011, ON THE FINAL DAY OF HIS NINE-YEAR TENure as head of the agency, Meir Dagan invited a group of Israeli journalists to Mossad headquarters. The members of the press thought they were about to hear a summary of Dagan's years in office, or perhaps an analysis of the situation vis-à-vis Iran's nuclear program. Instead, what they got was extraordinary criticism by a public official still in office of the military strike that Netanyahu and Barak had wanted to carry out against Iran, but that had been foiled by the Mossad director and others a few months earlier. Most of Dagan's comments, however, never made it into print because the chief military censor, Brigadier General Sima Vaknin Gil, banned publication on the grounds that the material was classified.

Always one to find another route to get what he wanted if the path was blocked, Dagan waited a few months, and in June said exactly the same things as he had to the journalists, but this time in front of a far wider audience at a conference at Tel Aviv University.

After all, in Israel, who could prosecute a national hero like Dagan once he came out and expressed his criticisms in public. In addition to questioning the wisdom of an attack on Iran, Dagan called on Israel to accept the Saudi peace initiative and to make progress on the Palestinian front.

The day after Dagan's impromptu January meeting with journalists, he was replaced by Tamir Pardo, who had come out of retirement after twice serving as Dagan's deputy and twice stepping down, despairing over the unlikelihood of ever getting the top job.

Like Dagan, Pardo came from a family of Holocaust survivors. His mother had lost her mother and father and brother, all killed by the Nazis. In his compulsory military service, Pardo served in Sayeret Matkal, Israel's elite Special Forces unit, which had declined to accept a young Dagan into its ranks. There, Pardo took part in one of the most famous commando raids of all time—Operation Thunderbolt. This was the celebrated rescue in 1976 of over a hundred Israeli and Jewish hostages along with the crew of an Air France plane that had been hijacked to Entebbe in Uganda on a flight from Tel Aviv to Paris. Pardo, who was the Sayeret Matkal's communications officer, was right next to the only Israeli commando killed in the operation, Yonatan Netanyahu, the older brother of the later prime minister.

Pardo completed his IDF service in 1978 with the rank of captain and joined the Mossad a year later, while still a history student at Tel Aviv University. He served initially in the research department sorting intelligence papers under Uzi Arad, who would later become the head of Israel's National Security Council. Pardo worked his way up the ranks, moving to, and later heading, Keshet, the eavesdropping unit, where the skills he had picked up in Sayeret Matkal proved useful. Then he was assigned to the agency's operational units, eventually becoming head of the special operations division, until, in 2002, he was appointed Dagan's deputy.

In 2006, Pardo stepped down from the Mossad to become an adviser to the IDF special operations division. During the Second Lebanon War in July that year, he was involved in planning operations against Iran's Lebanese proxy, Hezbollah, a force that he described as an "Iranian invention" aimed at giving Tehran a border with Israel. He returned to the Mossad in 2007, and when Benjamin Netanyahu was elected prime minister in 2009, he may have hoped that the position of director would soon be his.

Pardo had remained close to the Netanyahu family and had even named his own son Yonatan. Still, he didn't move to the top of the Mossad right away. Netanyahu first opted to extend Dagan's term, in part because Defense Minister Ehud Barak, a former commander of Sayeret Matkal, was opposed to Pardo getting the job. But in 2010, over Barak's objections, Pardo was named the Mossad chief.

However, there was a catch: Netanyahu demanded that Pardo appoint Yossi Cohen as his deputy. Pardo refused, arguing that Ram Ben Barak, currently in that position, was doing an excellent job and could not just be tossed out without a professional reason. In the end, an informal compromise was reached. Ben Barak would stay on for about a year and Cohen would become deputy after he stepped down.

Under Pardo, who had devised the program to target Iran's nuclear scientists, covert actions against Iran would, at least in the beginning, continue at an even faster pace than under Dagan.

The first major operation was on July 23, 2011. Two gunmen on a motorcycle drove up to a car driven by Darioush Rezaeinejad, a nuclear physicist and expert in high-voltage switches used to trigger nuclear warheads. The gunmen pulled up to the driver's side window and opened fire, hitting Rezaeinejad with five bullets, including one that went through his neck, severing his arteries and killing him on the spot. His wife, who was in the front passenger seat, sustained injuries, but survived.

While the Mossad, following usual practice, did not claim responsibility for the assassination, Western intelligence sources said that the agency had carried it out. Israeli sources told the German magazine *Der Spiegel* that it was the "first serious action taken by the new Mossad chief."

As with all previous assassinations of its nuclear scientists, Iran's state-run media initially claimed Rezaeinejad had nothing to do with the country's nuclear program and was just an innocent PhD electronics student.

Then, in November 2011, a mysterious explosion occurred at the Alghadir missile base at Bid Kaneh; it was so powerful that it shook windows in Tehran some thirty miles away. The blast also killed seventeen Revolutionary Guards; one of them Major General Hassan Tehrani Moghaddam, the architect of Iran's ballistic missile program.

The IRGC insisted that the explosion was not caused by foreign sabotage and had been the result of an accident during the transfer of munitions. But Israeli sources were quoted in foreign media outlets saying the incident at Bid Kaneh had resulted from a joint operation of the Mossad and the anti-regime MEK, the People's Mujahedin Organization of Iran. Officially, Israel declined to comment. However, Defense Minister Ehud Barak quipped, "May there be more like it." The former deputy head of the Mossad, Ilan Mizrahi, added: "God bless those who were behind it."

Certainly, Israel had every reason not just to hit an important Iranian missile base, but also to want Moghaddam dead. Born in 1959 in the Sarcheshmeh neighborhood of Tehran, Moghaddam was an engineering student when he joined the uprising against the Shah, making homemade bombs and grenades. With the triumph of the Islamic Revolution, he joined the IRGC and fought as a commander in the Iran-Iraq War. In 1981, he established the IRGC's artillery corps, but when Iran began an effort to acquire its own missile technology, he was assigned to reverse-engineer missiles acquired from North Korea, Libya, and Syria. In 2004, he went to Syria to study the Soviet-made Scud-B tactical ballistic missile. By 2006, he had been appointed commander of the IRGC Aerospace Corps Self-Sufficiency Jihad Organization, where he worked on ballistic missile development.

In addition to working on missiles that could potentially carry a nuclear warhead, Moghaddam also provided missile technology to Palestinian groups, and to Hezbollah. Khamenei credited him with "filling Palestinian hands with missiles instead of stones to strike these arrogant terrorists [the Israelis]." These anti-Israel actions made him honored. After his death, a huge crowd carried his coffin, draped in the Iranian flag, down one of Tehran's main boulevards to the Balal Mosque where Supreme Leader Ayatollah Khamenei attended a ceremony in front of uniformed officers. The epitaph on his gravestone reads, "Here Lies a Man Who Wanted to Destroy Israel."

Several years after his death, Hassan Tehrani Moghaddam's brother, Mohammad Tehrani Moghaddam, claimed: "This was not just a simple accident, but a carefully-planned operation. The Mossad was trying to assassinate my brother for many years." He was later forced to retract his statements and the IRGC aerospace commander, Amir Ali

Hajizadeh, issued a denial that there had been any Israeli involvement in Moghaddam's killing.

Other "accidents" were to befall personnel engaged in Iran's nuclear program during Pardo's time as the Mossad chief, but in the murky world of Middle East conflicts, it isn't always easy to tell what might truly have been accidents and what were operations by intelligence services. What is certain, given the Mossad's record, is that it is immediately suspected whenever any harm is done to Iran or to its supporters, though in some instances it genuinely wasn't involved.

In June 2011, for example, five Russian nuclear experts were among forty-seven passengers killed when a RusAir Tupolev-134 airliner hit a tree and crashed while landing in a thick fog at Petrozavodsk in the northwest of Russia. A week after the crash, reports emerged that the Russian experts had helped design the Bushehr nuclear power plant, where Iran was developing aspects of its military nuclear program.

Was the Mossad responsible? Pardo categorically denied that it had any involvement in the plane crash. "Mossad would never carry out such an action," he said, and this seems almost certainly true, if only given the heavy price that Israel would pay if it directly attacked a Russian target, especially inside Russia itself.

But at times the fog is almost impenetrable, in part because as a matter of policy, the Mossad keeps silent about its operations. It did under Dagan and it continued to do so under Pardo. But there is no doubt that the Mossad was responsible for numerous operations aimed at Iran's nuclear weapons program, even if sometimes the statements made by Israeli officials have been models of ambiguity or even self-contradiction. After retiring, Pardo was asked about the assassinations of nuclear scientists. His murky reply: "The Mossad isn't an organization for targeted killing. Sometimes you have to do that. . . . But you don't have to admit it." As for other operations, he said: "What people claimed the Mossad has done in that period isn't even a thousandth of what we did."

In the midst of all this, in October 2011, Netanyahu and Barak were once again pushing for the IDF to begin the countdown for an attack.

But as before, the prospect of direct military action against Iran provoked deep disagreement inside Israel. Pardo, like Dagan before him, was opposed to an attack, and he felt that Netanyahu was taking measures tantamount to launching a war without getting the approval of the cabinet, as required by Israeli law.

"I checked with legal advisers, I consulted with everyone I could to understand who is authorized to give the order to start a war," Pardo said in interviews with us and with Israeli TV. "I wanted to be certain if, heaven forbid, something incorrect happened, even if the mission failed, that there wouldn't be a situation where I carried out an illegal operation."

Pardo even mulled over whether to step down in the event that an order for a major aerial strike on Iran was given. But in the end, Netanyahu and Barak, under pressure from others in the security establishment, agreed to hold a vote in the inner cabinet. Pardo, along with then IDF chief of staff Benny Gantz and Shin Bet chief Yoram Cohen, all spoke out against a strike. There was a critical difference from 2010, when Netanyahu and Barak had first pressed for an air offensive against Iran's nuclear weapons program. Unlike during the earlier debate, the IDF chief of staff was sure his pilots now had the ability to achieve the complete destruction of the Iranian facilities necessary to produce a bomb. But Gantz, Cohen, and Pardo were against undertaking any action without coordination with the United States. Barak wasn't in theory opposed to notifying the Americans, but he wanted to do so as a kind of fait accompli, not providing the information early enough to allow them to pressure Israel to call it off. In any case, the vote went against Netanyahu and Barak, and there was no IDF attack.

Still, the differences expressed during the debate soured some relations at the top of the Israeli government. For one thing, Pardo fell out of favor with Netanyahu, who, according to some reports, asked Yoram Cohen of the Shin Bet to wiretap both Pardo's and Gantz's phones, supposedly to be sure neither man leaked any information from the Iran file. In a conversation with us, Pardo provided no clear evidence that his phone had indeed been tapped, but he was still clearly under the impression that some kind of investigation of the Mossad had taken place.

Netanyahu has denied ordering any wiretapping and Yoram Cohen denied to us that there had been any investigation targeting Pardo or Gantz.

While a military strike was ruled out, covert actions continued unabated.

On January 11, 2012, a nuclear chemistry expert working at Natanz, Mostafa Ahmadi Roshan, was killed when two assailants on a motorcycle attached a magnetic bomb to his gray Iranian-assembled Peugeot 405, the same tactic that had been used in the January 2010 assassination of Masoud Ali Mohammadi. The explosion, at 8:30 in the morning on Gol Nabi Street in a normally quiet neighborhood of north Tehran, killed the thirty-two-year-old scientist on the spot along with his driver. Another person in the car was injured. This time Iran acknowledged that one of its scientists had been killed, with Vice President Mohammad Reza Rahimi saying Israel was behind the assassination. A senior security official, Safar Ali Baratloo, also pointed a finger at Israel saying, "the magnetic bomb is of the same types already used to assassinate our scientists." It was the fourth assassination of a nuclear scientist in Iran in two years and Iranian media was speculating publicly that Israel was receiving help from inside the country.

That theory was backed up by a former chief of the CIA's counterterrorism operations, Vince Cannistraro, who asserted that the actual work on the ground was being done by Iranian opponents of the regime, not by Israelis directly. "The MEK is being used as the assassination arm of Israel's Mossad intelligence service," he said at the time. Cannistraro added that MEK operatives were in charge of carrying out "the motor attacks on Iranian targets chosen by Israel. They go to Israel for training, and Israel pays them."

In 2022, Iran put on display Ahmadi Roshan's car along with the wrecked vehicles of three other "nuclear martyrs," including that of Darioush Rezaeinejad, the so-called PhD student assassinated the year before. Exhibition plaques at the Sacred Defense Museum in Tehran state that both were killed by the Mossad.

The campaign against Iran's nuclear program led to calls for revenge within Iran, and in 2011 and 2012 there were several failed attempts, attributed to the Islamic Republic and its Lebanese proxy Hezbollah, to strike Israeli diplomats around the world. On January 24, 2012, for example, a three-man cell run by Iran that planned to assassinate the Israeli ambassador to Azerbaijan was exposed by Azeri intelligence. On February 13, the wife of an Israeli diplomat in New Delhi was wounded by a magnetic bomb attached to her car by an assailant on a motorcycle—the same method used in the assassinations of Iranian nuclear scientists. An Indian police investigation concluded the attack had been planned by five members of the IRGC. On the same day, an Israeli staffer at the embassy in Tbilisi, Georgia, found a bomb under his car, which was defused before exploding.

The following day, a bomb went off prematurely at an apartment in the Thai capital of Bangkok not far from the Israeli embassy. Three Iranians were convicted of planning that attack and sentenced to terms ranging from fifteen years to life imprisonment. They were eventually released in a prisoner swap for a British-Australian academic, married to an Israeli, who had been held for two years in the notorious Evin prison in Tehran. Then, in June in Mombasa, Kenya, police arrested two Iranian nationals in possession of 15 kilograms of RDX, an extremely powerful military-grade explosive. Kenya said the pair, who were sentenced to life imprisonment, were members of the IRGC Quds Force and had been planning attacks on Israeli and Western targets.

While Iran was unsuccessful in its attempts to attack these official Israeli outposts, on July 18, a Hezbollah suicide bomber managed to kill five Israeli tourists and their driver when he blew himself up in a bus transporting them to their hotel in the Bulgarian Black Sea resort of Burgas. Israel immediately blamed Iran for the bombing and eight years later a Bulgarian court sentenced in absentia two Lebanese nationals affiliated with Hezbollah to life imprisonment for their role in the assault.

Despite the assassinations, cyberattacks, and other covert actions that cannot be revealed, Iran's nuclear weapons program continued, to the point where Israel began worrying that it was reaching a dangerous new stage. Barak believed that by the end of 2012 or so, Iran would enter a "zone of immunity," meaning that it would have reached weapons-grade enrichment capacity at the Fordow plant, buried inside a mountain. Fordow was not yet operational, but it was nearing completion. Once it was up and running and all of the physical elements it needed were delivered, Israel, which did not have the U.S.'s bunker-busting bombs, might no longer be able to destroy it.

That worry again intensified the desire in Israel to hit the Iranians. But there was no agreement in Israel on exactly what to do, and the Obama administration, which by then had entered negotiations that would lead to the 2015 nuclear accords, was steadfastly opposed to further operations. On more than one occasion, Obama's secretary of defense Leon Panetta, a longtime friend of Barak who generally shared his politics (as well as a mutual hobby, playing classical piano), called the Israeli defense minister to give him the American reasoning. "Look, Ehud," Panetta said in a conversation in 2011, "the problem is that if you attack them now, you can only set their program back by a few years. It would come back. You'll give them a black eye. We, on the other hand, can deliver the knockout punch."

But Israel persisted, or at least seemed to. In mid-January 2012 it asked to postpone a major missile defense exercise, Austere Challenge 12, supposed to take place on Israeli territory in April of that year and involving the United States, Israel, the United Kingdom, and Germany. Speculation was rife that the delay was aimed at enabling Israel to plan and execute a strike, and making sure hundreds of foreign troops weren't on Israeli soil was a precondition for any operation.

Again, Panetta spoke to Barak, this time to see what Israel was planning.

"We haven't made a decision," Barak told him. "But I can't in good conscience hide the fact from our best ally that we are discussing it."

"If you do decide to attack the Iranian facilities, when will we know?" Panetta asked.

Barak told him that Israel wouldn't be able to provide the U.S. with more than a few hours' notice. "We'll make sure you have enough time to tell your people. We won't endanger a single American life, any of your personnel," he said.

In March, in a speech before the American Israel Public Affairs Committee (AIPAC), Netanyahu gave the impression that Israel might soon take action, with the Americans or without them. "Israel has waited patiently for the international community to resolve this issue," he said. "We've waited for diplomacy to work. We've waited for sanctions to work. None of us can afford to wait much longer. As prime minister of Israel, I will never let my people live under the shadow of annihilation."

Did Netanyahu and Barak really plan to strike Iran, or were their warnings and the postponement of Austere Challenge just a ploy to get the Americans to step up pressure on Iran? Either way, April went by, the exercises were held in October, and despite concerns and signs throughout the summer that Israel was planning something, the year ended without Israel making good on its threats.

During that time, the action shifted to the negotiations. The Islamic Republic was by now under unprecedented economic pressure due to sanctions. Iran was having trouble getting insurance to ship its oil and was blocked from some of its access to the global banking system. Covert actions by the Mossad and other Western agencies had set back its nuclear progress and it was worried that Netanyahu was close to ordering an overt aerial attack. So it was ready for some kind of a deal, at least to regroup and to gain a breather from the harm sanctions were causing to its economy and from the Mossad's assassination campaign.

Back in 2011, Khamenei had already consented to negotiations over the nuclear issue with the United States, after Sultan Qaboos of Oman offered to mediate between the sides. Oman also had a covert relationship with Israel, and traditionally sought to play all sides in the game. It took almost a year before the first talks were held, but beginning in July 2012, Iran and the U.S. held a series of meetings in Oman. There was another round of secret talks in Oman in March 2013 (Israel knew about them through its own sources), but it was only after June that year, when the "moderate" Hassan Rouhani was elected president of Iran, that the sides began to make progress.

The talks then moved out into the open and by August 2013 an interim nuclear deal between Tehran and the P5+1—the five permanent members of the United Nations Security Council plus Germany—had been struck. It took two more years for all the obstacles to be swept away and for the full nuclear deal known as the Joint Comprehensive Plan of Action (JCPOA) to be signed, but during all that time, the Mossad had put its more aggressive actions on the back burner.

The negotiations however were of course of intense interest to Israel and dominated much of Pardo's time as the Mossad chief. According to several reports, Israel reportedly spied on the talks in Vienna during an eighteen-month period—apparently using the Duqu worm, a variant of the Stuxnet virus that had been used earlier to destroy Iranian centrifuges—and even passed on information to U.S. lawmakers to try and turn them against the deal.

The interim accords made both the Netanyahu government and the Gulf states more alarmed over Iran's power and influence, with the Gulf states becoming more open to contacts with Israel. Pardo took full advantage. After the signing of the interim agreement, he met, secretly as always, with Bandar Bin Sultan, the former Saudi ambassador to Washington and now the head of Saudi Intelligence, in what a British diplomat described as a "long and boozy dinner" at a plush hotel in the fancy Knightsbridge neighborhood of London. They would meet again in late November in Geneva, where, according to Iranian sources, they would discuss "containing Iran by any possible means." A third meeting would take place early the following year, this time in the Saudi capital, Riyadh.

Bandar was the architect of Saudi Intelligence ties with Israel going back as far as former Mossad directors Shabtai Shavit and Efraim Halevy. He had met several times with Dagan and David Meidan in various countries across Europe with the Americans serving as intermediaries. When war broke out in 2014 between Israel and Hamas in Gaza, Bandar reportedly initiated a meeting with Israeli security chiefs at his palace in Jeddah, where the Saudis proposed a road map for peace with the Palestinians. Netanyahu, according to the reports in the press, met twice with Bandar in Europe to talk about the Saudi plan, but in the end, he decided not to pursue it, cooling relations with the Saudis for a while. But under Pardo and Meidan's successor as head of Tevel, Haim Tomer, the Mossad continued to try to push forward ties with the Gulf states, who for their part felt, like the Saudis, that Israel was holding things up by not making progress on the Palestinian front.

"There was a [Muslim] head of state who I spoke with while I was still in the service," Pardo told us after his retirement. "He said to me, 'We Muslims have a dream that one day we will wake up in the morning, and we are going to see that between the Mediterranean and the Jordan Valley there is not even one Jew.' I looked at him in shock, and he went on, 'You Jews have the same dream, but vice versa. You think that one day, you will wake up and there will be no Palestinians and no Muslims between the Mediterranean and the Jordan Valley. We woke up and understood that it was just a dream and will remain just a dream. You Jews still believe that it can happen.'"

But Netanyahu's attention wasn't on the Palestinians or the Gulf; he was now focused on trying to torpedo the impending nuclear deal. In March 2015, at the invitation of House Speaker John Boehner and Senate Majority Leader Mitch McConnell, Netanyahu made his now famous, or perhaps infamous, speech to Congress calling the looming agreement a "very bad deal" that left much of Iran's nuclear infrastructure in place and ultimately wouldn't stop it from getting the bomb. The speech was seen by Democrats as an outrageous violation of protocol, not only undermining President Obama's foreign policy, but also attacking his domestic support in the U.S. Several leading Democrats, including then vice president Joe Biden, stayed away in protest and the speech is seen to this day by many as having fractured Democratic support for Israel.

But while Netanyahu was raging against the accords, Pardo held to a different view. He wasn't completely for the deal. He felt it had grave flaws. But he was against Netanyahu's apocalyptic rhetoric and believed Israel should be working with the American administration to fix the flaws.

"Does Iran pose a threat to Israel?" he told an audience of Israeli ambassadors early on in his term. "Absolutely. But if one said a nuclear bomb in Iranian hands was an existential threat, that would mean that we would have to close up shop and go home. That's not the situation. The term existential threat is used too freely." On another occasion, as negotiations on the final accords were in full steam, he told a group of visiting U.S. senators that "More sanctions during the negotiations is like throwing a grenade into the room." Ten days after retiring, he told an Israeli defense establishment publication that "there is no existential threat today to Israel." In an interview with us, he said that Iran was a grave threat, but that calling it existential was a "significant exaggeration."

Paradoxically, at the same time that Netanyahu was trying to torpedo the JCPOA, Khamenei seemed to be involuntarily dragging himself into approving it. Khamenei had his own demons to battle. Way back in June 1981, he was knocked down by an explosion placed in a tape recorder meant to assassinate him as he delivered a speech at the Abuzar Mosque in Iran. He survived, though the attack permanently damaged his right arm and caused some damage to his vocal cords and lungs. As he lay on the floor wondering whether he was alive or dead, Khamenei must also have been astonished that he was again in such danger. Years before, during the Shah's regime, he'd survived six rounds of arrest and torture. His torturers, he was convinced, had been trained by the CIA and the Mossad.

This time, in 1981, his would-be assassins were Iranian opposition groups like the MEK and the Forqan Group, a fanatical religious faction that opposed theocracy. In Khamenei's eyes again, these groups derived the means to resist his rule from the Great Satan of America. And yet, suddenly, as the JCPOA signing date of July 14, 2015, approached, Iran's Supreme Leader was finding himself grudgingly agreeing to sign a deal with the same hated United States.

During the time that intense negotiations were taking place, Khamenei believed the Mossad operations would slow down, which was one of the reasons he moved forward with the talks between 2013 and 2015, despite his many reservations. Did the Mossad actually cease its anti-Iran operations in that period, which was after an interim accord was signed, but before the final version was ironed out? There were no reports during that time of any kinetic actions, or explosions, aimed at Iran's nuclear program, leading some to believe that the Mossad had indeed carried out no sabotage efforts. Not true, according to Pardo, who, without providing details, told us in no uncertain terms that operations continued all the way through the interim period.

How could that have been possible? The answer to that question is probably that the Israeli operations were simply never disclosed. Israel kept them quiet, as it had done before, and Iran downplayed them as well. With talks ongoing, the Islamic Republic didn't have an interest in telling the world about Israeli operations against it.

Once the JCPOA was signed, however, the Mossad's efforts were focused on gathering intelligence and on following up on Iranian compliance with the terms of the deal. Among those terms, Iran was required to give away approximately ten nuclear weapons' worth of enriched uranium, reducing its supply to 300 kilograms, or around one third of what it would need for one nuclear bomb. Even that one third could only be 3.67 percent enriched, as opposed to the 20 percent enrichment it had achieved through its significant investment of time and resources. It also had to put around 75 percent of its approximately twenty thousand centrifuges in storage, so that only around five thousand of them could be operated at any time.

Israel didn't like the JCPOA for several reasons, the main one being that it would expire in 2030, just fifteen years after it was signed, after which there were no limits on the amount of nuclear fuel that the Iranians could produce. The deal also said nothing about Iranian missile development or about its support of terrorist groups on Israel's borders. But the deal was now a fact, supported by the world's major countries, and Israel could do nothing about that. What it could do, acting through the Mossad, was watch Iranian compliance closely, and be ready to tell the world if and when Tehran violated its commitments, which it was sure it would do, sooner or later.

Chapter 5

CODE NAME CALLAN

IN JANUARY 2016, AFTER THREE YEARS AS PRIME MINISTER Benjamin Netanyahu's national security adviser, Yossi Cohen, was appointed director of the Mossad. Right away his promotion was clouded in controversy.

There had been intense competition for the job, one of the most important in Israel. The outgoing director, Tamir Pardo, had wanted "N," the deputy head of the agency, to be his successor, and believed he had convinced Netanyahu that he was the right man for the job. ("N's" identity, like that of most former Mossad agents, remains confidential. Any Mossad agents identified by name in this book received special permission [not connected to this book] to "unmask" themselves after their retirement.) The other two candidates on the short list were Cohen and Ram Ben Barak, a former deputy head of the agency under Pardo. N and Ben Barak were the betting favorites as the race loomed, but Cohen, also a former deputy head of the agency, felt his strong ties to Netanyahu would work in his favor, and he was right.

Still, while Netanyahu deliberated over his choice, Cohen was exploring a possible alternative that reflects a tendency on his part to engage in associations that some in Israel have found ethically dubious, especially for a director of the Mossad. During this time, Cohen, apparently unsure whether his career in intelligence would continue or was soon to come to an end, explored a private sector option that would have made him a wealthy man. Specifically, he entertained an offer of $10 million from two Netanyahu associates—the Australian casino billionaire James Packer and the Israeli-born secret agent turned Hollywood producer and business tycoon Arnon Milchan—to head a cybersecurity firm. Both men were, and are, expected to testify in one of the corruption cases brought by Israeli prosecutors against Netanyahu. Cohen has said that he met Milchan independently of Netanyahu as part of an earlier Mossad operation ordered by Dagan.

In one instance, Packer gave Cohen's daughter a $20,000 wedding gift, which certainly had the appearance of possible influence buying. On another occasion, Cohen accepted a gift of tickets to a Mariah Carey concert. Cohen later returned the $20,000 gift and has admitted that it was a mistake in judgment to associate closely with deep-pocketed individuals like Milchan and Packer, but a preliminary probe by law enforcement was closed after it found no basis even to question Cohen as a suspect, nor has any reliable connection been established between him and the allegations against Netanyahu. Just as important, if Cohen decides to pursue a political career in the future, a matter of ongoing speculation in Israel, none of this seems to have impacted his popularity with the right, his natural political home.

There were other allegations against Cohen that shadowed him as he embarked on the job. Right away troubling reports surfaced that he had won the competition over N and Ben Barak because he had been willing to pledge loyalty to Netanyahu personally, while the other two candidates were willing "only" to pledge their loyalty to the country. Cohen was also said to have charmed Netanyahu's wife, Sara, who, it was believed, had exaggerated influence on the prime minister. Cohen denies all these allegations and notes that neither N nor Ben Barak have come forward publicly to substantiate them. Moreover, there are reasons that Netanyahu would have chosen Cohen over the other candidates. The two men had been working together closely for three years and had developed a strong rapport. Netanyahu knew exactly what Cohen's position was on Iran and every other major national security issue, and he knew that they thought much more alike than he and his previous Mossad chiefs did. Cohen was in that sense a natural choice, and there would have been no need to ask him to pledge his loyalty.

Still, Cohen was an anomaly compared to previous Mossad directors. For one thing, he was the first director of the agency, made up almost entirely of secular Jews, to come from a religious background. Born in Jerusalem on September 10, 1961, into a deeply religious family, Cohen observed the Sabbath and kept strictly kosher. As a youth, he'd belonged to a religious Zionist youth movement and gone to a religious school in the disputed West Bank. He was first recruited into the Mossad thirty-four years before becoming its chief when he was a university student in England, and he'd been the only person in his class who wore a yarmulke. Ditto when he attended the Mossad course for collecting intelligence, earning him the somewhat derogatory nickname "Yossi Dossi"—Dossi meaning an old-fashioned religious person. Being a Mossad agent almost by definition meant for Cohen that he would have to remove his yarmulke, break the Sabbath at times, and eat non-kosher food. He remained religiously traditional all his life, but with time wasn't so overly punctilious about ritual details, such that it was said of him that he left Israel for his first assignment abroad wearing a yarmulke and returned without one. To this day he is not all that comfortable directly discussing his religious beliefs. But Cohen's religious background clearly played a major role in the thinking, philosophy, and predispositions he brought to office.

The Katamon-Rehavia neighborhoods where Cohen spent his childhood in the 1960s and 1970s were the center of fierce fighting in the War of Independence of 1947–1949, leading much of its population to leave. By the time Cohen was growing up there, the Jews who resettled the area were mostly refugees from the Holocaust or Jews who had been expelled from the Arab countries of the Middle East and North Africa. The former Palestinian-Christian majority was not allowed to resettle there. Cohen's family and many of the people he associated with in his youth were traditional right-wingers.

That many people in Cohen's neighborhood had survived the devastation of the Holocaust or anti-Semitic expulsions imbued them with a deep sense of the historical precariousness of Jewish life. All of this goes a long way to explaining Cohen's own differences with his predecessor Pardo and other former Mossad directors, which went beyond mere analytical disagreements. The difference also had to do with Cohen's deeply visceral feeling about Israel controlling its fate, and his willingness to sometimes let the risks, including alienating the United States, be damned.

It is not that Pardo was not a hawk on security. He ordered plenty of assassinations and risky operations. He was as committed to Israeli survival as Cohen or anybody else. But Pardo compartmentalized the dread experiences of the Holocaust and expulsion, and analytically he had a deep humility regarding enemies like Iran and friends like the U.S. Cohen, by contrast, had a fervor that echoed that of his family and the neighbors of his earlier years, so that when it came to Iran and the United States, he was naturally more aggressive toward the former and more defiant, when necessary, of the latter. Most important was the land-for-peace idea, favored by Washington and a decisive element for Israelis in choosing a political party. Cohen's home was the Likud Party, which has generally been uncompromising on that issue. Westerners talk dispassionately about Israel withdrawing from the West Bank, but the "Yeshiva" high school that Cohen attended was committed to settling the West Bank. "This Yeshiva has brought forth a line of extraordinarily strong Zionists," he said in a December 2014 speech to the school. He cited one such ardent Zionist in particular, Rabbi Haim Drukman, who has moved many religious Zionists in a more radically right-wing direction. He knew Drukman from this Yeshiva, Yeshivat Ohr Etzion, in the 1970s, as someone who spoke about three values. These were, as Cohen summarized them: "the Torah of Israel, the people of Israel and the land of Israel—and sometimes the order gets flipped. Regarding the importance of these three legs, we were raised exactly like you."

Cohen's willingness to "flip the order" of the three principles, so as to put commitment to the land of Israel even ahead of Torah, Jewish religious commitment, is important to understanding him. Remove the religious and emotional dimensions and the fervor taught to him at a young age, and you might be left with a pro land-for-peace Labor Party left-wing Zionist or center-left party Zionist, not a fiercely uncompromising, overtly right-wing figure who became head of the Mossad.

One effect of Cohen's own religious background has been his unusual push to recruit ultraorthodox Israelis, particularly talented ultraorthodox men between the ages of twenty-four and thirty-four, into analyst and cyber units of the security establishment. This has included the Mossad as well as the intelligence and cyber units in the Shin Bet and the police, all agencies that once adamantly avoided ultraorthodox recruits.

Other points made Cohen stand out. While previous Mossad directors preferred life in the shadows and dressed like drab bureaucrats, Cohen's fastidiousness about his appearance made him different. He was always perfectly groomed, showing his preference for expensive suits. A collection of anti-wrinkle face creams sat on his desk. And he loved the media, which, almost by definition, differentiated him from his predecessors.

His Mossad code name—which he chose for himself—was "Callan," after the hero of a 1960s British television drama about a secret service assassin.

Regardless of questions over the circumstances of Cohen's appointment and his background, he was considered a brilliant, even legendary, case officer. He had won the Israel Security Prize together with his successor David Barnea for their work on a Mossad operation that remains classified. One source who worked extensively with Cohen called him "one of the greatest case officers Mossad has ever known," adding that he was able to get "anywhere, no matter how hostile the environment." Another source who came through the agency's ranks at the same time as Cohen described his "phenomenal memory," obsession with perfection, and his 360-degree planning. His talents were also confirmed to us by former Mossad chiefs Shabtai Shavit and Danny Yatom.

As with previous Mossad directors since the turn of the millennium, Iran was Cohen's priority. With his position in sync with that of Netanyahu, he managed to obtain a massive increase in funding for the Mossad at a time when funds for the IDF and other security services were being cut back. The money was slated for technological acquisitions and development, mostly for what the Mossad called the "project," the fight against the nuclear program.

A government report, which nearly every media outlet missed, contained buried inside it pearls about how Cohen accomplished this. It includes exchanges he had with other members of the Mossad's high command about how to win funding for itself even as the IDF was getting pushed around by Israel's Finance Ministry.

The report is an extremely detailed disclosure of usually classified internal Mossad proceedings, including debates about how the Mossad's budget should be spent to advance its two principal objectives: fighting the Iran war and normalizing relations with the Sunni Arab countries.

Cohen's Mossad embarked on a relentless search for technologies to give the Mossad the edge in its contest with Iran—and to fight a host of other threats faced by Israel. To further that goal, he set up a venture capital fund, Libertad, to tap into the tech ecosystem of Israel, which is known as the "Start-Up Nation" for a reason. "We are looking for companies that are dealing in areas we are interested in, that are at the beginning stages, with a good idea and a good staff," a Mossad agent identified only as Aleph said in a conference call with Israeli journalists. "We want a relationship with them and invest in their idea, so that they can fulfill their dreams and we can get the technology that we can use." Among the fields the Mossad invested in were robotics, nanotechnologies, voice analysis, personality profiling, data-mining, high-speed encryption, robotics, and drones, all of which were added to the Mossad's already impressive toolkit.

In addition to arming itself against the Iranian threat, Cohen saw building a sense of common ground with Saudi Arabia as a high priority, and indeed, doing that was an essential ingredient in the long-range plan that resulted in the Abraham Accords in 2020. At an undisclosed date in 2016, a high-level Israeli delegation made a secret visit to Saudi Arabia which resulted in a concrete agreement that was among the first major signs of cooperation between Israel and the kingdom. Specifically, Israel consented to the transfer of two islands in the Gulf of Aqaba, Tiran and Sanafir, from Egypt to Saudi Arabia. The kingdom wanted the islands—which had ironically been the trigger for the Six Day War when Egypt blocked the Straits of Tiran to Israeli shipping—in order to build a $4 billion bridge to link the Saudi coast with the Sinai Peninsula. The bridge was part of a plan known as Vision 2030 formulated by Prince

Mohammed Bin Salman, commonly known as MBS, to modernize the country's economy. A Saudi pundit then raved about what a "pragmatic and progressive personality" MBS was, adding, "all indicators show that he is prepared and willing to develop real, enduring ties with Israel."

All of this was important to Israel's evolving, if still informal, relations with the Sunni Arab states. But perhaps the most important event for Cohen early in his Mossad tenure was one over which Israel had no control and for which it entertained no expectation. This was the election in 2016 of Donald Trump, an American president with a very different way of looking at the world, including the Middle East, and a very different way of doing diplomacy than his predecessors. Prime Minister Netanyahu and his close-knit circle of advisers, among them Cohen and Israel's ambassador to the United States, Ron Dermer, smelled an opportunity to change American policy on the Palestinian issue and the wider issue of peace between Israel and moderate Sunni states.

Under the Obama administration, the mantra—as it had been pretty much under every previous president—was: "Solve the Israeli-Palestinian conflict and you can solve the rest of the Middle East's problems." Retired four-star Marine Corps General Jim Jones, Obama's first national security adviser, put it this way: "I'm of the belief that had God appeared in front of President Obama in 2009 and said if he could do one thing on the face of the planet, and one thing only, to make the world a better place and give people more hope and opportunity for the future, I would venture that it would have something to do with finding the two-state solution to the Middle East."

What Israel was hearing from the Gulf Arabs during the Obama years, however, was something completely different. The people Israeli officials were talking to told them that the strategic environment had changed: Israel had emerged as a security and tech power, while the U.S. had withdrawn from the region.

What's more, Israel's Gulf interlocutors had also made a crucial shift in their posture on the Palestinian question. Before, like the Americans, they were saying that Palestinian rights were a necessary precondition to any improvement in relations with Israel. Now they were saying that they no longer wanted the question of Palestinian statehood to block their wider strategic and commercial interests, which included ending their nonproductive and failed attempt to isolate Israel. An Israeli diplomat involved in the talks put it this way: "Mohammed Bin Salman is thinking to himself, 'Why is the mayor of Ramallah affecting the future of my country? This plonker? He has the keys to all of the Middle East.'"

This change, stemming from the rise of a radical, aggressive, Shiite Iran determined to gain hegemony in the Middle East, was important, but not easy to translate into new agreements. In a way, the Gulf states were caught between Sunni and Shiite fanaticism. On the Sunni side, the Arab Spring had led to the rise of the Muslim Brotherhood—a political Islamist Sunni movement—in Egypt and Tunisia, and to ISIS, which had taken control of huge swaths of Syria and Iraq. On the Shiite side, Iran had also taken advantage of the chaos of the Arab Spring to gain ground in Syria, Iraq, Lebanon, and Yemen, working through Shiite proxy militias to advance its hegemonic aims. With both the Obama and Trump administrations moving to reduce the American presence in the Middle East, Israel's standing became more important.

As Ambassador Dermer told us: "The Arab states see Iran as the tiger and ISIS as the leopard; they see the eight-hundred-pound U.S. gorilla walking out, and then they see the gorilla with the *kippa* on, and say maybe we should deal with them." In other words, the Gulf Arabs were coming to see Israel as their protectors from Iran if the U.S. withdrew from the region.

From the Israeli administration's point of view, another factor that caused the Sunni Arab states to see Israel in this way was Netanyahu's speech to Congress in which he made a vociferous case against the nuclear accords with Iran. Netanyahu's critics saw the speech as a colossal failure; it did nothing to block the Iran nuclear deal even as it offended the Obama administration and potentially turned off a generation of members of the Democratic Party. But the moderate Sunni Arab states were won over on a whole new level by Netanyahu's assertiveness and readiness to act independently of the U.S. when it came to security issues with Iran.

Coming from countries that had been unremittingly hostile to Israel's very existence, this was a major change. And so was the message coming from the incoming Trump administration. At an event at Trump Tower in New York attended by the city's glitterati, Trump was introduced to a senior Israeli official by his then chief strategist, Steve Bannon. "Can you make peace?" Trump asked. The official responded: "With the Palestinians? No. But we can make peace with several Arab states."

Israel wasted no time. In December 2016, Netanyahu dispatched Cohen on a secret visit to meet with members of the president-elect's team, including his pick for national security adviser, Michael Flynn. Cohen's assignment was to brief them on the Iranian threat and on the opportunities that Tehran's dark shadow created for Israeli ties with its Gulf neighbors.

The extent of Cohen's entry into the world of high-stakes diplomacy was also new for a Mossad chief, but he had come into the job with some experience, partly thanks to his time as Netanyahu's national security adviser. Fluent in English, French, and Arabic, he soon became known as Israel's de facto foreign minister, shuttling secretly between Gulf capitals, sometimes on the Mossad's private unmarked plane.

The Mossad has always been involved in contacts with states with which it has no ties through its Tevel division. But Cohen now formed a separate task force known as the "strategic-diplomatic directorate" to identify and pursue peacemaking opportunities with the Gulf states and other Muslim countries, while Tevel continued to deal with covert ties to intelligence agencies elsewhere.

Meanwhile, Bin Salman was becoming ever stronger in the Saudi hierarchy. In June 2017, his aging father, King Salman, deposed his nephew Mohammed Bin Nayef as Crown Prince and MBS was elevated to that position, cementing his status as heir apparent and the kingdom's strongman.

MBS has been described to us by various intelligence and diplomatic officials who have been in contact with him as highly approachable, having a contagious youthful energy, and possessing a desire to shake up his country. Jason Greenblatt, the Trump administration's special representative for international negotiations who'd spent countless hours with MBS, said the Saudi Crown Prince had a "willingness to mobilize everybody and anybody" to achieve his vision, which is to modernize his country, adopt a more moderate version of Islam, and prepare it for a future no longer dependent on its production of oil.

From Israel's point of view, MBS's vision included a far greater readiness to engage with the Jewish state than his father, King Salman, ever showed. MBS was also far less tied down by historic commitments to the Palestinian cause. On Iran, he denounced Ayatollah Khamenei as "the new Hitler"; he excoriated the 2015 Iran nuclear deal cut by the Obama administration as "lousy"; and accused the Obama administration of "getting cold feet" in working together to save Yemen, the country on Saudi Arabia's southern border where Iran has supported the Houthis, a Shiite faction that has been fighting the Sunni-dominated government in a vicious civil war. Most important from Israel's point of view, MBS was looking to Jerusalem for a security alliance.

Cohen met with, spoke with, or texted with MBS and his top intelligence advisers often, starting in late 2017, and there was an obvious rapport between these men, each of whom thrived on disruption and tearing up of the status quo. The Mossad chief's earliest visits to Riyadh were not even leaked to anyone, and while some of his later visits were sometimes disclosed to the media after the fact, the details of what took place at them were always lost in fog and rumor.

As it is now altogether well known, MBS has also displayed a brutal, ruthless streak. He "jailed" as many as four hundred Saudi princes and other members of the elite at the gilded Ritz-Carlton hotel in Riyadh, subjecting many of them to beatings and interrogations, sleep deprivation, and blackmail. He accused them of corruption and, according to Saudi officials, eventually some $100 billion was recovered from them and paid into a state fund. Now they knew who was in charge.

Bin Salman would also force Lebanon's prime minister Saad Hariri to resign after luring him to Saudi Arabia and detaining him. But most notoriously, in 2018 he ordered the murder of the Saudi dissident and *Washington Post* contributor Jamal Khashoggi, who was killed and dismembered by Saudi agents in the country's consulate in Istanbul.

More than any other action by MBS, the Khashoggi killing shocked the world and, especially in the U.S. and Europe, produced qualms about cooperating with Saudi Arabia at all. Israel could afford no such qualms. The Mossad had long identified Bin Salman and the Saudis as the dominant power whose agreement would be required before any concrete steps toward normalization of ties could occur. Meanwhile, however, it was the United Arab Emirates that the Mossad saw as most likely to be the first to come out of the closet, while the Saudis were expected to lead from behind. But before Israel could move relations with the UAE out into the open, Cohen had to do one more thing to deal with the fallout of an event that had happened several years before his appointment as the Mossad director.

At 1:30 in the afternoon on January 20, 2010, a maid found one Mahmoud Abdul Raouf Mohammed dead in room 230 of the five-star Al Bustan Rotana Hotel in downtown Dubai. He appeared to have died of natural causes as he slept, most likely of a heart attack, and there was no reason for police to suspect that his death had been the result of foul play. But a few days later, Hamas officials in Damascus were becoming worried about a missing operative in Dubai, Mahmoud al-Mabhouh, with whom they had lost contact. Hamas sent one of Mabhouh's men to the Dubai morgue, where he identified the supposed Abdul Raouf Mohammed as the missing Mabhouh.

Mabhouh was a Hamas terrorist who had participated in the brutal kidnapping and murder of two Israeli soldiers, Avi Sasportas and Ilan Sa'adon, in southern Israel in 1989. A former car mechanic who had started his terrorist career torching gambling dens in the Gaza Strip, the burly forty-nine-year-old, who by now had acquired a taste for luxury, had risen through the ranks to become the group's point man smuggling weapons from Iran to the Gaza Strip. Mabhouh worked with Qasem Soleimani and his lieutenants in Iran's Islamic Revolutionary Guard Corps Quds Force, the brains and the tentacles behind the Iranian network smuggling weapons to its proxies and clients across the region.

The disclosure that the dead man was Mabhouh led Dubai's chief of police Lieutenant General Dhahi Khalfan Tamim to reopen the investigation, and what he found would send shockwaves through intelligence communities around the world and strain the covert ties between Israel and the UAE.

Security cameras at the Al Bustan hotel showed someone breaking into Mabhouh's room at around the time that pathologists had estimated his death to have occurred. Using CCTV footage, hotel and airport records, Tamim and his team of investigators meticulously pieced together what had happened.

At a press conference in February 2010, a month after Mabhouh was found dead, the tough-talking, camera-loving Tamim announced that the Hamas arms dealer had been murdered by a hit squad that broke into his room and smothered him to death. Later, the police would state he had been killed using a heart-attack-inducing toxin. Tamim accused the Mossad of being behind the killing and revealed that at least eleven British, Irish, German, and French nationals had been involved. The investigation would later find that a total of twenty-six European passport holders had played a part in the operation and that their identities had been stolen from dual-national Israeli citizens. Pictures of all the suspects were published worldwide, along with video footage showing the assassins in the hotel. Ironically, the security systems that exposed the alleged Mossad team were sold to the UAE in a deal brokered by the Israeli Foreign Ministry's roving envoy to the Gulf, Bruce Kashdan.

The incident caused huge embarrassment for Israel and was considered the major failure of Meir Dagan's storied nine-year career as head of the spy agency. Shortly after leaving his post in 2012, Dagan declined in an interview we did with him at his Tel Aviv apartment to confirm that the Mossad was behind the operation. But he also denied that it was a failure. "Did anybody get caught?" the gruff but gentle former general asked rhetorically. (Later that year, Dagan was diagnosed with liver cancer, and he died in 2016.)

The incident was a major setback to the goal of normalization. Haim Tomer, head of the Tevel foreign nations liaison unit at the time, and Mossad's senior man in the contacts, told us that he heard very harsh words from the Emiratis about the Mabhouh killing and how long it would take relations to recover. The Emiratis were aggrieved that Israel had taken the law into its own hands instead of asking them to take care of the issue. "We would have taken him out of the game one way or the other," they told Tomer. Fast-forwarding closer to the present, in 2020, Dan Shapiro, who served as United States ambassador to Israel during the entire Obama administration, would reveal that Mabhouh's assassination led to a year-and-a-half break in the covert ties between Israel and the UAE.

But eventually, starting around 2011, a very gradual process of rebuilding trust took place as common interests began to outweigh the UAE's sense of insult. Among these were fear of Iran, the civil war in Syria where Iranian militias were already becoming involved, and the fact that Arab monarchies were trembling as a result of the Arab Spring, the popular uprisings from Tunisia to Egypt to Syria that challenged the Arab world's authoritarian governments. Mossad officials held countless meetings with their Emirati counterparts, though it would take until around 2015 for full contacts to be restored, and even then the most important person on the UAE side, Mohammed Bin Zayed, MBZ, remained "unavailable."

"Nothing takes longer than gaining the trust of Bedouins and nothing is more sensitive than the honor of the Bedouins," Tomer told us.

To gain that trust, Israel had to pay. In addition to a commitment, made with American mediation, to never again conduct similar operations on UAE soil, Israel offered the Emirates strategic remuneration in the form of a basket of new technologies and systems it had previously declined to share.

Even with all that, however, when Cohen came into office, MBZ was still refusing meetings with Israelis. The highest-level contact at the time was with Abdullah Bin Zayed, the UAE's foreign minister and MBZ's brother.

Finally, it was Cohen who was able to build strong relations with

MBZ, thanks to his own capabilities and to a carefully orchestrated campaign supported both by MBS and by Cohen's new allies in Washington, like CIA director Pompeo and Jared Kushner, Trump's son-in-law and special adviser on the Mideast.

Israel's effort to overcome the break in relations was also helped by former British prime minister Tony Blair, who had arranged for talks between Netanyahu's personal lawyer and confidant Yitzhak Molcho, and an undisclosed Emirati minister. These talks eventually blossomed into direct phone contact between Netanyahu and Bin Zayed.

Then, just as Cohen was striving to get relations with MBZ back on track, something mysterious, but full of portent happened, or perhaps it didn't happen. Either way, it showed how rapidly things were changing.

According to multiple media outlets, on September 7, 2017, Saudi Crown Prince Mohammed Bin Salman paid a discreet visit to Tel Aviv. He arrived in Israel by private plane via a third country, the reports said, was then taken to Mossad headquarters in Glilot, north of Tel Aviv, and there he met with senior Israeli officials, including Yossi Cohen and Benjamin Netanyahu.

Within weeks, reports of the visit leaked to the media and the hashtag #Bin_Salman_Visited_Israel trended on Twitter.

A visit by MBS to Israel, if it really happened, would have meant a near revolutionary change in the balance of forces in the Middle East, a stunning recognition by the Arab world's wealthiest and most prestigious state that Israel was a reality and even a partner, an ally, in the struggle against Iran. But did MBS visit Israel or not? Multiple sources in Israel, including intelligence sources, the media in the Gulf states, and the international press, confirmed that indeed, the Saudi Crown Prince had come to Tel Aviv. The reports of the visit, moreover, were never officially denied.

Some senior Mossad sources told us, however, that the visit never happened. Former U.S. deputy national security adviser Victoria Coates agreed with these sources, leading her to wonder who gained what by broadcasting such positive, but fake news. Coates spent years living in Saudi Arabia and is an expert on the country. But even if MBS did not come to Tel Aviv, the multiple reports from multiple sources saying that he did indicate a concerted and highly sophisticated misinformation campaign aimed at convincing the world, including some medium-level Israeli intelligence agents, that he had—likely to create buzz, momentum, and a positive atmosphere for the normalizations process. Before, almost any high-level contact between Israel and Saudi Arabia would have seemed unthinkable. Now, it was viewed as logical, rational, even inevitable.

And soon, there was to be more.

In November 2017, the IDF chief of staff Gadi Eisenkot gave an interview to the Saudi paper *Elaph.* For a Saudi paper to publish an interview with a senior Israeli military officer was unprecedented. But what Eisenkot revealed was even more important. The two countries, he said, were sharing intelligence on Iran, which he called the "true and biggest threat" in the Middle East. The following month, as if making sure the message was getting through, Israel's energy minister Yuval Steinitz told Israeli Army Radio that covert ties existed with many Muslim and Arab countries, specifically naming Saudi Arabia.

These disclosures were the culmination of the nearly two years of work by Cohen since being appointed director of the Mossad, in which he had taken advantage of some key American efforts to break new ground diplomatically, even as Washington was drawing down from the region militarily.

How did the situation culminate with Eisenkot's and Steinitz's bombshell interviews? Rewinding back a few months to late March 2017, Jason Greenblatt, the Trump administration's special representative for international negotiations, had met with the Saudis, the Emiratis, and others on the sidelines of the Arab League summit on the Jordanian Dead Sea coast. Greenblatt and his team came away with the feeling that the Gulf states did not want to be held back anymore by the Palestinians from making progress with Israel. At the same time, the Arab leaders didn't want to be seen as giving up on the Palestinian cause, certainly not without being perceived as trying hard to get the Palestinians a fair deal. The summit ended with a statement reaffirming the Arab League's commitment to a peace plan the Saudis had first proposed in 2002 that laid out terms for an end to the Arab-Israel conflict. Essentially, the 2017 statement reiterated the demands of the 2002 Saudi initiative. It ruled out establishing formal ties between Israel and any of the Gulf states before Israel had withdrawn from the Occupied Territories and a Palestinian state had been established, two conditions that seemed very distant.

Greenblatt's analysis of this was that MBS, MBZ, and the Sultan of Oman, Qaboos bin Said, were moving closer to elevating their levels of cooperation with Israel, but they were not yet ready for full or formal ties, especially if establishing them gave the appearance of abandoning the Palestinians. Nevertheless, the wheels continued to turn. On May 20 and 21, 2017, Trump, accompanied by Greenblatt and Kushner, traveled to Saudi Arabia on the first foreign visit of his presidency. Trump, who had once claimed that the Saudis had blown up the World Trade Center and that the kingdom wouldn't exist without American assistance, was greeted like royalty with "red carpets, lavish meals and American flags flying everywhere."

The warmth of the Saudi welcome to Trump was already a hopeful sign that things were changing for the better, but the trip was noteworthy also for the way it demonstrated the complete reversal in style and substance that the new administration was putting into place. Where Obama had adopted a conciliatory tone with Iran and signed the nuclear accords with Tehran, Trump, although he had not yet withdrawn from the JCPOA, was bellicose in his statements on the Islamic Republic. Where Obama had put limits on arms sales to Saudi Arabia because of its involvement in the war in Yemen, Trump signed a $110 billion weapons deal with MBS, in response to which the Saudis agreed to invest $350 billion in the U.S. Obama had skipped Israel altogether on his first Middle East visit, going to Egypt instead and making his "A New Beginning" speech to mend America's ties with the Muslim world. Trump flew from Riyadh to Tel Aviv in what was the first official direct flight between the two nations. And where relations between Obama and Netanyahu had been strained to say the least, "Bibi" (nickname for Benjamin) and "Donald" got along famously, a veritable love fest between two long-lost brothers.

Trump's back-to-back visits to Israel and Saudi Arabia created a new dynamic and energy in the region. MBS now felt much safer and more optimistic about the future. And Trump and his team of Kushner and Greenblatt desperately wanted progress on Middle East peace. Ideally, they wanted the Saudis to rally the Gulf countries to press the Palestinians to cut a deal. But to start that process, they wanted aspects of Saudi-Israeli relations to finally be made public.

Enter Yossi Cohen, who made a series of secret visits to Saudi Arabia between May and November 2017, during which, sitting on large, elegant sofas in one of MBS's many palaces, he tried to persuade the Crown Prince and his advisers to go public with the two countries' budding security cooperation. In the open meetings, MBS and his advisers often repeated boilerplate statements, especially about Palestinian rights and Israel's occupation of the West Bank, and did not seem ready to move forward. But Cohen was savvy enough—and patient enough—to wait for the "after" meeting in one of the side rooms where the real deals got done.

Rookies in negotiations with MBS and his advisers might occasionally raise their voices, or even commit small offenses in etiquette, like receiving drinks with their left hand. Not Cohen, a seasoned player with the Saudis who knew exactly how to reel them in and who understood how delicate an open relationship with what used to be called "the Zionist entity" was for the Saudis. But Cohen also knew that once they made a commitment, it would be ironclad. Mountains of bureaucracy and red tape could vanish in an instant.

Along with these visits by Cohen, Kushner and Greenblatt made their own secret trips to Saudi Arabia to hold talks with MBS in October 2017, during which they tried to nudge the Saudi leader to allow aspects of the relationship with Israel to be made public. Finally, yielding to this full-court press, MBS agreed. The public statements by Eisenkot and Steinitz about Israeli-Saudi Intelligence cooperation were the result.

As Cohen reviewed the headlines that these statements made, he wondered whether he too should go public about his progress and plans for the region. After all, he knew that the Saudis were the "big brother" to the UAE, Bahrain, and other countries in the region that might normalize their relations with Israel, and that making things public might create movement elsewhere.

But Cohen didn't know at the time if the Saudis would be willing to be the first Gulf state to establish diplomatic relations with Israel, or if going public with security ties would, alternatively, encourage other countries like the UAE and Bahrain to be the first to take that momentous step—which was how things would turn out. Given that his goal was a broad shift in the region, he decided to keep silent, waiting for the countries in the region to get nearer to crossing the threshold before he made any public disclosures.

The moment for that would come in July 2019.

Chapter 6

THE REVEAL

AS THE DIPLOMATIC EFFORT WITH THE SAUDIS, THE EMIRAtis, and others continued behind the scenes, leading up to the 2019 and 2020 breakthroughs which emerged as the Abraham Accords, Israel continued pushing the Trump administration to withdraw from the Iranian nuclear deal. The aim was to get sanctions ramped back up and at the same time to have a freer hand to go after the Iranian nuclear program, which meant hunting down top officials like IRGC Quds Force chief Soleimani and Iran nuclear chief Fakhrizadeh. The major move tying these trends together came on January 31, 2018, with the Mossad's theft of the Iranian nuclear archive, which the Israelis hoped would catalyze a decisive shift in public opinion toward Iran. To achieve that goal, however, would take a great deal of preparation and a bravura press conference performance by Netanyahu.

Once the archives had reportedly made their way from Tehran to Azerbaijan and then to Israel, Farsi-reading analysts from the Mossad and Israeli Military Intelligence began reviewing the tens of thousands of documents and diagrams seized from the warehouse in Shirobad, while nuclear scientists were mobilized to gain a full understanding of their significance.

But even as the analysts did their work, Netanyahu and Cohen came to a conclusion about what Israel's next step should be. Normally, an operation like the nuclear archive theft, carried out with the full range of Israel's special operations forces, would remain a top national secret for decades, so Israel could evade responsibility for the raid and protect the sources and methods used to carry it out. Normal practice would have been for the Israelis to discreetly share the nuclear treasure trove only with friendly countries, in particular the U.S. and the Europeans that were party to the JCPOA. But on this occasion the prime minister and his spy chief understood that they needed to exploit the information disclosed by the theft not only to convince the world about the depths of Iranian deceit, but also to legitimize their economic, psychological, and covert warfare campaigns against its nuclear program. They decided on an unprecedented and radical move: they would publicize the theft and make a substantial amount of the information available for the whole world to see.

"How you use intelligence is even more important than the intelligence itself," Cohen said, in 2021, after his term as Mossad chief was over, explaining the departure from usual secret practice. "It was critical to send a clear message to the Iranians that they had been penetrated, they are being watched, and they cannot continue lying to the world."

Netanyahu, who even his detractors admit is one of the more PR-savvy politicians on the global stage, began to put together a team to prepare for what many later called "the reveal." He subcontracted the work to Eliezer Toledano, military secretary to the prime minister, who in Israel can be almost as influential as the national security adviser.

Around February 28, one month after the heist, Toledano brought in his first recruit to the team, Netanyahu's public diplomacy chief, Yarden Vatikai.

A slick PR veteran who had previously been a spokesman for the Jewish Agency and a media adviser to the defense minister, Vatikai had worked with the Mossad regularly, serving as a kind of public voice for an agency that typically doesn't have its own official spokesperson.

"I want to bring you in on a mega secret," Toledano, who would head the IDF's southern division and lead it in the Gaza War of May 2021, told a stunned Vatikai, informing him of the heist and of Netanyahu's plan for exploiting its public relations value. Vatikai was then briefed in full by Toledano's aide, Amnon Shefler. (Shefler later went on to head the IDF's foreign media branch.)

"I was super-shocked," Vatikai later told us. "It was mind-blowing. I had worked with professionals in the field of intelligence and operations for many years. I had been in many jobs involving security and diplomatic issues, whether in the IDF's spokesman's office or in the prime minister's office under Yitzhak Rabin and Shimon Peres. I thought I had seen everything!"

Once Vatikai had been briefed, Netanyahu called him in along with Toledano; National Security Adviser Meir Ben Shabbat; Yonatan Shechter, a diplomatic adviser to the prime minister; and a few Mossad officials (who are still serving and whose identities cannot be revealed) to view an initial presentation that the Mossad and other national security officials had worked on. "Your job is to get ready to present the operation's accomplishments to the broadest and most diverse possible global audience," Netanyahu told those present. "You need to do everything you can to use the information—from a public relations campaign to diplomacy.

"It's not enough just to present this to Trump," Netanyahu added. "We need to present this to the world."

"It was clear to us without the prime minister even needing to explicitly say it," Vatikai recalled, "that a major goal was to destabilize and wreck the very bad nuclear agreement with Iran, which everyone knew he opposed."

Nevertheless, the task was not going to be an easy one. Europe especially was pushing very hard to maintain the nuclear deal and was not going to welcome an effort by Israel to discredit it.

This is where Netanyahu's determination to make Iran's deceit public knowledge came in. The prime minister often said that "quiet diplomacy by itself is not enough, if it is not also public diplomacy."

In early March, the team, which now had added David Keyes, Netanyahu's English-language spokesman, along with Yonatan Shechter, Amnon Shefler, and the Mossad officials, got to work. They were given the original unfiltered material in Farsi. Recalling his shock, Vatikai told us how he said to himself: "How on earth will we convert this into something that can be presented to the world?" Translating mountains of nuclear material in Farsi was an unprecedented undertaking and significantly delayed revealing the heist to the world.

The Mossad officials gave the rest of the team a rundown of what they had found in the archive, and the PR people negotiated, as one source involved in the process put it, over "how we were going to do this, how often we would meet, and what would be the mechanism for getting and giving feedback to Netanyahu." The team met a couple times a week with the heads of the Mossad's different branches, its nuclear experts, and other specialists to decide what would eventually be included in Netanyahu's presentation, and which items would have to be dropped because they gave away too much. "Some items would have had amazing public relations value, but they were too dangerous from a proliferation perspective so we could not use them," our source told us. "Or we could only use them after parts of the photos or information had been blurred or blacked out."

On top of that, there were items that intelligence officials weren't going to publish because they "didn't want [the Iranians] to know that we know," Israel's ambassador to London, Mark Regev, who came on board later in the operation, told us. The team, he said, needed to be very careful not to indirectly or unintentionally reveal Mossad tactics.

Arguments broke out among the intelligence officials on one side and Vatikai, Keyes, and Shechter on the other, with the former concerned only with the intelligence value of the materials and the latter wanting only materials that would pack a public relations punch. One clash between the two, for example, was over whether to name Iranian nuclear scientists. The Mossad feared that naming names, especially lesser-known figures, would provide hints to the Iranians about Israeli intelligence sources and leaks. But Vatikai and the others were strongly in favor of naming these names. "It was very important that we name Fakhrizadeh," Vatikai told us. "The public deals with people. It is very different than talking about an organization like AMAD [Iran's clandestine nuclear project until 2003] or the SPND [Iran's Organization of Defensive Innovation and Research]" in a vacuum, adding, "if you connect faces and names to the organizations, you have a major public impact."

Once a week, the group met with Netanyahu, showing him a mix of videos, PowerPoint presentations, and computer graphs. In these meetings, Netanyahu would repeat some of the messages he had conveyed earlier: "Always focus on the message. The world must understand that Iran lied and continues to lie. The point is that this is not just a historical issue—it continues to happen." Iran, the message was, lies when talking about the distant past, and it lies again when talking about more recent events, for example, by concealing the military AMAD unit inside the SPND to give it civilian cover. The message, as one source put it to us, had to be: "Don't do business with these people," whether in the economic sector or in trusting them to follow diplomatic deals like the JCPOA.

"It took us a long time to figure out how to properly highlight this message using slides [in Netanyahu's eventual presentation]—not just of the archive," the source said.

Among Netanyahu's worries was that the presentation might come off as boring. "I want something very strong visually with images that help tell the story," he told the team. "Don't make me just a speaker who happens to have a slideshow in the background." There was also a debate about presenting a visual of the materials themselves. Would it be helpful to show the folders and disks taken from the Iranian warehouse? The compromise was to bring copies of the originals to the press conference, not the original physical documents themselves, to enhance security for an event with a room full of reporters and other people without security clearances.

But it was critical to Netanyahu to be able to say that he was actually pointing to information taken from Iran. He balked when he saw that some of the copies of documents to be shown to the world were pink in color, until Vatikai explained to him, smiling broadly, that this was the color of the actual stolen Iranian documents—Yes, the original color of many of Iran's nuclear secrets was pink!

All of these broader efforts came after Cohen and the others had worked on a private presentation to Israel's most important audience, the Americans. The goal here was simple: to convince them, using the information gained in the theft, to withdraw from the nuclear deal with Tehran. This effort started immediately after the theft had taken place, when Cohen called Secretary of State Mike Pompeo to give him an initial brief on the operation. After his first update from Cohen about the heist, Pompeo told National Security Adviser H. R. McMaster about the new Israeli information, and together they went to President Trump to fill him in.

Then, early in March, Cohen traveled to Washington where he gave Pompeo a more comprehensive briefing. It fell on receptive ears. "The entire basis of the nuclear deal was fundamentally flawed," Pompeo told us in an interview, adding, "The Iranians have no intention of ceasing to seek a nuclear weapon."

Cohen and Pompeo, as we've seen, had already built up a strong professional and personal relationship, based on their cooperation as heads of their countries' spy services and their common goals regarding Iran. But Pompeo was especially bowled over by the Mossad's achievement in getting Iran's nuclear archive. He said the operation "redefined daring and boldness."

On March 5, Netanyahu and Cohen showed Trump a short video summing up the main findings of the raid. He knew that he pretty much had the president on his side, when Trump pointed to other senior administration officials in the Oval Office and said, "Maybe they needed to see this. I didn't. I've already decided to leave the deal." The American side, McMaster told us, now had a "pretty good description about what was in the containers and what [the Mossad] found."

"What was significant about it," McMaster said, referring to the archive, "was it just confirmed you can't trust the Iranians about the nuclear deal. There was a completely inadequate verification and inspection regime. . . . These documents were history, but were of course indicative of what reliably is an ongoing nuclear weapons program. It helped because those looking for excuses or reasons to pretend with the Iranians that with a weak agreement, they could be convinced to abandon their nuclear program—this was a good corrective."

Despite that view, however, McMaster did not agree with the ultimate Israeli goal. He still believed, as he told Trump, that there were tremendous advantages to staying in the JCPOA, among them to use leaving it as a threat to convince the Iranians to agree to tighter restrictions. McMaster argued that new "snapback" sanctions aimed at isolating the regime financially and continuing to keep the public relations focus on Iran's proxy wars against Israel and the U.S. would be more effective than pulling out of the deal altogether.

But then, three weeks before the public revelation of the archives, Trump fired McMaster, with whom he had failed to "gel." McMaster had come into the job of NSC adviser with a reputation as a "warrior-thinker," but Trump saw him as gruff and condescending. McMaster's opposition to withdrawing from the JCPOA was probably also a factor. In any case, Israel had no problem with the change, especially because McMaster's replacement was the ultra-hard-liner John Bolton, who, in contrast to McMaster, had absolute contempt for the Iran deal and was strongly in favor of withdrawing from it.

Bolton told us that the archive material provided a huge justification for what Trump intended to do. It was "dynamite," he said. "Even a casual description of the material showed it was a potential game changer. It undercut twenty years of Iranian lies about what they were doing." The only disappointing element of the operation, he quipped, was that "the Mossad did not bring enough trucks into that warehouse to take the rest of the 'data.'"

Meanwhile, preparations for "the reveal" stepped up, with two contradictory goals needing to be achieved. One was to get the press conference ready and to be sure that both the domestic and international media would be present. That meant telling the press that something important was going to be disclosed but without telling it anything that might lead it to start asking the sorts of questions that could lead to a leak. In the end, they decided to announce the press conference only three hours before it was scheduled, to reduce the time for journalistic snooping. Vatikai had another worry, namely Netanyahu's reputation for making portentous pronouncements that turned out not to be as newsworthy as he thought they would be. This had at times led the sometimes jaded press representatives to accuse him of crying wolf, and Vatikai and his team wanted to avoid any suspicion that, when the press conference was called, they would suppose he was crying wolf again, and not show up. "We did not give them too much information which might help them guess what it was about, but we did want them to understand that it was important," Regev said. "There is always a tension there."

One thing that was decided: the press conference would be held in a large room at the Defense Ministry in Tel Aviv, close to many media headquarters. The presentation required technicians, drawn directly from the Mossad, to install audiovisual equipment, and Vatikai fretted that people seeing the preparations would start asking questions about what was in progress. He thought that would be especially likely if the venue was a hotel or the Foreign Ministry, which Vatikai felt was especially prone to leaks.

But everything was hidden from the higher echelons of the Defense Ministry as well, even as work getting ready for the press conference proceeded apace. Vatikai recalled to us how he used personal connections in the Defense Ministry Logistics Division to stop news about the temporary tenants, the Mossad technicians, from being known elsewhere in the ministry. "Every day, there were lots of people going in and out of the Defense Ministry," Vatikai told us, "and I was surprised it lasted for weeks without a major leak."

After months of planning and clandestinely setting the scene for the press conference, rehearsals began around April 20. Netanyahu has always been meticulous about his public presentations, practicing his speeches multiple times in private. For "the reveal," he rehearsed as many as fifteen times. But he still wasn't happy. Just a few days before the press conference, the prime minister decided to bring in Mark Regev, an Australian-born immigrant who had Hebraicized his name from Freiberg and had been Netanyahu's English-language spokesman. "We need you in Israel over the weekend," Vatikai told him over the phone. "I can't tell you what it's about, but it's really important. The prime minister needs you here."

Regev was not just any diplomat being recalled. As Israel's ambassador to England, he held one of the highest and most crucial positions in the Foreign Ministry. Jerusalem's relationship with London is arguably the next most crucial one after its relationship with the U.S., and here was Regev, one of the most senior diplomats in Israel's foreign service, being told to temporarily drop his ambassadorial post as well as his staff with almost zero explanation. But Netanyahu considered Regev to be the best explainer for Israel of the decade. He wanted him by his side.

Regev joined the team right away and worked day and night for three straight days without leaving the office, and, from Vatikai's point of view, rising to the occasion. Regev had a knack for helping Netanyahu nail down the wording, pitch, and themes that would get through to a varied global audience. Vatikai recalls that Regev was "almost militant about using the best phraseology for messaging."

For Cohen, who looked in from time to time, what was taking place was breaking new ground. The theft operation had been a thundering success, and he knew Netanyahu could present Israel's case effectively. Cohen would also enjoy basking in the public glory that would come from the revelation of that success, something that Mossad officials like him almost never got to do. But as good as he felt about disclosing the operation's success, which he also knew could eventually help launch a political career for him, part of him realized that public exposure carried risks, both personal and professional. It was one thing to have a knack for establishing trust and rapport with someone like MBS, or for planning bold, secret operations. It was a very different thing to risk exposure to the broad world, with all of the errors that could occur and all of the unintended consequences that could ensue.

And everybody involved knew what the message had to be and to whom it was directed. Netanyahu's disclosures needed to overcome whatever hesitations the Trump administration had about withdrawing from the nuclear deal, to push it over the hump. The American commitment to the deal had been based on the assumption that Iran would "come clean" about its past nuclear weapons activity and that it would halt a variety of nuclear activities for the fifteen years required by the agreement. Both the Israelis and the Americans knew that the IAEA had essentially given Iran a pass on its violations. Essentially, the IAEA had said the violations were too minor to require punitive countermeasures and certainly too minor to justify withdrawing from the JCPOA altogether. That's where the Israeli message had to make a difference, but it wasn't going to be easy. The material in the archive was technical, complicated, and not ready-made for a dramatic narrative. A forceful, incriminating presentation of that material had to be fashioned so as to expose the whole nuclear deal as the fake which Netanyahu and the Israelis believed it to be. "Everyone knew Iran was lying," Regev said, "but now they couldn't ignore it anymore."

So dedicated was Netanyahu to rehearsing his presentation that even important events in his staff's lives were thrown off.

Vatikai himself was supposed to be promoted to the rank of lieutenant colonel at IDF military headquarters. The ceremony was scheduled for one of the days when the prime minister would be rehearsing, but hours after he was expected to finish. Vatikai's whole family was at IDF headquarters, but Vatikai was in the rehearsal room with Netanyahu, and when the prime minister insisted on a whole new run-through, Vatikai, looking at his watch in helpless frustration, was more than an hour late for his own promotion. His cell phone, which he had to hand over to security during the rehearsal, was flooded with increasingly stressed-out messages from his wife and from the IDF. "And no one from the Prime Minister's Office would tell them where I was!" Vatikai said. "They did my whole ceremony without me! They gave the new rank and award to my wife, ate all of the refreshments and left!"

For all the elaborate, even obsessive preparations to create the perfect event, Regev recalled, just before it was supposed to take place a disturbing discovery was made: Netanyahu's microphone didn't work. This was because in order to keep everything hush-hush, the technical personnel who would normally perform standard checks didn't get there until the last second. With minutes to go, Vatikai suddenly began to worry that Netanyahu would knock over the copies of the archive disks when he took off the cover that had been placed over them so the assembled journalists wouldn't see them until the right dramatic moment. That had happened many times in rehearsal, leading team members to choke with laughter, despite the serious subject at hand.

On April 30, at exactly 8:00 p.m., coinciding with the prime-time evening news broadcast in Israel, Netanyahu walked out onstage in front of dozens of photographers and reporters from around the world, called to a press conference where "dramatic findings would be displayed."

Dressed in a black suit and blue tie, his graying hair carefully parted to one side and a dour expression on his face, Netanyahu began with video clips of Iran's Supreme Leader Ayatollah Khamenei, President Hassan Rouhani, and Foreign Minister Mohammad Javad Zarif all making public statements vigorously denying that Iran had a nuclear weapons program. Then a curtain was pulled revealing two words flashing on a giant white screen—"Iran lied." Standing at a podium at a calculated distance from a bookshelf holding parts of the stolen Iranian archive, Netanyahu told the world of Israel's possession of the full, heretofore secret record of Iran's effort to become a nuclear weapons power. Then, calmly, methodically, showing a series of slides, he presented the incriminating evidence demonstrating the falseness of its top leaders' assurances—photos, videos, microfilm, blueprints, and more—proving that Iran's "comprehensive program" to "design, build, and test nuclear weapons," and to mount them on a ballistic missile warhead, had never ceased, despite the requirements of the JCPOA.

It was one of the most dramatic news events in Israel in years.

It was also one of the most profoundly effective public presentations of intelligence aimed at shaping policy in recent memory, at least according to Netanyahu and Cohen. Not everybody agreed. Critics in the media and Netanyahu's political opponents argued that the press conference did no more than serve the prime minister's political needs, and they accused the Mossad director of pandering to them. Some senior officials were furious that Netanyahu had disclosed the theft at all, among them Lieutenant General Eisenkot, the chief of staff of the IDF, which had provided logistical support and intelligence via satellites, drones, and other air force assets for aspects of the operation. Eisenkot told us that Netanyahu had promised to keep the operation classified and that he would only share the results with friendly intelligence services and the IAEA. Netanyahu, he said, only revealed his plans to make it all public hours before the press conference. Regev defended Netanyahu, arguing that it was his prerogative to decide what to disclose to the public and when. He added that the prime minister had a broader vantage point than the IDF chief, who would be focused on more tactical security concerns.

Cohen's former boss, Pardo, was impressed by the operation's tactical success, but also incensed that it was made public. Both he and Eisenkot thought that in telling the world what had happened and providing details of the theft, Netanyahu had compromised the security of Israel's intelligence apparatus and unnecessarily poked a finger in the eye of the Iranians, something they feared could lead to retaliation.

Cohen, naturally enough, remained adamant in his defense of his and Netanyahu's actions. Privately, he derided Pardo's position as spineless. As for publicizing the operation, he argued that it was entirely justified as a way of influencing the U.S., the IAEA, and the European Union, as well as sowing chaos and confusion in Iran about how its security could have been so badly breached. As for the intelligence trove, Cohen said: "Put it in the Place de l'Étoile as far as I'm concerned," referring to the vast circle in the center of Paris dominated by the Arc de Triomphe.

Whatever the debate about the wisdom, or lack of it, in announcing the theft to the world, it was impossible to deny the significance of the information. The haul from the heist included 55,000 pages of documents and another 50,000 files stored on 183 compact discs—more original intelligence than the Mossad had ever received at any one time before. It proved that Iran's oft-repeated claim that its nuclear program was for civilian use was a fabrication, and that Iran not only had a weapons program but that it had destroyed essential documentation as part of a concerted effort at concealment. Much of this was already suspected by the U.S. and others, but the authenticity of the information made it impossible for Iran to continue its denials.

The trove also provided Israel with evidence on a "whole different level"—in the words of a senior intelligence officer who briefed the media, referring to the irrefutable nature of the materials. The documentation, furthermore, gave the international community the ability to confront Iranian lies with the cold hard truth regarding its nuclear ambitions. According to the officer, Israel was not able to make public all of the "truly incriminating photos" that it now had in its possession "because they clearly show how to build an atomic weapon."

Among the documents was a map that showed five secret nuclear test sites that Israel hadn't known about before, along with several other facilities involved in the nuclear chain. "Any tests Iran might now do at those sites will no longer remain secret," one official said.

Intelligence communities worldwide were stunned by the Mossad's operational accomplishment. But at a strategic level, observers and pundits broke in different directions, some hoping that the revelations would torpedo the 2015 nuclear deal, others wishing that they would just bounce off it. Those wanting to destroy the deal, like Netanyahu and Cohen, said the disclosures provided a smoking gun basis for doing so. In contrast, those who wanted to maintain the deal said the information referred to past actions and did not prove any new violations by Iran of the deal, and should have no impact on it.

There were strong points for each side. A careful analysis of the PowerPoint slides and a comparison of them to past IAEA reports shows that most of the Iran documents dated to the period 1999–2003, supporting the view that they failed to reveal much of anything new about Iran's nuclear activities. Indeed, a well-known IAEA report of December 2015 had already disclosed that Iran had a weapons program with Fakhrizadeh as its head. (Despite that earlier revelation, Netanyahu wanted to emphasize Fakhrizadeh's name to the general public, the media, and Western intelligence to draw greater scrutiny toward him since most of the world had completely ignored the 2015 IAEA report.) Still, many of the technical elements presented by Netanyahu could also be found in that same IAEA report. For example, Netanyahu presented slides showing designs for the development of nuclear cores as well as for a multi-point initiation (MPI) system—allowing for multiple detonations of a warhead—but this had been previously disclosed by the IAEA in 2015.

Netanyahu, however, also rattled off a list of specific claims Iran made to the IAEA that the new documents disproved. This gets a bit technical, but, for example, he showed documents contradicting Iranian claims that it had not done work on a shockwave generator, a critical component for initiating a nuclear explosion inside a spherical shell by using sophisticated technology. The IAEA in 2015 knew about some of this work, but not all.

There were other items of enormous importance. For example, while it was known before that Iran was doing experiments related to testing a nuclear explosive device at five sites, Western intelligence had no idea where the sites were. Now they knew that two were concealed in extremely hard-to-find locations in Semnan province near the Caspian Sea and three were in the Lut Desert in southeastern Iran. This information allowed Western intelligence to better follow suspicious activities at these sites.

What is more, Netanyahu's presentation provided previously unknown specifics about Iran's goal, which Netanyahu said was to build five warheads of 10 kilotons each. What that meant was that Iran was doing more than just striving to build a small nuclear deterrent. Five 10-kiloton bombs posed an undeniable threat to the Jewish state. That's why during his press conference, a lot of attention focused on one slide, made by the Israelis to call attention to what was for them the most important point: The caption on the slide read: "5 warheads, 10 kilotons TNT yield, on a missile."

One person who warmly welcomed Netanyahu's presentation was Donald Trump. He would use the evidence obtained by the Mossad to justify his decision to withdraw the United States from the nuclear accords, which he did on May 8, 2018, just over a week after Netanyahu's press conference.

"At the heart of the Iran deal was a giant fiction: that a murderous regime desired only a peaceful nuclear energy program," Trump said. "Today, we have definitive proof that this Iranian promise was a lie." He continued, "Last week, Israel published intelligence documents—long concealed by Iran—conclusively showing the Iranian regime and its history of pursuing nuclear weapons."

Trump's actions were praised by the Republican Party, some Democratic Party hawks, and Israel's political and defense establishment. But it remains a controversial move, vigorously opposed by most Democrats, most notably Joe Biden, who later campaigned for the presidency in part on a vow to find a way for the U.S. to reenter the accord.

"The bottom line is that Iran is closer to a nuclear bomb today than it was when Donald Trump took office," Biden wrote in an op-ed for CNN during the election campaign. "And Trump has no answer for that. Five years ago, even Russia and China stood with our European allies behind an American-led approach to Iran's nuclear program. Now, America stands alone." Cohen's predecessor Pardo would call Trump's leaving the JCPOA "a catastrophe" because there was no "Plan B" in place if his "maximum pressure" campaign against Iran failed to stop its nuclear progress.

From Israel's perspective in the Netanyahu-Cohen era, giving Trump the justification he needed to get out of the nuclear accords was far from the only benefit of the archive theft. Among the main finds in the archive, not yet released to the public, was "the map" showing the previously unknown nuclear sites. This facilitated a new comprehensive list of both the five test sites mentioned above and a wide range of other previously unknown sites which were part of Iran's nuclear cycle. Developed by the Mossad from the treasure trove of information, this map was and still is of critical importance. It allowed the Mossad to collect new intelligence before the Iranians had fully absorbed how badly they had been penetrated.

The Mossad was already hard at work using the map to prepare its new operational plans. In the following years, armed with new intelligence, it would strike Iran over and again.

The Mossad's raid on Iran's secret nuclear archives and the publication of the evidence on April 30, 2018, quickly put the International Atomic Energy Agency in an awkward position.

Though dismissed by much of the public as a boring group of technocrats issuing reports that have no influence on a country's actual behavior, the IAEA plays a very significant role. Its inspectors' privileged access to nuclear sites makes it the authoritative source of information on what individual countries, like Iran, are doing on the nuclear front. Its findings can shape the world's nuclear agenda, which is why Israel, the U.S., and Iran have for years engaged in a diplomatic dance around the agency. Israel and the U.S. have pushed it to be more aggressive and critical in its postures toward Iran, while the Iranians strive, naturally enough, for the opposite.

During much of the time that Iran has been the main, controversial focus of the IAEA, its head was Director General Mohamed ElBaradei, who was regarded by both the U.S. and Israel as an advocate of "appeasement" on Iran, avoiding conflict with Tehran even if that meant allowing the Islamic Republic to move closer to nuclear weapons.

In late 2009, ElBaradei was replaced as director general by Yukiya Amano, a former Japanese ambassador to the agency who was viewed initially by both Israel and the U.S. as being more prepared to be tough with Tehran. In fact, in November 2010, *The Guardian* reported on an American diplomatic cable supplied by WikiLeaks, detailing a meeting between Amano and an American ambassador in which Amano said he "was solidly in the U.S. court on every key strategic decision, from high-level personnel appointments to the handling of Iran's alleged nuclear weapons program."

Amano was deeply involved in lining up support for the July 14, 2015, JCPOA nuclear deal.

But that was a turning point in his handling of the Islamic Republic. From then on, at least from the American and Israeli points of view, Amano's top priority was no longer detecting Iranian violations, such as concealment of activities banned by the nuclear deal and reporting them to the world, but keeping the JCPOA in place.

And so, for example, in December 2015, Amano declared Iran's "past military dimensions" essentially a closed issue, despite the existence of numerous key questions regarding what Iran had done before and never disclosed.

When the Trump administration took office in January 2017, Amano remained supportive of the attitude of the previous Obama administration—defending the JCPOA against any attempt to weaken or withdraw from it. This meant that when, suddenly, the Mossad produced primary, strong evidence of actual Iranian cheating—backed by original Iranian documents proving that Amano had been hoodwinked by the Iranians in many ways—the IAEA director general seemed in no rush to admit fault and change direction. Instead, the IAEA's goal was to find a way to preserve the Iranian nuclear deal by limiting the impact of the disclosures.

Five months after "the reveal," for example, Netanyahu, speaking at the U.N. General Assembly in New York, disclosed some additional information that had been provided to the IAEA months before, namely that traces of illicit uranium had been found at a secret nuclear storage facility at Turquzabad in northern Iran. "The IAEA still has not taken any action," Netanyahu charged. "It has not posed a single question of Iran. It has not demanded to inspect a single new site discovered in that secret archive." That, Netanyahu continued, is why "I decided to reveal today something else that we revealed to the IAEA and to other intelligence agencies."

The IAEA did, finally, inspect Turquzabad in April 2019, six months after Netanyahu's U.N. speech and more than a year after the Mossad had told the IAEA about the existence of the site. When Amano was questioned about this, his reply was that the IAEA needed to take its time to verify any information provided by third parties. This appeared to be his way of trying to tone down any excitement over the Mossad's discoveries.

A few months after Netanyahu's September 2018 speech at the U.N., on January 30, 2019, Amano gave a more defiantly defensive speech. "The credibility of the Agency as a whole is our biggest asset," he said. "Independent, impartial and factual safeguards implementation is essential to maintain that credibility. If our credibility is thrown into question, and, in particular, if attempts are made to micro-manage or put pressure on the Agency in nuclear verification, that is counterproductive and extremely harmful." In other words, stop criticizing the IAEA for taking its time to verify information produced by the Mossad.

The impression that the IAEA had no appetite to go after Iran for its violations was strengthened by press leaks in April 2019. Among the disclosures: the IAEA in multiple visits to the Turquzabad site had found signs of radioactive material, but was refusing to publicize them. The IAEA did not respond to inquiries we made as to the apparent withholding of those results.

Meanwhile, the Trump administration, which had withdrawn from the JCPOA the year before, was tightening the screws on Iran. Until 2019, Trump had agreed to waivers from Iranian sanctions for eight key countries, including China, Russia, India, and others. This had kept Iran's economy above water even if it was suffering from the wider sanctions regime imposed by the U.S. and the Europeans. But in May 2019, Trump ended those waivers, closing a loophole by which the Islamic Republic had been able to sell oil, and it was at this point that Khamenei started to fight back much more strongly. From May 2019 to January 2020, Iran carried out a series of new violations of the nuclear deal. Most significantly, it started to build up its enriched uranium stock to a point where, if further enriched to higher levels, it could develop several nuclear weapons. In the fall of 2019, Cohen and Pompeo were hard at work coming up with contingency plans in case Iran went too far. They were in constant touch, so much so that Cohen, a fanatic about his own physical fitness, would sometimes text Pompeo both before and after he finished working out on his exercise machines.

In March 2020, Iran seemed to cross a red line. It now had enough low-grade enriched uranium to produce a nuclear bomb, if it chose to enrich that uranium to a higher weaponized level. Still, it didn't step up its enrichment activities to the point where it appeared to be close to an actual nuclear weapon. The American presidential election was looming, and Tehran, while continuing its enrichment program, probably didn't want to get too close to a bomb, hoping that by staying low-profile and not causing any alarm, it could help to oust the vehemently anti-Iran Trump administration.

But just as Khamenei and Fakhrizadeh were fine-tuning the country's nuclear strategy, the Mossad and Israel had been working on a diplomatic blow that Iran couldn't see coming.

Chapter 7

AN ALLIANCE EMERGES

THE HEIST OF THE IRANIAN NUCLEAR ARCHIVE AND PUBLIC disclosure of its contents in April 2018 had not only dealt a blow to Iran's prestige, it also boosted Israel's standing in the eyes of the Gulf Arabs. "MBS and MBZ were so impressed with the heist that it made them feel Israel was making them more secure and increased their readiness to move toward normalization," one senior member of the Netanyahu administration told us.

The next few months saw intensive diplomacy over what was, even before it was negotiated, being called—with Trumpian hyperbole—the "Deal of the Century," the utopian Israeli-Palestinian peace plan that the Trump administration was expected to announce at some point. The Trump team led by Jared Kushner and Jason Greenblatt visited the region several times to work on the plan and push Israeli-Gulf ties forward. The Saudis and Emiratis were still seeking progress on the Palestinian front before agreeing to any advance on normalization, and this was an obstacle given that the Palestinians themselves had unequivocally rejected the Trump initiative. "The Arab states did not want to be held back, but they did not want to give up on the Palestinian cause . . . they weren't quite there yet," Greenblatt told us.

Meanwhile, Yossi Cohen continued his contacts with the Gulf leadership. At a gathering of spy chiefs from around the region in Aqaba, Jordan, on the Red Sea coast, Cohen sat at the table with the head of the Saudi General Intelligence Directorate, Khalid bin Ali Humaidan, the intelligence chiefs of Egypt and Jordan, and Major General Majed

Farah, the head of the Palestinian General Intelligence Service. On the agenda was an explicit threat conveyed to Farah that the Gulf states could move forward in their relations with Israel without the Palestinians. The following day, Netanyahu flew to Amman to meet with King Abdullah of Jordan where the warning was repeated. Jordan formerly ruled the West Bank, a large percentage of its population is Palestinian, and the kingdom is often consulted on Palestinian matters.

Reports would later emerge that Netanyahu, accompanied by Cohen, met with MBZ in the UAE in 2018. Israel was becoming increasingly confident that a breakthrough in ties with the UAE and perhaps other Gulf states was only a matter of time.

But the murder of Jamal Khashoggi on October 2, 2018, caused a slowdown in the behind-the-scenes discussions that, until then, had been steadily moving forward. One disclosure about the murder was embarrassing to Israel. It turned out that the Saudi agents pursuing Khashoggi had infected the phone of his fiancée, Hanan Elatr, and other persons he was in contact with, including a Canada-based Saudi dissident Omar Abdulaziz, using a spyware program, allegedly Pegasus, developed by an Israeli company, NSO Group—although this has been denied by NSO. Sources have told us that providing NSO's spy tools was a sweetener for the Saudis, the UAE, and other countries with whom Israel wanted to develop ties.

After the murder, the Kingdom's license to use Pegasus was suspended, but Netanyahu and Cohen intervened to prevent the Khashoggi murder from derailing their larger diplomatic efforts. They may not have liked the actions of the tempestuous Crown Prince in eliminating nettlesome opponents, but they also felt Israel's long-term national interests were far more important. In his talks with senior Trump administration officials, Netanyahu called MBS a "strategic ally."

Still, there were repercussions over the brutal Khashoggi killing that were beyond Israeli control. Responding to the international outrage over the murder, MBS promised a full investigation. In the meantime, he fired two of his top advisers, Saud al Qhatani and General Ahmad al Asiri, both of whom were said to have been involved in the murder. But al Qhatani and al Asiri had also played leading roles in connections with

Israel. Al Qhatani, who was said to have overseen the torture and interrogation of Khashoggi, was the Saudi point man in the deal to purchase Pegasus from NSO, while al Asiri, a former deputy head of Saudi Intelligence and the alleged mastermind behind the assassination, had reportedly traveled to Israel several times to talk about the two countries' still secret security cooperation (al Asiri was later put on trial and acquitted; al Qhatani was investigated in the affair by the Saudi prosecution, but was not charged "due to insufficient evidence").

A few weeks after the Khashoggi assassination, Cohen and Netanyahu made a public visit to meet with Sultan Qaboos, the aging leader of Oman, a nation on the southern tip of the Gulf, with which Israel did not, and still doesn't, have diplomatic ties. They flew over Saudi airspace on their way to the sultanate at the mouth of the Persian Gulf, where it shares the vital oil shipping lanes of the Strait of Hormuz with Iran.

It was the first public visit by an Israeli leader to Oman in twenty-two years. Shimon Peres opened a trade office there in 1996, but it was shut down four years later amid the violence of the Second Intifada—although secret ties did continue. The Netanyahu visit in October 2018 was almost ruined when Netanyahu's wife, Sara, insisted on accompanying her husband, an embarrassing breach of Omani protocol that spouses do not join in state visits to meet with the unmarried and ailing Qaboos, who had been in power for five decades. But in the end, the Omanis accepted the breach, and in his public statements after the meeting, Netanyahu stressed the bigger picture. "You should not underestimate the openness and the thirst in the Arab world today for Israel," he said.

Cohen and other Israeli officials told us that if Qaboos had not been ill—he died on January 10, 2020—Oman would have pushed for full normalization of relations with Israel along with the UAE and Bahrain. However, Qaboos's cousin and successor Sultan Haitham bin Tariq has, while maintaining an unofficial relationship with Israel, opted to maintain its position of neutrality.

Just a few days after the 2018 Oman summit, Miri Regev, a hard-line minister from Netanyahu's Likud Party, was in the UAE as a spectator at an international judoka tournament. She paid a highly publicized visit to the Grand Mosque in Abu Dhabi, the Emirati capital, and then stood with tears in her eyes as the Israeli national anthem, Hatikvah, played after an Israeli competitor, Sagi Muki, won a gold medal.

Despite the slowdown of the conversations with Saudi Arabia stemming from MBS's firing of al Qhatani and al Asiri, Israel's icy relations with other Arab neighbors were thawing, and the shared fear of Iran was providing the heat. The thaw, however, was sometimes hard to detect, especially as the Saudis gave mixed signals, showing warmth toward Israel in private, but retreating into coldness in public.

In mid-February 2019, high-ranking officials from Saudi Arabia, the UAE, Qatar, Egypt, Jordan, Morocco, and Bahrain all attended an American-sponsored summit in Warsaw, Poland, that was billed as an event to discuss peace and security in the Middle East, but was really about confronting Iran. The meeting was also attended by Netanyahu and American vice president Mike Pence. Pence opened the meeting noting that an Israeli prime minister and various Gulf Arab representatives were "all breaking bread together." This signaled "a new era," Pence declared. Netanyahu's office posted a tweet making explicit the attendees' common interest. "This is an open meeting with representatives of leading Arab countries that are sitting down together with Israel in order to advance the common interest of war with Iran," Netanyahu's tweet said. It was posted for a short time to get the message across and then, in an act of diplomatic discretion, deleted.

In another act of leak-and-delete diplomacy, Netanyahu released a YouTube video from the closed-door sessions in which Bahrain's foreign minister, Khalid Bin Ahmed Al Khalifa, stated that confronting Iran was a far greater challenge than the Palestinian issue. "Iran smuggled weapons and explosives capable of wiping the Bahraini capital off the face of the earth," he said. The video was quickly removed from YouTube, but its brief showing provided a clear picture of the emerging Arab mindset.

A State Department official put it this way: "In Warsaw, we got the Arab foreign ministers and Netanyahu in the same room for dinner to talk about Iran, and it had never happened before, and they just loved it, and there was all this enthusiasm among the foreign ministries. The Arabs were, like, 'We got to keep this going.'"

But it was still "too much, too soon" for the Arab representatives to be seen in public in a cordial embrace with an Israeli prime minister or even to sit together on a stage participating in the same panel. The group photo reflected the Arabs' ambivalence. Netanyahu was in it, but carefully placed between Secretary of State Pompeo and Vice President Pence, as if to enable the Arab participants to avoid being too close to an Israeli prime minister. Even as the conference was taking place, Prince Turki Bin Faisal Al Saud, a former Saudi spymaster and ambassador to Washington and a confidant of King Salman, gave an interview to Israel's Channel 13 TV news in which he said: "Israeli public opinion should not be deceived into believing that the Palestinian issue is a dead issue. From the Israeli point of view, Mr. Netanyahu would like us to have a relationship, and then we can fix the Palestinian issue. From the Saudi point of view, it's the other way around."

But if the Saudis remained hesitant, caught between the contradictory goals of cooperation with Israel and fidelity to the Palestinians, the United Arab Emirates was less so. In late March 2019, the UAE foreign minister, Anwar Gargash, hinted broadly at where things were going. "Many, many years ago, when there was an Arab decision not to have contact with Israel, that was a very, very wrong decision, looking back," he declared. His comments, in which he predicted increased contact between Arab countries and Israel, were made with the approval of MBZ, who was rapidly emerging as an indispensable figure in the complicated effort to achieve normal relations between Israel and its erstwhile Arab enemies.

Tall, slim, and fit, MBZ, a British-trained helicopter pilot, had been the de facto ruler of the UAE since 2014 when his half-brother Khalifa Bin Zayed suffered a stroke. But as his father's favorite son, and as the Crown Prince of the Emirate of Abu Dhabi since 2003, he had been one of the most powerful figures in the Emirates for many years.

MBZ feared two enemies, the Muslim Brotherhood and Iran. He saw Israel as a counterbalance to Iranian power and an ally in the struggle against political Islam, as well as a supplier of security technology and a hedge in relations with Washington. MBZ was perhaps foremost among Arab rulers in realizing that their economies needed to develop beyond fossil fuels into tech and service industries. Israeli leaders who have met with MBZ describe him as "hugely impressive."

The Saudis and MBS are the powerhouses of the Sunni Gulf states. MBZ, though less charismatic than his Saudi counterpart, was considered for a long time to be a mentor and an inspiration for MBS, more than twenty years his junior. Both have emerged as sophisticated strategic thinkers committed to reshaping the Middle East. They fought the Iran-backed Houthis in Yemen; for several years they boycotted Qatar, a backer of the Muslim Brotherhood; and they supported the overthrow of the Islamist president Mohammed Morsi in Egypt in 2012. They firmly backed the man who ousted him from power, army chief Abdel Fattah El-Sisi, to whom they gave tens of billions of dollars in financial aid. Both men are socially liberal autocrats, who believe in a moderate Islam, and like Israel, both consider Iran the greatest strategic threat to their countries.

Though older than MBS, and though he exercises some influence over his Saudi counterpart, MBZ was unlikely to go ahead on the Israeli front without Saudi Arabia's agreement. This simply reflects the realities of the region. MBZ may have a military more advanced in some ways than that of Saudi Arabia and a sovereign wealth fund that is slightly larger even than that of Riyadh. But the Saudis have the world's largest oil reserves and much larger economic power overall. They have far greater geopolitical clout and, also important in the Muslim world, they are the custodians of the two holy mosques in Mecca, the holiest sites in Islam.

And so, when Gargash made his public prediction about future Arab ties with Israel, it's a virtual certainty that he did so with Saudi consent, even if the Saudis weren't ready to make such public comments on their own. Gargash's remarks, moreover, were followed up when the UAE Ambassador to Washington, Yousef Al Otaiba, privately told Jared Kushner that his country was ready for normalization with Israel. Kushner then flew to Israel to update Netanyahu, and things might have moved ahead quickly, but for another obstacle, this time on the Israeli side of things. Israel was deep in a political crisis. Netanyahu's government had collapsed and elections in April 2019 had failed to give either of the main party coalitions a parliamentary majority. Netanyahu therefore remained in power as head of a lame-duck caretaker government until a later round of elections, where once again neither political bloc managed to gain a majority. The Emiratis didn't want to press ahead when a major announcement could be seen as intervening in Netanyahu's favor. At the same time, trying to rally votes from the right, Netanyahu was reasserting the possibility of annexing portions of the West Bank, which also made it difficult for the Emiratis to move ahead toward formal relations.

Yossi Cohen would then fly to Washington for meetings with Secretary of State Pompeo to lay the ground for a meeting in June in Manama, the capital of Bahrain, another of the Sunni Arab states on the Persian Gulf. There, the Trump administration unveiled the economic portion of its peace plan—a massive $50 billion program, financed by the Gulf states, to upgrade the Palestinian economy. The Palestinians declared the plan DOA, "dead on arrival," but unlike in the past, failure to proceed on the Palestinian front was no longer an insurmountable stumbling block to progress. Despite the Palestinian snub, Bahrain, the host country, used the "Peace for Prosperity" conference in Manama to make its intentions regarding Israel pretty clear.

Bahrain, a small island kingdom, connected to Saudi Arabia by a fifteen-mile bridge, does nothing without the approval of its rich and powerful neighbor. And what it did now helped significantly to push normalization forward. Its foreign minister, Khalid Bin Ahmed Al Khalifa, gave several on-the-record interviews to Israeli media outlets who were allowed to attend the conference, even though Israel wasn't there. Khalifa asserted his support for Israel's right to strike Iranian targets in Syria; he said that Israel was "here to stay"; and he hinted that normalization was possible, even without an Israeli-Palestinian accord.

The Bahrainis also sent another message about the place of Jews in the region. In his interviews, Khalifa described the conflict between Israel and the Palestinians as one over territory, not religion, saying that any attempt to make it a Jewish-Muslim conflict was a return to "ancient times."

"We want to live today," he said.

There, in a symbolically important moment during the conference, some Israeli journalists and businessmen, accompanied by Jewish members of the American delegation, prayed in the Bahrain Synagogue in Manama, once used by the Bahrain Jewish community though by now it had fallen into disuse. It was a poignant signal that times were changing, "an example of the future we can all build together," as Jason Greenblatt, who was there, put it.

Why did Bahrain stake out such an advanced position? The Bahrainis have long had close relations with the United States, which it depends on for its security, most important by providing a home base for the U.S. Navy's Fifth Fleet. Now, the prospect of a deal with Israel gave them a way of adding a layer of security. Later, Israel would post a military liaison at Fifth Fleet headquarters, which is part of the effort by several Gulf states, the U.S., and Israel to develop a regional early warning and intercept system, based on Israeli technology, to counter Iranian missiles, drones, and naval threats.

By now, Cohen was confident that the time had come to announce Israel's ties with the Gulf, and he did so at another conference on July 1, 2019, shortly after the Manama conference. This one was an annual affair held in the Israeli town of Herzliya, which every year attracts droves of diplomats, journalists, and policy wonks—and a few spies. The atmosphere was electric in anticipation of Cohen's appearance, in part because any public speech by a sitting Mossad director is highly unusual. In fact, until Danny Yatom replaced Shabtai Shavit at the head of the agency in 1996, Mossad directors weren't even known by name.

Introducing Cohen at Herzliya, the conference chairman, Amos Gilad, a former IDF general, acclaimed the agency's most recent daring operation—"bringing the Iranian archives to Israel without coordinating with the Iranians." Cohen then took the podium, dressed nattily and expensively as usual. He opened by announcing that the very next day, "the Israel Security Prize will be awarded to the Mossad team that brought the Iranian atomic archive to Israel." He continued: "A few people, two women, and four men will go up on stage. Their names will not be mentioned; they will not be photographed; but they represent hundreds of our people who were involved in the operation for many long months."

The heist, he said, "showed that the impossible is possible and that the unbelievable can happen."

He then proceeded to give the Mossad's security assessment of the region, and it wasn't the usual bland intelligence analysis that says a lot and reveals nothing.

Israel, he announced, following "a long, secret process by the Mossad," had established formal ties with Oman. In fact, Israel had simply opened a new representative office in Oman, and didn't have full diplomatic relations with it, but Cohen's disclosure of "a long, secret process by the Mossad" was the first official confirmation of the Israeli spy agency's engagement with the Gulf states, which Cohen then suggested were ready for a truly historic change. "The Mossad today," he said, "identifies a rare opportunity, perhaps for the first time in Middle East history, to arrive at a regional understanding that would lead to a comprehensive peace accord. Shared interests, the fight against rivals such as Iran and jihadist terrorism, close relations with the White House, and channels of communication with the Kremlin all combine to create what might be a one-time window of opportunity."

The audience was abuzz; the media went into a frenzy speculating what exactly Cohen was talking about and what exactly was about to happen. Some dismissed the speech as detached from reality, saying that the Gulf Arab states were not ready to break with their past requirement that there be a peace treaty with the Palestinians before the normalization of relations with Israel could take place. But in retrospect, what Cohen said predicted the Abraham Accords pretty accurately. He may be a bit of a gambler by nature, but he understood better than his critics how much the situation in the Middle East was changing. After his countless meetings and encrypted text messages with Gulf leaders and intelligence officials, he knew they were ready for something historic. The only question from his perspective was timing. As far as he was concerned it could have happened that year. But Israel's political stalemate meant that progress was blocked.

Cohen's public disclosure of the Mossad's ties with the Gulf states grabbed the headlines. But the speech was focused mostly on Iran, its nuclear ambitions, attempts to strike Israeli and Jewish targets across the world, its aggression in the region, and its entrenchment in Syria—and the Mossad's role in confronting Iran on all of these fronts. The night before the speech, the Israeli Air Force conducted a massive strike on Iranian and Hezbollah positions in Syria. What Cohen didn't say, though it could be inferred from his remarks, was that the Mossad was making the final preparations for another series of spectacular attacks on Iran's nuclear program and personnel, and on the head of its global network of terror.

Chapter 8

DEATH OF THE SHADOW COMMANDER

ISRAEL AND THE MOSSAD DON'T USUALLY ANNOUNCE THAT they have conducted operations against Iran's nuclear weapons program or that they are responsible for the deaths of Iranian scientists, but they do often hint of their involvement. The public announcement of the archive theft was an unusual exception. There has, however, been an almost deafening silence about the Israeli role in perhaps the most significant strike ever against the Islamic Republic, which took place on January 3, 2020, when an American Reaper drone fired four laser-guided Hellfire missiles at two armored cars as they pulled out of Baghdad International Airport in Iraq, engulfing them in flames.

Ten people were killed, among them Abu Mahdi al Muhandis, the deputy commander of a pro-Iranian militia in Iraq, but the main target was Islamic Revolutionary Guard Corps Quds Force chief, Major General Qasem Soleimani, a man who had the blood of hundreds on his hands, according to former general and CIA director David Petraeus.

Known as the "Shadow Commander," Soleimani became a force to be reckoned with during the American invasion of Iraq in 2003. He provided training, funds, and weapons to Shiite militias in Iraq as Tehran sought to gain sway in the country through its fellow Shiites, who had been oppressed under the rule of Saddam Hussein. The Iraqi Shiites initially welcomed the Americans who overthrew their oppressor in the 2003 invasion, but over time pro-Iranian militias turned against

U.S. troops. It was Soleimani who provided them with the lethal roadside bombs that ripped through the armor of American vehicles and claimed the lives of at least 196 servicemen from 2005 to 2011 and wounded over 900 more. By 2007, Soleimani's broad-ranging activities had earned him a place on the U.S. Treasury's list of designated terror entities and persons.

The George W. Bush administration had him in its crosshairs. General Stanley McChrystal, a former head of U.S. Joint Special Operations Command, described how in 2007 he watched real-time drone footage of a convoy that included Soleimani traveling from Iran into northern Iraq. The drone was armed, and Soleimani could have been hit, but McChrystal decided against a strike. He wanted, he said, "to avoid a firefight, and the contentious politics that would follow," and Soleimani slipped into invisibility before a better opportunity arose. The policy generally observed was that nonstate actors were fair targets for intelligence agencies, but senior officials of governments were not, and Soleimani was a senior official of the Islamic Republic. To kill him might not only have violated international law, but also exposed top U.S. government and CIA personnel to similar retaliation.

In 2011, when President Barack Obama pulled most American troops out of Iraq, leaving residual forces at bases scattered around the country, he similarly ruled against a Soleimani assassination, even though before the withdrawal was complete, American officials accused Soleimani of overseeing a plot to assassinate the Saudi ambassador to the United States, Adel Al Jubeir, at Cafe Milano in Washington, a favorite haunt for diplomats and spies.

The reduction of American forces and the takeover of the government by Shiites with deep connections to Soleimani essentially turned Iraq, once a threatening Sunni challenger to Iran, into practically an Iranian satellite through which the ayatollahs could spread their influence and power. No Iranian was more associated with Iran's efforts to expand its influence and, eventually, to annihilate Israel, than Soleimani. The Americans kept track of the man who, as the commander of the Quds Force, became an ever more powerful figure in Iraq and the assumed mastermind of continuing attacks. But what exactly to do about him was a vexing matter on which successive American administrations remained both uncertain and divided for years.

Millions of people packed the boulevards of Tehran and other cities throughout Iran for Soleimani's funeral on January 7, 2020. Mourners beat their chests, carried photos of the slain leader, and cheered when his daughter called for revenge. In his hometown of Kerman where his body was buried, dozens of mourners were killed in a stampede. Similar processions were held in Iraq.

At a ceremony earlier in the day in Tehran, Supreme Leader Ayatollah Ali Khamenei performed the funeral rites for Soleimani and the other Iranians killed in the strike, visibly trembling and weeping, his voice quivering as he stood before their caskets and mourned in front of millions of Iranian viewers.

Khamenei's tears were genuine; he had lost his closest ally, his top adviser for his plans to dominate the region, and his most talented and creative operator. He knew that without Soleimani, all that Iran had invested in for years could be in jeopardy.

Others, including American analysts, agreed with that assessment. Petraeus went so far as to say that Soleimani's killing was more important than either the assassination of al-Qaeda chief Osama bin Laden, the architect of the 9/11 attacks on Washington and New York, or that of ISIS chief Abu Bakr al-Baghdadi.

For Israel, the death of Soleimani had perhaps even more significance than it did for the Americans. While Soleimani and the U.S. clashed indirectly in and around Iraq, for Israel, the Quds Force commander posed a multipronged direct threat to its home territory. As a consequence, he had been a target for Israel for many years and a major obsession for the Mossad. Yossi Cohen frequently spoke of Soleimani as a legendary figure, bringing destruction to the region. He viewed the Quds Force chief as the ultimate chess master against whom he was constantly exchanging moves and countermoves on several fronts.

Soleimani's grand strategy was to construct a "ring of fire" around Israel, mainly by smuggling advanced weapons, in particular rockets and missiles, to Iranian proxies in Syria, Lebanon, Iraq, and Yemen. This started with Hezbollah in Lebanon. Iran had founded Hezbollah in the early 1980s as it sought to export the Islamic Revolution to the Shiite population in Lebanon and to harass Israel, which had controversially invaded the country in 1982 with the stated aim of pushing back armed Palestinian groups who had been staging cross-border attacks into Israel. Hezbollah would eventually drive Israel out of Lebanon in 2000 after years in which it consistently inflicted heavy casualties on troops maintaining a buffer zone in the south of the country.

In 2001, in the midst of the bloody Second Intifada, Soleimani was one of the masterminds behind an audacious trilateral Iranian-Hezbollah-Palestinian plan to smuggle fifty tons of weapons, including powerful rockets, into the Gaza Strip, using a ship called the *Karine A.*

At that point, neither Israel nor anyone else had a viable missile defense system. The Patriot system, the only one available at the time, had been deemed ineffective. Israel's prized Iron Dome antimissile defense system was just an idea on paper and would only become operational in 2011, seeing its first major test during the 2012 Gaza War.

Working with Imad Mughniyeh, Hezbollah's military leader, and other IRGC agents, Soleimani helped devise an ingenious scheme in which the weapons would be dropped in special floating tubes in international waters near Gaza. By the time the IDF navy encountered these tubes closer to Israeli shores, the weapons would have disappeared into the boats of Gaza fishermen who would have quietly come by to collect them.

A combined effort by the Mossad, the CIA, and Israeli and American naval intelligence thwarted the plot. The formula served as a basis for decades of sea warfare and smuggling runs between Soleimani's forces and Israel. Much of the arms and munitions that Soleimani attempted to smuggle to Gaza did get through. He also adopted the creative tactic of using seemingly nonmilitary aircraft to smuggle weapons throughout the Middle East.

Soleimani then played a major role in the 2006 Second Lebanon War. Along with Mughniyeh, he spent most of the thirty-three days of the conflict in Hezbollah's underground command center in the Shiite strongholds of south Beirut. Hezbollah held Israel to a stalemate in the war which it celebrated as a victory.

In a rare interview with Iranian media, Soleimani described how during the war, he and Mughniyeh had decided to move Hezbollah leader Hassan Nasrallah out of the command bunker in the Dahiya quarter of Beirut, which had come under intense bombing by Israeli jets.

Two Israeli bombardments had struck very close to the building they had moved Nasrallah to, Soleimani recalled. "We felt that these two bombings were about to be followed by a third one . . . so we decided to get out of that building," he said. "We didn't have a car, and there was complete silence, just the sound of Israeli regime planes overflying Dahiyeh." He said that he and Mughniyeh hid under a tree from the heat-seeking drones sniffing out targets. Eventually they got a car, which they switched with another car in an underground garage to throw the Israelis off their tracks, thereby succeeding in getting Nasrallah, a priority Israeli target, out of danger.

After 2006, Soleimani and his lieutenants led a systematic campaign both to smuggle into Lebanon and to manufacture there an estimated 100,000 to 150,000 short-, medium-, and long-range rockets and missiles, some of them capable of reaching as far south as Israel's Dimona nuclear reactor, this despite the presence of a U.N. peacekeeping mission that was supposed to prevent any arms buildup. Soleimani's success made him irreplaceable in Khamenei's eyes.

According to *The New Yorker*, all of this, needless to say, attracted the attention of the Mossad, but the Israelis were well aware that the Americans had vetoed an assassination of Soleimani, observing the informal ban on killing government officials. There was one incident in 2008 early on the day on which Mughniyeh was killed. At one point in their surveillance of Mughniyeh, who was the intended target, the Mossad sighted him and Soleimani together, and with the two of them in its crosshairs, could have eliminated both. But then Prime Minister Ehud Olmert called off the operation, sparing them both. "I can tell you that not only did Soleimani owe me his life for twelve years," Olmert told us in an interview, "but there were circumstances that he couldn't have understood as a result of which he wasn't killed. I can't tell you what the circumstances were."

In the end, the Mossad reportedly caught up with Mughniyeh on his own later that day. He was killed in Damascus when a bomb placed in the spare tire of his jeep was detonated as he walked past.

The Syrian civil war, which erupted in 2011 in the wake of the larger Arab Spring movement, pitted the ruling Alawite majority led by the regime of Bashar al-Assad against the oppressed majority Sunni population. Soleimani and Iran, with critical help from Russia, helped save the Assad regime from defeat by organizing a mix of Iranian Special Forces, Hezbollah, and other Shiite militias to support it, thereby furnishing Soleimani and Iran a golden opportunity. In recognition of its help, Assad agreed to allow the Quds Force to establish its own bases in Syria for developing and planning drone and rocket strikes on Israel.

This meant that in a matter of only a few years, Soleimani had created for Khamenei two new fronts from which to attack and intimidate Israel, first via Hezbollah in Lebanon, now in Syria. Soleimani's plans, about which he kept Khamenei well informed, also included maintaining a force of tens of thousands of non-Syrian Shiite militias on Syria's border with Israel that could potentially attempt to seize some territory on the Golan Heights.

The overall strategy was audacious and far-reaching. It was to create a massive land bridge, a kind of Shiite Crescent, stretching from Iran through Iraq, Syria, and Lebanon, along which Soleimani's feared IRGC and massive quantities of weaponry would be able to move freely without having to worry about borders and sovereignty. The Shiite Crescent would surround Israel with grave threats on all sides.

Khamenei was thrilled and felt his gamble to cut the JCPOA nuclear deal might have been worth it, since it was giving Soleimani and Iran a free hand to reorder the region. He and Soleimani felt that the U.S., and even Israel to some extent, would be more hesitant than before about confronting the country or its proxies. Such confrontations, and especially military operations, would push Iran to stop complying with the nuclear deal. Indeed, in some ways, Soleimani's grand plan posed graver threats to Israel than the multi-front attacks it had faced during the Yom Kippur War of 1973 (the last war that was a truly existential threat) since drones and rockets could reach the Israeli home front more readily than Egyptian and Syrian aircraft and tanks could in 1973. Also, Soleimani and Co. had plans for Hezbollah to briefly take over small Israeli border villages using tunnels that Israel had not yet discovered.

The years between 2017 and 2020 thus saw a constant battle between Soleimani and Israel. IRGC forces tried to establish and deepen the land bridge plan and to use their presence in Syria to transfer more advanced weapons to Hezbollah, particularly precision-guided missiles able to strike targets in Israel with pinpoint accuracy. In a series of countermoves, the Israeli Air Force and Cohen's Mossad launched thousands of strikes and operations, mostly in Syria, but also some in Lebanon and Iraq.

It was during this "campaign between wars," as Israel's operations in Syria have become known, that Soleimani once again became a target for Israel. According to former IDF chief of staff Gadi Eisenkot, on an unspecified date, there was one missed opportunity to assassinate him during an operation against Quds Forces stationed in Abu Kamal in eastern Syria, when Israeli intelligence revealed that Soleimani was on the ground there. "We had a decision and we had confirmation that anyone taking part in this battle could be targeted," Eisenkot said. "Soleimani was there. We had approval to take him down if we could pinpoint his location and get him in our sights."

But Soleimani used up another of his nine lives: "We did not have him in our sights," Eisenkot said. "He survived by some miracle."

Soleimani would not be so lucky the next time.

By 2017, with Iran's entrenchment in Syria, the U.S. was beginning to rethink its policy keeping Soleimani off-limits because of his official government position. One major factor in this was likely various Israeli officials regularly pressing the issue with members of the Trump administration, which was still undecided whether Soleimani could be assassinated or not. Former IDF intelligence chief Tamir Hayman told us that he and Israeli intelligence officials provided the Americans with constantly updated information about the dangers Soleimani and the Quds Force posed to Israel, the U.S., and the world, returning again and again to the topic in order to hammer the point home. Cohen doesn't say so out loud, but he appears to view himself as the real catalyst on the matter of Soleimani, urging key decision makers in Washington to be open to taking more drastic action against the Iranian.

Perhaps in response to Israeli officials' reported pleadings, in 2017 Pompeo gathered officials from the CIA's Counterterrorism Mission Center and its paramilitary Special Activities Center to pursue concrete options to mount an operation. "Don't worry about if it's legal," Pompeo told the group, according to a source quoted by *Yahoo News*. "That's a question for the lawyers." Despite that, Trump himself as well as officials in the Defense Department still resisted an assassination, but things changed when John Bolton replaced McMaster as NSC adviser in 2018. Bolton was an advocate of regime change in Iran and was viewed as hawkish even among those who wanted to isolate the Islamic Republic. There was still resistance from the defense and intelligence establishments, both of which had reservations about departing from the principle that state officials like Soleimani are off-limits, and even with Bolton open to the idea, Trump was not yet ready to take on the defense officials opposed to it.

"The president wanted options, but they were always watered down" by the Pentagon, Victoria Coates, the deputy national security adviser, recalled. Killing Soleimani was one of them, she told *Yahoo News*, but "the Pentagon always equated it to nuclear war, and said there was going to be a backlash."

"The concern was on a bigger scale," said one former CIA official. The former official added that if Soleimani was killed, the Quds Force would try to "kill members of the Saudi or Emirati royal families," launch "attacks on oil infrastructure," or "foment coups" in the region. Another possibility was that Iran would respond to a Soleimani assassination by sending its proxies to attack an American consulate or embassy. In addition to those reasons for hesitation, Trump, at that point early in his administration, still thought he—the masterful negotiator that he considered himself to be—could get Iran to sign on to an improved, tougher nuclear deal. An aggressive action, like taking out Soleimani, Trump felt, would jeopardize that goal.

But then, as Coates put it, "the Iranians chose to do a whole host of things, extremely provocative and aggressive" and that changed everything as far as the Americans were concerned.

In 2019, Iran or its proxies launched more than a dozen separate rocket attacks on American military bases in Iraq. The Trump administration pointed a finger at Kataib Hezbollah, an Iraqi militia that was part of the Iran-backed Popular Mobilization Forces, but top American defense and intelligence officials said that the Soleimani's Quds Force was ultimately behind these operations.

Most of the attacks in this period were relatively small, involving 107mm or sometimes 122mm rockets, which were used against the Ain al Asad airbase in Anbar province, where American servicemen were stationed, although none were injured in the attacks. More provocative in its way was the downing by Iran of an American Global Hawk surveillance drone in June 2019. The drone, according to the U.S., was hit by Iranian surface-to-air missiles when it was flying over international waters above the Strait of Hormuz. Then, in September, Iranian missiles hit an oil processing facility in Abqaiq, Saudi Arabia. Up to that point, the Trump administration had responded to Iranian provocations with air strikes against Kataib Hezbollah in both Iraq and Syria. But now Bolton and Pompeo, citing the downing of the over $130 million U.S. drone, were urging Trump to kill the Quds force chief. Trump did not accept their recommendation. However, he did authorize a minor strike on Iran itself, which would have still been a marked escalation in American military responses. Then Trump backed down, calling off even the minor strike, stunning his advisers, who all believed it had been agreed upon. According to Bolton, Pompeo was so distressed that he called the president's actions "dangerous."

At most, Trump had been ready to increase sanctions on Soleimani, but not to assassinate him. But he did instruct U.S. national security officials to put together options for an assassination if Iran or its forces killed an American. On December 27, that's exactly what happened. Kataib Hezbollah launched thirty missiles against an Iraqi airbase in Kirkuk, the capital of the autonomous Kurdish region in northern Iraq, killing an American contractor and wounding four servicemen. This led Trump, finally, to put caution aside. Now he didn't want pin-prick retaliations. Now he wanted to take down a bigger fish, an Iranian whale.

"In the fall of 2019, there was Abqaiq," Coates told us, "and then attacking our people in Iraq, Trump realized even if he wanted to get a better deal with them, he would need to take extremely strong action to show we were serious." Interestingly, Coates did not seem to feel that Cohen had played a major role in this. "If there were CIA and Mossad discussions about [assassinating Soleimani], they did not reach the White House," she told us, speaking of the 2017 and 2018 period. "Yossi [Cohen] never raised it with me."

Bolton explained that much of Trump's handling of the Soleimani issue was emotional. "He did say at different times: 'What about Soleimani?' when he wasn't happy with something. It was his way of saying 'I really want to be tough' when he did not have to make a decision.

"But there are no consequences," Bolton continued. "It's all hot air. It's when he comes up to the brink of a decision that once he makes it irrevocably, that he begins to get nervous." In other words, when Trump was actually considering targeting Soleimani for real in late 2019, he was, according to his advisers, uncharacteristically reserved and restrained, because he knew that the consequences and risks of real-world action were much greater than mere bluster.

It "was not something that was thought of as a first move," said a former senior administration official involved in the discussions.

Despite his continuing hesitations, Trump was presented with four options for the Soleimani assassination: a long-range sniper shot; a tactical team in the field; the use of an improvised explosive device to blow him up as he passed in a car; or a drone or air strike. A senior Trump administration official said that the drone strike was picked, as it "made the most sense" and was viewed to be "the most likely path to success."

According to an Iranian television interview in early October 2019, Israel and the West had only shortly before attempted to assassinate Soleimani, but thanks to Iran's security services, the enemies of the country were foiled. This disclosure came from Hossein Ta'eb, the IRGC's head of intelligence from 2009 to June 2022. According to him, three would-be assassins had worked on their plan for a number of years, but the IRGC had been watching them even before they entered the Islamic Republic. The operation involved blowing up Soleimani at a memorial service during the Muslim month of Muharram, which began in early September 2019, in order to "trigger a religious war inside Iran."

"Frustrated by their failure to upset security in Iran or to harm the IRGC military bases, the enemies had hatched an extensive plot to hit Maj.-Gen. Soleimani in his home province of Kerman," Ta'eb was quoted as saying. The team planned to buy a house near a congregation hall where Shiite memorial prayers are held. The hall was built in the southern Iranian province of Kerman in honor of Soleimani's father, who died in 2017. The assassins, Ta'eb said, planned to tunnel under the building and detonate a 500-kilogram bomb during the mourning period of Fatimiyya—the period commemorating the martyrdom of Fatimah al-Zahra, the daughter of the Prophet Muhammad and wife of the Caliph Ali—"as soon as Maj.-Gen. Soleimani went to the mourning ceremony like every year." But all three were arrested before the plot could be carried out.

Is this true? We may never know for sure, but what might have happened is this: the Islamic Republic did somehow learn that the Mossad, the U.S., or allied forces were exploring a tunnel bomb operation, which they deemed too risky or unlikely to succeed and decided not to carry it out. The Iranians then used their knowledge of the plan, though never executed, to try to publicly embarrass the Mossad and the Americans.

The Iranians, as the Ta'eb interview indicates, were thrilled with their public relations show, but Cohen scoffed at their claims and called their conduct amateurish. On the other hand, neither Cohen nor the Mossad is likely to admit to failures where its agents' identities are not publicly exposed.

Either way, Cohen was disturbed that Soleimani was still on the playing field.

On January 1, 2020, at a little after 10:00 a.m., Secretary of Defense Mark Esper, Vice President Mike Pence, Secretary of State Pompeo, and other senior administration officials held a conference call to talk about Soleimani. Pompeo started by raising one of Trump's main worries about a possible assassination—that a mob would attack and perhaps overrun the American embassy in Baghdad. They all remembered what had happened in Benghazi, Libya, eight years before, when Islamic militants stormed the American consulate there, killing four people, including the ambassador, and severely embarrassing the Obama administration.

Pompeo informed the meeting that Trump had ordered the chargé d'affaires in Baghdad (since there was no ambassador there at the time) to repel all attacks. The directive was crystal clear: under no circumstances was the embassy to surrender.

The meeting then reviewed the latest intelligence on Soleimani, who was in Damascus with plans to travel to Beirut and then Baghdad. The intelligence said he was orchestrating multiple attacks against Americans in several locations with what could be "heavy consequences" for the United States.

Esper and others were worried that any such attacks by Soleimani could prompt Trump to overreact in return, which might lead to a wider war. In contrast, if Soleimani's attacks could be stopped—even with force—paradoxically the chances of war might be reduced.

That alone seemed like justification to kill Soleimani as soon as possible, but some inside the intelligence community weren't convinced.

Opponents of an assassination, including some within the CIA who spoke to the media, have said there was no imminent threat that would justify assassinating a high-ranking Iranian state official, as opposed to nonstate terrorists. But Pompeo told us, "If they said there wasn't [intelligence about imminent attacks], they didn't see what I saw. There was clearly an effort by Iraqi terror forces and the Quds Force to kill Americans. . . . As [Soleimani] was traveling from Beirut to Damascus to Baghdad, he was engaged in a project which, if fruitful, would lead to the death of Americans."

Early on Thursday, January 2, Esper and General Mark A. Milley, chairman of the Joint Chiefs, spoke to Trump again, giving a survey of the latest intelligence and the posture of forces in the region. Esper said that Trump was calmer than he had been earlier, but he was still nervous about the embassy. He asked for an update on American retaliatory options specifically against Soleimani.

At 1:00 p.m. that day Esper held a conference call with Pence, Pompeo, CIA director Gina Haspel, and others, with Trump himself participating. The discussion, as Esper recounted it, rapidly turned to Soleimani. The meeting was informed of new intelligence, which now placed Soleimani in Damascus; he'd traveled first to Beirut, contrary to prior information, and planned to fly to Baghdad within hours.

Esper said that Soleimani was pushing hard to strike the U.S. embassy and other American assets both inside and outside Iraq. He believed that the Quds chief would likely need to get a final green light from Khamenei before initiating the attacks, but American intelligence believed Khamenei would give that approval, meaning that the strikes could be only days away.

Some participants in the meeting, Pence and Pompeo in particular, supported taking out Soleimani as a response to this direct threat, but a mood of uncertainty nonetheless prevailed. According to Esper's account, Trump was "frustrated that the [Israelis] had not taken care of Soleimani earlier, as they had been pressing to do for months. He complained that [Netanyahu] was talking tough, but really wanted the United States to conduct the strike, which was a shrewd assessment." There was no firm consensus yet on what to do, until CIA director Haspel, asked by Trump for her views, dispelled the uncertainty. According to Esper, her answer couldn't have been clearer or more concise, and she gave it with confidence and authority: "The risk of doing nothing is greater than the risk of doing something," she said. That was the decisive moment, Esper told us.

"I would agree," Coates said in our interview with her. "Gina's role as CIA director was very powerful in assessing the information." She agreed that Haspel's support was a game changer, because unlike Pompeo, she was not a political appointee.

Pompeo sometimes complained about certain career CIA officials as being too cautious about taking action, but Haspel, who was a career CIA official, was pushing for action, which enhanced the impact of her recommendation. "The point that Gina made," Bolton told us, "came with considerable frustration. If you punt, you are not just punting for twenty-four hours necessarily. You could be punting for months." Everybody, as Bolton saw it, was aware that if Trump backed off this time, when a good opportunity was at hand, he might have been unwilling to consider killing Soleimani again for several more months, during which time the Iranian might have done serious damage to the United States.

At a follow-up meeting, military officials presented an estimate of civilian casualties that might result from the operation. They specifically detailed to Trump that killing Soleimani at the Baghdad airport, where he was due to land late at night on the Syrian private airline Cham Wings, would likely incur fewer casualties than other options.

Finally, Trump gave the order.

Soleimani flew from Damascus to Baghdad as the intelligence had predicted, although there was confusion about his travel during the day, with various reports representing different potential and contradictory itineraries he might take. First, he was going to Baghdad, then he wasn't going to Baghdad, then suddenly he was again.

"With an operation like this, until it's done, assume it is not going to get done," Coates, the former deputy NSC chief, said. "I really thought at midday that it was not going to happen."

In the end, Soleimani was several hours late, which, given the intricacy of the operation, could have thrown the whole thing off. But agents on the ground in Damascus had tipped off the CIA as to the exact plane Soleimani would be on, and Israeli intelligence had provided all the cell phone numbers for Soleimani, necessary in order to pinpoint his location with the exactitude needed for a drone strike.

In fact, the matter of cell phones was of critical importance, because in the six hours between his transit from Damascus to Baghdad, Soleimani switched them at least three times, precisely in order to throw off any enemy that was attempting to track him. But, back in Tel Aviv, the Israelis were reportedly passing Soleimani's numbers on to the U.S. Joint Special Operations Command in Tel Aviv, and using that information, the Americans zeroed in on the phone Soleimani was using when he arrived in Baghdad.

A remarkable bit of advance intelligence work had made this possible. Sometime before, as a former intelligence official told *Yahoo News*, "Israeli intelligence tipped off the CIA about a courier for Soleimani who would travel outside Iran to pick up clean phones for the Quds Force leader and his inner circle." The CIA learned that the courier would visit a specific market in a Gulf country to procure the devices. Using that knowledge, it installed spyware on a set of phones that it then planted in the market. The courier purchased at least one bugged phone, which was then used by someone who was often in the same room as Soleimani.

Meanwhile, personnel on the ground in Baghdad were taking their places. These included three Kurdish operatives, one impersonating a ground controller, another a baggage handler, and a third pretending to be an Iraqi police officer, which enabled him to positively identify Soleimani as the man killed in the attack, using photographic and DNA evidence. US Delta Force snipers, disguised as road workers, were positioned on the road leading from the airport to Baghdad or in nearby buildings.

In the minutes before the arrival of Soleimani's plane, three American drones moved into position overhead.

The drone operators did not need to worry about hovering in Iraqi airspace, since at the time it was still dominated by the U.S. military. Nor were they concerned about the noise that drones generally make, since in a large urban environment like Baghdad, their sound would be camouflaged by other noises.

The plane landed.

Abu Mahdi al Muhandis, the founder and commander of Kataib Hezbollah, and deputy commander of the Popular Mobilization Forces, an umbrella group of Shiite militias, dubbed "Iraq's Revolutionary Guards," ascended a set of stairs to greet Soleimani, his benefactor, as he emerged at the top of the ramp.

Those on the ground had no idea of what awaited. But in faraway America, senior officials from Trump on down were observing the operation as it unfolded.

CIA director Gina Haspel watched from agency headquarters in Langley, Virginia.

Secretary of Defense Mark Esper watched from an unspecified location.

President Trump followed from Mar-a-Lago in Florida, while officials on his team were at the White House.

U.S. Central Command watched from its forward headquarters in Qatar on the Persian Gulf.

Soleimani and al Muhandis descended the ramp and got into a sedan that promptly drove off. A security detail followed in a van.

As this happened, elite U.S. signals intelligence specialists from Task Force Orange, likely using data provided by Israel, reportedly homed in on the cell phones of the passengers, especially Soleimani, to confirm their identities.

Though a small number of other vehicles were on the road, there was little traffic. At Mar-a-Lago, as Trump told the story, military officials gave him a near second-by-second account of what then took place in Baghdad. "Sir, they have two minutes and eleven seconds to live, sir," one of them told the president. "They're in the car, they're in an armored vehicle going. Sir, they have approximately one minute to live, sir. Thirty seconds. Ten, nine, eight . . ."

On the road from the airport to Baghdad, the minivan with the security detail pulled ahead of the sedan and just then multiple Hellfire missiles were fired from overhead drones, destroying the vehicle carrying

Soleimani and al Muhandis. The driver of the minivan, seeing the sedan engulfed in flames, slammed on the gas to try to get away, but he ran into a trap only one hundred yards further down the road.

From concealed spots, the three teams of Delta Force commandos that had taken their positions earlier were following the convoy's progress through their scopes. They were set up so as to triangulate their target to maximize the ambush spot as a "kill zone." An elite Kurdish group that coordinates with U.S. Special Forces was measuring the wind factor to advise the snipers.

The sniper teams had their safeties rotated off their long guns with their fingers on their triggers.

The minivan driver skidded to a halt when a Delta Force sniper opened fire. As the minivan slowed, it was hit by a U.S. drone, and was blown to pieces.

Within seconds, both the sedan and the minivan were engulfed in fireballs.

"They're gone, sir," Trump recalled the military officer telling him. There were no survivors.

Despite this success, the reaction in U.S. military circles was somber as they wondered how Iran would respond. They didn't have to wait long. On January 8, Iran launched a huge barrage of missile strikes on American bases in Iraq. They injured dozens but killed no U.S. troops. There was no assault on the American embassy in Baghdad. But many officials in the U.S. and even in Israel would remain worried for some time about possible Iranian retaliation.

But Yossi Cohen didn't. He would always have a knowing and confident smirk on his face whenever the topic of the Soleimani assassination came up.

Soleimani was replaced by Major General Esmail Ghaani, his long-term former deputy who was never considered a star by Cohen or by other Iran analysts. But no matter who took the head of the Quds Force, as far as Cohen was concerned, Soleimani was irreplaceable.

Ghaani, who had been mostly involved in Iranian operations in Pakistan and Afghanistan, was less familiar with Israel and Middle East operations than Soleimani, whose absence, Cohen felt, would degrade the IRCG's ability to act boldly and creatively in risky circumstances. Cohen viewed Soleimani as an ingenious, talented rival, who he would tip his metaphorical hat to if he had not been an enemy, but he did not respect Ghaani nearly as much. The Islamic Republic's attempts to build a "ring of fire" around Israel would not suddenly end. But it would be slowed and managed in a much less agile manner.

Someone other than the Israelis had fired the missiles that killed Soleimani. Neither Cohen nor the Mossad as a whole could take credit for changing the balance of power or for raising the level of deterrence that the assassination had wrought. But reportedly Israel had for years been untiring and steadfast in its wish to take out perhaps its most potent enemy. With the U.S. taking the lead, after all those years, Cohen had gotten his man.

Chapter 9

CYBER WINTER IS HERE

BESIDES THE DEADLY PHYSICAL WAR WITH IRAN OF SABOtage and assassinations and engaging in secret diplomacy with pragmatic Sunni Arab states, there was another front: the virtual battlefield, which was breaking into the physical one in dangerous ways.

On the morning of April 23, 2020, workers at the command and control center of a water network somewhere in central Israel noticed something wrong with the pumps at a station responsible for two rural districts. They didn't think too much of the malfunction at first. It was probably just an underperforming pump, but amid unseasonably high temperatures, they sent a team out to the field to check, as required by protocol. It soon transpired that what was happening was far more ominous than a faulty pump.

Hackers had sought to trick the water system into pumping out a higher than normal volume of chlorine. The chemical is used in extremely low concentrations to disinfect drinking water, but in large amounts it can be poisonous, causing vomiting, internal bleeding, and respiratory damage, and, in extreme concentrations, even death. Cyber defenders succeeded in defeating the hack midstream before it could poison the water system.

The Israelis soon learned that Iran tried to hack several other water networks. Western intelligence agencies briefed on the hacks said they had originated in Iran, though they had been diverted through computer servers in the United States and Europe. Israel's intelligence assessment was that the source of the attack was the cyber offense units of the IRGC. "If the bad guys had succeeded in their plot, we would now be facing . . . very big damage to the civilian population," the head of Israel's National Cyber Directorate, Yigal Unna, said. Unna, a baby-faced cyber wizard, was a twenty-two-year veteran of the Shin Bet, having come up through the ranks in Unit 8200 (Israel's National Security Administration, its electronic espionage agency) before heading several units in charge of cyberwarfare in the domestic security service.

Speaking off the record, another Israeli official described it as "an attack that goes against all codes, even in war," because the sole target of the operation was the civilian population. It also signaled a new step in Iran's war against "the Zionist evil." Ever since the 2009–2010 Stuxnet hack against Iran's nuclear program, the Islamic Republic had been building up its cyber capabilities as part of its doctrine of asymmetrical warfare. Its hope was to employ hacking along with terrorism to inflict damage against opponents with superior military capabilities, while at the same time maintaining a measure of deniability to try to avoid severe repercussions.

Using an army of cyber groups, not working directly with the regime, but under its control, Tehran had earlier conducted a number of low-key cyberattacks against Israel and the United States, including a June 2015 theft of data from military suppliers in both countries. In April 2017, hackers working for Iran broke into the computer networks of 250 Israeli companies, and in March 2019 they were hacking top Israeli political officials' phones.

In going after the water system, moreover, Iran had shown a high degree of sophistication, an Israeli investigation concluded. It had prepared the attack over a period of months, possibly more, gathering intelligence and exploring infected networks piece by piece, moving slowly so that no sudden spike in unauthorized activity could be traced. The Iranians may even have infected updates by third-party software producers, forging digital keys so that malware detection programs could not catch them. Such capabilities are only possessed by state or state-sponsored actors.

Critical infrastructure, like a water network, is normally protected by what is known as air gapping—they have their own internal online networks isolated from the public internet, which makes them much harder to hack. In its own cyber espionage, Israel is believed nonetheless to have hacked into air-gapped systems, but Iran had not done the same to Israel, at least not yet. "Bridging these air gaps is quite a complex operational scheme to plan," Yaron Rosen, a former IDF cyber intelligence expert, told us. It requires a vast amount of intelligence to map out what is networked and what is not, then to tailor a plan to bridge each air gap. It may also require sending a team on the ground to effectuate the bridging.

To penetrate Israel's water system, Iran needed to have followed one of two methods. Either it directly hacked into the software that controls the balance among the different chemicals being released into the water; or else Iran took over the credentials of a third-party supplier, and it used those credentials to internally access and manipulate the mix of chemicals in the water. Such credentials are sometimes obtained by a seemingly much more innocuous hack of a private sector business months or years before to acquire key persons' personal data, which then becomes the doorway to credentials for hacking actual infrastructure.

The Iranian attack was also carefully calibrated. Whoever masterminded it could assume that the water system's fail-safe protections would have prevented actual large-scale chlorine poisoning from occurring, and this was almost certainly intentional. Iran probably didn't want to cause the sort of death and destruction that would have provoked a massive Israeli retaliation. They figured that Israel would respond to a nonlethal operation in a limited way.

In this, Iran miscalculated. Israel did strike back, but in a manner that caused far more physical damage than the Islamic Republic's failed attack on Israel's water networks had caused. Although Israel generally follows the law of proportionality during conventional conflicts, cyber is still viewed as a Wild West of sorts, and Israel's response wasn't a cyber "eye for an eye," but more like ten eyes for an eye.

The port of Shahid Rajaee, on the north shore of the Strait of Hormuz, is one of Iran's two most important sea terminals, responsible for over half the traffic of goods in and out of the country. It also has symbolic importance. It's home to the naval headquarters of the IRGC, which had used it on several occasions to ship weapons to Israel's enemies. And that's one of the reasons that, on May 9, a bit over two weeks after Iran's hit on Israel's water network, shipping traffic there came to a sudden halt. Computers that regulate the flow of vessels, trucks, and goods all went down at the same time. This meant a massive backup on waterways and roads near the port. The chaos lasted for days; an American official said that Iran was in total disarray.

Following its usual policy of intentional ambiguity regarding its covert operations, Israel didn't then, and never has, directly claimed responsibility for the Shahid Rajaee attack, but there have been broad official hints that Israeli intelligence was behind it.

About a month after the calamitous snarl at the port, Israel's Military Intelligence awarded "certificates of appreciation" to units that had participated in a "successful covert operation." Around the same time, Military Intelligence chief Tamir Hayman said that Israel had taken a "first and significant step on a long path," though he didn't specify exactly what step, nor did he specify the path he was referring to. Similarly, Israel Defense Forces chief of staff Aviv Kohavi announced, apropos of nothing specific, that "Israel will continue acting with a mix of instruments." Coming so soon after the Shahid Rajaee terminal attack, there seemed little doubt that the cyber sabotage there was both the "step" and the "instrument" referred to by Hayman and Kohavi.

If Stuxnet had been one of the earliest incidents of major state-versus-state cyberwarfare, the water network and Shahid Rajaee attacks—along with Russia's interference in the fall 2016 U.S. presidential election—provided glimpses into the likely persistence of this type of warfare in the future. There will almost certainly be an ongoing chess match where each side is constantly weighing its priorities, choosing when to make a sacrifice, when to respond, and when to attack. It's in this sense that Shahid Rajaee was "a first and significant step on a long path," and it would be one with an important psychological dimension. Indeed, in hinting at its responsibility for the attack, Israel, the Mossad, and IDF intelligence were also taking credit for it and thereby sending a message of deterrence to Iran. And that message was: Strikes at critical civilian infrastructure would not be tolerated. Don't underestimate the strength of Israel's determination to respond to future cyberattacks or our ability to scale up the degree of disruption. Our cyber capabilities are far greater than yours. Do not test us.

There was, in addition, a third element to the message: Retaliation could also cross over into actual military strikes or a mix of overt, covert, and cyber operations that would have a devastating cumulative effect.

Was Israel capable of making good on its warnings?

The IDF had been employing offensive cyber ops since the late 1990s when it started out using Trojan Horse malware to penetrate enemy computers, including, we were told, Iranian systems. At that time cyber capabilities were still rudimentary, and the operations were carried out by young computer whiz recruits from inside a couple of converted shipping containers at a base in the center of the country.

Gradually though, cyber became an important part of Israel's military strategy, coming to be seen as another critical aspect of its arsenal, alongside aircraft, tanks, and submarines, such as with the Stuxnet attack. In 2010, former Israeli major general Yitzhak Ben Israel helped Netanyahu become one of the first heads of state to comprehend the enormous importance that the digital sphere would have in the near future and the paramount need to invest vast national power and resources into that realm.

Budgets and new personnel do not appear overnight, but starting around 2014, the country again massively increased its efforts to become a world-class cyber power both in the military and civilian sides of the governmental sector. Israel's military and intelligence units would provide graduates for its civilian tech sector, creating a mutual knowledge transfer ecosystem. Netanyahu created a cyber bureau in the prime minister's office bringing in the cyber capabilities of the Shin Bet, Israel's domestic security agency, and other capabilities. In 2016, he appointed Buky Carmeli, a twenty-one-year veteran of the IDF's electronic surveillance operation, to take charge of it.

"Do you have the energy for this?" Netanyahu asked Carmeli in December 2015 as he handed him the keys to Israel's cybersphere. The prime minister was testing whether Carmeli was a match for the job of protecting a massive amount of the country's sectors from cyberattacks. By then, several such attacks had awakened the world to the danger, including WannaCry, which infected over 200,000 computers in over 150 countries in 2017. That same year there was also NotPetya, which primarily infected computers in Ukraine, but also hit the U.S. and countries all over Europe.

With twenty-one years in the IDF's Unit 8200 and the Defense Ministry under his belt, Carmeli assured Netanyahu that he was ready to dive into the job with whatever it would take.

In April 2017, an Iranian hacker group called OilRig instigated a cyberespionage operation against over 250 Israeli targets, using a vulnerability in Microsoft Word to gain access to both public and private sector systems.

Carmeli and Israel's National Cyber Directorate thwarted that one, but experts took it as a warning, namely that the hackers were using increasingly sophisticated methods. Michael Gorelik, vice president of the Israeli security firm Morphisec, said it was one of the most advanced cyber campaigns he had followed. "It was a targeted, large campaign using quite a big infrastructure," he said.

The cyber defense firms ClearSky and Profero later revealed that they had thwarted a large-scale cyberattack operation launched by MuddyWater, a group that previously worked for Iran's Revolutionary Guard.

But while Carmeli's efforts had met with success, his successor, Yigal Unna, knew that the challenge from Iran was only growing. "The cyber winter is coming, and it will arrive faster and stronger than the worst estimates," Unna told us in a series of interviews in November and December 2020. "Cyber weapons can be compared to nuclear weapons in their [destructive] power, but the ease with which they can be obtained or used makes them more similar to a spear or a bow and arrow." The attackers, he added, pay a low price when they fail, "since the weapon is usually a code based on man-made letters and numbers," and success can cause incalculable damage. "The World Economic Forum published an annual global risk report that rated the cyber threat as the highest rated man-made threat in the world," he told us.

In December 2020, we were given a tour of the massive infrastructure Israel has built to counter that threat. Our guide was "L," the head of the Cyber Emergency Response Team (CERT), whose identity is secret. Between Tel Aviv and Beersheba, a distance of about seventy miles, the Israel National Cyber Directorate has around 350 personnel with different specialties, each hotwired with the latest computers and networking technology. Blinking arrows on an electronic map in a classified operations center at a nondescript office in Beersheba show cyber threats moving across the globe from different locations to Israel. They stream in from multiple continents, though some of the locations were surprising because, as officials explained to us, hackers sometimes stage their attacks from a friendly third-party country to try to cover their actual origin.

"When I got to my interview with the prime minister, he explained to me that Israel needs to remain in the top five leading cyber powerhouses," Unna told us. "I asked him why only the top five and not the top three, so I looked into the issue.

"We worked on it in the cyber directorate," he continued, "and today I can tell you that Israel is among the two strongest, second only to the U.S. in certain areas, such as industry, global investment, and academic research."

But despite Israel's tremendous capabilities, cyber threats have continued to intensify, and the country's record in meeting them is mixed. Shortly after we met with Unna, Israel was hit by the first of a series of ever more sophisticated mega hacks. On December 2, 2020, the giant Israeli insurance company Shirbit, which provides insurance to much of Israel's defense establishment and whose files contain personal information on thousands of military personnel, was hacked by a group called Black Shadow. The hack became known when ID numbers, driver's licenses, and registration forms of Israelis leaked from the insurance company's files.

Black Shadow later claimed credit for the attack in a tweet that read: "A huge cyberattack has been taken [*sic*] place by Black Shadow team. There has been a massive attack on the network infrastructure of Shirbit Company, which is in Israel economic sphere [*sic*]." The next day, Black Shadow demanded that Shirbit send fifty bitcoins (at the time, almost a million dollars) to their bitcoin wallet within twenty-four hours or else they would leak more information. The group warned that if the money was not sent, the ransom demand would rise to one hundred bitcoins, and to two hundred if another twenty-four hours passed.

"After that we will sell the data to others," warned the hackers, adding that more data would be leaked at the end of every twenty-four hours.

The warning caused panic in Israel, which was intensified because of the awareness that Black Shadow, though ostensibly an ordinary criminal hacking enterprise, had links to Iran. The group publicly says its goals have to do with money and extortion, in the same way that groups use ransomware to hold the computer systems of companies and agencies hostage. But its targets and long-term activities show that the country's anti-Israel ideology is its true foundation. With one round of leaks following another, the alarm gripping Israel, a tiny country of only nine million, was palpable. Still, two days after Black Shadow's ultimatum, Shirbit announced that it would not pay the ransom.

Although nominally only a threat to private data in the business sector, and not to physical infrastructure, Black Shadow's operation along with some similar private sector cyberattacks had major national security implications for Israel. First, as mentioned earlier, personal data can be the doorway to later large infrastructure hacks. Second, the data of Mossad and other Israeli intelligence agents, or that of their families, could sometimes be accessed through private sector insurance or other service agencies. Though the personal data of Israeli spies may not be labeled as "spy," powerful artificial intelligence and data mining techniques can now be used to discern when personal data of specific persons connect to security sectors. Third, ransomware attacks against large and influential businesses are the soft geopolitical underbelly of democracy. Israel's economy is so small that hacking a large insurance company like Shirbit or a single medium-size hospital can potentially destabilize the economy, the health system, and the foundations of the country itself. This is why Israel counters with physical-world infrastructure hacks as if its national security is at stake.

And so, the question arises: how did Iran get to the point where it could make such serious trouble for the Israeli cyber juggernaut?

In the background is a major, little understood aspect of Iranian society: that among its highly educated population of 80 million people, it has enormous human resources to draw on in developing its own cyber sector. Iran is fifth in the world in the number of STEM graduates, behind only China, India, the U.S., and Russia.

In addition to its considerable human resources, two events prompted Iran to make developing its cyberwarfare capacities a priority.

One was the 2009 Green Movement, in which protesters took to the streets to challenge the victory of the hard-line incumbent Mahmoud Ahmadinejad over the "moderate" Mir Hossein Mousavi, an election widely believed to have been rigged. The protests were the largest since the 1979 Islamic Revolution, powered as they were by social media, both to organize the demonstrations and to get information about them out of the country. As many as 1,500 protesters were killed in a brutal crackdown, and in the end the movement was crushed by the firepower available to the state-sponsored thugs of the Basij paramilitary force. But the use of social media by the protesters was a kind of wake-up call to the Iranian authorities, who realized that they had been caught napping in cyberspace and needed to be able to control information and communication technologies.

The following year, 2010, saw the second formative event, the Stuxnet attack against Iranian nuclear facilities (discussed in Chapter 2). In damaging some one thousand uranium enrichment centrifuges, Stuxnet is believed to have postponed the progress of Iran's nuclear program by one to two years. By September 2010, moreover, the Stuxnet worm had infected some thirty thousand computers across at least fourteen Iranian facilities—including those at the crucial Natanz nuclear facility.

But there was a flip side to Stuxnet. It may have delayed Iran's nuclear program, but it also woke up the sleeping Iranian cyber lion. It made Iran's authorities acutely aware of the vulnerability of their systems and of the urgent need to protect and defend themselves in cyberspace.

Furthermore, Iran's response to Stuxnet illustrated a phenomenon unique to the cybersphere that many cyber intelligence officials have warned about: it is that when digital weapons are used, their workings are almost always revealed to the enemy side and thus can be adopted as part of its own arsenal. In addition, cyberwarfare is a means by which a small attacker using asymmetric guerrilla tactics can greatly damage a larger adversary, and for that reason, the Islamic Republic came to see it as an important means by which it could compete against its most formidable internal and external adversaries.

That explains why the Iranians increased their security budget by 1,200 percent. As Frank Cilluffo, formerly vice president and cyber center director of George Washington University, put it in 2017, "In recent years, Iran has invested heavily in building out their computer network attack and exploit capabilities. Iran's cyber budget has jumped twelvefold under President Rouhani, making it a top-five cyber-power. They are also integrating cyber operations into their military strategy and doctrine."

On October 28, 2018, the head of Iran's civil defense agency claimed success in neutralizing a "new generation" of the Stuxnet virus that had been used in an attempt to damage Iran's communications infrastructure. Iranian officials blamed Israel. Then, in March 2019, Iranian intelligence hacked the cell phone of Benny Gantz, one of two leading candidates running for prime minister in the country's upcoming elections. According to a Microsoft survey also published in March 2019, in a two-year period, Iranian cyber groups hacked more than two hundred companies around the world, causing an estimated hundreds of millions of dollars in damage.

Given all this, one might have thought that by 2020, Israel would be ready for Iran's cyber onslaught. It was not. It was especially not prepared for hacking attacks on real-world infrastructure.

In fact, the main lesson of the cyberattack and counterattack tit-for-tat between Israel and Iran that took place through most of 2020 was that there was no telling where the new escalated digital conflict would lead.

If anything, the Israel-Iran conflict heated up during the course of 2020 and then peaked after major assassinations and attacks on Iranian nuclear facilities in 2021 and 2022. In retaliation, Iran attacked a number of Israeli ships at sea and attempted to assassinate several Israeli businesspeople during their travels outside of Israel. All through this time, in pursuit of its "ring of fire" objective, Iran persisted in trying to smuggle precision-guided missiles to its militias on the Syrian-Israeli border or to Hezbollah on the Lebanese-Israeli border, and the IDF persisted in launching air strikes and other operations to intercept the shipments.

In June 2021, the hard-liner Ebrahim Raisi, a man charged with crimes against humanity by international human rights organizations, was elected Iran's president with nearly 63 percent of the vote, taking over from the somewhat more moderate Hassan Rouhani. Not surprisingly, under Raisi Iran took on more aggressive postures, whether in promoting terrorism, in its nuclear negotiations with the world powers, or stepping up in its use of cyberwarfare to execute a number of increasingly sophisticated and damaging attacks.

In March 2021, TA453, a hacking group aligned with the IRGC—also known as Charming Kitten and Phosphorous—cleverly impersonated a prominent Israeli physicist and sent phishing emails to medical researchers in both Israel and the U.S.

The tactics and techniques used in the attack mirrored those of previous IRGC intelligence collection campaigns and goals. In May 2021, Israeli analysts using a forensic analysis traced another series of hacks to an Iranian-linked group, which had earlier gotten credit for hacks of the Israeli cybersecurity company Portnox and defense giant Israel Aerospace Industries.

The situation presented a new challenge to Israel and to the men responsible for the country's security: Prime Minister Naftali Bennett; David Barnea, who had succeeded Yossi Cohen as the head of the Mossad; IDF Chief of Staff Aviv Kohavi and his various other security chiefs. The new leadership not only maintained Israel's existing cyber networks, but also intensified its effort to develop new tools to meet the increased challenge from Tehran, which it used during the course of 2021 to strike back.

On July 9, 2021, hackers threw Iranian train stations across the country into disarray, posting fake messages about canceled trains on the stations' display boards. These fake messages encouraged passengers to call 64411, which was a hotline number for Supreme Leader Khamenei's office. On July 10, websites linked to Iran's Ministry of Roads and Urbanization went down. Then, on October 26, 2021, Israel struck harder, and in creative fashion. Suddenly on that day, there were outages at every one of Iran's 4,300 gas stations. The outages stemmed from a cyberattack aimed at a networked system that normally allowed millions of Iranians equipped with government-issued cards to buy sixteen gallons of gas each month at half price.

Chaos soon ensued.

Snapp and Tapsi, Iran's app-based taxi companies, seeing that drivers would have to buy expensive, unsubsidized gas, doubled and tripled their standard prices. Enormously long lines formed at stations. Tensions intensified between the regime and average Iranians already unhappy with the government's oppressive religious policies and its warlike priorities. There was even a danger of mass rioting in a country where, in the past, price hikes had led to unruly protests on the streets.

In fact, rumors spread that the crisis had been manufactured by the government as a sneaky way of raising fuel prices and being able to blame the rise on an external enemy.

That was exactly the sort of turmoil and distrust that the hackers hoped to sow. It was psychological warfare. At the same time as the gas stations were imploding, some "smart" digital billboards in Tehran and Isfahan started to display the message, "Khamenei! Where is our gasoline?" Others read, "Free fuel in Jamaran gas station." Jamaran was Khamenei's home neighborhood.

President Raisi, the hard-line cleric who formally took office in August 2021, essentially confirmed the psychological warfare element of the hack in his response to it. He asserted that the disruption of fuel sales was part of a plot conceived to manufacture disorder. "There should be serious readiness in the field of cyberwar and related bodies should not allow the enemy to follow their ominous aims," he said.

In the end, there was no widespread uprising. Still, the government had to scramble to defuse the situation. Following emergency meetings in the Oil Ministry and the National Cyber Council, Iran Oil Minister Javad Owji issued a remarkable and rare public apology on state tele-

International Atomic Energy Agency (IAEA) Director Rafael Grossi shows a camera system employed to check on Iran's Karaj Nuclear Facility during a press conference in Vienna, Austria on December 17, 2021. DEAN CALMA / IAEA

Iranian President Ebrahim Raisi views high-speed IR6 centrifuges, used to enrich uranium, at an exhibition for Iran's National Nuclear Technology Day.

Prime Minister Benjamin Netanyahu speaks at a press conference in Tel Aviv revealing the Mossad's heist of the Iranian nuclear archives, on April 30, 2018.
MIRIAM ALSTER/FLASH90

Mossad Director Meir Dagan attends a meeting of the Knesset Foreign Affairs and Defense Committee, shortly before ending his nine-year tenure in January 2011. Dagan formulated a policy of assassinations, covert actions, sabotage and cyberwarfare to slow down Iran's nuclear weapons program. MIRIAM ALSTER/FLASH90

Mossad Director Tamir Pardo at an event in Jerusalem in 2013. A former commando, who had participated in the famed Entebbe operation, Pardo continued Dagan's policy on Iran, which he had helped devise as his deputy. DAVID VAAKNIN/FLASH90

Mossad Director Yossi Cohen delivers a speech at an award ceremony for outstanding Mossad operatives in 2018. As head of the spy agency, Cohen led the heist of Iran's nuclear archives and has been blamed by Iran for many other operations against it. KOBI GIDEON/GPO

Israeli President Isaac Herzog inspects an honor guard together with the Crown Prince of Abu Dhabi, Sheikh Mohammed bin Zayed Al Nahyan (MBZ) during the first official visit to the United Arab Emirates by an Israeli leader, January, 2022. MBZ was the first Arab leader to sign on to the Abraham Accords.
AMOS BEN GERSHOM/GPO

Saudi Crown Prince Mohammed Bin Salman. The Saudi Crown Prince has gained a reputation as an erratic, but paradoxically pragmatic leader willing to engage with Israeli officials behind the scenes. Some view him as the key Arab leader behind the Abraham Accords.

A photo of the warehouse in the Shirobad neighborhood of Tehran from where Mossad agents stole Islamic Republic nuclear secrets on the night of January 30, 2018. ISRAELI PRIME MINISTER'S OFFICE

Fireproof vaults holding the Iranian nuclear archive. A Mossad team used special blow torches, heated to at least at 3,600 degrees Fahrenheit to burn through six of the 32 Iranian-made two-meter-high vaults to extract the files they needed. ISRAELI PRIME MINISTER'S OFFICE

The bullet-ridden car of Iran's nuclear program's chief nuclear scientist Mohsen Fakhrizadeh *(top)*. Iran accused Israel of carrying out the assassination using a remote-controlled gun operated through a satellite link.

Major General Qasem Soleimani headed the Islamic Revolutionary Guard Corps Quds Force. Known as the Shadow Commander, he was blamed by former CIA director David Petraeus for having the blood of hundreds of Americans on his hands.
WIKIMEDIA COMMONS

Millions of Iranians turned out for the funeral ceremony in Tehran for Soleimani, nemesis of the Mossad and the CIA.

Iran's Supreme Leader Ali Khamenei (with Hassan Rouhani, at left) stands over the casket of Qasem Soleimani, the Supreme Leader's closest ally and his top adviser for his plans to dominate the region.

vision. He also promised an extra ten liters of subsidized fuel to all car owners. The ministry rushed technicians to every single gas station across the country's vast territory in order to get them working again. It was a multistep process, since even after the pumps had been reset, most stations could still sell only unsubsidized fuel, which is twice the price of the subsidized product.

It was not until October 30, four days after the hack, that about 3,200 out of the country's 4,300 stations had been reconnected to the central distribution system. Only then could subsidized sales resume. Even then, nearly one quarter of the gas stations remained affected, some for up to another two full weeks.

Who carried out the gas station attack?

The Israeli government made no statement on the matter. Instead, an obscure group of hackers known as Predatory Sparrow formally claimed responsibility. The group said in a Telegram post that it was responding "to the cyber actions by Tehran's terrorist regime against the people in the region and around the world."

But most Iranian officials who commented publicly referred to another country as likely being responsible and it's not hard to guess who got the blame. "We are still unable to say forensically, but analytically I believe it was carried out by the Zionist regime, the Americans, and their agents," Brigadier General Gholamreza Jalali, the head of Iran's Civil Defense Organization, said on October 30.

This analysis was supported by evidence that the hack had goals beyond the tensions it created between the regime and the public. A senior manager in the Oil Ministry and an oil dealer with knowledge of the investigation said that Iranian officials believed the hackers may have accessed its data on international oil sales. Put differently, the cyber attackers may have seized a closely held state secret about exactly how Iran evades international sanctions.

This crucial data is saved on the ministry's computer servers, which is an air-gapped system.

In any case, Iran's retaliation against Israel wasn't long in coming.

On the same day that Jalali pointed the finger at "the Zionist regime," Iran's Black Shadow hacker group attacked Cyberserve, the host for the online presence of a number of significant Israeli companies.

One such company was the Israeli LGBTQ dating site Atraf. Black Shadow threatened to leak highly personal and sensitive user data, including their HIV status, sexual orientation, and unencrypted passwords.

Simultaneously, cyber attackers hacked the medical files at Machon Mor Medical Institute, an Israeli network of private clinics. Black Shadow then posted on the Telegram messaging website the personal information of some 1.5 million Israelis, fully 16 percent of the country's population and about 20 percent of the more targeted majority Jewish population (not including the more than two million Arab citizens of Israel).

"Hello Again! We have news for you," the hackers wrote in a message on Telegram.

"You probably could not connect to many websites today. 'Cyberserve' and their customers [were] hit by us," they said. "If you don't want your data leak(ed) by us, contact us SOON."

Later another message read: "They did not contact us . . . so [the] first data is here." A massive online data dump followed.

The Iranian counterattack also hit the large Israeli bus companies Dan and Kavim, a children's museum, public radio's online blog, and others, including the tourism company Pegasus and Doctor Ticket, a service that could have sensitive medical data. Although these Iranian hack attacks could be dismissed as less effective than attacks attributed to Israel against Iranian physical infrastructure, given Israel's much smaller population (nine million Israelis versus 80 million Iranians) the significant social and economic disruption led Israeli officials to view the attacks as a national security threat.

The Israel-Iran cyberwar is perhaps the most shadowy element in the ongoing conflict between the two countries. There is almost always an element of uncertainty in cyberattacks: Who was really responsible? What was the goal? Was the hacker state-sponsored or a private entity?

Was the intent to steal national security secrets or financial extortion? And where was the attack from? Iran, or another mischief-maker, like Russia or China?

Just weeks before Israel penetrated Iran's subsidized gas supply system, for example, Israel's Hillel Yaffe Medical Center's computer systems were compromised. In some ways, it was the worst infrastructure cyber strike Israel has faced, considering the scale and sensitivity of the data that was compromised.

Next was the damaging Black Shadow attack of October 30, 2021, on Cyberserve. According to cyber chief Yigal Unna, the Israel National Cyber Directorate had warned the company of the likelihood of an attack four days before it took place, telling it that immediate measures needed to be taken to plug some holes in its cyber defenses. Astoundingly, the Cyberserve official contacted by the INCD told the agency that he would be away for the weekend and would take care of the problem when he got back. INCD had the power to order critical infrastructure companies to protect their digital space, but not private sector companies like Cyberserve.

With Black Shadow, all Israeli authorities could do was ask Telegram to block the hacker group's channel posting the compromised data, which it did. But that didn't foil the hackers—they immediately reposted the material on a new channel, and hopped from channel to channel every time they were blocked.

All of which is to say that the status of cyberwarfare between Israel and Iran remains somewhat murky, but we're left with the feeling that Iran's counterattacks have led to a greater level of parity between the two adversaries. Even though Iran lags far behind Israel in global assessments of cybersecurity, the ayatollahs can threaten Israel in the cybersphere in a way that they cannot on most of the other military fields of play. Why is that the case? Three factors offer some explanation.

In cyberattacks there is a general principle: cyber offense always beats cyber defense. Any digital wall or defense has vulnerabilities that, given unlimited time and sufficient resources, any adversary can eventually find and exploit. Secondly, as Kevin Mandia, the CEO of the cybersecurity firm Mandiant, points out, on the playing field of technology, there's an asymmetry between Israel and Iran: Israeli society is much more dependent on technology. Hence, they have much more items of value worth stealing and, therefore, far more to lose. And finally, the technology gap between the heavyweights in the cybersphere—China, Russia, the U.S., and Israel—and the rest of the world is narrowing.

That is not the only reason why Israeli hospitals like Hillel Yaffe, insurance companies like Shirbit, defense companies like Israel Aerospace Industries, and server hosts like Cyberserve will continue to be hacked. As cyberweapons continue to spread, "democratizing" the digital sphere, there are more and more cyber groups, and some of them end up causing geopolitical trouble even without state sponsorship. For the U.S. over the past two decades, combating ISIS and al-Qaeda felt like an endless game of Whac-A-Mole. Now, fighting these expanding nonstate cyber outfits with nation-state-like capabilities is becoming increasingly unmanageable.

A March 2022 hack is a case in point. That was when an Iranian group managed to hack the old cell phone of the current Mossad director, David Barnea—even though to date there's no evidence that any national security was exposed. A few days after that, Israeli cyber experts blamed Iran for an attack that led to the activation of the siren system Israel relies on to provide early warning of rocket attacks in the Jerusalem and Eilat regions after a massive hack of the Tehran municipality computers, including those controlling traffic cameras and other electronic surveillance presumably by Israel. So far, cyber clashes have amounted only to the virtual equivalent of border skirmishes. But it seems likely that in time one side or another will be able to mount a cyberattack that would undermine state security in a more existential way.

Chapter 10

OPPORTUNITY FROM STRANGE QUARTERS

ON JUNE 25, 2020, AS THE COVID-19 PANDEMIC WAS CAUSING panicked countries across the world to close their borders, Benjamin Netanyahu announced a new opening. Israel and the United Arab Emirates, he said, after "extensive and intensive contacts," had reached an agreement to exchange supplies and medical knowledge aimed at combating the virus in their countries. Israel would get supplies of personal protective equipment, reactive agents, swabs, and ventilators from the UAE, which in turn would receive medical know-how from Israel.

The agreement wouldn't have been extraordinary had it been between countries with normal relations, but that wasn't the case with Israel and the UAE, and for that reason it was noteworthy. As Netanyahu put it when announcing the cooperation agreement in a speech at a graduation ceremony for a class of new Israeli Air Force pilots, "Our ability to work against the coronavirus pandemic . . . creates opportunities for us for open cooperation that we have not known so far with certain countries."

The country in question on this occasion, the UAE, adopted a more muted tone in its statements about the deal, pointing out that it was between private companies in the two countries, not between the two countries themselves. The caution came partly from the same source as always on the Arab side of the diplomatic dance it had conducted with Israel for years, a fear of a public backlash against any dealings whatsoever with the Jewish state, which was locked in a decades-long conflict with the Palestinians. But for the UAE there was also a new cause of concern having to do with the Palestinians. Just at the time the Covid deal was struck, Israel's cabinet was due to debate extending Israeli sovereignty to Jewish settlements in the West Bank, a euphemism for annexing some 30 percent of the territories that it had occupied since its victory in the Six Day War of 1967. And this was something that the UAE would not be able publicly to accept—nor even tacitly appear to condone by entering into any kind of a deal with Israel. Nonetheless, the medical cooperation agreement broke new ground, injected some momentum into the halting pace of the normalization process, and in the end, when Israel dropped the annexation plan, the road was open to the historic agreement known as the Abraham Accords, signed just a few months later.

Normalization doesn't just happen out of nowhere; many trust-building steps need to be taken in the background leading up to the final agreement, and in this instance, the steps came from an unexpected direction, the chief of Israel's intelligence service. Short on sleep and red-eyed, drinking coffee heated up in a microwave, Yossi Cohen on March 21, 2020, was working the secure phones at his home in Modi'in, a satellite city midway between Jerusalem and Tel Aviv. The Covid-19 virus that had emerged in China was already spreading across the globe. A battle was under way to secure the various scarce supplies around the world which were desperately needed to protect against the disease, and in Israel, the Mossad was drafted into the fight.

Why was the spy agency, rather than the Health, Foreign, and Defense ministries, taking charge of this procurement effort? Many people guessed that the Mossad got involved because some of the equipment was being obtained from countries with which Israel did not have diplomatic relations, and such relations had always been part of the Mossad's agenda. However, in March 2020, no one would have guessed that Israel had specifically sought out cooperation with some of those countries in order to catalyze a broader diplomatic breakthrough. That's the reason Cohen was working hard that night to acquire 10 million surgical masks from the UAE in exchange for Israeli medical know-how and security assistance. He multitasked, issuing orders to his agents, telling them that this "coronavirus diplomacy" with the UAE would be critical to getting Israel's relationship with the country out of the shadows, at the same time providing reassurances to top Emirati officials, talking on the phone while his white poodle scampered around the house barking incessantly. Eventually, he made eye contact with his wife, Aya, who was sitting next to a high chair that they kept for grandchildren's visits, who understood she needed to take the dog away.

When the deal was finalized in late March 2020, Cohen had to work out ways for the UAE's deliveries to be done in such a way that it would not be perceived as having helped Israel. Cohen would have preferred for everything to be publicly announced, but he also knew that a crisis creates space for bold moves and that exchanging UAE medical equipment for Israeli medical knowledge and security assistance could be a turning point in history. On June 25, he watched with satisfaction as Netanyahu publicly announced that cooperation between Israel and the UAE in combating the virus was taking place.

In fact, Cohen had written Netanyahu's speech. He had negotiated with his UAE counterparts over the text and when the speech could be delivered, taking into account the UAE's intense concern about the blowback it might get after being outed for cooperating with Israel. Cohen later told colleagues at the Mossad that the normalization announcement with the UAE that came only two short months later, in August 2020, might not have been possible without these important steps to build trust and cooperation.

But first, Netanyahu's plan for annexation loomed as a major obstacle to the normalization objective. Netanyahu had been promising since the start of the campaign for the September 17, 2019, snap elections to annex a large number of Israeli settlements on the West Bank and the Jordan Valley, which Israel had occupied since its victory in the Six Day War in 1967. The idea, which was a main plank in Netanyahu's election campaign that year, got a boost in January 2020 when President Trump announced the political portion of his Middle East peace plan that he had promised would resolve the Israel-Palestinian conflict once and for all, as well as pretty much all the other problems of Israel's relations with its neighbors. The Trump plan was officially called "Peace to Prosperity: A Vision to Improve the Lives of the Palestinian and Israeli People." It provided essentially for the U.S. to recognize the West Bank annexation that Netanyahu was proposing in exchange for the Palestinians getting their own independent state on the remaining 70 percent of the territory. The plan also gave the Palestinians some special arrangements relating to Jerusalem, but far less than prior plans proposed by the U.S.

But while Netanyahu seemed ready to press ahead with annexation, his plan ran into stiff opposition, and not just in the Arab world. The European countries, led by the United Kingdom, a staunch Israeli ally, condemned it. So did King Abdullah II of Jordan, who warned that the move could lead to "massive conflict" and endanger Israel's peace treaty with his country. Even within the new coalition government Netanyahu had formed with former IDF chief of staff Benny Gantz and his Blue and White party, there was stiff opposition to annexation. And furthermore, even some Israeli West Bank settlers were opposed to accepting the Trump plan, fearful that Israel would then have to move ahead finally with recognition of a Palestinian state on the nonannexed portions of the territory. "Either the settlements have a future, or the Palestinian state does—but not both," the far-right Religious Zionist leader Bezalel Smotrich said.

The settlers were correct in their analysis. American officials soon made it known that recognition of Israeli sovereignty over the 30 percent of the Occupied Territories envisaged by Netanyahu could only come if Israel agreed "to negotiate with the Palestinians along the lines set forth in President Trump's vision." The American ambassador to Israel, David Friedman, though a supporter of the settler movement, slammed home this message when he told aides to Netanyahu, "The U.S. wants to implement a peace plan, not an annexation plan." Jared Kushner, Trump's son-in-law and chief adviser on the Middle East, would later reveal that the U.S. had even considered going so far as to abstain from using its veto at the United Nations to block any international sanctions against Israel if Netanyahu went ahead with annexation.

But perhaps the most important factor sinking Netanyahu's plan was opposition from the UAE. Any annexation of the West Bank, Yousef Al Otaiba, the UAE ambassador in Washington, warned in talks with the American peace team, would be "really dangerous." The UAE made clear that, while such things as medical cooperation over stopping the Covid pandemic were a positive step toward the normalization of relations, Israel extending sovereignty to any of the West Bank would kill the prospect of normalization. As one senior American diplomat put it, "Annexation was really beginning to make the situation fall apart."

Otaiba's role was critical in saving normalization. An American-educated diplomat from a wealthy Emirati merchant family, he had been the UAE ambassador to the U.S. for twelve years and, as one American media observer put it, he "understands Washington, its DNA and its rhythms incredibly well." It didn't hurt that besides his ambassadorial post, he was also a minister in the Emirati government and considered close to MBZ, Crown Prince Sheikh Mohammed Bin Zayed.

Otaiba had been in contact with Israeli officials since coming to Washington in 2008. These early contacts were usually held in secret or came about serendipitously. One such meeting took place in 2012 after the Israeli prime minister gave a speech at the U.N. General Assembly. With a flair for the theatrical, Netanyahu held up a cartoonlike drawing of a bomb with a fuse and called on the U.N. to draw a red line "before Iran completes the second stage of nuclear enrichment necessary to make a bomb."

After the speech, Otaiba accompanied the UAE's foreign minister Sheikh Abdullah Bin Zayed to Netanyahu's hotel room at the Loews Regency in midtown Manhattan. The two entered the hotel through the parking lot and were taken up in a service elevator to Netanyahu's suite. The conversation centered on the Iranian threat.

Six years later, the parties felt comfortable enough to lift the veil of secrecy. In November 2018, Otaiba sat conspicuously at the same table as Israel's ambassador to Washington, Ron Dermer, during a kosher dinner at the Jewish Institute for National Security of America (JINSA), where Secretary of State Mike Pompeo was the keynote speaker. It was one of the earliest public signs that Israel-UAE ties were warming up.

Now, after the deal on Covid was signed and sealed, Otaiba was pushing the UAE leadership to start talking openly to the Israelis, in part to tell them, "All the things you want to do with us are going to be at risk if you proceed [with the annexation plan]." At the same time, Otaiba pursued another idea: to publish an op-ed in an Israeli newspaper. He approached Haim Saban, a billionaire Israeli-American media mogul and a major donor to the Democratic Party, who funds the Saban Forum at the liberal Brookings Institution in Washington, D.C.

"If you really want to speak to the Israelis, it has to be published in Hebrew," Saban advised Otaiba. Eventually, he paved the way for publication of an open letter to the Israeli public written by Otaiba and spread across the entire front page of *Yedioth Ahronoth*, one of Israel's largest-circulation dailies. "Israeli plans for annexation and talk of normalization are a contradiction," Otaiba wrote. That was the stick. The carrot promised a bright new future: "With the region's two most capable militaries, common concerns about terrorism and aggression, and a deep and long relationship with the United States, the UAE and Israel could form closer and more effective security cooperation." The letter's conclusion reflected the remarkable changing attitudes toward Israel in some parts of the Arab world: "In the UAE and across much of the Arab world, we would like to believe Israel is an opportunity, not an enemy. We face too many common dangers and see the great potential of warmer ties. Israel's decision on annexation will be an unmistakable signal of whether it sees it the same way."

The door had been opened. Now Israel had to decide whether to walk through it.

In late June, Jared Kushner sent aide Avi Berkowitz to Jerusalem for talks on the annexation issue. At that point, the only option on the table from the American perspective was to push ahead with the Trump plan, namely to get Netanyahu to agree to major concessions to the Palestinians in exchange for the extension of Israeli sovereignty to large parts of the West Bank. In a four-day period, Berkowitz met three times with Netanyahu, as well as separately with Defense Minister Benny Gantz and Foreign Minister Gabi Ashkenazi. But already after the second of his meetings with Netanyahu, Berkowitz realized that the Israelis and the U.S. government weren't talking the same language.

The Americans felt that Netanyahu, if given a choice between annexation of the West Bank or normalization with the UAE and perhaps other countries, would have opted for annexation. This may have been true—it probably was—but whether true or not, the Americans understood that Netanyahu wasn't willing to make the concessions that Kushner wanted for the Palestinians, such as recognition of Palestinian independence—without which Washington wouldn't agree to any "extension of sovereignty." Moreover, the Americans were nervous about the potential violence that annexation was likely to spark just a couple of months before the U.S. presidential elections.

To break the impasse, the American and UAE teams came up with the same idea around the same time: normalization of relations with the UAE and other Gulf states in exchange for the suspension of the West Bank annexation plan. Otaiba had suggested normalization to Kushner in 2019, but the U.S. didn't pursue it at the time because the fragmented Israelis were having trouble forming a government. Now, it seemed to Kushner and Berkowitz that the time for such a solution had arrived, that, indeed, it was the only way to move forward. Netanyahu, to the frustration of the Americans, remained skeptical. His instructions to Dermer were to continue pushing for American acceptance of annexation, while keeping the normalization option alive as a backup if annexation fell through. But by then, Kushner, Berkowitz, and company had stopped pretending that annexation was any longer an option.

Berkowitz flew back to the U.S. on July 1, which was also the first date that the Israeli government's coalition agreement allowed the annexation plan to be presented to Israel's cabinet. Because of coronavirus restrictions, there were no direct flights to Washington, which meant that Berkowitz had to take a roundabout return flight that turned into an eighteen-hour ordeal. As he was headed from the airport to the White House, the first call he received was from Otaiba, who suggested to Berkowitz, "What do you think about normalization in exchange for Israel dropping annexation?"

"You might not believe this, but I had a very similar thought the other day," Berkowitz replied.

Berkowitz arrived at the White House, took his Covid test, and rushed in to brief Kushner. The two affirmed their earlier conviction that annexation was a dead end. From then on, they decided, their efforts would be focused on a normalization deal between Israel and the UAE. Over the next few weeks diplomacy moved into high gear in Washington, with Berkowitz meeting with Dermer and Otaiba around thirty times in the space of a month. Despite years of close relations, because of the high stakes, many of the meetings involved shuttle diplomacy in which Kushner and Berkowitz met in one White House room with Otaiba, and then in another room with Dermer.

Dermer would report back at least once a day to Netanyahu and would also update National Security Adviser Meir Ben Shabbat every few days. Netanyahu also secretly updated close Likud minister Yariv Levin. Cohen told us that he was given updates by Netanyahu, but Netanyahu himself did not list Cohen as one of those he gave secret updates to. Either Cohen was left out of a loop for a short period down at the wire or Netanyahu doesn't want to disclose all of the Mossad's diplomatic activities. Kushner spoke on the phone several times with both UAE Crown Prince Mohammed Bin Zayed and with Netanyahu. Cohen and Secretary of State Pompeo, taking advantage of the close friendship they'd formed when Pompeo was director of the CIA, were also in frequent contact. Cohen made a number of crucial trips to the Emirates, meeting with MBZ and with his counterpart at the head of UAE intelligence, Sheikh Tahnoon Bin Zayed Al Nahyan, MBZ's brother. Tahnoon is also the chairman of Group 42, a conglomerate that has done several defense deals with Israel and was the company with which Israel signed the deal on coronavirus cooperation.

Cohen and MBZ had met many times, but one time close to the deal's signing was different. Cohen had shown infinite patience in the past, hoping that an incremental marathon approach would win over the cerebral MBZ. But MBZ still had the same concerns that they had discussed numerous times. Would he face emboldened domestic opposition in a UAE revolt against him for being the first Arab leader to cross the normalization line to Israel? Would other Arab nations throw him under the bus because he was partially throwing the Palestinians under the bus? He knew that even in the best case, he would get some serious pushback. So, the real questions were, would the economic, technological, and security benefits of getting closer to Israel outweigh the pushback? In twenty-five years, would people look back and praise him as a bold visionary or would they spit at the mention of his name as a traitor to the pan-Arab-Palestinian cause? Cohen had prepared responses on every point. He especially emphasized that the coronavirus diplomacy had gone off without a hiccup. The two countries had undertaken massive cooperation, and no one had tried to tear MBZ down. Plus, Cohen said, based on his close relationship with Pompeo, the U.S. would come through and make it worth it to MBZ and the UAE for taking some risk. In addition, Cohen warned that Trump might not win reelection and some of the benefits MBZ could lock into place might not be available in another six months. Likewise, MBZ assured Cohen that the UAE was ready to move quickly on a path to peace and normalization, with fast-tracked government, business, and tourism exchanges ready to go. MBZ did not make the final decision during that meeting with Cohen, but the Israeli could tell that he was getting ever closer.

Both sides had doubts and needed reinforcing at different points. Reassuring Israel was a mix of MBS, MBZ, UAE foreign minister Abdullah Bin Zayed Al Nahyan, Saudi General Intelligence Directorate head Khalid bin Ali Humaidan, Tahnoon Bin Zayed Al Nahyan, and Otaiba. Meanwhile, Otaiba in particular pushed forward publicly with the idea now being pressed on both sides by the Americans—normalization with Israel in exchange for an Israeli suspension of Netanyahu's annexation plan. At critical points when Kushner was nervous, he would call Saudi Arabia's MBS, who would laugh off his concerns that the UAE would in the end reject the agreement, reassuring him that he would personally make certain that didn't happen. Each side had interlocutors who were longtime trusted partners and who quietly and craftily gave the other side a push, while never pressing so hard that they would retreat. Over and over again, each side got close to normalization but pulled back at the last moment.

That was until August 2020. At that point, a mix of reassurances came together at the same time as Cohen and Israel offered additional cyber, technology, or defense gifts. Also, the Netanyahu-Dermer tandem agreed to delaying the West Bank annexation. All of these trends converging brought the UAE across the finish line.

All of this was taking place simultaneously with another development, the sale by the U.S. of F-35 fighter jets to the UAE. Technically, this important weapons transfer had nothing to do with the UAE-Israel negotiation. But Cohen, without ever being explicit, let it be known that Israel would support it if it would lock in normalization.

Netanyahu's annexation plan was never presented to the Israeli cabinet.

By the beginning of August, an agreement in principle had been reached, and what was left were tortuous negotiations over the wording of a joint statement to be made by the United States, Israel, and the UAE. In total, 130 versions of a draft were passed from side to side as the UAE and Israel wrangled over the minutiae—how, for example, exactly to word Israel's agreement not to annex parts of the West Bank. Israel also wanted to make sure it was getting the real deal in the normalization agreement, including all aspects of economic cooperation.

Incidentally, the accords were given their name by Miguel Correa, a U.S. general on the National Security Council, who had been put on the American team thanks to a previous acquaintance with Otaiba. Correa had been stationed in the UAE and it so happened that he had orchestrated a rescue mission to extract a UAE Special Forces team whose helicopter had crashed during a mission against al-Qaeda in Yemen. Among those rescued was MBZ's son-in-law. After that, Correa had built up a special relationship with the Emiratis.

Correa recalled that he came up with the idea of calling the agreement the "Abraham Accords" literally at the very last moment, on the morning of August 13, 2020, the day that Trump, Netanyahu, and MBZ were scheduled to make a three-way conference call to announce normalization. The name came to him, he said, because Abraham is revered by the three monotheistic religions of Judaism, Islam, and Christianity. The word Accords was in the plural to make way for other countries to join the circle.

The Accords came almost twenty-five years after the Oslo agreement, when Israel and the UAE had first begun their covert ties. The final wording stated that "Israel will suspend declaring sovereignty over areas outlined in the President's Vision for Peace and focus its efforts now on expanding ties with other countries in the Arab and Muslim world." Israel and the UAE would "sign bilateral agreements regarding investment, tourism, direct flights, security, telecommunications, technology, energy, healthcare, culture, the environment, the establishment of reciprocal embassies, and other areas of mutual benefit."

Immediately after the announcement, talks with Bahrain moved into high gear, but Cohen had already prepared some of the groundwork for that with several trips to meet with officials in the Bahraini capital of Manama.

The Mossad had maintained active ties with the kingdom since the early 2000s, and Israel had maintained a secret diplomatic presence there since 2009 through a Bahraini-registered front company named the Center for International Development—which acted as a de facto embassy. It had been opened following several behind-the-scenes meetings between Bahrain's then foreign minister Khalid Bin Ahmed Al Khalifa and his Israeli counterpart at the time, Tzipi Livni.

In early August, with the UAE talks in their final stages, Cohen spoke by phone with Bahraini prime minister Khalifa Bin Salman Al Khalifa, and within a month an agreement to establish diplomatic relations was signed. As one Israeli official put it: "All we had to do is change the sign on the door"—meaning on what had until then been the de facto embassy. It all seemed to happen fast, and Netanyahu and Cohen basked in the limelight of publicity that accompanied the accords, but in truth their achievements were the culmination of more than two decades of work by the Mossad, the Israeli Foreign Ministry, and others.

It would be hard to overstate how important the Abraham Accords were for Israel and for the Israelis who worked on them over the years. In the space of a few months, Israel had established full relations with a group of Arab countries, united in their fear of Iran, but also united in a certain vision of a future in which the waging of ancient tribal conflict seemed archaic and futile and the only viable way forward was some sort of accommodation with each other. The Abraham Accords shifted the balance of power in a still volatile region, but one in which Israel was ever more a normal part of the picture. No longer an enemy and perhaps not exactly an ally, but as a kind of partner. Nearly forty years before, Egypt's Anwar Sadat had been assassinated by Islamic extremists largely because of his willingness to accept the Jewish state's permanent presence. Now, figures like MBZ, and informally MBS, had done much the same thing, still with risks and dangers and opposition, but in an environment far more accepting of Israel.

On September 15, 2020, a month after the official announcement, there was a signing ceremony at the White House. As Cohen stood on the South Lawn of the presidential residence, he thought back to some of his early meetings with MBS and MBZ. He remembered how he had touched down in the Gulf in the middle of the night so as to remain invisible. He'd been driven past the Great Mosque in Abu Dhabi on the way to the Qasr el Watan royal palace there and been received at the opulent royal palace in Riyadh, Saudi Arabia—places he would never have dreamed of seeing, from the inside, when he joined the Mossad almost thirty years earlier.

Success has many fathers and each of the main actors in the Abraham Accords story tells the events from their own point of view. From Washington, the view was that the Otaiba op-ed was the "big inflection point" and that following publication the Americans were able to come in and broker the deal. Benjamin Netanyahu and Ron Dermer would push their own claims for credit. President Trump has pointed to the Abraham Accords, as well as to his decision to move the American embassy from Tel Aviv to Jerusalem, as among the major achievements of his presidency. Predictably, Kushner too has described in book form his role, presenting himself as the key player in getting to an agreement.

Trump and Kushner deserve considerable credit for the Accords. Kushner was the key day-to-day player on the American team, he and his aides tirelessly maintaining contact with all sides, easing their anxieties, cajoling them into taking a chance. Even though the Palestinians felt that Trump was biased toward Israel, the Trump administration still played a critical role by resisting Netanyahu's annexation plan, unless it came with agreement to a truncated Palestinian state. Kushner also deserves credit for his aggressive role in arranging for each country to get major benefits from the Accords—for example, getting approval for the sale of F-35s to the UAE (even though that deal was later frozen sometime after the signing of the agreement).

But it's also true that none of his contributions would have been possible if the historical circumstances had not lined up so favorably. He and Trump took advantage of a situation that had evolved over many years. Kushner, moreover, was merely the top adviser to just one of four national leaders, all of whom were critical to cutting the deal—MBS, MBZ, Netanyahu, and Trump, any one of whom could have sabotaged the Accords at any time.

Cohen too has not been hesitant to claim his share of the credit, and both Netanyahu and Dermer were generous in their praise of the Mossad director's role. Netanyahu specifically noted Cohen's talent in converting "the hearts of the leaders of the region . . . long before the emotional ceremony in Washington, and by the way, also after." According to Dermer, Cohen's contribution, appropriately for a spy agency, had been below the radar: "It is easier to surface when there has been strengthening of ties. If you are standing on an iceberg, you only see the perspective from the top. But what makes an iceberg strong is underneath the surface. He [Cohen] spent time strengthening underneath."

As for Cohen, he believes that very likely no deal would have been possible without the blessing of Saudi Arabia, where he had spent years building his contacts and an element of trust, especially with MBS, the Crown Prince. The fact that Cohen's grandparents spoke Arabic and that he was highly fluent in the language and culture allowed him to make MBS as well as MBZ feel that they had a trusted and reliable partner in him. Otaiba, MBS, and MBZ's sophistication, innovative streak, and years of quietly investing in getting to know the West helped Cohen and Netanyahu feel secure enough to take their own risks. Cohen highlights his and prior Mossad officials' countless trips to the Gulf as contributing to the later Kushner-Dermer-Otaiba breakthrough. The Mossad, says Cohen, "worked for many years, during my time there and even before me, and built up bilateral relations between the countries. Then the U.S. entered and said 'come and sign.' You only sign at the climax when you have built a foundation below based on high levels of trust." Agreeing with that, a senior Israeli diplomat familiar with the long history of Israeli-Gulf relations told us, "Peace with the Gulf was built layer on layer, no one single person built it."

Sitting in his office in Tel Aviv on August 13 watching the news that the UAE and Israel were formalizing ties, Ehud Olmert, who was prime minister when Meir Dagan had first sensed the shifting winds in the Gulf, received an email from a "very senior" Mossad official who had served as his emissary to the UAE.

> Hello Ehud,
>
> It's a very important day. De facto peace with the Emirates began fifteen years ago. Successful secret business ties showed them the beautiful face of Israel. I remember your contribution and reporting to you after each trip.
>
> Peace is better than war.
>
> Yours

Olmert, who has never revealed the identity of his correspondent, replied:

> One day your role will be known. Not everyone who shows off is worthy; you never did, but I know what you did and the value of your contribution.

In a dig at Netanyahu and Cohen for claiming full credit for the Abraham Accords, the Mossad official wrote back: "Dagan believed very strongly in the relationship. We invested a lot in it. I'm very happy with the agreement, less so that Bibi is celebrating."

Similarly, in an interview with us, Olmert argued that while things came into public view during the time of Netanyahu and Cohen, the ground had been prepared before. The breakthrough with the UAE was the product of "strategic thinking and a very long and patient process of ties" with the Gulf state, he said.

Trump negotiator Jason Greenblatt used the analogy of a Rubik's Cube to describe the process by which the parties came together over the years. "You don't finish the Rubik's Cube until you touch all the pieces and get them in the right order," he told us.

As for Cohen, he told us in a public interview at the *Jerusalem Post* conference in October, 2021: "I think that was one of the greatest diplomatic moves [in] the Middle East ever. It helped in pushing the evils away and working with the good guys, working with the good states. It was . . . not less than a miracle or a beautiful move for us Israelis in the Middle East."

In late October 2020, Sudan followed the UAE and signed an agreement to normalize relations with Israel. In some ways, the breakthrough with Sudan, which followed some complex diplomacy led by the United States, was even more of a break with a bleak past than the one with the UAE. Sudan had once been at war with the Jewish state; for most of the first two decades of the new millennium, it had been a client state of Iran and a way station on its weapons supply route to Hamas and Islamic Jihad in Gaza. Now it had been removed from that circle of hardline, unremitting hostility to Israel.

In the wake of the agreement, President Trump removed Sudan from the list of state sponsors of terrorism. Normalization documents were signed in January and March 2021, but only after Sudan paid a symbolic $335 million settlement to the victims and families of various terror attacks. With that done, Washington then helped Sudan receive a gargantuan $50 billion in debt relief from the International Monetary Fund, with the Paris Club writing off a further $14 billion.

But it was not just this financial benefit to Sudan that had secured the deal; there was a backstory in Sudan, where several warlords were vying for power as the country's long-ruling dictator faced popular unrest, while disputes among key Israelis threatened to sabotage their ability to pursue a united strategy.

In early February 2019, according to foreign sources, Yossi Cohen met with Sudan's intelligence chief Salah Gosh on the sidelines of the Munich Security Conference to discuss the possibility of a normalization process with Israel. In parallel, and unknown to Cohen, the country's embattled Islamist dictator Omar al-Bashir, whose regime was on the verge of collapse amid an economic crisis and rioting on the streets, met with a former Shin Bet officer, Ronen Levy, working at the time under the code name Maoz. Levy, under the auspices of Israel's National Security Council, had opened up a channel to Bashir via connections in Chad. Levy and his boss, Meir Ben Shabbat, would also eventually be in contact with another Sudanese leader, military chief Lieutenant General Abdel Fattah al-Burhan.

Cohen meanwhile, following his conversation with Salah Gosh, and helped by his contacts with the United Arab Emirates and Saudi Arabia, had arranged meetings with top Sudanese officials, especially with warlord and power broker Mohamed Hamdan Dagalo. When Cohen learned that Levy and Ben Shabbat were establishing their own channels in Sudan, open war broke out between Cohen and Ben Shabbat. At one point, the Mossad and Cohen threatened to cut off contact with Levy because they viewed his talks, first with Bashir and later with Burhan, as undermining their broader efforts. Levy and others, however, accused Cohen of nearly sabotaging their developing ties with Sudan. Ben Shabbat told Cohen that it was Netanyahu himself who brought him in to create multiple power centers for diplomacy. The Mossad director appealed to Netanyahu in protest.

Eventually, a compromise was hammered out, which satisfied the combative Cohen, if perhaps only partially. Sudan and Morocco would be handled mostly by the NSC team of Ben Shabbat and Levy, the Mossad would retain responsibility for the UAE and Bahrain, and the Mossad also got a green light to continue connections with Dagalo.* Meanwhile, Bashir was ousted in April 2019 in a military coup after almost thirty years in power.

At this point, another figure emerged out of the blue, Nick Kaufman, a Cambridge-educated British-Israeli lawyer. Kaufman had represented Sudanese victims of Bashir's regime and was advising the new Sudanese government on a case against Bashir at the International Criminal Court.

A year earlier, at an airport business lounge in Addis Ababa, Ethiopia, Kaufman had a chance encounter with a Sudanese woman named Najwa Gadaheldam, a well-connected diplomat. As chance would have it, Gadaheldam had become an adviser to Burhan, who now headed the military council supposedly leading a transition to democratic rule.

She told Kaufman that the Sudanese wanted to be taken off the U.S. State Department's list of state sponsors of terrorism. The new Sudanese regime saw a path to Washington passing through Israeli prime minister Benjamin Netanyahu. Gadaheldam proposed an exchange of letters between Israel and Sudan to be facilitated by Kaufman.

Kaufman approached contacts in the NSC who put him in touch with Ben Shabbat, who in turn agreed to raise with Netanyahu the idea of a three-way negotiation among Sudan, Washington, and Jerusalem. Netanyahu gave a letter to Kaufman expressing a wish to open diplomatic relations, and Kaufman then traveled to Sudan, still officially an

* The arrangement kept the Mossad in the game, while also providing a backup option if the NSC failed. In any event, Netanyahu promised Cohen that anytime something major happened with Burhan, he would get to weigh in. The promise would prove valuable in February 2020, when the talks with Sudan were at a critical make-or-break point, and it was Cohen's personal connections, in his own telling, that helped get both Dagalo and Burhan across the finish line. The alternative view gives far more credit to Ben Shabbat and Levy for the Sudan breakthroughs.

enemy of Israel. Kaufman was told that if anything went wrong, he was "on his own."

In Khartoum, Kaufman delivered the letter in person to Burhan, receiving in return a letter that he had jointly drafted with Gadaheldam, welcoming normalization between the two countries. Burhan gave Kaufman a letter in response, which remained with Kaufman at all times. At one point, he told us, he even stuffed it down his trousers for safekeeping—a lucky move as his hotel was broken into at one point when he took some time off to tour Khartoum with his minders. Following the exchange of letters, Gadaheldam coordinated with Maoz-Levy to secretly arrange a meeting in Uganda between Burhan and Netanyahu.

The meeting took place on February 3, 2020. Burhan was prepared to proceed immediately with normalization. But following the ouster of Bashir, there was now a third key player in Sudan's leadership, the top civilian leader, transitional prime minister Abdallah Hamdok—who had been left in the dark about the meeting—and he vehemently objected to any deal with Israel. Cohen had played a role in setting up the meeting and was present during the Burhan-Netanyahu talks, but Hamdok's ability to obstruct a normalization agreement convinced Cohen that the Burhan track might not produce the desired result. He calculated that the real power in Sudan was held by General Dagalo, an illiterate former camel trader who had allegedly carried out atrocities in Darfur and who had become the deputy chairman of the Sudanese Sovereign Council. Former intelligence minister Eli Cohen has confirmed to us how critical the Mossad-Dagalo front was to maintaining support for any major normalization initiative in Sudan.

In May, Gadaheldam died of Covid. Ironically, this tragedy led to renewed momentum on the diplomatic front. Learning that she was sick, Levy flew to Sudan on an emergency plane to bring her medicine, and though he failed to save her, it was on his unexpected trip that Burhan confirmed his commitment to normalization, overriding Hamdok's opposition. "I am with you to the death," he supposedly told Levy.

Yet another major obstacle appeared in the path of a deal in September, when American-Sudanese relations broke down. The Americans were deadlocked on the issue of removing Sudan from the terror list as well as over Sudan's demand for a monetary payment. A month later, Israeli and American officials, including Levy and Aryeh Lightstone, chief of staff to American ambassador to Israel David Friedman, went to Khartoum to convince Sudan that the deal on offer was the best they would get. It was a repeat of what Cohen had told the Sudanese a few months before, and suggests that, coordinated or not, he and Levy had used a good cop–bad cop approach to reel Khartoum in.

Levy, it seems, was letting Sudan think they would get more dollars from the U.S. than Washington was willing to give, while Cohen was shooting that down to keep expectations realistic. This last meeting in September finally brought Sudan to sign in October.

In December 2020, another domino fell as Israel and Morocco announced normalization. The two countries had long-standing informal ties and close cooperation between their intelligence agencies. The deal was sealed when the Trump administration agreed to recognize Moroccan sovereignty in the Western Sahara as a quid pro quo for normalization with Israel. Alone among the elements in the Abraham Accords, the agreement with Morocco was not connected in any way to the Iranian threat.

Of the four normalization deals, the Sudan-Israel agreement has led to the least amount of progress. This lack of movement is mostly due to continuing political upheavals in Sudan. Indeed, relations with Sudan became totally unmanageable after October 2021, when military chief Burhan toppled the civilian leader Hamdok, thereby making himself a pariah in the West. The U.S. has condemned Burhan, threatening to keep the Western aid spigot to Khartoum shut until a civilian leadership is reinstated. At the same time, Washington has clearly signaled its desire to hold on to the improved relations by maintaining its diplomatic presence in Sudan. This was true at least until mid-April 2023, when Burhan and Dagalo's forces started fighting, leaving the country's future in an even greater state of uncertainty.

Jerusalem is less concerned about Sudanese democracy, but cannot publicly ignore when the West recasts Sudan and Burhan as persona non grata. Still, in the shadows, the Mossad, under Cohen and his successors, has maintained quiet ties, keeping ready for the day when normalization can get back on track. In fact, there were glimmers of this future with a visit by Israeli foreign minister Eli Cohen to Sudan on February 2, 2023, about further advancing the normalization between the countries.

In any event, the breakthrough with Sudan in 2020 remains at least symbolically the most important of the Abraham Accords deals. More than half a century after the Arab League met in Khartoum in the wake of the stinging defeat inflicted on the combined Arab armies, including Sudan, in the 1967 Six Day War to announce the infamous "Three No's"—No peace with Israel, No recognition of Israel, No negotiations with Israel—Jerusalem and Khartoum do recognize each other, negotiate with each other, if quietly, and, most important, are at peace.

Chapter 11

THE MOSSAD SENDS A MESSAGE

TWO AND A HALF YEARS AFTER ISRAEL GOT ITS HANDS ON Iran's nuclear archives, another of the major goals it had set for the raid materialized. Already the archive materials had helped induce the United States to withdraw from the JCPOA, and provided Israel with new operational intelligence. Now it had the International Atomic Energy Agency back on Iran's case with full force and intent.

And the IAEA did take more direct action on Iran, though not just because of the materials seized in the archive raid. There was also a change at the helm of the organization that led it to alter both its style and its substance. In July 2019, a few months before he was due to step down, the IAEA's long-term director, the Japanese diplomat Yukiya Amano, who had headed the nuclear watchdog for almost a decade, died from an unspecified illness. He was replaced later that year by an Argentinian diplomat, Rafael Grossi.

Whereas Amano was tight-lipped, Grossi was loquacious. If Amano preferred a slow pace, laboriously investigating every detail, Grossi was high-energy and worked on instinct. More importantly, from Israel's perspective, whereas Amano summoned all of his powers as a low-key, toned-down bureaucrat to pour cold water on any attempt to rally excitement or intensity against Iran on the basis of the Mossad's findings, Grossi knew exactly what the material the Mossad had shown the IAEA was worth, and he wasn't going to stick his head in the sand.

Born in Buenos Aires in 1961, Grossi joined Argentina's foreign service in 1985. He served a spell as IAEA chief of staff under agency chief

Mohamed ElBaradei, handling negotiations with both North Korea and Iran. From 2010 to 2013, he was the agency's deputy director general, and became the new agency head on December 3, 2019.

Grossi immediately started to confront the Islamic Republic to resolve the questions about its undeclared nuclear activities that had been revealed after the Mossad's archive heist. The ayatollahs tried to push back, insisting that by accepting the Mossad's information as valid despite Iran's denials, the supposedly neutral IAEA was effectively taking sides. But Grossi was unwilling to look at a red light and pretend it was green. At issue was whether Iran was concealing from the world: uranium enrichment, past nuclear experiments, and other potential nuclear weapons activities.

Grossi pressed Iran on this issue at the end of 2019 and again in early 2020, when he said that Iranian deputy foreign minister Abbas Araghchi had not explained the violations. Grossi again pressed Iran in public statements on February 10, 2020, though he did not support punitive action, such as reimposing sanctions. Western sanctions against Iran had been relaxed when the 2015 nuclear deal was signed, as long as Iran kept its nuclear violations to a level that did not get it substantially closer to developing an actual nuclear weapon.

But on March 3, 2020, a leaked document showed that Grossi had privately reported a high-level violation to IAEA member states, namely that Iran had almost tripled its stockpile of low-enriched uranium and was now just 30 kilograms short of the 1,050 kilograms required to go to the 90 percent enrichment level needed to produce a nuclear bomb.

"Iran must decide to cooperate in a clearer manner with the agency to give the necessary clarifications," Grossi said publicly. He talked about the rapid pace of Iran's enrichment and also, finally, acknowledged that the Mossad's claims of a secret uranium storage facility at Turquzabad in northern Iran were true. (See Chapter 6.) "The fact that we found traces [of illicit uranium at Turquzabad] is very important," Grossi added publicly, noting an additional violation beyond the enriched uranium which Iran openly admitted to. "That means there is the possibility of nuclear activities and material that are not under international supervision and about which we know not the origin or the intent.

"That worries me," Grossi added.

Those were fighting words coming from the normally "no drama" IAEA, and they signaled the difference between Grossi and his predecessor.

In early June 2020, Grossi leaked a report that in the three months since his last warning, Iran had produced another 500 kilograms of low-enriched uranium. He noted that if Tehran maintained that enrichment rate, it would probably have enough low-enriched uranium for two nuclear weapons within three months. The Israelis, as both Intelligence Minister Eli Cohen and Mossad director Yossi Cohen told us, were pleased that Grossi was showing a willingness to be publicly tough with the Iranians.

Finally, on June 19, the IAEA Board of Governors condemned Iran for the first time since before the 2015 nuclear deal. From Israel's perspective, the condemnation took away any fake "moral high ground" the Islamic Republic could have tried to claim, citing its compliance with other aspects of the deal.

If Israel achieved its goal regarding the IAEA, it still had to contend with the progress Iran had made in its now not-so-secret enrichment activities. In fact, for the two and a half years following the archive raid and the American withdrawal from the JCPOA, Cohen had been itching to hit Iran, practically salivating over the opportunities he knew existed to exploit the gaping holes in its security. But he was forced to exercise uncharacteristic restraint because it would have been unthinkable for the Mossad to destroy a major Iranian nuclear facility as long as the IAEA and the JCPOA signature countries were crediting the Islamic Republic with compliance. Now, however, the tide had turned and created sufficient moral cover to take new, risky operations.

Cohen, an avid marathon runner, felt as if the pistol had been fired for the start of a race. He could finally unleash the agency's potential.

From June 25 until July 19, the Islamic Republic's facilities were pummeled almost nonstop by more than ten mysterious explosions, fires, and other "accidents." Among the sites hit were the country's most advanced centrifuge assembly facility, a petrochemical plant, a power grid, and its largest missile site.

It was almost as if the entire country was suddenly surrounded by volcanoes and all the Islamic Republic could do was wait in futility until the next eruption. For Cohen, it might have looked like someone was shooting fish in a barrel: one after another a nuclear or IRGC installation burst into flames. His intelligence counterparts from other countries and Iran analysts across the globe watched in awe as the seemingly unending show continued.

The first incidents occurred on June 26, 2020, exactly a week after the IAEA condemnation of Iran, when a fire broke out at a power station in Shiraz, Iran's fifth most populous city, causing major blackouts. Later that same day, a huge blast ripped apart the Khojir missile production facility in the mountains some twelve miles east of Tehran. The National Council of Resistance of Iran, an opposition group, has claimed that Khojir is an Iranian Defense Ministry secret facility code named B1-Nori-8500 and is "engaged in the development of nuclear warheads for intermediate-range ballistic missiles."

There were multiple reports of sabotage or strikes against Khojir by Israel, the U.S., or Iranian dissident groups, but four days after the June 26 blast, Israeli and American officials, speaking off the record, denied they had been involved in that specific incident.

Whoever carried out the attack on Khojir, there seems little question that it was part of Iran's constellation of facilities related to its nuclear weapons development. The same is true of other sites where sabotage or explosions have taken place, including Natanz, the Sina Hospital at the University of Tehran, and on the cities of Ahvaz and Karun, former U.S. Air Force cyber intelligence official Jeff Bardin told the authors. He added, for example, that Sina Medical is tied to the University of Tehran's Nuclear Medicine Department, and Ahvaz has a nuclear facility that is identified on the map obtained in the Mossad heist. Bardin also theorized that the Karun chemical plant likely has some ties to the nuclear supply chain, but said evidence to prove this was less present in open-source information.

Iran, in an almost Pavlovian reaction, claimed the Khojir blast was caused by a gas explosion, not at Khojir itself, but at the nearby Parchin military complex, both about twenty miles from Tehran. When the incident occurred, the entire night sky over Tehran was lit up, giving some credibility to the idea that a huge gas explosion had occurred. However, satellite images showed clearly that a shed housing two subsidiaries of Iran's space industries at Khojir was completely destroyed, as were a number of unidentified facilities. One of the companies, the Shahid Bagheri Industrial Group, produces solid fuel for Iran's rockets, while another, Shahid Hemat Industrial Group, makes the liquid fuel for its ballistic missiles. Several sources both in Israel and overseas speculated the strike was carried out by Israel using a kinetic cyberweapon, meaning malware that causes physical damage, like the Stuxnet virus used in 2009 to sabotage centrifuges at the Natanz nuclear development cite. An American analyst, Theodore Karasik, told a Saudi paper, "The consensus appears to be a cyber-strike by Israel. . . . The Khojir event is a continuation of the Stuxnet virus used 10 years ago to disrupt and deter Tehran's military industry."

The Iranian refusal to admit that the strikes at Khojir and others were acts of sabotage and not accidents was of a piece with its reluctance to admit its security weaknesses. But Western intelligence officials and sources inside Iran said that while some were indeed accidents, several were the result of covert Israeli actions, sometimes with American help. "The entire point is for the Iranians to feel considerable stress trying to decide what might have been our work," said an Israeli defense official. European intelligence officials speculated that Israel might be "trying to provoke Iran into military confrontation" before the U.S. November presidential elections when President Trump might be voted out of office (as indeed he was). Netanyahu and Cohen feared they would not be able to strike so hard and fast with a Democratic president in power.

A few days after the explosion at Khojir, an explosion occurred at a site ostensibly not associated with any nuclear or military program. This was an attack that killed nineteen people and injured six at the Sina Athar clinic in northern Tehran, which specializes in nuclear medicine. The Iranian authorities had previously issued safety warnings to the facility's administrators, and it is likely that the blast was an accident. Still, it contributed to growing pressure on the Iranian authorities at a time when there was a feeling of rising insecurity among the Iranian public.

Meanwhile, on June 27, amid the hits Iran was taking on its territory, Israel also struck Iranian proxies in Syria. At least nine pro-Iranian militia members were killed in an alleged Israeli air strike targeting military positions in Syria's al-Bukamal, a crucial point on the Iraqi border used for trafficking weapons. This attack took place just hours after IRGC Quds Force commander Esmail Ghaani had reportedly been at the site. The trip was his first to Syria since Soleimani's assassination, and he was there at least in part to convey the message that, despite the loss of Soleimani, Iran would continue its post-2017 strategy of opening a Syrian front against the "Zionist regime." All of this was happening as Netanyahu was supposedly about to make his announcement to annex part of the West Bank on July 1, but then did not. The Syria strike and the Khojir blast, which occurred within twenty-four hours of each other, dealt further serious blows to Iranian prestige and also may have helped distract the Israeli public from Netanyahu's balking on his annexation promise. But if these operations were also distractions, they were just preliminaries to a more important strike a few days later. This one was at Natanz, the small city in the center of Iran where a critical part of Iran's program to make an atom bomb is located.

At first, it was unclear if anything significant had actually happened. Initial reports, including the Associated Press quoting an Iranian nuclear spokesman, were of an unspecified "incident" taking place on the morning of July 2, 2020, at a building under construction near the Natanz nuclear facility, but not at the nuclear facility itself. In fact, since whatever happened was on a Thursday, which is part of the Iranian weekend, local websites didn't report the incident at all.

An Iranian nuclear spokesman eventually said there was no damage to the actual nuclear facility or to its reactor. Despite that denial and the hazy picture of what exactly had occurred, it became clear that something did go awry at Natanz and that there had been a fire or an explosion. This gave rise to speculation that someone had physically sabotaged the site, perhaps hacking it with cyberweapons, as had happened with the Stuxnet virus ten years earlier. Or perhaps Iran itself had experienced some kind of technological failure and the reported damage at the plant wasn't caused by foreign interference at all.

Also, it was unclear from the start—since Iran often lies about setbacks—whether the damage was really only to nearby construction or also to the main Natanz facility.

Natanz is in Isfahan province, about two hundred miles south of Tehran, a region well known for its exquisite pears as well as for the stunning natural beauty of the nearby snow-tipped Karkas mountain range.

The Natanz enrichment facility is located near a major highway some twenty miles northwest of the town. From the air, if the large antiaircraft gun emplacements nearby are ignored, it looks like a series of ordinary, nondescript flat-topped warehouses. Inside, the main building contains an armada of many thousands of tall gray tube-shaped machines where uranium hexafluoride gas is spun at ultra-high speeds to produce enriched uranium, a process that is key to Iran's nuclear future.

Exactly what type of centrifuges spin at Natanz is a crucial question. In the years before the 2015 nuclear deal, and during the long period when Tehran denied even having a nuclear weapons program, Iran used relatively slow IR-1 centrifuges. In more recent times, intelligence sources warned us about its major efforts to install new, more advanced machines that could enrich uranium anywhere between four to fifty times faster. But there was one critical problem that had to be solved, getting the latest prototypes to work. In this, Iranian scientists ran into trouble, though whether this was caused by sabotage engineered from outside the country or by simple technical failure has been difficult to determine.

The IAEA's June 2020 report said that Iran had deployed cascades of 164 IR-2m and IR-4 centrifuges, representing its most successful advanced centrifuge types. However, Iran was also experimenting with even more advanced IR-8s and even IR-9s. In the past, when Tehran had tried to up its game in the centrifuge arena, it had many failures and large numbers of broken centrifuges, which were not the result of hacking by foreign powers but ordinary technical failures.

All of this raised the possibility that the "incident" at Natanz on July 2 was simply an equipment breakdown, not the consequence of sabotage or an attack. But in the middle of the night of July 2 to 3, a previously unknown dissident group calling itself the "Homeland Cheetahs" sent emails to *The New York Times* and the BBC claiming responsibility for sabotaging the Natanz nuclear facility. The Homeland Cheetahs said they had somehow caused a fire that dealt extensive damage to a building there. The group described itself as an "underground opposition within Iran's security apparatus." It is unclear whether this organization genuinely existed or was part of a classic spy world disinformation campaign to throw the Iranians off the scent of the true saboteurs. Separately, it was reported that an unnamed Middle Eastern intelligence official had said that the blast was the result of an explosive placed in a part of the facility where centrifuges are balanced before going into operation. Sometimes the anonymity of comments like that is code for the Mossad. However, it remained unconfirmed; it was still possible that whatever took place at Natanz was an accident, as Iran continued to claim.

Accidents, however, don't happen at these kind of facilities, David Albright, the president of the Institute for Science and International Security, told us. "They get subcomponents and put them together," Albright said. "You wouldn't have a lot of flammable liquids. The assembly operations are not dangerous per se. It seems like it could be sabotage. It's a high-value site for the Iranians. It's a very important building."

So, what actually happened at Natanz, and who was responsible for it?

NASA satellite images showed there had been a fire at Natanz. Moreover, the damage caused by the fire there corresponded with details contained in the emails from the Homeland Cheetahs.

Observers of Iran and the Mossad noted, for example, that the Homeland Cheetah group's message included a propaganda video about attacks on strategic sites it said it had carried out inside Iran. Making the video would have required hours, if not days, of planning by people with a high level of expertise. Its appearance so soon after the event strongly suggested that whoever produced it knew in advance that the Natanz explosion was going to happen, which would indicate that a sophisticated sabotage operation had been carried out by a powerful intelligence agency—even if there were also local Iranian dissidents potentially involved.

In other words, it seemed like a Mossad operation from start to finish; Cohen himself publicly hinted as much in a later television interview in June 2021.

After the 2020 Natanz attack, Cohen referred in his first full public interview to numerous instances over the course of his career where the threat of assassination succeeded in convincing some scientists to leave the weapons program or actually to work for the Mossad—though the scientists may often have thought they were working for an Iranian dissident group or an Arab foreign intelligence service. The key in every operation to flipping anyone, he said, no matter what their nationality, is to figure out how to get them to trust you and then to get them to need you. The Israeli clandestine agency reportedly made sure to spirit any scientists who helped them to secret safe locations, presumably under new identities.

In addition to working directly on the nuclear scientists, the Mossad also renewed its practice of using agents posing as construction wholesalers to infiltrate the Iranian nuclear supply chain. This enabled the Israelis to place explosives inside the A1000 centrifuge hall at Natanz when it was being constructed. Some bombs were in the hall; others were hidden in the food on a catering truck. These were the explosives that went off in the Natanz facility that the Iranians attributed to an "accident."

The supply chain trick was something the Mossad had pulled off many times before against the Iranians, the Palestinians, and others. In fact, multiple intelligence officials have said the Iranians even know how deeply penetrated their supply chains are, but have been powerless to do anything about it.

Albright has theorized that from 2020 and forward, when the Iranians were choosing which advanced centrifuges to put into service, one consideration was which models could operate with Iranian-made parts.

On Sunday, July 5, 2020, a spokesman for Iran's nuclear energy body finally admitted that there had been a fire at Natanz and that it had caused "significant damage." He did try to tone down the significance of the incident by saying there had been no casualties. Bizarrely, he also said that the cause of the Natanz blaze had been determined, but he gave no details, an indication that Khamenei and Fakhrizadeh still did not want to let on about how poor Iranian nuclear security was. But Behrouz Kamalvandi, a spokesman for Iran's Atomic Energy Organization, admitted that "the incident could slow down the development and production of advanced centrifuges in the medium term." Striving to put the situation in the best possible light, he added, "Iran will replace the damaged building with a bigger one that has more advanced equipment," but it was clear that Iran had suffered a major loss.

The Iranian statements still left open the question whether the costly explosion was the result of an Israeli operation, or was due to something else. On July 6, the day after the Iranians admitted there had been a fire at Natanz, a Middle Eastern intelligence official told us that Israel was behind the explosion, which, he said, was caused by a "powerful bomb." A member of the IRGC confirmed that an explosive was used in the incident as well, though he didn't say it was an Israeli attack. Both officials spoke on condition of anonymity.

The IRGC member also discounted the likelihood that a cyberattack had caused the damage, thus ruling out the possibility that the Israelis had used the same method as they allegedly did in the strikes against Natanz a decade earlier.

In its official remarks, Israel remained coy about the new sabotage of Iran's nuclear program. Asked about it, Foreign Minister Gabi Ashkenazi said at an online conference of *The Jerusalem Post* and the newspaper *Maariv*, "We take actions that are better left unsaid."

On July 9, four days after the Iranians admitted there had been a fire at Natanz, David Albright revealed to us that there was not just "some damage" to the facility, but that three quarters of the main centrifuge assembly hall had been destroyed. Albright said his finding was based on two new satellite overviews showing a much fuller picture than footage obtained from the lower-resolution photos the weekend before. It was in the destroyed building that the rotor assemblies, the rapidly spinning part of the centrifuge that is its most crucial component, were put together, and that the extent of the damage meant Iran's nuclear program regarding advanced centrifuges had been set back far more significantly than originally understood. In fact, the earlier estimates of days or weeks of delay were suddenly changed to years (in the end the delay proved to be about nine months, longer in certain areas).

"It is clear that a major explosion took place, destroying nearly three quarters of the main centrifuge assembly hall, generating a fire that blackened a major portion of the building, the blackening visible where the roof had been blown away," Albright said. His assessment of the damage and its consequences was accepted by Sima Shine, the former Mossad Iran Research and Analysis chief, when we met with her. She told us in 2021, "The main harm to Iran from damage to its advanced centrifuges near the Natanz nuclear facility is connected to its future capabilities and options for breaking out to a nuclear weapon." She acknowledged that the loss of advanced centrifuges did not affect the stock of uranium that the Islamic Republic had already enriched, itself enough for at least one nuclear bomb, once it had been weaponized. However, she called advanced centrifuges "very important," pointing out that most of Tehran's centrifuges enrich uranium at a very slow speed. This requires a large number of centrifuges to get to fissile material. In contrast, she said, "advanced centrifuges allow for a faster breakout," and since you do not need as many of them to enrich uranium, "it is easier to hide them."

Developing faster centrifuges is important to the Iranians for reasons other than speed, Shine and other Israeli intelligence officials told us. At the time of the explosion at Natanz, Iran was anticipating making a new deal on the JCPOA with Joe Biden, if he was elected president in November 2020. To be ready for that, Shine said, it would be crucial for Tehran to already have their advanced centrifuges established, since that would make it more difficult to take them away in any negotiation. "They want more and more cards," she said, cards meaning strong positions used to gain advantages in negotiations. At least as of mid-2021, she projected, "At the end of the day, they want an agreement. . . . It is better for them to come to the table when they have better cards."

Why would any party that attacked Iran have gone after the advanced centrifuges instead of the already threatening and existing uranium stock? Shine's answer was simple: the attacked facility was likely more vulnerable.

Coincidentally or not, in the middle of the night of July 5 and 6, Prime Minister Netanyahu announced that he would extend Cohen's five-year tenure as Mossad director for six months, meaning that Cohen would now end his term in June 2021. Was the timing of Netanyahu's order to blow up Natanz three days earlier, on July 2, partially due to politics? Did Netanyahu extend Cohen's term as a way of thanking him for changing the subject from Netanyahu balking on annexation to Netanyahu succeeding against Iran? As a highly successful Mossad chief, with successes against Iran in 2018, in combating Covid, in operations against Hamas, and in quiet diplomatic progress with Sunni Gulf countries, Cohen certainly qualified for an extension of his term. Besides which, Cohen was known to be Netanyahu's favorite of the five Mossad chiefs he had worked with. Or maybe his extension was announced then because there was a pause in multiple rounds of Israeli elections.

Promoting Cohen right after the Natanz explosions might have seemed an indirect way for Netanyahu to take credit for the operation, and that may have risked Iranian retaliation at a time when Israel appeared to be trying to lower its profile—by, for example, possibly inventing an Iranian group, Homeland Cheetahs, and having it take credit. We may never unravel these questions.

Yet another explosion took place, on July 9, this time in southwest Tehran. As with the "incident" at Natanz, Iranian officials initially denied that anything had happened, though they did admit that power had been cut off. Analysts said that the blast had hit an area with underground facilities associated with IRGC chemical weapons research and an unidentified military production site. Once again, Western intelligence services speculated that Israel was behind the attack.

It was the third explosion in three weeks to hit an Iranian military target, but some nonmilitary targets were also struck. There was an incident at the Shahid Medhaj Zargan power plant in Ahvaz on July 4, a fire at the Mahshahr petrochemical plant on July 12, and an explosion at an industrial complex near Mashad the following day. In all, in July after the Natanz attack, there were explosions on eight different days, and some additional incidents in August 2020.

On July 11, we published an article in *The Jerusalem Post* disclosing that Iran was facing a total intelligence breakdown. The question was not only how had anyone pulled off so many attacks in the brief span of a few weeks, but also how had the Islamic Republic's counterintelligence forces repeatedly failed to detect or prevent them.

By the time of our article, for example, the IRGC ought to have had time to ferret out the cell or cells that were making these attacks happen, but it had gotten nowhere, and the attacks continued. This seemed to be the case even though, in general, Iranian counterintelligence is known to have performed at a much higher level than most Israeli adversaries. Tehran's counterintelligence service has made mistakes, as when it arrested political opposition members falsely claiming that they were Mossad agents. But it has also flushed out spies at a level closer to that of the world's top powers. Indeed, until Israel's January 2018 archive theft, Iranian territory was deemed much harder to penetrate than, say, Syria's, where Israel has admitted to thousands of intelligence and air strike operations. True, in the days when Meir Dagan headed the Mossad, a score of attacks on Iranian nuclear scientists was attributed to the agency, and Iran had been unable to prevent them. But much of that was over a decade before, and many of the operations that Iran had not been able to stop were directed against scientists who were killed alone and outside their workplaces. They were presumably easier targets than major highly protected plants like Natanz. But now, the Mossad, possibly with the help of dissident Iranian proxies, was allegedly hitting Iranian nuclear sites, conventional weapons, and IRGC facilities practically at will. In that light, what the world witnessed in the summer of 2020 was a second-tier counterintelligence force up against a premier intelligence or cyber power.

As Cohen repeatedly emphasized to Iran, with his typical rhetorical flourish, Israel is not going to let you get nuclear weapons—what don't you understand?

One reason for the Mossad's success was that Iran's intelligence establishment was being torn apart by a brutal and self-defeating internal turf war. Between 2009 and 2021, Iran's Islamic Revolutionary Guard Corps completely eclipsed Iran's Ministry of Intelligence and Security (MOIS), which had previously had a near monopoly on intelligence gathering. This development was highlighted in a November 2020 report from the Meir Amit Intelligence and Terrorism Information Center, among whose findings was that the IRGC's takeover of intelligence operations was continuing despite the assassination of its chief, Qasem Soleimani, on January 3, 2020. The turf war between the two Iranian agencies benefited Western intelligence in general, and the Mossad in particular, in large part because the MOIS has been more professional and talented than the IRGC.

One reason for this is that the IRGC entered the world of intelligence relatively recently, and mainly for the purpose of gathering information on Iran's domestic situation, especially on internal dissent. In contrast, the MOIS has a long history as a serious and professional service familiar with tactics to recruit foreign agents and for using sophisticated counterintelligence techniques to catch Iranians who are spying on the Islamic Republic. It was the MOIS, for example, that announced in August 2020 that it had dismantled five teams of spies working for foreign intelligence services that, the intelligence ministry's counterintelligence deputy said at the time, were planning to spy on Iran's nuclear, political, economic, military, and infrastructural projects. The accuracy of this statement can't be confirmed, but it is certainly the case that the MOIS has conducted successful counterintelligence operations in the past, including its dismantling of much of the CIA's network in Iran between 2010 and 2013.

In November 2019, *The Intercept* published a series of reports about the IRGC and the MOIS activities in Iraq and elsewhere, based on leaked MOIS internal cables and reports, that confirmed the different focuses of the two competing organizations. According to the cables, the MOIS was assigned to "keep Iraq from falling apart, from breeding Sunni militants on the Iranian border, from descending into sectarian warfare that might make Shiite Muslims the targets of violence, and from spinning off an independent Kurdistan." By contrast, the cables showed that the IRGC was working to "eradicate the Islamic State"—meaning the radical Sunni Muslim faction, otherwise known as ISIS, that tried to take power in Iraq and Syria some years after the American invasion of Iraq and during the Syrian civil war. But the IRGC's main focus was "on maintaining Iraq as a client state of Iran and making sure that political factions loyal to Tehran remain in power." The factions loyal to Iran would be Shiite groups that, before the American invasion, had felt oppressed by the Sunni majority in Iraq.

What the report showed, however, was that in pursuing its main goals, the IRGC undermined other goals. For example, in using the dark arts of espionage and covert military action to maintain Shiite power and control in Iraq, the Shiite IRGC disenfranchised the Iraqi Sunni majority, leading them to look to others, whether to the U.S. or ISIS, to protect them. And so, in 2014, the IRGC and its proxies, trying to destroy an ISIS stronghold, massacred Sunnis in the farming community of Jurf al-Sakhar near Tehran. Cables from the MOIS made it clear that they viewed such IRGC actions as disastrously harmful to the longer-term Iranian goal of maintaining predominant influence in Iraq. This is, ironically perhaps, much the same way that the CIA interpreted the massacre and similar events.

At one level, the MOIS criticism of IRGC policies in Iraq signaled divisions within Iran between the pragmatic camp of then Iranian president Hassan Rouhani and the more militant and sometimes megalomaniac Soleimani and the IRGC, supported by the hard-line Supreme

Leader Khamenei. According to this analysis, the division inside Iranian intelligence mirrors the larger division between moderates and hardliners in Iran in general. It's in this context, moreover, that Khamenei has purposely pitted the IRGC and the MOIS against each other, as a way to ensure that none of his lieutenants could emerge as a potential challenger for national leadership. According to this analysis, Khamenei gave the IRGC a greater role as a way of weakening Rouhani, who controlled the MOIS.

Khamenei has also favored the IRGC over the Iranian military, whose budget in 2016 to 2017 was actually less than that of the spy agency. By 2018 and 2019, the IRGC was receiving three times the budget of the entire army.

Over the years, Khamenei's favoritism has made the IRGC undoubtedly more powerful than any other agency or ministry of the Iranian government. It even has a parallel aerospace division that competes with Iran's version of NASA; it also runs a special cyber division and an elite division involved in the country's ballistic missile program and other nuclear-related capabilities. But the very multiplicity of the IRGC's duties has distracted it from its critical counterintelligence mission, preventing spying by foreign powers. Its various, sometimes amorphous responsibilities diminished Iran as it played its broader international game, even as the sidelining of the MOIS opened the door for Israeli special operations and helps explain their remarkable proliferation.

Coming back full circle to the Mossad, the upshot is that by the time Israeli spies were pulling off audacious operations in Iran in 2018 and 2020, the IRGC had likely worsened the country's capacity to catch and thwart espionage, laying down a red carpet for the Mossad.

By late July 2020, there had been so many explosions in Iran that some geopolitical analysts raised the question of whether the regime's very control of the country could be slipping. But in fact, as several Iran experts have argued, the regime remains resilient despite the manifold challenges it faces, including the seemingly endless and unstoppable sabotage taking place at nuclear and military installations around the country.

If all this explains why Iran hasn't been able to stop the attacks against it, the question remains: Why was Iran's response to the Israeli attacks, especially the very damaging one at Natanz, so weak? Why has there been nothing in the way of serious retaliation? Israeli experts disagree about this. Some argue that Iran didn't have the capacity for a tit-for-tat retaliation; others believe that Iran is biding its time and that it will strike against Israel when it feels the time is right.

"They have reacted before, for example, with their cyberattack against the Israeli water sector," Tel Aviv University professor Meir Litvak said, referring to Iran's sabotage operation in 2020. They may, Litvak continued, simply be "waiting until they can hit harder from Syria," or for some other opportunity. Litvak pointed out that Tehran's response to the American assassination of IRGC Quds Force leader Qasem Soleimani was limited, in the sense that there was no equally dramatic counterattack.

"The Iranians will not wait forever," he said. "It is not smart to try to embarrass them."

Ori Goldberg, of Reichman University in Herzliya, argues, by contrast, that the Iranians "didn't have many good options for vengeance.

"The Iranian public is not up in arms for vengeance," he said, though he added that Jerusalem should be careful not to "run out of control with tactical attacks and gains without thinking things through."

Meanwhile, whatever retaliation Iran may eventually undertake, the strike against Natanz had an unmistakable immediate meaning for Israel. Khamenei and Fakhrizadeh's dark plot to use advanced centrifuges to sprint to a nuclear bomb—at a much faster pace than the conventional three-to-four-month estimate—was off the table for the foreseeable future. Iran's plan was premised on the idea that advanced centrifuges capable of producing a nuclear weapon quickly would scare the Biden administration into making new concessions. The Mossad had literally blown up these plans and Iran's hoped-for leverage in the looming negotiations, forcing Iran nuclear chief Fakhrizadeh to scramble to provide Khamenei with a new scheme.

Chapter 12

THE FATHER OF THE BOMB IS NO MORE

ON NOVEMBER 27, 2020, THREE WEEKS AFTER JOE BIDEN WAS elected president, the Mossad, according to Iran, carried out one of its most important operations. Mohsen Fakhrizadeh, the head of Iran's military nuclear program, traveling in a black Nissan Teana sedan some forty miles east of Tehran, was gunned down in a hail of bullets. Mortally wounded, Fakhrizadeh spilled out of the car and collapsed in a pool of his own blood.

Fakhrizadeh was evacuated by helicopter, but at 18:17 local time, the Ministry of Defense of the Islamic Republic issued a press release revealing that he'd died. He was declared a martyr, and the next day his coffin, draped in the green, white, and red–striped Iranian flag, was carried by an honor guard on a kind of pilgrimage to Iran's Islamic holy sites that could only be accorded to a hero. Fakhrizadeh's remains went first to the holy shrine at the magnificent Imam Reza Mosque in the northeastern city of Mashhad. There, the casket was carried around the Imam Reza tomb; then it was brought to the shrines of Fatima Masumeh in the holy city of Qom and of Imam Khomeini in Tehran, then to a state funeral at the Defense Ministry in the capital. Three days after the assassination, Fakhrizadeh was finally interred at the shrine of Imamzadeh Saleh in Tehran.

With the coronavirus raging in the country and deaths climbing into the tens of thousands, the state funeral was attended only by family and military commanders. An imam sang religious songs comparing the assassinated scientist to Imam Hossein, Shiite Islam's most important martyr, who was slain in the battle of Karbala in the seventh century. Though aging Supreme Leader Ayatollah Khamenei couldn't attend, his representative, Ziaeddin Aghajanpour, read a eulogy and warned that the enemies of the Islamic Republic would "never put an end to their hostilities toward us." Defense Minister Amir Hatami kissed the casket and promised revenge.

The elaborate ceremonies, the eulogy composed by Ayatollah Khamenei, the comparison to Imam Hossein, and the vows of revenge showed just how important Fakhrizadeh was. It also indicated that the assassination was of major significance in the Mossad's ongoing war against Iran's efforts to build nuclear weapons.

Mohsen Fakhrizadeh Mahabadi lived his life out of the public spotlight. In an age of mass media—even in Iran under the ayatollahs—there were barely any photos of him; even his date and place of birth were uncertain. A rare image of him, included in a 2011 report by the exiled opposition group the National Council of Resistance of Iran (NCRI), showed him as a middle-aged man with dark hair and a graying stubble of beard. The report said that Fakhrizadeh was born in Qom in 1958. He joined the Islamic Revolutionary Guard Corps after the revolution of 1979, although it is unclear if he fought in the bitter battles of the Iran-Iraq War that raged from 1980 to 1988. Fakhrizadeh studied nuclear physics at Shahid Beheshti University in Tehran, and went on to do graduate studies and earn a PhD in nuclear engineering from the University of Isfahan. He was believed to have an interest in the relationship between physics and philosophy.

Fakhrizadeh went on to what appeared to be an academic career, teaching at Imam Hossein University. But at the same time, he held the rank of brigadier general in the Revolutionary Guards. His supposed job teaching at a university was, according to the CIA, no more than a front. He also operated under the alias Dr. Hassan Mohseni.

It was only after his death that Iranian officials opened up about Fakhrizadeh's role in the nuclear program. He was posthumously awarded the Order of Nasr (Victory) for his role in "defending the Islamic Revolution," and photographs were released showing him receiving an award from President Hassan Rouhani for his part in helping secure the nuclear deal that Iran signed with the U.S. and other countries in 2015. But while other members of the team such as Ali Akbar Salehi, the head of the Atomic Energy Organization of Iran, and Defense Minister Hossein Dehghani were honored in public, Fakhrizadeh received his award in a side room without an audience.

Still, Fakhrizadeh was well known to experts outside of Iran. His name had come up in several United Nations and IAEA reports, and he was one of eight Iranians connected to the country's clandestine weapons program who were sanctioned in 2007 under U.N. Resolution 1747. The IAEA reports in 2008 and 2011 confirmed him as the head of the AMAD program to develop nuclear weapons. Foreign intelligence sources would later claim that he headed the SPND, the Iranian Ministry of Defense's Organization of Defensive Innovation and Research, the successor program to AMAD, something that would be confirmed by documents seized in the 2018 nuclear archives heist—and after his death by Defense Minister Hatami. He had also been instrumental in taking Iran's nuclear program underground in 2003, when, after the American invasion of Iraq that year, the mullahs feared Iran could be next in line.

A 2010 investigative report by the German magazine *Der Spiegel* labeled Fakhrizadeh the "Robert Oppenheimer of Iran" after the American physicist who in World War II headed the Los Alamos Laboratory that developed the atomic bombs dropped on Hiroshima and Nagasaki. A 2014 Reuters report quoted a Western diplomat as saying, "If Iran ever chose to weaponize, Fakhrizadeh would be known as the father of the Iranian bomb." The same report quoted Mark Fitzpatrick, director of the nonproliferation program at the International Institute for Strategic Studies, saying, "If the IAEA had a most-wanted list, Fakhrizadeh would head it."

Fakhrizadeh had been instrumental in the Islamic regime's nuclear program from early on. He traveled several times to North Korea, where he watched a nuclear test, and cooperated with Libya before it abandoned its nuclear program. He met with A. Q. Khan, the father of

Pakistan's nuclear weapons program, who sold Iran the know-how to manufacture uranium-enriching centrifuges; he was an expert in obtaining black-market nuclear materials; and he worked with Russian technicians to build the nuclear core at the Bushehr nuclear facility.

The former head of Israel's Military Intelligence, Major General Aharon Ze'evi Farkash, told us that Fakhrizadeh had "built Iran's Atomic Energy Agency into a larger and more professional body. He had control over all aspects of the nuclear fuel cycle, over the acquisition of required foreign materials, of the process to convert metals into yellow cake, an intermediate step in processing uranium ores, and to move that to Isfahan for processing,"

In addition, he said, Iran's nuclear chief "also maintained nuclear ties with China, which helped to build the Isfahan conversion facility" where, as Farkash noted with some dark irony, there was a dedication plaque at the front entrance recognizing Beijing's contribution to the project.

The assassination took place just outside of Absard, a town of about ten thousand in the countryside of Damavand province, set among apple and cherry orchards, where modernist villas and Persian-style palaces serve the Iranian elite, the businessmen and government officials whose lives are unaffected by the poverty of ordinary Iranians.

Several versions of how Fakhrizadeh's killing was carried out were reported in early official statements and in the press. Given the secrecy that still surrounds the operation, no version has been definitely confirmed, though recent evidence points to one as most likely. What is certain is that Fakhrizadeh was killed in or near Absard, and that his assailants knew his travel routes, his schedule, and details about his security. One of his sons, Hamed, would later claim that Iranian intelligence had received alerts that his father had been targeted for assassination that day and asked him not to leave his house. "But Mohsen Fakhrizadeh did not obey the security team," his son said. Instead, he went by car to his villa in Absard for the weekend, together with his wife, Sedigheh Ghasemi, as he often did on a Friday.

After a series of fantastical reports in the Iranian media about how the assassination had taken place, including assassins on motorcycles, a truck bomb, and a platoon-size hit team with backup group, the truth gradually emerged, although it too was initially greeted with ridicule and skepticism. Official Iranian sources, including IRGC General Ali Shamkhani, the secretary of Iran's Supreme National Security Council, speaking at Fakhrizadeh's funeral on November 30, said the nuclear scientist had been killed by a remote-controlled, satellite-linked machine gun. Israeli intelligence sources later confirmed to us that this was not science fiction, and a remote-controlled gun was in fact the weapon used.

It would later transpire that the weapon together with explosives had been smuggled into Iran in pieces and secretly assembled there over a period of some eight months by a team of twenty operatives that also tracked Fakhrizadeh's every movement. As one agent put it, the Mossad "breathed with the guy, woke up with him, slept with him, traveled with him. They would have smelled his aftershave every morning if he had used aftershave."

About a week after the funeral, Revolutionary Guards Deputy Commander Rear Admiral Ali Fadavi revealed further details about the assassination. Fakhrizadeh had indeed been traveling to his holiday home in Absard, he said, and was driving his own car with his wife sitting alongside him while heavily armed bodyguards traveled in cars behind and in front. Iranian agents working for the Mossad had parked a blue Nissan Zamyad pickup truck along the Imam Khomeini Boulevard, which connects the main Fikruzh highway to Absard. Hidden in the back of the pickup was the weapon, a 7.62millimeter U.S.-manufactured M240C machine gun that had been doctored to work by an operator thousands of miles away using facial recognition technology to zoom in on the nuclear scientist. Another car, seemingly broken down on the main road, was also equipped with cameras and had confirmed Fakhrizadeh's arrival about three quarters of a mile before the designated hit spot some five hundred meters south of the junction. The Mossad knew from its intelligence gathering that as the convoy drew off the main road, the front car would head into town to check that Fakhrizadeh's house hadn't been compromised, thus opening up a line of sight. Fakhrizadeh was exposed and the machine gun opened fire, shooting in total thirteen rounds before the weapon self-destructed, also blowing up the vehicle it was placed on.

"They focused only on martyr Fakhrizadeh's face in a way that his wife, despite being only 25 centimeters away, was not shot," Fadavi said. Sources have since confirmed to us that avoiding killing his wife was indeed a major consideration for how the operation was designed, including the use of the remote gun.

Fakhrizadeh's personal bodyguard had also taken four bullets when he threw himself on the scientist, but he survived his injuries, Fadavi told reporters. Iranian media later revealed the bodyguard to be Hamed Asghari, who belonged to the Ansar al-Mahdi Security Corps and had previously been the personal bodyguard of Iran's foreign minister. He was said to have trained Iranian forces and proxies in Beirut, Baghdad, and Syria. Like dozens of people in Fakhrizadeh's close circle, Asghari was repeatedly interrogated after the killing, and was even temporarily suspended despite his "battle scars."

The operation to eliminate Fakhrizadeh was a long time coming. In fact, the Mossad and other Israeli intelligence agencies had been tracking Fakhrizadeh for more than a decade. About a month after the assassination, the Israeli newspaper *Yedioth Ahronoth* revealed that twelve years earlier, at a dinner in honor of visiting American president George W. Bush, then Prime Minister Ehud Olmert played a recording of Fakhrizadeh discussing Iran's nuclear weapons efforts. "I'm going to play you something, but I ask that you not talk about it with anyone, not even with the director of the CIA," Olmert was reported to have said to Bush. The prime minister pulled out a miniature digital media player and played the president a recording of a man speaking in Persian.

It was, according to the report, since confirmed to us by Olmert, the voice of Mohsen Fakhrizadeh.

In the recording, Fakhrizadeh complains that his bosses "want five warheads," but aren't giving him the resources he needs to carry out his work.

Olmert, whose goal was to achieve unprecedented intelligence cooperation with the U.S., told Bush that Israeli intelligence services had an Iranian agent close to Fakhrizadeh who had been feeding them information on the nuclear scientist for years. It was this agent, recruited by Yossi Cohen, then a case officer (and later the head of the Mossad), who had provided the recording Olmert played for Bush. Cohen has not confirmed that he recruited the agent, but after he retired, he said: "Mossad has been closely monitoring Fakhrizadeh for years, including close surveillance." He took pride in the alleged hand he had in Fakhrizadeh's demise.

As Olmert's disclosure to Bush indicated, Fakhrizadeh had been one of Israel's most important intelligence targets going back to the mid-2000s, when he was put on Dagan and Pardo's list of Iranian scientists Israel wanted to assassinate. The Mossad's penetration was so deep that, according to foreign sources, it knew Fakhrizadeh's address, his phone number, and even his passport number. "We knew everything about him, about his every movement, how he would switch the names of agencies, all the subterfuges they tried with him, all the trickery he tried, everything about the nuclear program," Pardo would say in a 2018 TV interview a couple of years after he retired.

But whether to assassinate Fakhrizadeh right away was at the core of a fierce dispute within the agency. Dagan had a reputation for fearlessness such that, according to former IDF chief of staff Shaul Mofaz, when Prime Minister Ariel Sharon appointed him head of the Mossad, he asked Mofaz to "keep an eye on him." Dagan wanted to take Fakhrizadeh out as early as 2009. But there was opposition to that idea both within Mossad's high command and among the leadership of Military Intelligence. Pardo, then Dagan's deputy, felt that, based on the circumstances at the time, as long as the Mossad had its eyes and ears on Fakhrizadeh's every move it was better to leave him alive.

"If a particular person is a source because someone can talk to him and extract information from him, and on the other hand someone says 'well if he ceases to function that could help,' this is something that always has to be placed on the scales," Pardo told us in an interview. This comment, while somewhat cryptically formulated, describes the difficult choice faced by spy agencies in the case of someone like Fakhrizadeh, an enemy figure who has been penetrated and therefore might unknowingly provide valuable information, and yet continues to pose a danger and is therefore a candidate for assassination. There has also been and continues to be an often acrimonious debate at top levels of Israeli politics and intelligence over the costs and benefits of assassinations of such senior figures.

In the end, Dagan's position seemed to win the day and the Mossad prepared a mission to assassinate Fakhrizadeh. But on the very night in 2009 when the strike was to take place, agents on the ground in Tehran spotted suspicious movements. They feared that the plan had been compromised and that Iranian intelligence was planning an ambush. Even so, Dagan wanted to go ahead with it despite the risk, but then, with the operation already in motion, he called it off, reportedly after a call from Olmert.

The former prime minister told us, "There were operational reasons that we had to call off an operation that had already been launched."

Olmert also revealed without elaborating further that there were "two other times when he was very close [to being killed] but due to circumstances we had to call it off."

Ever since then, Israeli intelligence experts have pondered whether the decision to wait years before eliminating Fakhrizadeh was the right one. Looking back from the perspective of over a decade, Pardo and Aharon Ze'evi Farkash, the former head of Military Intelligence, both told us that Fakhrizadeh's impact on the nuclear program in previous time periods was far greater than in 2020 when he was finally killed. Farkash describes this as a paradox because Fakhrizadeh reached his highest level of influence and direct connection with Khamenei in the 2010–2020 period, especially from 2012 to 2015, the time Tehran negotiated the nuclear deal. Farkash revealed to us that Fakhrizadeh held a crucial meeting with Russian president Vladimir Putin right around the time of the signing of the JCPOA. He implied that the two discussed long-term grand nuclear strategy and confrontations with the West, though Russian and Iranian priorities also sometimes clash in this area.

But after the JCPOA was signed, Fakhrizadeh became more replaceable on a technical level. True, Khamenei still needed his strategic help in configuring a nuanced nuclear policy, one that adhered to the deal at minimal cost, but that also preserved as many future options as possible for Iran. However, at the same time as Fakhrizadeh's broad impact on policy went up, he was no longer the only one with unique technical expertise. In the early 2000s, when he was just launching its nuclear weapons program, Iran had at best a small number of less advanced centrifuges and few scientists with the experience to operate them and to coordinate the parallel processes required to move forward toward a nuclear weapon.

By the time Fakhrizadeh was assassinated in 2020, Tehran had thousands of operating older generation centrifuges, hundreds of advanced centrifuges, and many scientists with experience in enriching uranium to the medium levels of 20 percent and 60 percent. In other words, according to this logic, Fakhrizadeh's assassination came only after he had played his most significant role.

"There is no doubt that if he had disappeared off the map earlier, killing him would have caused graver damage," Pardo told us.

The Iranians would have concurred with the former Mossad chief's analysis. "He created a network of scientists that will continue his work," Fereydoon Abbasi, an Iranian nuclear scientist and former head of Iran's Atomic Energy Organization, told Iranian media.

Nonetheless, his killing in 2020 was an enormous blow to Tehran's prestige and removed a talented manager with unparalleled experience and organizational knowledge, one who had been part of the Iranian nuclear project from the start and was one of the only people able to see the whole picture, to know where every component fit. While his technical scientific knowledge was no longer as unique, many analysts still compared the loss to that of Qasem Soleimani at the beginning of 2020 because of his influence on policy. Netanyahu had singled him out at the press conference in 2018 when he revealed the nuclear archive theft, saying simply, "Fakhrizadeh—Remember that name."

Israeli Major General Amos Yadlin, who succeeded Farkash as head of Military Intelligence, wrote in the wake of the strike that the damage caused to Iran's nuclear weapons program by the assassination, while "very significant, is not necessarily due to the loss of scientific knowledge, but due to the loss of project leadership, managerial experience, and access to Iran's top political echelon—salient Fakhrizadeh assets."

Former Mossad Iran analysis chief Sima Shine told us that Fakhrizadeh had a unique ability to keep talented scientists and coordinate among them, even after much of the nuclear program had to go underground or pause in 2003.

Moreover, she said Fakhrizadeh was a master at raising funds and laundering money to continue clandestine progress and maintain whatever nuclear achievements had already been attained.

Former CIA Iran desk chief Norman Roule concurred that "what was lost with Fakhrizadeh's death was a uniquely experienced manager of nuclear weaponization, as well as a hard-line voice on nuclear issues who could engage the Supreme Leader directly. Any successor will not have the same level of trust with the Supreme Leader and the IRGC leadership but will still likely be charged to maintain dual-use programs that could support a covert weaponization program.

"Most important," Roule continued, "should Iran ever decide to restart its covert nuclear program, Fakhrizadeh's successor won't have his experience—and perhaps not even the authority—to conceal the many related aspects of this undertaking."

Roule added: "Finally, it's worth considering why Western governments paid so much attention to this individual, why the IAEA repeatedly sought access to him, which Iran vigorously denied. And, finally, why some party undertook a sophisticated surgical and risk-laden attack to remove him. . . . I think the message to Iran is that first, your most sensitive operations are probably known, or will be quickly known, to your most capable adversaries. Next, if someone is involved in operations that threaten the lives of others, that person should consider himself or herself at mortal peril, and Iran's security services cannot provide protection."

In the days and hours before he died, Israeli intelligence estimated that Fakhrizadeh felt a mixture of arrogance about being too valuable to be targeted and a smugness that he had brought Iran back to having more than enough enriched uranium for a nuclear bomb, along with some lingering fears that most Iranian security officials have felt since Qasem

Soleimani was killed—that he could be next. He was at the height of his power and influence with Khamenei and had a twenty-five-year-long iron grip on the Islamic Republic's nuclear moves.

Yossi Cohen cannot publicly admit to his role in Fakhrizadeh's death. But in the moment that he learned that the trigger was pulled and the kill was confirmed, the Mossad chief felt Israel was safer than the situation he had been handed in early 2016.

Both Soleimani and Fakhrizadeh were gone, enemies of Israel who had for decades avoided the Mossad's legendary capacity for vengeance. Cohen had a serious and grudging respect for the two as worthy adversaries, but that respect did not hold him back from relishing in their deaths.

Chapter 13

A BEAUTIFUL ATTACK

"I WILL OFFER TEHRAN A CREDIBLE PATH BACK TO DIPLOmacy," declared Joe Biden on September 13, 2020, less than two months before the presidential election. "If Iran returns to strict compliance with the nuclear deal, the United States would rejoin the agreement as a starting point for follow-on negotiations. With our allies, we will work to strengthen and extend the nuclear deal's provisions, while also addressing other issues of concern."

Biden labeled Trump's Iran policy—withdrawal from the 2015 nuclear deal and a "maximum pressure" campaign—an abject failure, and he announced a formula that sounded tougher and wiser to the world than the 2015 deal cut by the Obama administration. He would return to the nuclear deal jettisoned by his predecessor, but he'd fix the deficiencies that critics of the original Obama deal had pointed out.

The differences between the Americans and Israelis on Iran stemmed from the nature of the nuclear deal signed in 2015, and what Israel felt were its positives and negatives. The deal was successful in that, until 2019, when Iran resumed nuclear enrichment beyond agreed limits, it kept the ayatollahs at least twelve months from a nuclear bomb. But from the Israeli standpoint, the agreement failed because in dealing only with enriching uranium and a potential plutonium nuclear weapon, it left out other matters of pressing importance. At the top of that list was testing dual-use missiles which could deliver either a conventional warhead or potentially eventually a nuclear warhead, to Israel. The 2015 agreement was silent on this issue. In fact, as top IDF officials told us, they considered Iran's effort to transfer precision-guided missiles and the technology to build them to its proxies in Lebanon and Syria a far greater threat in the short and medium term than nuclear weapons. Precision-guided missiles from Hezbollah-controlled territory in Lebanon, Syria, Iraq, or elsewhere could cause massive death and hit strategic industries on the Israeli home front, and such an attack was more likely than a nuclear one. Indeed, Israeli analysts believed that Tehran's intention was to reach the nuclear threshold, but not go past a certain point so as not to risk Israel's wrath and a preemptive strike.

That had been a key point in the Khamenei-Fakhrizadeh nuclear strategy, and intelligence officials believed that it was still the case, though Fakhrizadeh was gone and was replaced in January 2021 by a new nuclear weapons chief, a top Iranian commander known to intelligence officials only as "Farahi," who had previously been a senior figure in the country's space program.

Farahi's high status was a sure indication that the nuclear program remained a top priority for Iran. Indeed, some Israeli intelligence officials used to talk about the directorship of the program as having gone "from Fakhri to Farahi," with a special reverence usually reserved for giants of Jewish history like the biblical Moses. While Farahi's identity was first revealed by *The Jerusalem Post* in January 2021, it was not until December 2022 that further details about him were made public. IRGC Brigadier General Mahdi Farahi was formerly deputy of Iran's Ministry of Defense and Armed Forces Logistics (MODAFL) and managing director of the Defense Industries Organization (DIO), and head of the Aerospace Industries Organization (AIO). He was also reportedly involved in the development of an eighty-ton rocket booster being jointly developed by Iran and North Korea and traveled to Pyongyang during contract negotiations.

Still, Cohen and the rest of Israeli intelligence didn't think Farahi would change Iran's basic policy against risking an Israeli preemptive strike. For that reason, Netanyahu and Israel's military and intelligence services wanted Biden to restrict other aspects of Iran's activities, not just its nuclear weapons program.

Israel had other criticisms of the 2015 deal. It didn't do anything to stop Iranian support of terrorism in the region, something that might mildly annoy the U.S., but was a major concrete daily threat to Israel. The 2015 agreement also had an end date of 2030, after which almost all the restrictions on Iran would stop. Theoretically, Iran was still banned from developing a nuclear weapon after 2030, but there would no longer be any sanctions "teeth" or concrete JCPOA consequences if it ignored the ban. Finally, the 2015 agreement made no mention of a military option, meaning the use of force against Iran in case of noncompliance. And force was something Biden might need to threaten at some point to get the Iranians to agree to anything new.

For all these reasons, the Israelis from Netanyahu on down watched Biden's statements very closely, and they didn't always like what they saw. In an interview with *The New York Times*'s Thomas Friedman in December, after he won the election but before he was inaugurated, Biden said that he would deal with Iran's nuclear weapons first, which to both Netanyahu and the nonpolitical defense establishment meant he would give secondary importance to other matters, like missile development, and perhaps lift sanctions in exchange for progress on the nuclear front alone.

But Biden in his interview with Friedman also seemed to try to provide reassurances that he was mindful of the other issues. The administration would open negotiations with Iran about the American return to the 2015 nuclear deal, but with necessary changes, and, Biden said, if Iran did not cooperate, sanctions could be snapped back. After Trump pulled the U.S. out of the JCPOA in May 2018, large aspects of global sanctions were reimposed on Iran, thanks to the unilateral power of the U.S., but sizable chunks of the sanctions regime were not, because the U.N. Security Council blocked a snapback. Further, key countries like China, Russia, and others selectively cooperated for or against U.S. sanctions on Iran, depending on broader geopolitical considerations. There was a possibility that if Biden offered Iran a fair return to the JCPOA and Iran rejected it, perhaps the president could even rally support for full Security Council sanctions. A full snapback by Biden would hurt Iran far more than even what Trump had done in reimposing some sanctions.

But how would he accomplish this, the Israelis asked, unless Biden was willing to go for a unilateral "maximum pressure" campaign of the sort the Trump administration had followed, which Biden did not want to do? All in all, Israeli officials, such as Meir Ben Shabbat, the head of the National Security Council, and others were slightly less worried about the incoming administration than they had been by the Obama administration, which, in their view, had simply refused to recognize the holes in the deal it negotiated and signed. Biden at least recognized the deal's deficiencies. Still, they were nervous that Biden would rush back into the deal by February or shortly after in order to make the issue go away and leave him free to focus on China and Russia. Israel in that case would be alone dealing with Iran's terror, ballistic missile testing, and the expiration of some of the limits on Iran's nuclear development, starting in 2025.

But then on January 19, 2021, with Biden about to take office, some of Israel's worries receded a bit. Using almost identical language, both incoming director of national intelligence Avril Haines and incoming secretary of state Antony Blinken said that the Biden administration wanted to rejoin the deal, but was "a long way" away from doing so. Both officials expressed vehement and unqualified opposition to Iran getting a nuclear bomb and both cited a need to somehow rein in the Islamic Republic's ballistic missile program and its destabilizing of the Middle East. This was music to the ears of Israel as well as to the moderate Sunni states in the region, like the United Arab Emirates and Saudi Arabia, especially given that Haines and Blinken were among the officials who would have a major impact on Iran policy in the new administration. And there were more favorable signs besides their statements.

Less clear was whether they intended "a long way" to mean they would not rush to cut a deal before Iran's June 2021 elections, at which time many analysts assumed (correctly) that anti-diplomacy hard-liners would replace the relatively moderate and pragmatic administration of Hassan Rouhani. While that question hung in the air, there was some other good news for Israel and the moderate Sunnis. Blinken did not merely say he opposed the ayatollahs getting a nuclear bomb, but twice stated the U.S. would prevent them from getting to the uranium enrichment threshold for a bomb.

This put down clear benchmarks for a future Biden administration policy, which, until then, had been vague on exactly what stopping Iran from getting a bomb meant in practice. When officials talk about preventing a country from getting nuclear weapons, they could mean preventing it from any preparation for a bomb, including any degree of nuclear enrichment. But it could also mean allowing it to proceed with enrichment and only stepping in when the country has actually gained the wherewithal to become a nuclear weapons power quickly.

Blinken's multiple statements seemed to clarify that Biden intended to stop Iran at an early enrichment stage to ensure it did not get to the point of enough enriched uranium for a bomb. That was good news, but it was the end of the good news.

The incoming secretary of state upset the Israelis by being pretty explicit that as long as Iran was not foolish and did not make excessive demands unrelated to the nuclear deal, Biden would return to the 2015 agreement, without insisting on up-front concessions on such issues as ballistic missile testing and Iran's regional behavior. This for the Israelis again meant giving up all of the U.S.'s leverage before achieving any major fixes to the 2015 deal.

Moreover, despite its public statements, the Biden administration seemed in no hurry to start negotiating with Iran, and one element in the picture may have been the Israeli election that was set for March 23, 2021. It was an open secret that Biden was hoping someone would finally beat Netanyahu, and signing a new Iran deal just before election day would have enabled Netanyahu to rally undecided voters to his side based on their fear of a Shiite nuclear Armageddon against the Jewish state.

This was a gift Biden did not want to give.

In addition, even if negotiations restarted, the Biden team knew that it could take months for any new accord to bear fruit. A formal document could be signed restoring limits on enrichment and ending sanctions, but it would take Iran months to put in the necessary changes to its nuclear facilities to make them compliant with the nuclear limits. Likewise, it would take months after a signed deal before the complex U.S. Treasury financial war machinery could be fully undone. So if a deal was signed "quickly" in February or March, the Iranian public would not see the earliest benefits trickle down to them until the summer. Given that a new Iranian government would take office after Iran's elections on June 18, 2021, Biden seemed in no rush to wrap up a new nuclear deal with what would soon be the outgoing government.

Despite being shut out by Iran for much of 2020, in August IAEA chief Rafael Grossi had achieved access to certain disputed nuclear sites and received a more detailed explanation from Tehran regarding its nuclear deviations. This had followed the IAEA board's June 2020 condemnation of Iran and the Mossad's alleged campaign of blowing up Iranian facilities. But from the Israeli perspective, Grossi's victories were fragile and temporary. By 2021, the sands had shifted once again and Grossi started a new dance with Iran and the Mossad. Grossi's new policy seemed to fall someplace in between Amano's willingness to look the other way even in the face of smoking-gun evidence of Iranian violations and Grossi's earlier readiness to confront Tehran.

Grossi's new policy of avoiding a crisis with Iran was motivated in part by his desire to forestall any military action against it, but simultaneously he wanted to publicly and repeatedly call out Tehran for its inadequate answers to questions about its nuclear program. He coined the phrase "not technically credible" when characterizing Iran's statements, which was a diplomatically euphemistic way of calling the ayatollahs liars. But in being somewhat ambiguous and nonconfrontational, the phrase gave Grossi room to maneuver.

In February 2021, he held an almost exuberant press conference announcing the results of his efforts to resume IAEA inspections, which Iran had been threatening to stop in the wake of the American reimposition of some sanctions. Now, Grossi said, Iran would "only" reduce its cooperation to around 70 percent of the IAEA's normal inspection regime. Grossi made this remarkable announcement in the middle of the night Israel time between Sunday and Monday, which seemed designed to deflect attention from the fact that Iran was reducing IAEA inspections by almost a third. Grossi, in other words, seemed to be striving to lessen the potential for an explosive crisis. Yet, to accomplish that, he not only disclosed his new information in the middle of the night, but also left unclear how much Iran was really cooperating and to what extent it was reserving the right to conceal its activities.

Grossi, moreover, didn't make this critical element in the picture much clearer in subsequent statements. At a press conference on March 9, 2021, he was questioned repeatedly about the evidence of Iranian cheating he'd received from the Mossad. His response:

"There is an urban myth that we get information and I send inspectors running to check whether it is true or not. When we act on something like that, it's when we have credible indications." Asked in several different ways by journalists whether he was engaging in "wishful thinking," given that Tehran was not giving any concrete sign that it would change its tune, he shrugged and said, "I am an optimist."

Suddenly, Grossi was sounding like Amano, trying to put as much distance as he could between himself and the evidence of Iranian deception that everyone knew he'd gotten from the Mossad. Evidently, Grossi had realized by March 2021 that the critical issue for him was, as it had been for Amano, to keep the JCPOA alive and to devote the IAEA's resources and credibility to that effort. To do that he could not get tied down to the Mossad or force a crisis with Iran.

For Israel, this was deeply disconcerting. The arrangement that Grossi had agreed to in February—in which Iran would allow 70 percent of a full inspection regime—was due to expire on May 21, and even though Grossi soon announced that the arrangement would continue until at least June 24, Jerusalem was worried that Grossi's knees were buckling.

Adding to the uncertainty was the prospect of Iranian elections coming up only a few weeks after the newest inspection agreement would end. As the election approached, contradictory statements coming out of Tehran indicated that a power struggle was under way over the inspections between President Hassan Rouhani's pragmatist camp and the hard-line camp led by Ebrahim Raisi, the favorite of Khamenei, who would ultimately win the election. Rouhani declared that Tehran's negotiations with the U.S. and the world powers would continue until a deal was reached. His statement seemed to be a rebuke to the hard-line position expressed by Iran's parliamentary speaker, threatening to further limit international inspectors' access to nuclear sites and data. Some of these contradictory statements, analysts felt, could be a kind of political theater for Western consumption, given that all sides had to report to Supreme Leader Khamenei. But the way that the different statements were made public in an uncoordinated fashion seemed to indicate some real substantive differences between the Iranian officials.

These internal Iranian battles also caused the IAEA to zigzag around the issue, calling press conferences and then canceling them, apparently waiting for some clarity on what Iran's true position was. In hindsight, it appears that the hard-line camp had started to take control of policy and that the one-month extension of the inspection regime that Grossi announced was the last moment in which the outgoing pragmatist camp was able to somewhat moderate Iranian policy.

By June 16, 2021, Grossi finally acknowledged in an interview with the Italian daily *La Repubblica* that "Everyone knows that, at this point, it will be necessary to wait for the new Iranian government," to revive the 2015 Iran nuclear accord. Grossi said this in reply to a question about where the negotiations on the nuclear deal stood. The new Iranian government was elected on June 21, and as expected Ebrahim Raisi won with more than 70 percent of the vote (although with the lowest voter turnout in Iranian history, 49 percent). Given that the hard-liners had all along been opposed to the nuclear deal, those results did not bode well for greater Iranian cooperation or openness, toward the IAEA or anybody else.

For Cohen, this was history repeating itself. Years earlier when he was still Netanyahu's National Security Council chief and leading into the 2015 nuclear deal, Amano had broken a personal promise to him that he would make Iran follow through on disclosing all of its possible military dimensions (PMDs).

Amano may not have kept his word to Cohen, yet the intelligence which the Mossad obtained from the nuclear archives was exactly what empowered Grossi—for some period of time—to insist on new inspections. Likewise, the Mossad's evidence regarding these sites and of Iran's lying led to Grossi's stronger stance with Iran and laid the groundwork for the reported Mossad operations against Iran's nuclear program in 2020–2021. But it was unclear how much this would help in the new era of the hard-liner Raisi.

Meanwhile, Israel was learning that, remarkable as the July 2, 2020, sabotage of the aboveground Natanz nuclear facility had been, Natanz was still up and running. On March 17, a leaked IAEA report indicated that Iran had started enriching uranium there, no longer aboveground as before, but now at a new underground plant using an array of advanced IR-4 centrifuges. The IAEA report "verified that Iran had begun feeding the cascade of 174 IR-4 centrifuges already installed at the Fordow Enrichment Plant with natural UF6," a reference to uranium hexafluoride, the form in which uranium is fed into centrifuges for enrichment. In addition, Iran, the IAEA said, planned to install a second cascade of IR-4 centrifuges, though that had not yet been done.

This was highly significant for the simple reason that IR-4 centrifuges could shorten the ayatollahs' timeline for breaking out to a nuclear weapon. From Israel's point of view, this meant that Iran had made an almost impossible comeback from the setbacks of the year before, including the attack on Natanz in July 2020, the assassination of Fakhrizadeh in November, and his replacement by Farahi, who Israel saw as less competent than his predecessor. Between Fakhrizadeh and Farahi, the Iranians had succeeded in recovering most of what had been lost and they had now moved on to an underground installation protected by forty feet of concrete and iron. This would make it much harder, if not impossible, to strike the same way that the aboveground Natanz facility had been hit nine months earlier, since Israel lacked the U.S.'s unique "bunker buster" bomb that could tunnel deep beneath the surface.

Despite these factors, as we reported in *The Jerusalem Post* on March 18, 2021, Israeli intelligence did not feel that the earlier attacks had amounted to nothing. The numbers of advanced centrifuges that

Iran had now installed paled in comparison to what Iran would have had if the destruction of the old Natanz facility had not taken place. On top of that, while an underground facility might be more secure, it created logistical problems and slowed down virtually all elements of nuclear progress, our sources told us. Nuclear expert David Albright told us that even if Iran had made a partial recovery since July, they still lacked the capacity to mass-produce advanced centrifuges. Although it had more advanced IR-4 centrifuges, it was still well behind where it had been in July 2020, and it would need additional time to recover to that point.

What the new situation really showed, as Cohen himself told us, was that Israel's program to prevent Tehran from obtaining a nuclear weapon was never ending and that there was no site, old or new, which he could not reach. A plan for a new stage in the Mossad's war, it seemed, was in place.

In fact, the plan was already advanced. In the early morning of April 11, 2021, a spokesman for the Atomic Energy Organization of Iran, Behrouz Kamalvandi, told the Iranian Fars News Agency that an "accident" had occurred in the electricity distribution network at the Natanz nuclear facility. As we later learned, Khamenei was aghast at what appeared to be yet another successful Israeli operation, and he instructed his spin doctors to deny reports about the extent of the destruction. As a result, early accounts in Iran downplayed the incident, with Kamalvandi saying there had been no injuries and that no radioactive material had been present at the site.

However, as we revealed in *The Jerusalem Post* only hours later, the Islamic Republic's attempt to portray the "accident" as internal and unimportant was wildly misleading and the consequences of what had happened were far graver than Kamalvandi was letting on.

Kamalavandi would learn at his own expense just how wrong he was. When the spokesman went to visit the site, he fell down a seven-meter hole and broke his ankle. Nuclear experts said this was a sign that the site had been seriously compromised. "Nuclear installations normally are very safe," Olli Heinonen, a former United Nations nuclear weapons inspector, said. "There are no open places where you can go down seven meters just like that. . . . So probably he went to some area that is damaged, and that is a bad sign."

Later in the day on April 12, reports citing two anonymous intelligence officials came out saying that the "accident" consisted of an explosion at Natanz that had destroyed its internal power system. According to the report, the damage was so severe that it could take nine months or more to restore production.

Following these reports, Iranian nuclear official Ali Akbar Salehi changed Iran's tune, confirming that the incident was an attack. Soon thereafter, Iranian foreign minister Mohammad Javad Zarif blamed Israel. "The Zionists want to take revenge because of our progress on the way to lift sanctions. . . . We will not fall into their trap. . . . We will not allow this act of sabotage to affect the nuclear talks," he said according to state TV. "But we will take our revenge against the Zionists."

In an effort to minimize the event's importance and to deny Israel any public relations victory, Saeed Khatibzadeh, a spokesman for the Iranian Foreign Ministry, stated that the affected centrifuges were only old, first-generation ones. "All the centrifuges that were shut down were of the IR-1 type, which will be replaced with advanced machines, and Iran will not fall into their cunning trap," he said.

Later in April, Iranian officials were beginning to give further details of the destruction. The attack had targeted an electrical substation located around 165 feet underground and damaged thousands of centrifuges. Fereydoun Abbasi-Davani, a former head of Iran's Atomic Energy Organization, who had survived an assassination attempt attributed to the Mossad in 2010, acknowledged that damage both to the power distribution system and to the power cable leading to the centrifuges had taken place. In a distinctive and odd rhetorical flourish, Abbasi-Davani even allowed not only that an operation like this third one against Natanz takes years of preparation, but also that "the design of the enemy was very beautiful." Abbasi-Davani added that the substation was built underground in order to protect it from air and missile strikes, but that the new attack had been carried out either via cyber, by sabotaged equipment, or by agents in place. One intelligence official, who is a big advocate of using new technologies, has told us that no matter how advanced technology gets, "boots on the ground still has extraordinary importance."

For Israelis like Cohen this "tipping of the hat" by an adversary was a source of pride. Netanyahu too was buoyed by the success of the operation, which came at the exact time when it could shake Iran's position in its negotiations with the West, given that now the existence of Iran's newly built underground installation at Natanz was no longer even an open secret; it was simply open, a proven fact.

If the Mossad did it, how did they do it?

We reported on the very day of the attack that it was carried out by smuggling an explosive device into the facility and detonating it remotely. The Israelis had used this method before according to none other than Abbasi-Davani, who disclosed that at least part of the first sabotage attack at Natanz, on July 2, 2020, had been caused by explosives placed in a desk at the site. The inference was that a supply chain method, similar to that used in 2020, had been used in the new attack. Certainly, the Mossad had on other occasions been able to tamper with equipment before it was shipped to Iran. On one occasion, the director of Iran's Parliament Research Center, Alireza Zakani, said, three hundred pounds of explosives were embedded in machinery that was refurbished abroad and then brought into an Iranian facility, where it blew up.

Indeed, Israel has gone all over the world to track down equipment destined for Iran, and then reportedly concealed listening or sensing devices in it for the collection of intelligence, or explosives to be triggered at some later date as has been revealed to us by senior officials.

Former Israeli prime minister Ehud Olmert hinted as much in an interview after the Natanz explosion, saying that it may well have been prepared many years before. "I don't know what happened there, who set it off, if it was planted in that year or another, ten years ago or fifteen, I don't know," he said. "These kinds of missions, whether we carried them out or not, are not somebody broke in two nights ago and planted things there. These things happen when all sorts of machines, long before they are even installed, are already booby-trapped and waiting for the right time," Olmert added.

In an interview with us, Olmert suggested that "perhaps further surprises await." Cohen has also boasted about the repeated success of this method.

Plastic explosives such as C4, which have the benefit of being extremely stable over an almost infinite period of time, have been routinely used by the Mossad, the CIA, and other intelligence agencies. They can survive being transported and implanted long before use and detonated at just the right moment. C4 can easily be molded into any desired shape and thus easily concealed. While standard issue C4 has a taggant, a chemical marker, that makes it detectable, it can be made without the taggant, making it extremely difficult to detect. In 2016, the CIA concealed some C4 so well inside the engine of a school bus loaned for a training exercise that sniffer dogs failed to find all of the hidden explosives. Later, when the bus returned to its regular function of ferrying around schoolchildren, it made several runs before mechanics chanced upon the devices, which the agents had forgotten to remove.

Most of the saboteurs involved in such operations have remained nameless, but Iran state television channels identified a possible Israeli agent who it has named a lead "culprit" in the sabotage of the underground Natanz nuclear site. The Iranian media displayed a passport-style photograph of a forty-three-year-old man it identified as Reza Karimi, saying that he was born in the nearby city of Kashan, Iran, and that he had left the country after the Natanz operation. In addition, they showed an Interpol-style "red notice" indicating that Iran was seeking his arrest and saying that he had traveled to Spain, the United Arab Emirates, Kenya, Ethiopia, Qatar, Turkey, Uganda, Romania, and one other country whose name was illegible.

Mysteriously, Karimi does not appear on Interpol's public database, and the organization declined to confirm that it was seeking his arrest, suggesting the Iranian "red notice" could be fake, perhaps part of a disinformation effort to distract attention from their inability to track the true saboteurs. Nor did Iranian television provide any information describing how Karimi would have gotten access to the critical nuclear facility.

But Ali Rabiei, another spokesperson for the Iranian government, had earlier said that the attack on Natanz was not "external" and that a "traitor" had been identified, adding that "the necessary measures are being taken" presumably to capture or kill Karimi. There has been no sign that the Islamic Republic has succeeded at locating him, and it remains unclear, despite Iran's rare identification of a working Israeli agent, what, if any, role he may have played in planting or smuggling in the explosives to Natanz or in enabling some other aspect of access to the Natanz facility.

Months went by before the damage caused in the new Natanz attack could be accurately assessed, and when it was, it became clear that neither the original Israeli estimates, of a nine-month delay to Iran's nuclear program, nor Iran's assertion that the impact was minor, were true. The truth was somewhere in the middle. On June 1, 2021, the IAEA released a report saying that between February and May that year, 335.7 kilograms of 5 percent enriched uranium was produced at Natanz, an average of 107 kilograms per month. That amount showed that Iran finished the quarter with significantly more LEU, or low-enriched uranium, than it had at the beginning. While that might seem like a significant advance, it actually wasn't. Progress was in fact much more limited, taking into account all the relevant factors. On the one hand, Iran lost aspects of its program that could have propelled it forward faster. On the other hand, the Islamic Republic increased the speed of those aspects of its program that had not been damaged. Taken together, Iranian nuclear progress was a wash. In addition, the question of how many of Iran's arrays of centrifuges were damaged by the explosion remained unanswered.

Trying to give an answer, David Albright, using the figures on the reduced production of LEU, estimated that as many as fifteen cascades, each containing around 164 to174 centrifuges, may have been damaged or destroyed by the April explosion. He also noted that even when a cascade is not destroyed, if deposits of debris make their way into the piping, replacement of various machinery becomes impractical. The upshot is that the attack by no means ended Iran's nuclear program, which had about 5,060 operating IR-1s between the Natanz and Fordow facilities, along with another 13,000 or so in storage. For Iran to have lost the 2,400 or so centrifuges estimated by Albright would have left the Iranians with plenty of others to continue the enrichment program. But it would nonetheless have been a much more significant blow than Tehran wanted to admit. Albright speculated that perhaps as many as three of the six cascades of more advanced IR-2m centrifuges that Iran had may have been destroyed, which would also be a considerable setback. Moreover, in a later June 2022 report, Albright estimated that the collective impact of the two Natanz explosions—in June 2020 and April 2021—was to reduce Iran's fleet of thousands of advanced centrifuges to a fleet of only hundreds.

A final major question raised after the Natanz attack was the perennial one about Iran's nuclear program: how far was it from being able to produce a bomb? The question took on additional meaning with the reports that Iran had started enriching uranium to an all-new high of 60 percent.

As of June 1, 2021, Iran had only enriched around 2.4 kilograms to the 60 percent enrichment level in the seven weeks following the April attack. But according to Albright, it would take 40 to 50 kilograms of 60 percent enriched uranium to make a nuclear explosive—since going from 60 percent to the weaponization level of 90 percent can be done relatively quickly. This meant the Iranians had produced a mere 5 to 6 percent of what they needed for a bomb, a further indication that the Islamic Republic's nuclear program had been greatly weakened in both quantity and quality by the April explosion, and this also reduced some of its ability to pressure the West into concessions on the diplomatic front.

Even when the plans have been made and the technical challenges met, there is always an art in choosing the right moment to strike, and, assuming it was indeed the Mossad that carried out the Natanz operation,

Cohen had chosen the April 11 date for the strike with great care and for maximum effect. The Biden administration was in its first few months; it was also just before negotiations for a renewed nuclear deal opened between Iran and the United States, with the other signatories to the agreement, France, Britain, Russia, China, and Germany, also present.

By striking then, Cohen would have accomplished several purposes. First, he would have shown Iran he could reach them underground as well as aboveground. The Iranians would now understand that even burying their facilities didn't make them immune from sabotage. The meticulous plan that Fakhrizadeh had crafted for Khamenei after the first Natanz explosion in July 2020 was based on a nuanced premise. Fakhrizadeh believed that Iran could outflank Israel despite that setback. He had ordered moving forward with new advanced centrifuges that would bring Tehran close enough to a nuclear bomb to force the West to crumble into Iran's hands. Their plan was to violate the nuclear deal faster and more aggressively with advanced centrifuges at the new underground facility, and this would scare the U.S. into new concessions. Though Tehran would make an impressive comeback, it was still once again far behind from where it would have been.

Second, the Mossad would have embarrassed the Iranians just as a round of the Vienna nuclear negotiations was starting. The Islamic Republic had always made gains by arriving at the negotiating table with credible fresh threats of reaching a nuclear weapon in months, if it did not get the deal it wanted. Now, given the wreckage at Natanz, the U.S. and its allies in the talks could brush off any imminent threat. It was a remarkable achievement and it added to others. From the 2018 archive raid, to the July 2020 aboveground Natanz explosion, to the April 2021 underground sabotage, if Cohen was pulling the strings, each time he pulled, it was to devastating effect.

Chapter 14

DEATH BY A THOUSAND CUTS

AS SOPHISTICATED AS THE MOSSAD'S CAMPAIGN OF SABOtage was, nothing is forever in this contest. In the past, Iran had shown a remarkable capacity to recover from sabotage and it did so again after the April 11 strike on Natanz. Later that month, IAEA reports came to frightening conclusions: the number of cascades operating at Natanz now exceeded their pre-sabotage level, and new cascades, including advanced IR-4s, had been installed at Fordow, all of them being fed with uranium. More important, perhaps, Iran had enriched more uranium to the 60 percent level. This significantly shortened the scientific "distance" to weapons-grade uranium at the 90 percent purity level.

Even as the Israelis reportedly carried out the April 11 attack on Natanz, they were getting ready on the diplomatic front to persuade the new Biden administration to live up to its promise not to return to the nuclear accords without remedying some of its flaws. At the end of April, only weeks after the Natanz attack, a high-powered delegation of Israeli security officials came to Washington. Their goal was to get across the message that if the Americans left Israel convinced that it faced a choice between fighting a significantly weakened Iran now or a much stronger Iran on a glide path to nuclear weapons a few years from now, no one should be surprised if Israel decided to act before disaster hit.

The Israeli delegation included Cohen; National Security Council chief Meir Ben Shabbat; head of the IDF intelligence directorate General Tamir Hayman; and Brigadier General Tal Kelman, an Israeli Air

Force officer in charge of the Iran file. The Israelis held meetings together and separately in different combinations with Secretary of State Antony Blinken, National Security Adviser Jake Sullivan, CIA director William Burns, and other senior officials. These meetings came just six weeks before the elections in Iran, a prospect that intensified Israel's worries about what the Americans would do. With President Hassan Rouhani's term coming to an end, Israel feared the U.S. might cut a deal before Ayatollah Khamenei's pick and the favorite to "win the vote," the hard-line Ebrahim Raisi, moved into office.

From Israel's standpoint, the Americans were back to giving mixed signals regarding their intentions on Iran. Jerusalem had been somewhat reassured by statements from Secretary of State Blinken and others that they would be firm in demanding concessions from Iran, not only on its uranium enrichment activities, but also on its ballistic missile program and its support of regional terrorism. Still, the primary thrust of American policy was to return to the deal, and that worried the Israelis. Moreover, even before the Israeli delegation arrived, Biden's press secretary, Jen Psaki, questioned whether anything the Israelis might say would alter the administration's position on a return to the JCPOA, had answered with a point-blank: "No."

That statement from Psaki, and more discreet comments by other administration officials, led to a profound skepticism in Jerusalem about whether Biden would stick to his promise for a better deal. How, the Israelis continued to wonder, could the U.S. lift its most powerful sanctions on one hand and maintain its leverage against Iran on the other hand? Jerusalem did not accept Washington's argument that it could force Iran into new concessions merely by virtue of a threat to snap back the sanctions at some later unspecified date. This skepticism was fueled in part by the Israelis' awareness that every senior administration official from Biden on down had excoriated Trump in 2018 for reimposing sanctions at a time when Iran was judged by international inspectors to be fully complying with the nuclear deal. In addition, the Biden team on the Iran issue was largely a reboot of the Obama administration team that negotiated the 2015 deal in the first place. Biden's special adviser on Iran was Robert Malley, who had been one of President Obama's lead negotiators in the original negotiations on the JCPOA. Malley was seen by his critics as dead set on a return to the accord and willing to overlook Iran's involvement in terrorism in order to achieve that.

In their various meetings in Washington that April, the members of the Israeli delegation made their arguments for a tough Iran policy. But they did not feel like they were convincing anyone.

But then, on the sidelines of this "mini-summit" on Iran, Cohen had an hour-long face-to-face meeting with Biden. In fact, the State Department refused to comment on this meeting or even to confirm that it had taken place. In a slight variation on this theme, the National Security Council said that Biden had merely dropped in on Cohen during one of the Israeli's other meetings. The Americans evidently wanted to give the impression that Biden had just come by to say hello, but not to engage in a substantive discussion with the head of Israel's intelligence service. But we were the first to confirm that the Biden-Cohen encounter, which also included the new CIA chief William Burns, was more than just a drop-in affair. For that matter, it was the only meeting between President Biden and any Israeli official in the first four months of his administration.

Exactly what words were spoken in the meeting we don't know, but surely Cohen updated Biden with Israel's most recent intelligence on Iran's advanced centrifuges and on its progress toward being able to weaponize its stock of enriched uranium. Whatever words were used, after the meeting, the U.S. surprised the Israelis by standing tough on the advanced centrifuges, on Iran's nonnuclear activities, and on the holes in the JCPOA. Israel's worry that there would be a quick deal with Iran while Rouhani was still in office proved unfounded. There was no deal at all, so that when Raisi came into office in August 2021, he faced a hardened American position. The talks on the JCPOA were put off for about six months. The U.S.'s tougher stance may have contributed to delaying a deal for even longer than that—though by August 2022, the Biden team—in its cyclical zigzag on Iran policy—started to show greater flexibility toward Iran once more regarding the advanced centrifuges issue. If Iran had been willing to compromise on some of the IAEA probe issues, there probably would have been a deal before Labor Day.

Did Cohen help convince Biden to hold his ground?

For now, nobody but Biden himself can know with any certainty the answer to that question. Whatever it was, Cohen's trip to Washington was pretty much his parting shot as Mossad chief. A month later, with Mike Pompeo in the audience at Mossad headquarters at the end of May 2021, Cohen, speaking at his retirement ceremony, summed up his term in office. The Mossad, he said, had "penetrated into the heart of hearts of the enemy, Iran," "undermined its self-confidence and haughtiness," and exposed its "fraud and lies."

Cohen's successor, David Barnea, was in some ways cut from the same cloth as Cohen in the area of intelligence, having taken a similar path on his way to the top. Like Cohen, he began his career as a case officer, spending most of it in the Tzomet division, recruiting and handling enemy agents—except for a two-year spell as deputy head of Keshet, the Mossad's eavesdropping division. After returning to Tzomet, he spent much of his time dealing with the Iran file and served as its head from 2013 to 2019 when Cohen made him his deputy, also heading the special operations division—that would have seen him involved in the planning of the assassination of Mohsen Fakhrizadeh, if, as Iranian sources claim, Israel was behind it.

As a teenager, Barnea had spent a few years in New York, where his father, a lieutenant colonel in the Israeli Air Force, was stationed, working on weapons acquisitions from the United States. He would return to the U.S. later, studying first for a bachelor's degree at the New York Institute of Technology and then for an MBA at Pace University. Following his studies, Barnea worked as an investment banker in Israel for several years before applying to join the Mossad in 1996.

Within two weeks of becoming Mossad chief, Barnea started working for newly elected Israeli prime minister Naftali Bennett, whose mixed coalition made up of parties from both the right and the left, as well as an Arab party, ousted Netanyahu on June 13, 2021.

Like Netanyahu and Barnea, Bennett was an alumnus of Sayeret Matkal, a key Israeli army Special Forces unit. He had gone on to serve as an officer in another Special Forces unit, Maglan, which was tasked among other things with hunting down Hezbollah rocket launching squads during the Second Lebanon War. His experiences very much shaped his worldview on how to deal with Israel's enemies. Indeed, it was Israel's failures in the Lebanon war that had pushed him into politics.

He told us that when he came into office, even though he had chalked up countless hours studying Iran in his short spell as defense minister under Netanyahu, he was going to "relearn Iran from scratch." For about five weeks, he invested tremendous amounts of time meeting with the full range of Israeli intelligence and national security officials and various other Iran experts in order to forget his preconceptions and revisit everything. This version of events was confirmed to us by officials who said he had visited key locations and met with Israeli intelligence officials an unusual number of times to be briefed on Iran—even for a prime minister.

Bennett came out of this "policy review" with various insights: chief among them that Israel had been fighting a one-sided war. "We've been suckers," he told us, explaining, "Their goal was to weigh us down fighting in Gaza and Lebanon, and they sit back happy in Tehran." Iran, he said, had "to pay a direct price when they use proxies to hit us. Every time Hamas or Islamic Jihad shoots a rocket at Sderot, someone pays a price in Iran," and that price could be disproportionate. "Just as important," he told us, the policy review taught him that the regime was "profoundly corrupt and fairly incompetent right now. Large swaths of land don't get water. You turn on the faucets and you get mud. You have all these demonstrations and people are very frustrated with the IRGC." There were opportunities, he felt, to take advantage of the regime's weaknesses, but according to one account, he also impressed on Barnea and the Mossad that they needed to be more creative about being more aggressive. Bennett wanted to make his mark on the new office and would encourage Barnea's aggressive instincts.

According to a parallel narrative those instincts were not only well developed, but it was Barnea who pressed Bennett to be even more daring and alter the rules of the game with Iran more in Israel's favor. Like Cohen, Barnea had earned a reputation for his eagerness to carry out daring operations, and former Mossad officials speaking to Israeli media predicted he would continue with covert actions against Iran.

They were right. Even the Israeli media was shocked at how fast Barnea and Bennett threw their first punches. Only three weeks after Yossi Cohen handed over the reins at the Mossad to Barnea, a week and a half after Netanyahu's twelve-year term in office finally ended, and just a few days after hard-liner Ebrahim Raisi was elected president of Iran, the Mossad reportedly carried out another attack on an Iranian nuclear facility. This time it was on a plant manufacturing parts for centrifuges used at the Natanz and Fordow enrichment plants.

At first, as always, the Iranian security forces said the attack, which was on a facility associated with the Atomic Energy Organization of Iran near Karaj, some twenty-five miles west of Tehran, had been foiled. Iranian media reported that a quadcopter drone carrying a parcel bomb had been shot down "thanks to tight security measures," and that, while there had been some damage to the roof, it was "slight."

However, we were told by senior intelligence sources that the attack had caused significant damage to the Iran Centrifuge Technology Company, or TESA, which had been on a list of potential targets connected to Iran's nuclear program that Israeli intelligence had shown to senior American officials when the Trump administration was still in office.

Mossad sources said a joint Israeli-Iranian team had gotten to a point ten miles from the target, launched the drone, flown it toward the facility, and fired, partly destroying it before guiding the drone back to the launch location and removing it for possible future use.

Significantly, after the attack, Iran blocked the IAEA's access to the site for nearly six months, until the agency held a press conference at which it disproved bogus Iranian claims that it had spied for the Mossad. To this day, it is unknown what Iran may have covered up in that half year when the IAEA inspectors were barred from the site.

The operation targeting TESA, which took months to prepare and carefully considered the probability of whether it would lead to a broader escalation, bore the signatures of Netanyahu and Cohen, but it was carried out with Barnea and Bennett at the helm, and in that sense it prefigured where things were headed under the new leadership.

In fact, the Barnea-Bennett pairing led to one of the most intense periods of Israeli operations against Iran ever. As had been the case with Netanyahu and Cohen, their operations were not just tactical feats but were also designed to influence or even decisively shape the strategic posture of the Islamic Republic's nuclear program and its negotiations with the world powers. As top intelligence sources told us about the purpose of the Karaj hit, "you need to understand the language of the Middle East. You need to strike back unequivocally. If you equivocate, Iran will come after you." However, while Netanyahu and Cohen had worked for the most part with Donald Trump, a president who saw eye to eye with them on Iran, Barnea and Bennett were acting on a playing field dominated by President Biden. Despite the fact that Biden's team had not rushed into a return to the JCPOA, they still wanted to get back into the nuclear deal that Trump had walked away from.

This could have led to a rerun of the nasty and destabilizing open conflict over the JCPOA that had taken place between the Netanyahu and Obama administrations. But it didn't. It wasn't that the Bennett-Barnea tandem agreed with Biden on Iran. They did not. In August, Bennett traveled to Washington to talk with Biden at the White House. Other than the under-the-radar meeting that Cohen had had with Biden in April, Bennett's talks were the first any Israeli official had with the new American president, and it didn't bode well as far as the Israelis were concerned. Bennett and his team quickly came to the conclusion that the administration's talk of a "longer and stronger deal" was empty.

One impression that the Israelis did get from their first encounter with Biden was encouraging. In contrast to Obama, Biden wasn't going to be publicly antagonistic to Israel's continued operations against Iran, which had infuriated Obama, who saw them as sabotaging the JCPOA negotiations. For Bennett, despite his reservations about American firmness toward Iran, that left the road open to establishing common ground with the U.S. and a better relationship than Netanyahu had had with Obama. Bennett certainly didn't want to burn bridges in the way Netanyahu had. "I said to them 'we don't yet see eye to eye,'" he told us, adding nonetheless that the two countries would work openly and not sneak behind each other's back.

Trying to establish that common ground, Bennett told the American president that the conflict between Israel and Iran mirrored that between the United States and the Soviet Union during the Cold War, with Israel playing America and Iran the corrupt and decaying Soviet Union. In the same way that the Soviet Union had eventually fallen apart under the weight of an embittered and impoverished population and an inability to keep up economically, Iran too would eventually collapse.

Besides hoping to get the Americans not to return to the JCPOA, Bennett also wanted an understanding with Biden about a Plan B. Barnea also worked hard on this issue behind the scenes with CIA director William Burns, with whom he had high levels of mutual professional respect. What would happen if negotiations fell apart, or if Khamenei ordered a jump in the enrichment of uranium from 60 percent to the weapons-grade level of 90 percent as a way of trying to pressure the West into new concessions? Bennett, Barnea, Foreign Minister Yair Lapid, Defense Minister Benny Gantz, and other top Israeli officials expected that if Iran took that dramatic step, there would be a snapback of all sanctions from both the European Union and the United States. A senior American official confirmed to us that if Iran enriched to 90, or if there was intelligence showing it was currently moving forward with a nuclear test or developing a nuclear missile delivery system, that this would be a "different path, a different universe." But this official did not specify exactly how Washington would respond. Moreover, at the time of this writing, April 2023, Iran had already stockpiled enough 60 percent enriched uranium for multiple nuclear bombs and even briefly enriched a very small volume of uranium to the 84 percent level. Although only 90 percent enriched uranium is weapons-grade, 60 percent is already a jump of three or more levels closer to weapons-grade than the enrichment level limits on Iran under the JCPOA—which means the transition to weapons grade can be much faster. The 84 percent enrichment was so close to the 90 percent level that there was almost a major crisis, before the Islamic Republic convinced the West either that the 84 percent enrichment was an accident or that it was such a small amount it could be mostly ignored. Iran had also significantly reduced its cooperation with international nuclear inspectors, yet the Biden administration had not even referred the matter to the U.N. Security Council. Given all of these events, it is safe to say that the Biden administration's ideal of a "different path, a different universe" differed significantly from Bennett's.

While he wasn't certain of the U.S., Bennett wanted to be sure that the Mossad would engage in constant attacks that would undermine the Iranian regime's confidence. He called his strategy "death by a thousand cuts." The Bennett-Barnea strategy was "to weaken the Octopus" using the Cold War–style tactics that the U.S. employed against the Soviet Union, that is dozens of different measures. Bennett, Barnea, and others could only guess whether Iran was more like the 1960 Soviet Union, a metaphor for looking weak, but managing to pull through for three more decades, or more like the Soviet Union of 1988, a metaphor for looking like it might last for decades, but then suddenly falling apart. Either way, weakening an authoritarian regime, Bennett believed, required not months or years, but sometimes decades, eroding it piece by piece.

After Karaj, the next major Israeli operation reportedly carried out by the Bennett-Barnea tandem came in late September when an explosion and fire occurred at the Shahid Hemat Industrial Group (SHIG), part of the IRGC-run Iran Aerospace Industries Organization, which heads Iran's liquid-fueled ballistic missile program. This includes the medium-range Shahab-3 missile, which is based on North Korea's No-Dong missile. Designed to be capable of carrying a nuclear warhead, and with a range of over six hundred miles, it can reach Israel if fired from Iran. Two people were reportedly killed in the incident and satellite imagery showed serious damage.

Who did it? On this occasion, Iran refrained from blaming Israel and said the incident resulted from an accident, but *The New York Times* named Israel as the culprit. The Biden administration may have been overjoyed at no longer having to deal with Netanyahu, but it was nonetheless unhappy about the new Israeli attack. It did not have a public conflict with the Bennett administration, which might have happened in the Obama era. But it did break protocol, leaking to the *Times* that Israel was responsible for it as a form of a lighter rebuke. It has been generally assumed that the attack, on a part of the Iranian program that was of major concern to Israel, was a joint Mossad-IDF operation, and it reflected Bennett's and Barnea's determination to continue what previous Israeli governments had done, whatever the U.S. thought about it.

Three months later, in December 2021, the U.S., the European Union three, Russia, China, and Iran returned to nuclear talks after an approximate half-year freeze. Iran only agreed to resume negotiations, which the U.S. and the EU-3 desperately wanted, after the West and the IAEA Board of Governors threatened to condemn it for only the second time since 2012.

But these talks were different from the April 2021 to June 2021 talks or the 2015 talks, which had been led by then Iranian foreign minister Javad Zarif, and had been under the administration of then Iranian president Hassan Rouhani. Now, the new Iran president Ebrahim Raisi and his team were running the show and pushing for all kinds of new concessions and a tougher deal.

With overwhelming support from Khamenei, who had handpicked Raisi and disqualified any real potential challengers, Raisi had ignored pleas for more negotiations throughout his term and his team tore up many of the deals that had been reached in earlier 2021.

After the Americans and Europeans resisted most of Iran's new demands, Tehran eventually showed a readiness to return to the understandings the sides had reached in 2021 before the talks had been frozen. But Raisi's new team of negotiators had one concession that they were still demanding in order to break the logjam: a deal could be made, they hinted through leaks to the press, if the U.S. were amenable to "merely" removing the IRGC from its list of terrorist organizations. While elements of the Biden administration were ready to do this, many top officials were not, and Biden himself made it clear from the outset that he did not like the idea. The talks remained stalled.

Based on our multiple interviews with the U.S.'s chief negotiator on

Iran Rob Malley, a mix of collected public statements by key U.S. officials and private comments by U.S. officials told to us by multiple top Israeli officials, the one formula that Biden might have endorsed was what was called "more for more." Meaning that the U.S. might remove the IRGC from the terror list if the IRGC made commitments to avoid terrorism against American forces worldwide, including attacks carried out by Iranian proxies against American forces in Syria and Iraq.

As of December 2022, Malley told us, "The central pillars of President Biden's policy regarding Iran's nuclear program are, first, that he will not allow Iran to acquire a nuclear weapon; second, that diplomacy is by far the best and most sustainable way to achieve that goal; but, third, that should diplomacy fail, he will not take any other option off the table in pursuit of that core objective."

Meanwhile, Barnea privately fought hard in talks with CIA director Burns, and Bennett fought hard in a mix of public and private statements against any deal that involved delisting the IRGC. When Khamenei also signaled that he would not agree to the American condition, involving not just the IRGC itself but Iran's proxies elsewhere, the freeze in the talks continued. In any case, a senior U.S. State Department official told us that it was doubtful whether the IRGC issue had ever genuinely been make-or-break for Iran, or whether it was "just something they wanted" and that they were willing to use to drag out talks.

While Iran and the powers were talking early in 2022, Iran attempted to fly two Shahed-136 suicide drones from Iraq at targets in Israel. The attack failed when the drones were identified by the American-led coalition in Iraq and reportedly intercepted by American fighter jets. Israel's reported response to the attempted strike illustrated the conclusion that Israel had come to after Barnea and Bennett decided to alter the paradigm of responses to Iran. Before, Israel would have retaliated against an Iranian operation by a counterattack on the originating point of the attempt—in this case Iraq—or on an Iranian or proxy base in Syria. Now that was no longer deemed sufficient. Israel would strike inside Iran itself, at the head of the octopus, not just at its tentacles. And so, in February 2022, over 125 Iranian drones parked at a base in Western Iran were blown up. A top Israeli official confirmed to us foreign reports that Israel was responsible for the strike, carried out by six suicide quadcopter drones that crashed into a drone warehouse near Kermanshah in western Iran.

In his interview with us and in interviews or published briefings by other Israeli intelligence officials, Bennett and others stressed the speed with which Israel had moved against Iran's drone hub, hitting it only twenty hours after Iran's failed attempt to launch a drone strike at Israel. It was like a giant boom that resonated all around the Middle East, said multiple officials.

Iran too claimed to have responded against Israeli targets. In mid-March, following the Israeli attack on its drone warehouse, Iran launched a dozen ballistic missiles at what it called "Israeli strategic centers" in Erbil, the capital of the autonomous Iraqi Kurdish region. Iranian officials claimed that Israeli agents had operated out of the building targeted, a lavish mansion belonging to a Kurdish-Iraqi oil tycoon.

Tehran also scored a psychological blow when later that month Iranian hackers, operating under the name Open Hands, posted online a video showing pictures of Barnea's house, as well as personal and financial documents they had obtained by breaking into his wife's phone. While the group failed to obtain any classified documents, it did show that Barnea's family had been lax in protecting their personal data and prompted a shake-up of security procedures and protection details.

On April 8, 2022, Biden rejected Tehran's demand that the U.S. remove the IRGC from its terror list.

Following that decision, Bennett and Barnea let loose the most intense public relations campaign against Iran's nuclear program since the Dagan and Cohen years. In one major element of this campaign, in April, a Mossad team abducted Mansour Rasouli, an official of the IRGC's Unit 840, a secretive IRGC force operating outside of Iran against Western targets and opposition groups. Apparently tricking Rasouli into believing that he was talking not to Israeli operatives, but to Iranian intelligence, the Mossad got him to confess to planning terrorism plots against an Israeli diplomat in Turkey, an American general in Germany, and a journalist in France. On April 30, the Israeli media released an audio recording of Rasouli making his confession. A few weeks later, a video was released from an unknown source in which Rasouli, apparently no longer in Israeli hands, said he had been coerced into making the confession and that his abductors had threatened to kill him and his family.

On May 22, according to foreign reports, the Mossad's long arm then reached the head of Unit 840, Colonel Hassen Sayyad Khodaei, who was gunned down by two assailants on a motorcycle as he sat in his car outside his home in downtown Tehran. Images on social media showed him slumped in the driver's seat with the front passenger window shot out. Khodaei had reportedly been behind the plots admitted to by Rasouli. Khodaei was no stranger to Israeli intelligence. He was reportedly behind the series of attempted revenge attacks against Israeli targets in 2012 that followed Israel's assassination of Iranian nuclear scientists around that time. Now, ten years later, the Mossad seemed to have struck back. The assassination was the first on Iranian soil of an official not connected to Iran's nuclear program. Once again, it was a strike at the head of the octopus.

Officially, Israel declined to comment on the assassination, but a report in *The New York Times* said that Israeli officials had informed their American counterparts that Israel was responsible. Iran said the killing was "definitely the work of Israel" and promised revenge. The following day Fars News, a press agency affiliated with the IRGC, published a list of five Israelis with backgrounds in Israel's military and cybersecurity sectors under the title "Zionists Who Must Live Secretly," warning they could be targets.

Fars said the five, including Amos Malka, a former head of the IDF Military Intelligence directorate, had been "involved in sabotage against Islamic countries and the assassination of activists of the Islamic Resistance" and that they were "under close surveillance day and night." The report also claimed that many other Israelis were being monitored and were potential targets.

On May 25, Iran was hit again when a quadcopter drone punched through the roof of a building at the Parchin military compound, a nuclear site, killing a mechanical engineer.

On the same day, *The Wall Street Journal* published a report based on a leak from Israeli officials that Iran had hacked the IAEA in earlier rounds of nuclear inspections. The report, which the Israelis had gotten from the 2018 theft of Iran's nuclear archive, quoted internal Iranian emails in which officials discussed how they could use the materials they hacked from the IAEA to outfox and outwit the nuclear inspectors.

These newly released materials underscored Israel's ongoing contention that Iran never stopped lying, never ceased to run circles around IAEA inspectors, and never halted its efforts to progress with its nuclear weapons program. The timing of Israel's disclosure of these documents is interesting. Yarden Vatikai, who had headed the "reveal" of the Mossad's 2018 heist of Iranian nuclear documents, told us that the email exchanges among Iranian officials were not yet known in 2018. He reminded us that translating tens of thousands of documents in Farsi about technical nuclear details was an enormous and time-consuming task.

However, the exact timing of their disclosure to the U.S. was clearly part of an effort to weaken the Biden administration's wish for a new deal with Iran, since it showed not only Tehran's fundamental untrustworthiness, but also undermined any confidence the U.S. might have in the ability of the IAEA to conduct full inspections inside Iran. Bennett told us that he picked that particular moment to release the intelligence about Iran's hack of the IAEA because he thought it could push the U.S. away from the nuclear negotiations. But he also said he had purposely not released the materials earlier in 2022 when they might have had less effect. Waiting until Biden's patience with the Iranians was already waning was a better bet.

A week after the Parchin attack, on May 30, a senior IRGC Unit 840 official who served with Rasouli and Khodaei died after falling from the roof balcony of his home in the Jahan Nama area of Karaj. Speculation was rife that the IRGC had liquidated him as the possible mole who had helped Israel track down and kill his two colleagues.

These operations against Unit 840, taking place in such a short time, would have gotten worldwide attention on their own. But they also changed the game. Unit 840 was heavily involved in Iran's response to any Israeli hits on the Islamic Republic's nuclear and drone scientists, which gives a preemptive quality to Israel's strikes against it, as if to warn Iran that retaliation against Israel would itself generate retaliation.

And strange things kept happening. Several officials connected to Iran's aerospace, drone, and nuclear programs died in mysterious and unexplained circumstances.

Amid all these incidents, Israel obtained intelligence that Iran was planning to attack Israelis in Istanbul. On June 13, Israeli tourists were advised to evacuate Istanbul immediately or stay in their hotel rooms. Turkey's National Intelligence Organization (MIT) later revealed that it had arrested eight members of an Iranian-led cell, some of them Iranian nationals and others local criminals, who had been planning to kidnap a former Israeli consul and his wife while they were at a hotel in the Beyoğlu district of the capital. The Turks said the group planned other attacks against Israeli tourists in the same neighborhood.

A former senior official knowledgeable about the affair told us that in one of the incidents, Turkish agents had seized armed members of a cell outside a store, seconds before they planned to enter and kill their targets.

We asked intelligence sources in Israel about the timing of disclosures about these attacks, which, as it happened, took place after Bennett learned—probably in a conversation with Biden in April—that the Americans would reject Iran's demand that the IRGC be removed from the U.S. list of terrorist organizations. Following the U.S. rejection, negotiations with Iran stalled again. Ultimately our sources indicated that the two issues were not connected. However, Biden's telling Bennett about his decision regarding the IRGC certainly created a major opening for Israel's operations, and the Western countries were unusually silent about them.

In late July 2022, negotiations with Iran were alternately stalling and jumping forward again. In August 2022 it suddenly seemed that a joint U.S.-Iranian return to the nuclear deal was at hand. However, EU chief negotiator on Iran Enrique Mora told us that, "In July and August 2022, all of the P5+1 were in favor of bringing the JCPOA back to life. We had an agreement and a text. But at the key moment, the Iranians came back" with multiple impossible requests which they knew would not be agreed to. A senior U.S. State Department official gave us what he thought of as guidelines for when a return to the JCPOA would be warranted, and when it wouldn't. If a deal meant that Iran's nuclear breakout time would be extended to several months, as opposed to some shorter period, it might still be acceptable. But the U.S. was resigned to the fact that they could not recapture the one-year breakout time achieved by the original JCPOA because of the irreversible knowledge Iran had gained after the Trump administration withdrew from the deal. It's not clear whether Israel knew about these American guidelines, but they would have taken no comfort in these reduced American expectations.

Bennett also confirmed to us that Israel was ready to hit back against Iran disproportionately in the cyber realm, and, as if making good on that threat, on June 27, Iran's steel industry came to a sudden halt because of a cyberattack, attributed by many to Israel.

Did the Bennett-Barnea campaign succeed?

The strategy seemed to be an all-out blitz to both keep the Islamic Republic far away from a nuclear weapon, despite its worrying progress in uranium enrichment, while also hamstringing its ability to respond with overseas terror.

While Iran had clearly suffered serious damage, its determination to go ahead, and even to develop new offensive weapons, didn't weaken. Already in February 2020, the Islamic Republic unexpectedly executed a successful launch of its Zuljanah solid-fuel rocket, capable of carrying a satellite into space. Around the time that Israel's attacks were taking place, an Iranian defense official said that Iran was planning more tests of that missile. Iran did then attempt launches in December 2021 and March 2022, and while they failed, they still worried Israel and the U.S. that it was developing the skills needed to deliver an ICBM with a nuclear warhead.

In addition, between 2020 and 2021, Tehran, also unexpectedly, nailed down how to operate advanced centrifuges like the IR-4 and IR-6 after years of failing to do so and being stuck using the much slower IR-1 and IR-2m. The two technologies are unrelated, but the question was raised whether Iran would, following the time-honored method of trial and error, achieve success in both of them. True, the country had lost some of its most elite scientists, which certainly made it harder to progress, but it nonetheless seemed likely to reach a point where enough of its people had the necessary technical knowledge so that isolated assassinations would have less of a decisive effect.

Biden administration officials, asked their views on this possibility, deemed it too sensitive to go on record about it, but it is clear that Israeli hits against Iran that are not coordinated with the U.S. and that take place when negotiations are ongoing is generally not welcomed in Washington. Further, many, and likely most, Biden administration officials regard the hits as strategically ineffective, and potentially damaging in that Iran might use such an incident as an excuse to further exceed nuclear limits. They were trying to push forward with negotiations even as Iran's nuclear facilities and personnel were being struck repeatedly.

The view of many Biden administration officials is that Bennett and Barnea undoubtedly succeeded in further delaying Iran's nuclear progress, but it was simply not clear how long the delays would keep Israel and other threatened countries safe. Also, it was unclear how much Khamenei had managed to progress in rocket development despite the assassinations.

Another way to measure the success or failure of Israel's overall program against Iran had to do with the IAEA. It was whether its efforts to convince the agency of Iranian misbehavior, especially the lies that had been exposed by the theft of its nuclear archive, had pushed it to take a firmer position on the country, and here too the results were mixed.

In a gesture extremely damaging to Iran's reputation and prestige, the IAEA board in June 2022 formally condemned Iran's lack of cooperation with inspectors to resolve the questions raised by the Mossad's 2018 raid and the Islamic Republic's ongoing nuclear violations. In doing that, the IAEA followed through on the warnings it had been issuing in 2021 and 2022, though it had not done so until then for fear of derailing the negotiations taking place on a renewed JCPOA. This was not only a huge diplomatic and public relations embarrassment for Iran, but could lead to global sanctions if the matter makes its way to the U.N. Security Council.

Tehran immediately responded to the condemnation by shutting off twenty-seven IAEA surveillance cameras (leaving over forty still working). And even though Israel has reportedly continued to hit the Iranians' nuclear program, there is no sign that they are ready to turn the IAEA cameras back on. Nor have the IAEA or the world's major powers taken additional meaningful steps to force the country into compliance with the inspections required by the 2015 nuclear deal.

Responding to Iran's ongoing shutdown of cameras, IAEA director general Grossi did set a deadline of the first week of July 2022 for them to be turned back on—or, he said, the JCPOA would suffer a "fatal blow." The concern is what's called "continuity of knowledge," the ongoing, uninterrupted tracking of activity so that there are no significant gaps in the data about Iran's nuclear program. Once those gaps become too big, the IAEA would no longer be able to assure the accuracy of its inspections, and that, Grossi said, would effectively put an end to any chance of a return to the JCPOA. Israel liked that possibility, but when Grossi visited Israel in early June, he seemed to brush off the significance of Iran's obstructionism and its hacking of his agency. When Grossi's deadline of July passed and Iran had still not turned any cameras back on, there was no notable response from the IAEA or the major powers.

Moreover, the Americans felt that Iran's shutdown of the IAEA cameras, while concerning, could be temporarily remedied to some extent. A senior U.S. State Department official told us that the American side's major concern was "continuity of knowledge," and the idea that the IAEA could reconstruct Iran's activities without any significant gaps. But the Biden administration's hope was that, once a deal on the JCPOA were reached, Iranian transparency would be restored, consistent with the original deal. Israel's fear that Iran's acquisition of even a single atomic bomb would pose an existential threat is understandable. But Israelis believed that the U.S. was less worried than Israel that Iran would actually "break out" to nuclear weapon status. Israeli officials believed that when push came to shove America would downplay Iran merely being ready to produce a single bomb, and would only be more focused on Iran being ready to produce several of them, regardless of public statements to the contrary. Since that time was still considerably in the future, Iran's temporary noncompliance with IAEA inspections could be tolerated.

There had, Malley claimed, been no disagreement with Israel about the seriousness with which the U.S. views Iran's nuclear advances. "From our perspective, a deal that includes the most intrusive international monitoring ever negotiated, and that would extend Iran's breakout time [the time Iran would need to obtain enough weapons-grade uranium for a bomb] from where it currently lies—a mere, very uncomfortable handful of weeks—to many months, is very much in our national security interest. It would give us the time and space necessary to know what Iran was doing and to react to what it was doing if need be," Malley told us.

Meanwhile, regardless of Grossi's dramatic pronouncement which almost ended nuclear negotiations, the IAEA chief later partially walked back his deadline. In addition, the United States believed continuity of knowledge could be restored—although with each passing day it would require Iran to divulge more to the agency if a deal were reached. The Biden administration's hope was that, once a deal on the JCPOA was reached, Iranian transparency would be restored consistent with the original deal (which would cure the partial blackout periods). However, with each passing day it would require Iran to divulge more to the agency if a deal were reached.

In short, like with the Netanyahu-Cohen era, the Bennett-Barnea era had some remarkable achievements and engineered continuing delays of Iranian nuclear progress. At the same time, the Islamic Republic has by no means given up its ambition to become a nuclear weapons power. The Mossad's secret war, in other words, is not over. Indeed, it may never end.

Chapter 15

THE ABRAHAM ACCORDS, THE SAUDIS, AND THE FUTURE

ISRAEL AND THE UAE, THEN ISRAEL AND BAHRAIN SIGNED the Abraham Accords in September 2020, and almost before the ink had dried, the countries involved were moving ahead to a level of cooperation inconceivable only a few months before. It started with reports that Israel was selling some of its most advanced defense military hardware—radars, missile defense batteries, anti-drone systems—and the UAE and Bahrain were snapping them up.

In other words, just as Israel and the Mossad were stepping up their operations against Iran's nuclear weapons development infrastructure, they were also moving full steam ahead in forging a kind of informal military alliance with Iran's Sunni rivals. Already in December 2020, just three months after the Abraham Accords were signed, Moshe Patel, a senior official at the Israeli Ministry of Defense, was suggesting that Israel and its new Abraham Accords partners might cooperate in the high-tech realm of missile defense, an area normally shrouded in national security secrecy. Noting that Israel and the Gulf states share the same enemies, Patel said that synchronizing radar and missile defense systems would be advantageous "from an engineering point of view."

More generally, personal relationships built up during the years of secret negotiations were becoming visible and very friendly. A few months after Patel's remarks, we attended an Israeli-UAE business conference in Abu Dhabi where Yossi Cohen made his first public appearance in the Emirates since his years of secret visits. There, he expressed the view that Iran's threat was even more serious for the Sunni Arabs than it was for Israel, saying that "there are imminent threats as we speak to the stability of nations in the region." While this comparison is debatable, the Sunni Arab countries do feel extremely threatened and they also feel less able to defend themselves from Iran than Israel is able.

After the speech, we watched as Cohen slipped off to the side where he huddled with the chief of the UAE's secret police. The two, clearly very familiar with each other, spoke together like longtime partners.

Meanwhile, in the year following the signing of the Accords, Israeli defense officials were reported to have held dozens of meetings with their Emirati and Bahraini counterparts. By the end of 2021, Israel's annual arms sales had soared to a record of over $11 billion, with the UAE and Bahrain accounting for $1 billion of that total, all in that year alone.

It would be the following year though that these ties would really take off.

In January and February 2022, the UAE came under attack at least three times from drones and ballistic missiles fired by the Iranian-backed Houthis in Yemen. On one of those occasions, a missile was intercepted while President Isaac Herzog was paying the first official visit by an Israeli leader to Abu Dhabi. The UAE immediately stepped up its requests for detection, early warning, and defense systems. Israel was happy to oblige, the only issue was which systems and technologies it would be willing to share.

When exactly the first major post–Abraham Accords arms sales to the UAE were made and what systems have been delivered is classified. However, in a two-week period in April 2021, eight UAE Air Force heavy transport planes landed at the Nevatim airbase in southern Israel. A couple of months later a Ukrainian transport aircraft reportedly used by the UAE Air Force touched down at the same base. In October, satellite images showed that Israeli-made Barak-8 aerial defense batteries had been stationed around Abu Dhabi. Another, unconfirmed report said Israel had agreed to provide the UAE with its truck-mounted SPYDER mobile interception system, capable of engaging drones and precision-guided munitions.

In February 2022, Israel's defense minister Benny Gantz and his Bahraini counterpart, Abdullah Bin Hassan Al Nuaimi, signed a formal security agreement. Gantz, together with Vice Admiral David Salama, the head of Israel's navy, visited the American Fifth Fleet ahead of its biennial International Maritime Exercise 2022, in which the Israeli Navy participated publicly alongside Saudi Arabia and Oman. Bahraini sources also told *The Wall Street Journal* that the Mossad and the Shin Bet were training Bahraini intelligence officers and that Israel had agreed to provide the country with anti-drone systems.

Then, in early March, the U.S. reportedly convened a meeting at Sharm el-Sheikh, Egypt, that brought together top military officials from Israel, Saudi Arabia, Qatar, Egypt, Jordan, the United Arab Emirates, and Bahrain. Among those said to be present were Lieutenant General Aviv Kohavi, the IDF chief of staff, and General Fayyadh Bin Hamed Al Ruwaili, the chief of staff of the Saudi armed forces.

On the agenda was the coordination of aerial defenses against the common threats that Patel had hinted at, namely Iran and its proxies, but also Sunni militant groups that might possess drones capable of hitting Gulf state targets. The year before, Israel had been absorbed into the area of responsibility of the U.S. Army's Central Command, CENTCOM, a move that helped Israel coordinate their defense structures with the Gulf states. Previously, Israel had been under the umbrella of the European Command, but now the idea would be for Israel and all of the Gulf countries to pool resources to identify aerial and missile threats.

The UAE was already in possession of the U.S.-made Terminal High Altitude Area Defense antimissile system, known by its acronym THAAD, and it is believed to also operate Israeli systems. The Saudis operate the U.S. Patriot antimissile system and have signed a deal to purchase the THAAD system. We have also learned from top Israeli officials that the Saudis have already placed joint radar systems on their soil.

"The task in the theater is really how do you knit those together so you create more than the simple sum of the component parts," General Frank McKenzie, the head of CENTCOM and the top American commander in the Middle East, said in a Pentagon briefing in March. "So everybody sees the same thing; everybody gets early warning; everybody can be prepared to react very quickly to a potential Iranian attack."

We have also learned that radars and antimissile systems were not the only weapons discussed at the Sharm el-Sheikh meeting. A presentation on Israel's futuristic laser defense system, the "Iron Beam," which had undergone a successful operational test a month earlier, left the Gulf military chiefs thunderstruck, and their wish to acquire the system when it becomes operational has played a major role in advancing Israeli agreements with the Gulf states.

Naftali Bennett, Israel's prime minister at the time of the Sharm el-Sheikh meeting, told us that Israel hopes to have the laser system ready to deploy near Hamas-controlled Gaza by the first half of 2023. While this date has passed, the IDF still believes the system will be deployed in the near future. When the system is operational, he said in public statements, it will "nullify Iran's ring of fire," meaning that the basic strategy pursued at great cost by Iran to surround Israel with hostile, missile-equipped proxies could essentially flop. Even more significant perhaps than its ability to defend against missiles and rockets in the hands of Iranian proxies, the Iron Beam at its more advanced stages could be equipped with drone-mounted and even space-based laser weapons capable of intercepting ICBMs, possibly carrying nuclear warheads, outside of the atmosphere.

Meanwhile, in testimony to the Knesset Foreign Affairs and Defense Committee in June, Gantz disclosed that Israel and the Gulf states had formed what he called the Middle East Air Defense Alliance (also significantly envisioned and developed by Bennett), saying it was part of a shared vision "in the face of Iran's attempts to attack the region's countries using rockets, cruise missiles, and UAVs," referring to drones, or unmanned aerial vehicles.

Gantz said that the program was already operative and had "enabled the successful interception of Iranian attempts to attack Israel and other countries." He might have been referring to at least one of two incidents. One was a March 2021 incident in which Israeli F-35 stealth fighter jets shot down two Iranian drones, each capable of carrying a payload of close to two hundred pounds, believed to have been on their way to the West Bank and Gaza to deliver arms to Hamas. The IDF did not reveal where the drones were shot down, only that the interception was "in coordination with neighboring countries, thus preventing intrusion [of the drones] into Israel," hinting that it happened to the east of Israel. The other could have been the February 2022 shooting down of Iranian drones on their way to attack Israel (in response to which Israel reportedly carried out the attack in western Iran that destroyed 125 Iranian drones).

In any event, U.S. lawmakers have sought to establish a concrete framework for a regional defense umbrella. A bipartisan bill introduced in the House and Senate in June 2022 and known as the DEFEND Act aims at realizing what its text calls "the full potential of the Abraham Accords." It would require the "Secretary of Defense to seek to cooperate with allies and partners in the Middle East . . . to implement an integrated air and missile defense capability to protect the people, infrastructure, and territory of such countries from cruise and ballistic missiles, manned and unmanned aerial systems, and rocket attacks from Iran, and for other purposes." The Senate Armed Services Committee (SASC) has marked a similarly worded bill as part of the 2023 National Defense Authorization Act.

The most public demonstration of the growing ties between Israel and the Gulf states came in March 2022 when Secretary of State Antony Blinken convened a meeting in the Negev in Israel with several Arab countries either in the Abraham Accords or with which it already had diplomatic relations, namely Bahrain, Egypt, Morocco, and the UAE. The goal was to formalize cooperation among them, or as Israel's foreign minister at the time, Yair Lapid, put it, to build a "new architecture" and "shared capabilities" that "intimidates and deters our common enemies—first and foremost Iran and its proxies." Even just a year or two earlier, for Israel and its Arab neighbors to publicly declare an informal alliance involving intelligence sharing and military cooperation would have been hard to imagine. But that has now become a fact of Middle East politics. The goal of bringing all the parties of the Middle East together, a senior U.S. State Department official, Hady Amr, told us, was to have "not just the salad, but the whole salad bar."

Recounting the events of the Negev summit in a September 2022 speech to the U.N., Lapid, by then Israel's prime minister, said, "There were six of us—the Secretary of State of the United States, Foreign Ministers of Egypt, the United Arab Emirates, Bahrain, Morocco, and Israel. A dinner that only two years ago no one would have believed was possible.

"And then," Lapid continued, "the door opened, someone came in and said, 'I am sorry to disturb you, but there was a terror attack not far from Tel Aviv. Two Israelis were murdered.' In an instant, we all understood that the goal of the attack was to destroy the summit, to create anger among us, to cause us to argue, and to divide this new partnership between us. . . . I said to the Foreign Ministers, 'We have to condemn this terror attack, right now, together. We have to show the world that terror will not triumph.' The room fell silent. And then one of the Arab Foreign Ministers said, 'We are always against terror, that's why we are here.' And five minutes later we put out a joint statement from the six of us condemning the attack and sanctifying life, cooperation, and our belief that there is a different way."

The Negev summit was followed in September by a visit to Israel by the United Arab Emirates foreign minister Abdullah Bin Zayed Al Nahyan marking the second anniversary of the Accords. It was the first visit by a top-level official, since Israel's coronavirus restrictions had prevented it from taking place earlier. Welcoming the foreign minister, Israeli president Isaac Herzog called the Abraham Accords "a paradigm change in the Middle East, of sounding new voices, of painting new horizons for our children and their future and a celebration of life and change."

That same month, Israel Atomic Energy Commission chief Moshe Edri said in a speech to the IAEA in Vienna that Israel may share aspects of its nuclear technology and knowledge with countries who are part of the Abraham Accords trend.

"We are hopeful that the new spirit in our region, as demonstrated in the 'Abraham Accords,' will mark a path forward for meaningful direct dialogue within our region, including in the nuclear fora." Edri's statement referred to civil nuclear technologies, not to nuclear weapons; still, even to mention such a possibility showed how relations have entered a new and different era.

Alongside defense cooperation, business and tourism ties with the UAE and Bahrain have also leaped ahead since the signing of the Abraham Accords. Dubai with its glamorous resorts and luxury shopping malls has become a popular destination for Israeli tourists—overall more than 500,000 Israelis visited the Emirates and Bahrain in the first two years since normalization—this despite coronavirus-era restrictions. On the business side, Israel and the UAE, which is on the verge of becoming one of Israel's top ten trading partners, signed a free trade agreement in May 2022 and talks are under way with Bahrain on a similar deal. In 2021, trade soared by 600 percent, and within a few years trade numbers are expected to hit between 2,000 and 5,000 percent of what they were at the beginning of that year.

According to Bennett, a big piece of this was also personal relationships. He said that his business background and strong meetings with MBZ at Sharm el-Sheikh helped set a productive tone for much of 2021 and 2022, including cutting a major economic deal at a rapid pace that normally could have taken most of a year.

All of this suggests the transformation of Middle Eastern politics, much of it, somewhat ironically, catalyzed by Iran's aggressive hostility both to Israel and to Sunni Islam, but while this has certainly been dramatic, perhaps the greatest prize for Israel has, at least in the formal sense, remained out of reach—namely a full, open, official relationship with Saudi Arabia. Even though they are outside the Abraham Accords framework, the Saudis have given it critical support. That alone is perhaps the most revolutionary change in Israel's international situation since it made peace with Egypt in the Camp David Accords of 1978 (just a few months before the mullahs came to power in Iran). But full success on the Saudi front can only come with full Saudi recognition of Israel, and many factors will determine if and when that happens.

Among those factors are the Saudis' relations with the United States, which have, to say the least, been fraught since President Biden entered the White House. Among the main reasons was how the Biden administration has handled the matter of Crown Prince Mohammed Bin Salman's responsibility in ordering the murder of the *Washington Post* columnist Jamal Khashoggi in 2018, during Trump's term.

During his campaign for the presidency in 2020, Biden made clear that he saw support for the Abraham Accords as a bipartisan issue, even giving credit to his opponent Trump for helping to bring them about. But Biden also vowed to make MBS into what he called "a pariah" for the Khashoggi killing.

After entering the White House, Biden upped the ante by allowing the public release of an American intelligence finding that the Khashoggi killing was carried out "on behalf" of and "approved" by MBS. While the report was common knowledge, its release was seen as a move intended to humiliate the Crown Prince. The administration refrained from taking any direct measures to penalize MBS because the diplomatic cost was "too high," but it did say that it would "recalibrate" relations with the kingdom and it effectively downgraded MBS's status. The Americans made clear their view that Biden's counterpart was the elderly King Salman, who is still technically Saudi Arabia's supreme ruler, and that the president would be speaking to him, not the Crown Prince. Biden even thought he would be able to convince King Salman to shunt MBS, his son, aside, but that gamble was dangerously misplaced. Not only did Biden fail in that bid, but MBS also tightened his grip on power in September 2022 when his father issued a royal decree naming him prime minister. The Biden administration had wrongly thought that it could be both in favor of the Abraham Accords and against MBS, but the glaring error in this was failing to recognize the critical role MBS continued to play, quietly supporting the emerging alliance between Israel and the Gulf countries. This gave the Sunni Arab states a kind of authorization for joining the arrangement.

While analysts likened the Saudi-American relationship to a troubled marriage, they didn't expect it to end in divorce. When a year after Biden entered the White House, Russia invaded Ukraine, this abruptly dictated a rethink of the American position regarding Saudi Arabia. With Russia shutting off gas supplies to Europe, the West needed its allies, the Saudis most important among them, to increase their oil production. But when the White House tried to arrange a call with MBS, now recognizing that he was the real power broker in Saudi Arabia, he declined, leaving Biden to talk to King Salman, and the spigot remained firmly shut. In July 2022, Biden was forced to swallow his pride. He headed to Saudi Arabia on a direct flight from Israel, where he had made a previously planned trip, his purpose being to warm up Saudi-American relations.

The U.S. president's meeting with MBS marked the most closely covered moment of Biden's major trip to the Middle East. Neither Saudi Arabia's King Salman nor the Crown Prince came to King Abdulaziz International Airport to meet Biden when he landed. Yet, when Biden arrived at Al Salam Royal Palace, MBS greeted him as he stepped out of his limousine and the two leaders fist-bumped one another in what became an infamous moment for critics of the Saudis' human rights record. *Washington Post* publisher Fred Ryan said, "The fist bump between President Biden and Mohammed bin Salman was worse than a handshake—it was shameful. . . . It projected a level of intimacy and comfort that delivers to MBS the unwarranted redemption he has been desperately seeking."

Biden's responses to the criticism alternated between trying to make light of the moment and being apologetic, while making it clear he thought he was doing what was necessary "to deal with the security and the needs of the free world, and particularly the United States."

Despite Biden's grand gesture, which led to heavy criticism from some at home, MBS, deeming that his honor had been seriously offended, was not about to give Biden a quick victory, especially after Biden announced to the press that when MBS claimed he did not bear responsibility for the Khashoggi murder, the American president told him he thought he was responsible. The Americans did agree in July to massive new arms sales to the Saudis, officially announced a couple of months later, but Biden left without any promises that oil production would be increased.

Then, at a critical meeting of OPEC, the organization of oil-producing states, in October, the Saudis not only failed to up oil production, but in coordination with Russia, they agreed on a cut in output to protect prices, infuriating the Americans.

Throughout the ongoing crisis between the Biden administration and the Saudis, Netanyahu, Ben Shabbat, and Cohen, and later Bennett, Lapid, and Barnea, all worked assiduously at separating themselves from American criticism of MBS, focusing on the common interests that made the Abraham Accords possible in the first place. And the tactic has worked, and Israeli relations with the Abraham Accord countries have continued to develop.

A senior Biden administration official claimed in his interview with us that the administration deserves some credit for this, claiming that some progress made on the Palestinian issue, which even if the Democrats were bunting for small advances instead of swinging for home runs, had convinced the Arab states to continue the normalization process. In contrast, many Palestinian supporters have thought the Biden administration has done much too little for the Palestinians.

Meanwhile, Biden's trip to Saudi Arabia yielded a benefit for Israel—MBS's approval for Israeli airlines to fly over Saudi airspace on the way to India and the Far East, a move that significantly cuts travel time and costs.

Nevertheless, while Israeli prime minister Yair Lapid, who had replaced Bennett on July 1, called the measure "the first official step in normalization," the Saudi announcement was carefully worded to avoid any mention of Israel.

Moreover, Saudi foreign minister Prince Faisal Bin Farhan, at least publicly, shot down any hint of a broader move, saying, "This has nothing to do with diplomatic ties with Israel."

Several aspects of Saudi culture and politics play a role in the country's continued hesitation to move to formal diplomatic relations with Israel, or even to publicly acknowledge the full extent of the informal relations that do exist. Among the elements in the picture are Saudi Arabia's intrinsic conservatism, its status as the center of the *Ummah*, or Islamic community, and the fact that it is a traditional Arab monarchy, with a traditional Arab monarch, King Salman, at its head. It is pragmatic enough to want informal cooperation with Israel to balance the growth of Shiite Iran's power—hence its encouragement of the Abraham Accords—but its status as the de facto head of Islam limits what it can do in regard to a Jewish state still in a dispute with the Palestinians over the West Bank and Gaza.

Can this change?

At one point while he was still the Mossad chief, Yossi Cohen, according to sources close to him, believed that MBS was ready to cross the Rubicon of formal relations with Israel as early as late 2021, early 2022. That optimism, however, was based on his belief that President Biden, despite his tough campaign rhetoric about the Saudi leader, would be pragmatic and forge warmer ties with the Saudis. This might, in turn, have induced MBS to be bolder in his approach to Israel. But that clearly did not happen.

While Cohen had believed that the Saudis could be pushed to make the breakthrough with the right incentives, a senior former Mossad official with extensive knowledge of the Israel-Saudi relationship told us that normalization is out of the question as long as King Salman is alive, unless, unexpectedly, there is a definitive solution to the Palestinian situation. According to that source, MBS in this sense would not allow his commitment to the Palestinian cause endanger Saudi security in the face of the twin threats of Iran and Sunni Arab radicalism. He would still maintain a degree of cooperation with Israel. But the Saudi state, the Mossad analyst explained, because of the conservative nature of its society, especially its status as the upholder and defender of the traditions of the Prophet Muhammad, will be the last country to change on almost any issue.

This is not the wish of MBS, who wants to change everything, the official added. But he is still King Salman's son and he can't break abruptly with either the king's directives or the role that his country plays in the Islamic world. MBS, from this point of view, is seen to be extremely respectful of Israel's achievements and keen to develop a cadre of young professionals who can reflect Israel's dynamism. He meets a lot of people who he knows are Israeli but have passports of other countries, and partially through these contacts he stays familiar with developments inside Israel.

According to this view, MBS will wait for a generational change to take place. He understands that being in a stand-in leadership position is different from being king. Once he is king, however, assuming no conservative opposition emerges in Saudi Arabia to stop him, he will be able to further develop covert cooperation and contacts with Israel and possibly even full relations. Change in this situation can only come slowly, one step at a time.

Nevertheless, the government of Benjamin Netanyahu that came to power in December 2022 promised to make progress with the Saudis one of its top priorities. Top intelligence sources told us at the time that "all of the remaining [potential Muslim] countries are looking to Saudi Arabia [for when to normalize with Israel]," adding that "the Saudis will not be the last" to cut a deal. Those sources also said that MBS's decision not to increase oil production in October 2022 was not necessarily a move to switch from a U.S.-Western alliance to a Russian-Chinese alliance as some commentators wrongly suggested. They say that MBS felt somewhat bound to the OPEC group momentum and thought he could escape U.S. anger by blaming this decision on OPEC as an organization. Alternatively, MBS did want some more revenge against Biden for earlier perceived mistreatment, but after he saw how the U.S. public reacted, he may have realized that he miscalculated and tried to play down the OPEC move.

But then, there was another twist in the tale: in March 2023, Saudi Arabia and Iran announced an agreement to restore diplomatic relations after a break of eight years.

Many commentators saw this surprising announcement as a blow to the chances that Israel might establish normal relations with the Saudis and even potentially slow or undermine those normalization processes already underway. Their view was that if their relations with Iran improved and the tensions eased, the Saudis would have less incentive to build ties with Israel, especially without an agreement to establish a Palestinian state. But Israeli intelligence officials, who don't need or care much about general public approval like so many politicians who might be incentivized to give overly rosy predictions, were mostly united in their belief that the move would not affect the wider long-term picture of Israel's relations with the Sunni Arab countries, including Saudi Arabia. Meir Ben Shabbat, whose recent tenure as Israel's national security adviser had given him deep contacts in the Sunni Arab world, argued that the resumption of ties with Tehran could, paradoxically, give Saudi Arabia more leeway to take risks in other areas, including moving forward in some way with Israel.

In fact, the day before the Saudi-Iranian deal was announced—it was brokered by China in what was seen as a setback to America's standing in the Middle East—Saudi Arabia, according to *The Wall Street Journal*, told American officials its terms for moving ahead with normalization with Israel. Riyadh's demands reportedly included American security guarantees for the kingdom and help in establishing a civilian nuclear-power network.

Indeed, we had been told by intelligence officials that MBS may ditch waiting for a final deal with the Palestinians and agree to some kind of interim normalization with Israel if Netanyahu helps convince Biden to sell the Saudis large volumes of weapons and to commit to the Saudis' future needs in a less qualified way. Days after the Saudi-Iran deal, Riyadh signed a $37 billion deal with Boeing. Regarding the Palestinians, they added, MBS may merely request some kind of face-saving gesture from Israel, such as when the UAE got Netanyahu to back off of any possible West Bank annexation, as opposed to insisting on a major and permanent breakthrough.

Israeli sources said meanwhile that the Chinese-brokered deal would "not make it difficult for the Abraham Accords to proceed" and that there was "more going on below the surface that is not being seen." Analysts and intelligence officials said that while the deal could signal a resumption of talks on a renewal of the nuclear accords, the wider strategic picture remained as before: Shiite Iran and Sunni Saudi Arabia remain divided by a gulf of sectarian hostility and the Saudis remain threatened by Iran's continued aggressive drive for regional hegemony. Moreover, the Saudis still have economic and defense interests in building ties with Israel. It should also be noted that when the UAE normalized with Israel it maintained its diplomatic ties with Iran.

Perhaps more detrimental to Israel's hopes of a deal with the Saudis in the short-term at least is the ongoing divide within Israel over the judicial overhaul initiated by Netanyahu's hard-right coalition. This has led reserve pilots and special forces to threaten not to serve, thus undermining the perception of Israel as invincible, with the plans for reform also leading to daylight between Israel and the U.S.

Whatever happens with the Saudis, Riyadh's input will be crucial to whether other Muslim countries join the Abraham Accords.

To sum up, despite Saudi Arabia and Iran restoring ties, the overall situation in the Middle East now is very different from what it was when the Mossad's war against Iran began nearly three decades ago, and those differences are largely to Israel's advantage. The Abraham Accords is the biggest such difference. Despite a number of setbacks, Israel and its new Sunni allies are far more united regarding joint security and diplomacy versus Iran than they were prior to the normalization wave. This is a testament to the Gulf countries' fear of Tehran, a fear that continues despite some recent Iran-Saudi diplomatic progress, but also to Israel's skill in advancing its interests simultaneously on two separate but related fronts: forging a historic peace with former enemies and waging a bitter, gritty, risky shadow war against Iran.

Despite some positive trends, as of this writing, Israel's new Arab partners, and its older ones, like Egypt and Jordan, are somewhat disillusioned over Israel's failure to undertake any new major peace initiatives with the Palestinians. This is likely always to be a significant point of difference. At the same time, many Sunni Arab leaders are also waiting for the day when the eighty-seven-year-old president of the Palestinian Authority, Mahmoud Abbas, passes from the scene. They believe, or hope, that Israel could make progress with a new Palestinian leader who has less historical baggage, and thus make room for more countries to enter the Accords, perhaps even an interim deal with Saudi Arabia.

That is one note of optimism. Another is the hope that other countries might soon join the Abraham Accords even if efforts to resolve the Israeli-Palestinian conflict remain stuck.

Near the end of the Trump administration, Kushner's team was reportedly close with Mauritania and Indonesia, and while neither country has moved visibly ahead on relations with Israel, it seems possible that before the 2024 presidential election, one or another of the wider circle of Islamic countries will, at the urging of the Americans, join the Accords. We were told by a senior Biden official that the administration thought it had a done deal with another country to normalize its relations with Israel, with agreements drafted and all but signed, only to see the country pull out at the last second.

Nevertheless, that feeling of a broadening horizon in and of itself puts an optimistic spin on the prospects for the future. There will no doubt be obstacles to continued progress for Israel as it tries to establish normal relations with its Muslim neighbors and with the wider Islamic world. The Iran-Saudi deal could be a large obstacle. But already the Abraham Accords appear to have brought about a seismic change that has accomplished a critical Israeli objective, namely the forging of a functioning and effective, if informal, alliance of regional powers determined to stand against Israel's most lethal and determined enemy. Because of this fundamental shift in Israel's relations with the Arab world, the Islamic Republic of Iran, even with its deal with the Saudis, now faces the most powerful opposition that has ever existed to its messianic ambitions to destroy Israel and to spread radical Shiite Islam and terrorism throughout its region.

CONCLUSION

THE MOSSAD'S PROMISE

The first wave of Israeli planes penetrated Iranian air space at 0400 on a late September morning in 2024. The ten quartets of specially modified extended range F-35 stealth combat jets—christened "the Mighty Ones" by the Israeli Air Force—had flown by separate routes to hit sites across the massive country, some as far as 1,200 miles from Israel. Some of the aircraft flew along the border between Syria and Turkey and then streaked across Iraq; the others went over Saudi airspace and the Persian Gulf, all of them arriving simultaneously over Iran where their mission was to take out air defenses at dozens of Iranian nuclear sites, selected from information provided by the Mossad and IDF Military Intelligence. At the same time, the IDF deployed electronic and cyberwarfare intended to disable Iranian communications and weapons systems and create chaos within Iran.

Almost immediately a second wave of F-15 Eagles, F-16 Fighting Falcons, and this time less stealthy but more weapons-heavy F-35s carrying recently supplied 5,000-pound American GBU-72 bombs arrived over the targets, now devoid of their usual complement of ground-to-air missiles, to drop their payloads. And then a third wave hit with another round to penetrate deep into the ground and demolish the heavily protected facilities, including those at Fordow and Natanz. A large number of intelligence-collecting and attack drones along with surface-to-surface ballistic missiles were also used in the attack.

Fordow's main chamber is believed to be buried some 80 meters underground, a depth that only the 30,000-pound "bunker buster" bombs in the American arsenal could reduce to rubble. But the U.S. had never supplied those devastating weapons to Israel, which instead relied on repeat strikes, one bomb creating a crater and then others deepening it until the target is reached. Even without entirely obliterating a facility, repeated strikes are able to block its access to power, bury its exits, and in so doing effectively switch it off.

Israel wreaked devastating damage to its targets, though it paid a price in lost planes and casualties among the Special Forces troops that had been infiltrated across the border to assist in the operation. The heavy water reactor at Arak was also disabled, along with a uranium conversion plant near Isfahan, research reactors at Bonab, Ramsar, and Tehran, and other facilities where Iran conducted its nuclear weaponization experiments.

"This morning, we removed an existential threat against the state of Israel," the prime minister declared shortly after the surviving planes and Special Forces had returned home safely. Flanked by the head of the Mossad, the IDF chief of staff, and the air force commander, he addressed the nation from the underground command bunker at military headquarters in Tel Aviv. "We decided to act after obtaining intelligence that Iran was close to arming missiles with nuclear warheads. The sword was at our necks and we could wait no longer."

The prime minister continued: "Dark days are ahead of us, but we shall show resilience and fortitude. After the Holocaust, we know that only self-reliance and sometimes preemptive self-defense will preserve our existence from those who would seek our destruction."

Israelis were listening to the speech from their bomb shelters because even as the prime minister spoke, Iran's proxies had already begun to execute Tehran's revenge. Missiles fired from across the border in Lebanon and Gaza were raining down on Israeli cities and towns, sorely testing the country's much heralded Iron Dome missile defense system.

This massive air assault on Iran, carried out by over one hundred Israeli aircraft and perhaps a similar number of drones, the destruction of dozens of Iranian nuclear sites, the casualties, the revenge attacks—for now, all of this is an imagined scenario. It hasn't happened, but it could. It has a high level of plausibility.

While a direct military strike is the option of last resort, Israel has been preparing itself for exactly that eventuality, building up its forces and capabilities and conducting drills as it continues to face a determined effort by a far bigger nearby state to wipe it off the Middle Eastern map.

A critical part of the preparation involves intelligence, to know what Iran is doing, how it is adapting to Israel's sabotage, and where in its vast territory it is concealing the uranium enrichment centers and missile development sites making up its decades-long effort to become a nuclear weapons power. In May 2022, the IDF conducted its largest-ever military exercise, Chariots of Fire, in which dozens of Israeli fighter jets simulated aerial attacks on Iranian nuclear targets (the U.S. Air Force provided refueling services for the Israeli jets) while Special Forces struck "deep within enemy territory." The month-long drill resembled a war fought on several fronts. With much of the exercise made public, it was a thinly veiled warning to Iran. A similarly massive joint US-Israeli military exercise called Juniper Oak took place in January 2023.

There are, of course, other options besides full-scale war available if Iran deepens its effort to become a nuclear weapons state. In one scenario, the West refers Tehran to the U.N. Security Council, where, because of a special feature of the JCPOA, neither Russia nor China can veto a snapback of worldwide sanctions against Iran. The EU and the Biden administration have wanted to avoid taking that route on the grounds that it risks the Islamic Republic completely losing any incentive to cooperate. But if nothing else is working, and the West is still reluctant to use force, that could be their most likely path forward.

Even so, without an ironclad agreement between Iran and the world powers guaranteeing that Tehran will not be able to become a nuclear weapons power, the chances of a crisis grow with every month; many people believe that such a crisis is inevitable and that this would be the case even if the United States and Iran succeed in negotiating an American reentry into the JCPOA. Indeed, this is the fundamental reason for Israel's opposition to the Iran nuclear deal. It simply does not believe that Iran will stop pursuing the development of an atomic bomb. In fact, the Mossad's theft of the nuclear archive proved to many that it never completely stopped, even when they were part of the JCPOA.

Iran knows that as long as the agreement is in effect and it appears to be observing the limits set by the pact, it will be politically harder for the Mossad to carry out operations than it would be if there were no pact and Iran is blatantly violating the limits that the pact had set.

Moreover, in the old deal from which the U.S. withdrew, aspects of the limits on the number of centrifuges Iran can assemble expire in October 2025. So even if there is a new accord and it maintains the basic provisions of the old one, a crisis could develop toward the end of 2024, in anticipation of an Iran now permitted to possess a larger number of centrifuges and thus able to break out to weapons-grade uranium at a much faster speed. Theoretically, the agreement keeps Tehran several months from a nuclear weapon by not allowing the centrifuges in use to enrich uranium beyond a volume of 300 kilograms. However, the Israelis believe that once Iran acquires a certain number of centrifuges and enrichment sites, it would be far more difficult for either its intelligence services or the West's to be able to find out about a breakout with enough time to do something about it. Israel would probably address such a prospect first through covert sabotage led by the Mossad, and if that didn't work, the IDF would be assigned to mount an aerial strike.

And if that doesn't happen, the new deal would still expire in 2030, and the crisis would hit then.

Not everybody agrees, however, that a crisis is either imminent or inevitable. The American position, as expressed to us by a senior U.S. State Department official, is that the fear of a crisis in 2025 is overblown. The American view is that restoring the JCPOA or IAEA monitoring combined with Western intelligence gathering would, they argued, be enough to defer any crisis until 2031, which, according to the old deal, is the earliest when the main restrictions on Iran drop. But, of course, that has from the start been the main reason for Israel's opposition to the 2015 deal; whether the crisis comes in 2025 or 2031, it will still be existential for Israel.

So, where do we stand? In some ways, the conflict between Israel and Iran seems in its essence sadly unchanged, and perhaps unchangeable. Barring the collapse of its theocratic regime, Iran will continue to do two things: one, strive to become a nuclear weapon state, and two, for reasons of religious ideology and national grandeur, seek the destruction of Israel. The U.S. will try to support Israel in a variety of ways, but the Biden administration has carefully avoided any promise of real military action on its behalf. Israel, naturally, will continue to struggle to stop Iran from achieving its linked objectives, which, despite the extraordinary, creative, and audacious achievements of the Mossad and the IDF, have only slowed, not stopped, Iran's progress on the nuclear front.

And yet, the overall situation in the Middle East is now very different from what it was when the Mossad's war against Iran began nearly twenty-five years ago, and those differences largely favor Israel. The Abraham Accords is the most significant such difference. The Middle East Air Defense Alliance is the most concrete change, but many other diplomatic and business aspects of the Abraham Accords have strengthened Israel's position in the region and enhanced its list of allies in the event of a regional conflict with Iran.

In the best-case scenario, Israel's advances with its Sunni neighbors will deter Iran from making more trouble than it does today. But for many analysts there is nothing inevitable about any best-case scenario.

If the Israel-Iran chess game is played out further, things could become ominous. If Iran knows that Israel knows that it might try to break out a nuclear weapon before October 2025, then it might decide to do so even earlier, before any possible preemptive Israeli strike. In turn, Israel might decide to strike before the Iranians have had more time to prepare—in other words, before October 2025. At that point, the sides would be locked into unending rounds of suspicion and preemption, which is why some, in disagreement with prevailing views within the Biden administration, expect a new crisis to arrive in 2024.

Another element in the picture: Iran might prefer to create a nuclear crisis while the Biden administration is still in charge. Though Biden is committed to preventing Iran from obtaining a nuclear weapon, he has shown significant aversion to using American military power (reversing what Biden officials have said was the Trump administration's neglect of diplomacy). The ayatollahs may worry that almost any potential Republican president coming to office in January 2025 would be more aggressive in confronting an Iranian nuclear threat, whether by imposing harsher sanctions, increasing Iran's diplomatic isolation, or showing more willingness to use American military and cyber power against Iranian interests.

To prepare for the eventuality that it may have to act alone, Israel has been allocating billions of dollars to beef up its long-range offensive capabilities, as well as stocking up on batteries for its Iron Dome missile defense system in preparation for any potential Iranian revenge conducted via missiles or drone attacks by local proxies. The IDF has ordered an additional squadron of F-35 jets, four Boeing KC-46 Pegasus refueling aircraft, twelve new CH-53K King Stallion helicopters, and large stockpiles of interceptors for the Iron Dome.

Iran does not possess a modern air force and relies on fourth-generation MiG-29 jets acquired from Eastern European countries after the collapse of the Soviet Union in the early 1990s. But while Tehran has been unable to modernize its air force, its aerial defenses have significantly improved since Israel originally considered a strike on Iran's nuclear program in 2010. At the time, Iran's radar network was incapable of tracking the F-16s and F-15s that Israel could have used for a strike. Israeli and American aircraft reportedly made frequent sorties into Iranian air space. But in 2017, after a year-long saga that involved a $4 billion lawsuit that Iran brought against Russia's state-run arms export company Rosoboronexport, Iran finally took delivery of an advanced Russian S-300 air defense system.

It has also invested heavily in upgrading and manufacturing its own surface-to-air missile systems possessing anti-stealth capabilities. Israel has shown in countless past strikes in Syria that it has the ability to circumvent the S-300's defenses, but it and the more advanced Iranian systems would at least challenge Israel's F-15s and F-16s. As a result, Israel would have to rely on its radar-evading F-35s, along with cyber and electronic attacks, to take out Iran's defenses ahead of a second and third wave of strikes with fourth-generation fighters. Israel might confront a greater problem if Russia were to sell Iran the S-400, which Moscow claims has the ability to track and destroy fifth-generation stealth fighters. In March 2023, Iranian state media reported that Iran and Russia were moving forward on a pact under which Moscow would supply Tehran with potentially twenty-four Sukhoi Su-35 SE 4.5-generation fighters that had originally been destined for the Egyptian air force and two S-400 SAM batteries.

No time frame for delivery was noted and there was no confirmation from Russia at the time. The sale follows the emergence of a Russian-Iranian alliance as a result of the Ukraine war; Iran is believed to have sold Russia hundreds of suicide drones, other types of drones, surface-to-surface missiles, and other weapons.

As of April 2023, when this book was completed, over twenty years had passed since experts predicted that Iran was just a few years away from breakout. This long delay represents a significant success for Israel's elite spy agency, but Tehran, by its own admission, is now a skip and a jump away from the 90 percent purification level required for weapons-grade fissile uranium. Yet, even if Iran has seemingly mastered the enrichment cycle—a critical step for any would-be nuclear power—it is still between six months to two years from being able actually to deploy a nuclear weapon, which involves not only creating the uranium explosive but also mastering detonation, the miniaturization of a warhead, and placing it on a ballistic missile.

Mastering the enrichment cycle, as we were told by both former U.S. national security adviser John Bolton from the right side of the spectrum and former Israeli prime minister Ehud Barak from the left, has another advantage for a would-be nuclear breakout state: highly enriched uranium (at least 60 percent) is much easier to hide in smaller nuclear facilities than lower-level enriched uranium.

Former IDF intelligence chief Amos Yadlin has told us, "Israel should make the assumption that maybe we lost the opportunity to stop Iran on the fissile material threat, and we have to concentrate more on the weaponization group, on the weaponization activities—[to] know where they are, when they will be activated, and how to stop them." Yadlin was referring to ballistic missiles that could deliver nuclear payloads.

While Israel ponders its future strategy, the negotiations over the American reentry into the 2015 nuclear deal with Iran have continued, but with uncertain results. As of April 2023, after multiple rounds of negotiations, the various participants—the U.S., Iran, and the other world powers—had reached agreement on about 95 percent of the issues related to an American return to the JCPOA. According to leaked accounts of the negotiations, the fundamentals of the original JCPOA would be restored. Iran would suspend its nuclear weapons program until 2030 in exchange for a lifting of sanctions, and it would undo some of the progress it made after the Trump administration left the agreement in 2018. As in the original agreement, there would be limits on the volume of enriched uranium that Iran can possess as well as on the number of centrifuges that it can continue to operate.

But according to the leaked accounts, there were some important concessions made to Iran, most notable perhaps, it could put hundreds of the new advanced centrifuges it has built since 2018 in storage, rather than destroy them. Iran, according to the leaked information, would also be allowed to maintain a small level of 60 percent enriched uranium. This and the right to keep advanced centrifuges in storage are of great concern to Israel, since it would leave Iran only a few months away from a nuclear weapon, if and when it returned the centrifuges to operation.

"If they will go back to the same parameters of 2015, Iran is much closer to the bomb, due to the advanced centrifuges, especially if they are not destroyed," Yadlin told us. "There is knowledge—you cannot destroy knowledge."

Centrifuges and uranium stockpiles have not been the only spoke in the wheels at the talks. At one point in 2022, Iran was insisting that the U.S. take the IRGC off its official list of terrorist organizations, which Washington has refused to do. Some observers, including ourselves, believed that Iran would eventually drop this demand, which reports indicated it had done. But then it reopened another old issue, demanding that the IAEA close its investigations into any of the prior incidents of cheating regarding nuclear limits which were exposed by the 2018 Mossad heist. At this point, some analysts swung to the view that Iran might be delaying a final agreement in order to buy more time for clandestine activities aimed at enabling it to build a nuclear weapon quickly once the pact has expired. These clandestine activities could vary from hiding some of the 60 percent enriched uranium to performing new detonation and missile delivery experiments.

Meanwhile, multiple new developments emerged in 2022 that have downgraded the immediate prospects of a deal. One is the ongoing conflict between the U.S. and Russia over Ukraine, in which the Islamic Republic, as noted, has taken Moscow's side and has become a major weapons supplier to Russia. "The absolute key moment [for indefinitely delaying a deal with Iran]," EU chief Iran negotiator Enrique Mora told us in February 2023, "was the presentation of evidence in mid-October 2022 that the Iranians were providing drones to Russia. It became a very difficult question about if there was a way to endorse the JCPOA. I doubt implementation could happen in the new situation," even if a deal was signed. Besides the Ukraine developments, a fresh wave of domestic protests in Iran erupted in September 2022 following the regime's modesty police torturing and killing a woman for allegedly violating its modesty laws. The Iranian regime responded with violent repression and hundreds of people have been killed with the protests still ongoing.

Nevertheless, we have been told by several senior Israeli military and intelligence sources that Israel still sees the U.S. and the West as likely to seek a way back to the JCPOA if and when circumstances allow.

For Israel, as for the rest of the world, there is no clear agreement on how best to stop Iran from acquiring nuclear weapons.

A public dispute that erupted between Tamir Pardo, the former Mossad director, and Yossi Cohen, his former deputy and successor, illustrates the two opposing schools of thought within Israel. Essentially, Pardo believes that Netanyahu and Cohen made a catastrophic mistake in convincing the Trump administration to withdraw from the Iran deal. True, the withdrawal reimposed crippling sanctions on Iran, which have brought it back to the negotiating table. But, as proponents of the JCPOA have correctly pointed out, Iran has used the time to advance its nuclear ambitions and is now closer to a bomb than it was when Trump yanked the U.S. out of the pact. Fundamentally, while Cohen accuses Pardo of being passive regarding Iran, too reluctant to take the aggressive actions that can cripple its nuclear program, Pardo believes that tiny Israel needs to be more modest about its abilities to challenge the ambitions of a nearby country with ten times its population. He believes that Netanyahu's willingness to defy the U.S. and go its own way on Iran is futile; there can be no solution on the question without American support.

"What American diplomats needed to do," Pardo told us, was "to say [to the Iranians]: Sweetie, the agreement is an agreement, but you need to stop with this big Satan stuff, putting the Little Satan issue off on the side. . . . And I want to open an embassy in Tehran and I want to open a consular office in Tabriz and a consular office in Isfahan. And I want to open McDonald's in Iran . . . a Halal-equivalent like in Israel. . . . If you want Iran to change its policies then you need to transform the entire game."

There are a wide range of opinions about how best to handle Iran, and none of them offer black-and-white clarity, which means that the debate will go on even as the three major protagonists in this drama, Iran, Israel, and the U.S., continue to respond to new situations as they arrive.

Yadlin, a left-of-center moderate, told us Israel should have stayed in the nuclear deal despite its faults, at least until 2024—he said Trump pulled out too early—when some of the limits on enrichment were to have expired. He said Israel would have no choice but to comply if the Biden administration were to return to a deal. Jerusalem, he said, should focus its efforts on making sure the wording of any deal leaves no potential loopholes for the Iranians to exploit and demand that "Washington fulfills the commitments of the three last presidents—that Iran will not have a nuclear bomb."

Similarly, on the American side, former national security adviser H. R. McMaster, a right-of-center moderate who opposed Trump's exit from the nuclear deal in 2018, told us that now that the Americans have withdrawn, it would be "ludicrous" to return to the 2015 pact, noting that its expiration is only a few short years away, and a few years in the life of a nation is practically no time at all. Moreover, he added, just extending the deal by five or ten years would also be no solution, unless there were specific benchmarks that Iran had to meet for removing the restrictions on its nuclear program.

But there is a bigger issue that the focus on this or that provision of the JCPOA tends to miss. The big question is not whether the JCPOA was or will be good or bad or about Obama, Trump, or Biden. The question is what measures would actually stop Iran from getting a nuclear weapon in both the short and long term. Anyone honest will admit that there is no perfect way to achieve this objective and that a mix of diplomatic, military (at least viable threats), and covert methods are necessary. In this mix, the covert actions of the Mossad have been the most successful way to slow down Iran, while avoiding all-out war.

No one can completely dismiss those who say Israel should have relied more on diplomatic approaches which Netanyahu and Cohen rejected, given where Iran's nuclear program is today. But it is far from clear that such approaches would have delayed the Islamic Republic as long as the Mossad already has. Pundits may well debate these questions forever. Regardless, Israel and the Mossad have made it clear that they will not accept a situation of a nuclear-armed, theocratic Shiite state determined to destroy it.

As the United States and Iran met in Vienna in November and December 2021 to discuss a possible return to the nuclear accords, David Barnea spoke at an awards ceremony for twelve outstanding Mossad agents.

"Iran will not have nuclear weapons" he vowed, "not in the coming years, not ever. That is my promise, that is the Mossad's promise."

SUPPLEMENTAL CAST OF CHARACTERS

UNITED STATES

Mike Pompeo successively CIA director and secretary of state, 2017 to 2021.

Mark Esper secretary of defense, July 2019 to November 2020.

Gina Haspel CIA director, 2018 to 2021.

Antony Blinken secretary of state, 2021 to the present.

Jared Kushner senior adviser to President Trump and primary American architect of the Abraham Accords.

Robert Malley chief negotiator with Iran, January 2021 to the present

Hady Amr senior official assigned to the Abraham Accords and Israeli-Palestinian issues.

Avi Berkowitz aide to Kushner, deeply involved in the Abraham Accords, 2019 to 2021.

Jason Greenblatt aide to Kushner on the Abraham Accords, 2017 to 2019.

John Bolton Trump's national security adviser from 2018 to 2019, favored an aggressive posture toward Iran, including the Soleimani assassination.

H. R. McMaster Trump national security adviser from 2017 to 2018, advised Trump against exiting from the nuclear deal.

OTHER NATIONS

Ram Ben Barak former deputy director of the Mossad and rival of Yossi Cohen.

Gadi Eisenkot IDF chief of staff from 2015 to 2019, including during the theft of Iran's nuclear archive.

Yukiya Amano IAEA chief from 2009 to 2019, seen by Israel and the U.S. as too soft on Iran.

Mohamed ElBaradei IAEA chief from 1997 to 2009, seen by Israel and the U.S. as too soft on Iran.

ACKNOWLEDGMENTS

FROM BOTH AUTHORS

From the bottom of our hearts, we would like to thank all of the many people who agreed to be interviewed on the record, off the record, on deep background, and who otherwise contributed to this book. This includes top political and diplomatic officials, but especially to "the people in the shadows" for whom speaking about their experiences and views is usually extraordinarily difficult and complicated.

Our agents, Peter and Amy Bernstein, provided constant insight and experience to guide us through the many twists and turns we went through to bring this project to fruition.

Working with Bob Bender and Johanna Li and the talented staff at Simon & Schuster has not only been an honor, but helped push us both to reach higher standards than ever before. Bob's comments and profound understanding of the material elevated the book to a whole new level. Fred Chase led the copy editing of this book with clarity and precision. Working on manuscript drafts, Richard Bernstein substantially enhanced the content, structure, and style of the book.

FROM YONAH

I would like to thank *Jerusalem Post* editor-in-chief Yaakov Katz for his inspiration and ideas.

I would also like to thank my mother, Joan Bob; my father, Harold Bob; and my wife's parents, Martin and Ruth Lockshin. Significant aspects of what is worthwhile in this book are an outgrowth of my parents raising me to be dedicated to integrity, seeking truth, excellence, and dreaming big. I was blessed to marry into a family who shares similar principles; and my in-laws have been a tremendous source of support.

Special thanks are due to my wife, Channa, and our children, Natan, Shahar, and Ayala. Channa is not only my life partner, but her deep insights and incisive mind as well as her support and love during the sometimes incredibly intense process of writing and editing this book (and two prior books) were invaluable.

FROM ILAN

I would like to thank Steve Linde, my successor as editor-in-chief of *The Jerusalem Report* and former editor-in-chief at *The Jerusalem Post*, for his words of encouragement.

I would also like to thank my wife, Orit, and our three girls, Lia, Amit, and Adva, for their love, patience, understanding, and support; my mother, Daphne Bruckner, for planting the seeds of curiosity and nurturing a love of reading; my dog, Roza, for taking me out on long walks; and my uncle Dan Price for always being there.

Both of us would also like to thank the many other friends and colleagues who supported us through this project in countless ways.

NOTES

NOTE ON SOURCES

This book is based on years of interviews as well as numerous articles, books, and documents. The interviewees in the book cover the full spectrum of Israeli intelligence and diplomatic officials, some of whom have supported Israeli government policy on Iran over the last decade, but also some who have been critical of it, and the book describes some of the ferocious arguments among these officials. In addition to this spectrum of Israeli officials, we also interviewed a dozen or so top officials in both the Trump and Biden administrations as well as intelligence and diplomatic officials from a mix of other countries, some of whom were directly involved in the events that took place over the twenty-year span covered in the book.

A central source was former Mossad chief Yossi Cohen, who granted us extensive and unprecedented access. Access and closeness to any source presents special challenges for journalistic objectivity; nevertheless objectivity and independence were our goals. There are parts of this book where Cohen will agree with our interpretations, but others we suspect that will probably disappoint him. Many of the other interviewees for the book were supportive of Cohen and his policies and actions. However, we also interviewed and collected information from his critics, and their views are represented in the text. We hope that our own introspection, combined with input from a variety of readers, editors, and our agent, were sufficient to give the reader not only an exciting story, but an objective one. Getting current and former Mossad, CIA, and other intelligence officials to talk to us was challenging. Sometimes we succeeded only by promising anonymity or partial anonymity, and there are places where we had to avoid disclosing when and how we learned certain information.

Sources citation presented challenges. As authors who live in Israel, we come under the jurisdiction of Israeli censorship regulations. We won many battles with the censor, but there were small parts of the book which we were required to cut. In other instances, we credited foreign sources rather than our independent Israeli sources to avoid censorship problems, provided that the information from foreign sources was accurate. There were some rare cases where we granted anonymity not only to intelligence officials, but also to a small number of political officials who were providing exclusive revelations. In such cases, we did our best to verify information they provided through other means. Nevertheless, our notes are extensive and provide as much detail about the sources of the information in the book as possible. None of this is perfect, but it facilitated our presenting what we believe to be a great story, which includes new and valuable reveals.

A final note: After he retired from the Mossad, Yossi Cohen underwent a whirlwind of media interviews, including with us in October 2021, seemingly as a trial balloon for an eventual run for prime minister heading the Likud Party, where Netanyahu has already declared him one of his two likely successors. Subsequently, claims emerged that he had disclosed classified information, had an extramarital affair with a flight attendant, and carried out problematic activities in Congo. While these allegations took a toll on his public reputation, none of the probes into these issues led into the criminal sphere.

INTRODUCTION

1 *declared the annihilation:* Udi Evental, "Why the Islamic Regime in Tehran Calls for the Destruction of Israel?," February 10–17, 2019, Reichman University, Institute for Policy and Strategy, https://www.runi.ac.il/en/research-institutes/government/ips/publications/spotlight-13-2-19/; Dr. Yossi Mansharof, "Qods Day Advances Iran's Regional Aspirations," Jerusalem Institute for Strategy and Security, June 21, 2020, https://jiss.org.il/en/mansharof-qodsday-advances-irans-aspirations/.

1 *a concerted effort:* "Iran Nuclear Overview," Nuclear Threat Initiative, June 25, 2020, https://www.nti.org/analysis/articles/iran-nuclear/.

2 *This disclosure:* Mark Fitzpatrick, "The IAEA's Diligent Investigation of Iran's 'Atomic Archive,'" Institute for Science and International Security, March 20, 2019, https://www.iiss.org/blogs/analysis/2019/03/the-iaeas-diligent-investigation-of-irans-atomic-archive.

2 *to withdraw:* Tom DiChristopher, "Trump Announces He Will Withdraw US

from Iran Nuclear Deal and Restore Sanctions," CNBC, May 9, 2018, https://www.cnbc.com/2018/05/08/trump-to-announce-he-will-withdraw-us-from-iran-nuclear-deal.html.

4 *to strike and destroy:* "Air Strike at Osirak," *Air Force Magazine*, April 2012, https://www.airandspaceforces.com/PDF/MagazineArchive/Documents/2012/April%202012/0412osirak.pdf.

4 *enunciated the policy:* Israeli and Iraqi statements on raid on nuclear plant, Reuters/*New York Times*, June 9, 1981, https://www.nytimes.com/1981/06/09/world/israeli-and-iraqi-statements-on-raid-on-nuclear-plant.html.

4 *"will be a precedent":* "CBS News: An Interview with Prime Minister Menachem Begin," *Face the Nation*, CBS, June 15, 1981, in Leonard S. Spector and Avner Cohen, "Israel's Airstrike on Syria's Reactor: Implications for the Nonproliferation Regime," *Arms Control Today* (July/August 2008), https://www.armscontrol.org/act/2008-08/features/israel%E2%80%99s-airstrike-syria%E2%80%99s-reactor-implications-nonproliferation-regime.

5 *bombed and destroyed:* David Makovsky, "The Silent Strike: How Israel Bombed a Syrian Nuclear Installation and Kept It Secret," *The New Yorker*, September 10, 2012, https://www.newyorker.com/magazine/2012/09/17/the-silent-strike.

5 *heavy water plant:* Marianne Nordahl, "Heavy Water Mission That Failed," *ScienceNorway*, November 7, 2011, https://sciencenorway.no/forskningno-history-norway/heavy-water-mission-that-failed/1373337; Timothy J. Jorgensen, "Operation Gunnerside: The Norwegian Attack on Heavy Water That Deprived the Nazis of the Atomic Bomb," February 23, 2018; Olav Njolstad, Ole Kristian Grimnes, Joachim Ronneberg, and Bertrand Goldschmidt, "The Allied Heavy Water Operations at Rjukan," IFS Info 4/1995, https://fhs.brage.unit.no/fhs-xmlui/bitstream/handle/11250/99533/INF0495.pdf; Dan Reiter, "Preventive Attacks Against Nuclear, Biological, and Chemical Weapons Programs: The Track Record," Emory University Department of Political Science, 2006–8, https://www.files.ethz.ch/isn/46216/Reiter_Preventive_Attacks.pdf.

5 *WMD Free Zone:* Paolo Foradori and Martin B. Malin, "A WMD-Free Zone in the Middle East Creating the Conditions for Sustained Progress," Belfer Center for Science and International Affairs, December 2012, https://www.belfercenter.org/sites/default/files/legacy/files/WMDFZ_PDF.pdf.

5 *sustained criticism:* "UN General Assembly Says Israel Must Get Rid of Its Nuclear Arsenal," *i24 News*, October 30, 2022, https://www.i24news.tv/en/news/israel/diplomacy/1667131405-un-general-assembly-says-israel-must-get-rid-of-its-nuclear-arsenal.

5 *Israel's nuclear arsenal:* "Israel Nuclear Overview," Nuclear Threat Initiative, May 2014, https://www.nti.org/analysis/articles/israel-nuclear/; "Fact Sheet: Israel's Nuclear Inventory," Center for Arms Control and Non-Proliferation, March 31, 2020, https://armscontrolcenter.org/fact-sheet-israels-nuclear-arsenal/.

6 *strategic deterrence:* Louis René Beres, "Israel's Nuclear and Conventional Deterrence," BESA Center Perspectives Paper No. 814, April 29, 2018, https://besacenter.org/wp-content/uploads/2018/05/814-Israeli-Deterrence-Beres-final.pdf.

6 *Samson Option:* Seymour M. Hersh, *The Samson Option: Israel's Nuclear Arsenal and American Foreign Policy* (New York: Random House, 1991).

6 *nuclear program:* Viktor Esin, "Advantageous Ambiguity: Israel's Nuclear Arsenal," Carnegie Endowment for International Peace, September 25, 2020; William Burr and Avner Cohen, "The US Discovery of Israel's Secret Nuclear Project," Wilson Center, https://www.wilsoncenter.org/publication/the-us-discovery-israels-secret-nuclear-project.

CHAPTER 1: THE HEIST

Most author interviews mid-2019–November 2022; some 2016–mid-2019

9 *moment had arrived:* Author interviews with Israeli intelligence officials and other government officials; live press conference of Prime Minister Benjamin Netanyahu of April 30, 2018; presentation to the media of Israeli intelligence officials.

10 *contained the entire record:* Author interviews with Israeli intelligence officials and other government officials; Netanyahu press conference April 30, 2018; presentation to the media of Israeli intelligence officials; Ilana Dayan, Interview with Yossi Cohen, *Uvda,* June 10, 2021 (Hebrew), https://www.mako.co.il/mako-vod-keshet/uvda-2021/VOD-20cd4083fc4f971026.htm.

10 *hadn't a clue:* Author interviews with Israeli intelligence officials and other government officials; presentation to the media of Israeli intelligence officials; Dayan, Interview with Yossi Cohen.

11 *The Mossad director understood exactly what his prime minister meant:* Author interviews with Israeli intelligence officials and other government officials; Dyan, Interview with Yossi Cohen.

12 *Cohen met with his top spymasters:* Author interviews with Israeli intelligence officials and other government officials; see Nadav Eyal, Interview of former deputy Mossad chief Ehud Lavi in *Yediot Ahronot,* March 4, 2021.

12 *risk of the operation:* Benjamin Netanyahu, *Bibi: My Story* (New York: Threshold, 2022), 596–98.

13 *a former Mossad source:* Author interviews with Israeli intelligence officials; Yossi Melman, "How the Mossad Recovered a Secret Iranian Archive," *Moment Magazine,* June 13, 2018, https://momentmag.com/how-the-mossad-recovered-a-secret-iranian-archive/.

13 *and many others:* Ronen Bergman, "Fakhrizadeh's Secrets: New Revelations About Assassinated Nuclear Scientist" (Hebrew), *Yedioth Ahronoth,* December 4, 2020, https://www.ynet.co.il/articles/0,7340,L-5854571,00.html; Melman, "How the Mossad Recovered a Secret Iranian Archive."

13 *Ali Yunesi warned:* Jiyar Gol, "Israel's Mossad Suspected of High-Level Iran Penetration," BBC News, February 5, 2022, https://www.bbc.com/news/world-middle-east-60250816.

13 *he was aware:* Author interviews with former Mossad chief Tamir Pardo.

14 *a "very bad deal":* Krishnadev Calamur, "In Speech to Congress, Netanyahu Blasts

'A Very Bad Deal' with Iran," NPR, March 3, 2015, https://www.npr.org/sections/thetwo-way/2015/03/03/390250986/netanyahu-to-outline-iran-threats-in-much-anticipated-speech-to-congress.

14 *even more terrified:* Author interviews with former IDF intelligence chief Tamir Hayman.

15 *"The conflict today":* Author interviews with Israeli intelligence officials.

15 *unparalleled Intelligence sharing:* Author interview with Mike Pompeo; Mike Pompeo, *Never Give an Inch* (Sydney, Australia: HarperCollins, 2023), 25–26, 31–33.

15 *a team professionally:* Author interview with Mike Pompeo; Ronen Bergman, "Interview with Mike Pompeo," *Yediot Ahronot,* June 6, 2011 (Hebrew print edition); Pompeo, *Never Give an Inch,* 25–26, 31–33.

16 *whenever Yossi called:* Pompeo, *Never Give an Inch,* 25–26, 31–33.

16 *tireless ruler:* Damien McElroy and Ahmad Vahdat, "Iran's Ayatollah Khamenei Loves Caviar, Vulgar Jokes," *Daily Telegraph,* December 31, 2009, https://www.telegraph.co.uk/news/worldnews/middleeast/iran/6913069/Irans-Ayatollah-Khamenei-loves-caviar-and-vulgar-jokes-defector-claims.html; Dexter Filkins, "The Twilight of the Iranian Revolution," *The New Yorker,* May 18, 2020, https://www.newyorker.com/magazine/2020/05/25/the-twilight-of-the-iranian-revolution; James Reynolds, "Profile: Iran's 'unremarkable' supreme leader Ayatollah Khamenei," BBC News, August 4, 2011, https://www.bbc.com/news/world-middle-east-14362281; Golnaz Esfandiari, "The Frugality of Iran's Supreme Leader," *Payvand,* November 20, 2012, http://www.payvand.com/news/12/nov/1174.html; Frud Bezhan, "Leaked Video of Khamenei Raises Questions About Iran's Supreme Leadership," Radio Free Europe, January 11, 2018, https://www.rferl.org/a/iran-khamenei-leaked-video-1989-questions-leadership/28969517.html; and The Office of the Supreme Leader website, February 6, 2010, https://www.leader.ir/en/biography.

17 *self-effacing speech:* The Office of the Supreme Leader website.

17 *killed by poisoning:* Shaul Shay, *The Axis of Evil: Iran, Hizballah and the Palestinian Terror* (London: Routledge, 2017), 226–37; Robert Tait, "Grandson of Ayatollah Khomeini Leaves Iran to Avoid Presidential Inauguration," *The Guardian,* July 21, 2019, https://www.theguardian.com/world/2009/jul/21/iran-khomeini-ahmadinejad-inauguration.

17 *had been a mistake:* Author interviews with former Israeli Military Intelligence chief Aharon Ze'evi Farkash, former Mossad Iran research and analysis chief Sima Shine, and other Israeli intelligence officials.

18 *persuaded Khamenei:* Author interviews with Ze'evi Farkash, Shine, and Institute for National Security Studies Iran scholar Raz Zimmt; Yossi Melman and Ilan Evyatar, "Sipping the Poison Chalice," *Jerusalem Report,* December 16, 2014, https://www.jpost.com/jerusalem-report/sipping-the-poisoned-chalice-384831; author interviews with other Israeli intelligence officials.

18 *relied on most:* Author interview with Ze'evi Farkash; author interviews with Israeli intelligence officials; April 30, 2018, Netanyahu press conference; David

Albright and Sandra Burkhard, *Iran's Perilous Pursuit of Nuclear Weapons* (Washington, D.C.: Institute for Science and International Security, 2021), first mention p. 18 but throughout the book; author interviews with Israeli intelligence officials.

18 *surveillance on Fakhrizadeh:* David Kirkpatrick, Ronen Bergman, and Farnaz Fassihi, "Brazen Killings Expose Iran's Vulnerabilities as It Struggles to Respond," *New York Times*, April 13, 2021, https://www.nytimes.com/2020/11/28/world/middleeast/iran-assassinations-nuclear-israel.html; Bergman, "Fakhrizadeh's Secrets"; Dayan, Interview with Yossi Cohen; author interviews with Israeli intelligence officials.

18 *the last minute:* Author interviews with Ehud Olmert; Dayan, Interview with Yossi Cohen; author interviews with Israeli intelligence officials.

19 *secret intensive meetings:* Primary Iranian secret nuclear documents released by the Israeli government following the Mossad 2018 raid; April 30 Netanyahu; Albright and Burkhard, *Iran's Perilous Pursuit of Nuclear Weapons*, 281–90; and author interviews with Israeli intelligence officials.

19 *embedded into the civilian program:* Primary Iranian secret nuclear documents released by the Israeli government following the Mossad 2018 raid; April 30, 2018, Netanyahu press conference; Albright and Burkhard, *Iran's Perilous Pursuit of Nuclear Weapons*, 281–90; author interviews with Israeli intelligence officials.

19 *go even further underground:* Albright and Burkhard, *Iran's Perilous Pursuit of Nuclear Weapons*, 281–90; author interviews with Ze'evi Farkash and other Israeli intelligence officials.

19 *the defense minister and the nuclear chief:* Author interviews with Israeli intelligence officials.

20 *among the hostage takers:* "Hassan Rouhani's Choice for Defence Minister Is a US Embassy Hostage Taker," *Iran News Update*, August 12, 2013, https://irannewsupdate.com/news/terrorism/iran-hassan-rouhani-s-choice-for-defence-minister-is-a-us-embassy-hostage-taker/; National Council of Resistance of Iran, "Iran's New Defense Minister Behind the 1983 Attack on the US Marine Corps Barracks in Beirut," August 13, 2013, https://jcpa.org/irans-new-defense-minister-behind-the-1983-attack-on-the-u-s-marine-corps-barracks-in-beirut/.

20 *figure out everything else:* Author interviews with Israeli intelligence officials.

20 *cultivating relations with:* NBC News, "Israel Teams with Terror Group to Kill Iran's Nuclear Scientists, U.S. Officials Tell NBC News," *Rock Center with Brian Williams*, February 9, 2012, https://www.nbcnews.com/news/world/israel-teams-terror-group-kill-irans-nuclear-scientists-u-s-flna241673; author interviews with Israeli intelligence officials; author interview with former U.S. national security adviser John Bolton.

21 *played a role:* NBC News, "Israel Teams with Terror Group to Kill Iran's Nuclear Scientists, U.S. Officials Tell NBC News."

21 *to be a woman:* Michael Bar-Zohar and Nissim Mishal, *The Mossad Amazons: The Amazing Women in the Israeli Secret Service* (Hebrew edition, Rishon Lezion, Israel: Yedioth Books, 2020), 270–73; author interviews with Israeli intelligence officials.

22 *made a diplomatic effort:* "Trump and Macron Hint at New Iran Nuclear

Deal," BBC News, April 25, 2018, https://www.bbc.com/news/world-us-canada-43887061; "Trump Aims Blow at Iran and Threatens Landmark Nuclear Deal," BBC News, October 13, 2017, https://www.bbc.com/news/world-us-canada-41613314.

22 *operation itself was frozen:* See Nadav Eyal, Interview of former deputy Mossad chief Ehud Lavi in *Yediot Ahronot,* March 4, 2021; author interviews with Israeli intelligence officials.

23 *Pompeo made clear:* Author interview with Mike Pompeo; Bergman, "Interview with Mike Pompeo"; author interviews with Israeli intelligence officials.

23 *Netanyahu revealed to Trump:* "Netanyahu Says Trump Knew in Advance of Israel's Iran Archive Mission," Reuters, July 2, 2019, https://www.reuters.com/article/us-mideast-iran-israel-usa/netanyahu-says-trump-knew-in-advance-of-israels-iran-archive-mission-idUSKCN1TX2EJ.

23 *rare public speech:* Yossi Cohen, address to Herzliya Conference, July 1, 2019, https://www.youtube.com/watch?v=wJvHuyAA1Jw.

23 *Cohen enunciated*: Author interview with Israeli intelligence officials.

24 *vaults had to be cut:* Presentation to the media of Israeli intelligence officials; Dayan, Interview with Yossi Cohen; David Sanger and Ronen Bergman, "How Israel, in Dark of Night, Torched Its Way to Iran's Nuclear Secrets," *New York Times,* July 15, 2018, https://www.nytimes.com/2018/07/15/us/politics/iran-israel-mossad-nuclear.html; Gerald F. Seib, "Inside Israel's Raid to Seize Nuclear Documents in Iran," *Wall Street Journal,* July 15, 2018; Joby Warrick, "Papers Stolen in a Daring Israeli Raid on Tehran Archive Reveal the Extent of Iran's Past Weapons Research," *Washington Post,* July 15, 2018.

24 *intelligence experts surmise:* Author interviews with officials whose identity and background must remain anonymous.

25 *had precisely:* Presentation to the media of Israeli intelligence officials; Dayan, Interview with Yossi Cohen; Sanger and Bergman, "How Israel, in Dark of Night, Torched Its Way to Iran's Nuclear Secrets"; Seib, "Inside Israel's Raid to Seize Nuclear Documents in Iran"; Warrick, "Papers Stolen in a Daring Israeli Raid on Tehran Archive Reveal the Extent of Iran's Past Weapons Research."

25 *things had been moved:* Presentation to the media of Israeli intelligence officials; Dayan, Interview with Yossi Cohen; Sanger and Bergman, "How Israel, in Dark of Night, Torched Its Way to Iran's Nuclear Secrets"; Seib, "Inside Israel's Raid to Seize Nuclear Documents in Iran"; Warrick, "Papers Stolen in a Daring Israeli Raid on Tehran Archive Reveal the Extent of Iran's Past Weapons Research"; author interviews with Israeli intelligence officials.

25 *using special blowtorches:* Presentation to the media of Israeli intelligence officials; Dayan, Interview with Yossi Cohen; Sanger and Bergman, "How Israel, in Dark of Night, Torched Its Way to Iran's Nuclear Secrets"; Seib, "Inside Israel's Raid to Seize Nuclear Documents in Iran"; Warrick, "Papers Stolen in a Daring Israeli Raid on Tehran Archive Reveal the Extent of Iran's Past Weapons Research"; and Author interviews with Israeli intelligence officials.

26 *loaded onto two trucks:* Al Jarida, "A Small Truck Took Netanyahu's Evidence out of

Tehran" (translated from Arabic), May 3, 2018, https://www.aljarida.com/articles/1525285879421497900/; Dayan, Interview with Yossi Cohen, 2021; Sanger and Bergman, "How Israel, in Dark of Night, Torched Its Way to Iran's Nuclear Secrets"; Seib, "Inside Israel's Raid to Seize Nuclear Documents in Iran"; Warrick, "Papers Stolen in a Daring Israeli Raid on Tehran Archive Reveal the Extent of Iran's Past Weapons Research"; author interviews with Israeli intelligence officials.

26 *no cinematic pursuit:* Jarida, "A Small Truck Took Netanyahu's Evidence out of Tehran"; Dayan, Interview with Yossi Cohen; Sanger and Bergman, "How Israel, in Dark of Night, Torched Its Way to Iran's Nuclear Secrets"; Seib, "Inside Israel's Raid to Seize Nuclear Documents in Iran"; Warrick, "Papers Stolen in a Daring Israeli Raid on Tehran Archive Reveal the Extent of Iran's Past Weapons Research"; author interviews with Israeli intelligence officials.

26 *complex decoy scheme:* Dyan, Interview with Yossi Cohen; author interviews with Israeli intelligence officials.

27 *substantial drug trade:* Jarida, "A Small Truck Took Netanyahu's Evidence out of Tehran"; author interviews with officials whose identity and background must remain anonymous.

27 *to be extracted:* Interview with former IDF chief Gadi Eisenkot; author interviews with Israeli intelligence officials; Dayan, Interview with Yossi Cohen.

28 *Netanyahu met with members:* Netanyahu, *Bibi: My Story*, 598.

28 *Fakhrizadeh immediately conducted:* Author interviews with Israeli intelligence officials.

28 *kept the heist secret:* Author interviews with Israeli intelligence officials.

28 *An Iranian drone:* Maayan Lubell and Lisa Barrington, "Israeli Jet Shot Down After Bombing Iranian Site in Syria," Reuters, February 10, 2018, https://www.reuters.com/article/us-israel-iran/israel-launches-heavy-syria-strikes-after-f-16-crashes-idUSKBN1FU07L; Michael Eisenstadt and Michael Knights, "Crossing Redlines: Escalation Dynamics in Syria," Washington Institute for Near East Policy, February 13, 2018, https://www.washingtoninstitute.org/policy-analysis/crossing-redlines-escalation-dynamics-syria.

29 *proxy conflict:* Anshel Pfeffer, "After Years of Covert Proxy Wars, Iran Shifts to Direct Contact with Israel," *Haaretz*, February 13, 2018, https://www.haaretz.com/israel-news/2018-02-13/ty-article/after-years-of-covert-proxy-wars-iran-shifts-to-direct-contact/0000017f-e75d-d62c-a1ff-ff7ff5c00000.

29 *avoid any permanent:* Author interviews with Israeli intelligence officials; Ze'evi Farkash interview.

CHAPTER 2: DIVINE INTERVENTION

Most author interviews 2018–November 2022; some 2012–2018

31 *"Today Iran, tomorrow, Palestine":* James M. Markham, "Arafat, in Iran, Reports Khomeini Pledges Aid for Victory over Israel," *New York Times*, February 19, 1979.

32 *"turn to the issue of victory over Israel":* Ibid.

32 *"erase Israel":* "Ahmadinejad: Israel Must Be Wiped Off the Map," *IRIB News*, December 26, 2005; "Iranian President at Tehran Conference: 'Very Soon, This Stain of Disgrace [i.e., Israel] Will Be Purged from the Center of the Islamic World—and This Is Attainable,'" MEMRI, October 28, 2005, https://www.memri.org/reports/iranian-president-tehran-conference-very-soon-stain-disgrace-ie-israel-will-be-purged-center; Uri Friedman, "Debating Every Last Word of Ahmadinejad's 'Wipe Israel Off the Map,'" *The Atlantic*, October 5, 2011, https://www.theatlantic.com/international/archive/2011/10/debating-every-last-word-ahmadinejads-wipe-israel-map/337064/.

32 *"inconsistent with Islam":* Gareth Porter, "When the Ayatollah Said No to Nukes," *Foreign Policy*, October 16, 2014.

32 *Mohsen Rafigdhoost:* Ibid.

33 fatwa: Mehr News Agency, August 10, 2005, https://nuke.fas.org/guide/iran/nuke/mehr080905.html.

33 *"the art of deception":* Author interview with former American intelligence official Harold Rhode.

33 *Shabtai Shavit:* Yossi Melman, "How Pakistan's A. Q. Khan, Father of the 'Muslim Bomb,' Escaped Mossad Assassination," *Haaretz*, October 13, 2021, https://www.haaretz.com/israel-news/2021-10-13/ty-article-opinion/.highlight/pakistan-a-q-khan-father-of-muslim-bomb-escaped-israel-mossad-assassination/0000017f-f15f-d487-abff-f3ffe5ed0000.

33 *soil samples:* Ronen Bergman, *The Secret War with Iran: The 30-Year Clandestine Struggle Against the World's Most Dangerous Terrorist Power* (New York: Free Press, 2008).

33 *NCRI:* Remarks by Alireza Jafarzadeh on "New Information on Top Secret Projects of the Iranian Regime's Nuclear Program," August 14, 2002, https://www.iranwatch.org/library/ncri-new-information-top-secret-nuclear-projects-8-14-02.

34 *too cerebral:* Author interview with former Mossad official David Meidan.

34 *Gotthard Lerch:* David Albright and Paul Brannan, "CIA Recruitment of the Three Tinners: A Preliminary Assessment," Institute for Science and International Security, December 21, 2010.

34 *Ali Mahmoudi Mimand:* "Tehran Loses Key Arms Figure," *Intelligence Online*, July 19, 2001, https://www.intelligenceonline.com/threat-assessment/2001/07/19/tehran-loses-key-arms-figure,2122487-art; OEA Team Threat Report, "Attacks Against the Iranian Nuclear Program," February 15, 2012, https://info.publicintelligence.net/USArmy-TRISA-IranNukeProgram.pdf.

35 *"Dagan's specialty":* Ilan Evyatar, "The Art of Espionage: Former Mossad Head Meir Dagan Discusses How Israel Should Respond to the Iranian Nuclear Threat," *Jerusalem Post*, April 5, 2012, https://www.jpost.com/features/magazine-features/the-art-of-espionage-265000.

35 *man of contrasts:* Author interviews with Meir Dagan and Israeli intelligence and military officials; Evyatar, "The Art of Espionage."

35 *Michael Morell: Intelligence Matters* podcast, May 22, 2019, https://www.cbsnews

.com/news/transcript-tamir-pardo-talks-with-michael-morell-on-intelligence-matters/.

36 *chilling advice:* Leon Panetta with Jim Newton, *Worthy Fights: A Memoir of Leadership in War and Peace* (New York: Penguin, 2014), 272.

36 *The Azeris:* Author interview with former U.S. intelligence officer Harold Rhode.

36 *top former military officer:* Author interview with former top-ranking IDF official.

36 *"supply chain":* Author interview with former Israeli prime minister Ehud Olmert.

37 *irst known sabotage attack:* William J. Broad and David E. Sanger, "In Nuclear Net's Undoing, a Web of Shadowy Deals," *New York Times*, August 24, 2008, https://www.nytimes.com/2008/08/25/world/25nuke.html; "Attacks Against the Iranian Nuclear Program," OEA Team Threat Report, February 15, 2012, https://info.publicintelligence.net/USArmy-TRISA-IranNukeProgram.pdf.

38 *"resides in the brains":* Author interview with former Mossad chief Meir Dagan.

38 *"divine intervention":* Author interview with Haim Ramon; Haim Ramon, *Against the Wind* (Hebrew) (Tel Aviv: Yedioth Books, 2020), 515–19.

38 *Dr. Ardeshir Hosseinpour:* Yossi Melman, "Mossad Killed Iranian Nuclear Physicist," *Haaretz* via Stratfor, February 4, 2007, https://www.haaretz.com/2007-02-04/ty-article/u-s-website-mossad-killed-iranian-nuclear-physicist/0000017f-e10b-d9aa-afff-f95bb2100000.

38 *Masoud Ali Mohammadi:* Alan Cowell, "Blast Kills Physics Professor in Tehran," *New York Times*, January 12, 2010, https://www.nytimes.com/2010/01/13/world/middleeast/13iran.html; "Israel and US Behind Tehran Blast—Iranian State Media," BBC, January 12, 2010, http://news.bbc.co.uk/2/hi/middle_east/8453401.stm.

39 *hanged an Iranian citizen:* "Iran Hangs 'Mossad Agent' for Scientist Killing," Reuters, May 15, 2012, https://www.reuters.com/article/iran-execution-majid-jamali-fashi-idINDEE84E09I20120515; "Behind the 'Mossad Plot' Against Iranian Scientist," BBC, January 15, 2011, https://www.bbc.com/news/world-middle-east-12191203.

39 *Majid Shahriari:* "Iranian Nuclear Scientist Killed in Motorbike Attack," BBC, November 29, 2010, https://www.bbc.com/news/world-middle-east-11860928.

39 *Another attack:* Ibid.

40 *sanctioned:* "Security Council Toughens Sanctions Against Iran, Adds Arms Embargo, with Unanimous Adoption of Resolution 1747," U.N. Security Council, March 24, 2007, https://press.un.org/en/2007/sc8980.doc.htm.

40 *disappearance:* Uzi Mahnaimi, "Defector Spied on Iran for Years," *Sunday Times* (London), March 11, 2007 (subscription), https://www.thetimes.co.uk/article/defector-spied-on-iran-for-years-spprdnxwqns.

40 *Among Asgari's revelations:* Von Erich Follath und Holger Stark, "How Israel Destroyed Syria's Al Kibar Nuclear Reactor," *Der Spiegel*, November 2, 2009, https://www.spiegel.de/international/world/the-story-of-operation-orchard-how-israel-destroyed-syria-s-al-kibar-nuclear-reactor-a-658663.html; "Iranian Defector Tipped Syrian Nuke Plans," Ynet/Associated Press, March 19, 2009, https://www.ynetnews.com/articles/0,7340,L-3689320,00.html.

41 *proof was obtained:* David Makovsky, "The Silent Strike: How Israel Bombed a

Syrian Nuclear Installation and Kept It Secret," *The New Yorker*, September 10, 2012, https://www.newyorker.com/magazine/2012/09/17/the-silent-strike.

41 *"following him"*: "Tamir Pardo Talks," *Uvda*, May 31, 2018 (Hebrew), https://www.mako.co.il/mako-vod-keshet/uvda-2018/VOD-d2c7779e1f5b361006.htm.

41 *publicly admitted:* Judah Ari Gross, "Ending a Decade of Silence, Israel Confirms It Blew Up Assad's Nuclear Reactor," *Times of Israel*, March 21, 2018, https://www.timesofisrael.com/ending-a-decade-of-silence-israel-reveals-it-blew-up-assads-nuclear-reactor/.

41 *an open threat:* "Israeli Minister Says 2007 Strike on Suspected Syrian Reactor a Message to Iran," Reuters, March 21, 2018, https://www.reuters.com/article/uk-israel-syria-nuclear-katz-idUKKBN1GX0MO.

41 *another daring hit:* Adam Goldman and Ellen Nakashima, "CIA and Mossad Killed Senior Hezbollah Figure in Car Bombing," *Washington Post*, January 30, 2015; Ronen Bergman, *Rise and Kill First: The Secret History of Israel's Targeted Assassinations* (New York: Random House, 2018), Chap. 34, Kindle.

42 *Dutch intelligence:* Kim Zetter and Huib Modderkolk, "How a Secret Dutch Mole Aided the U.S.-Israeli Stuxnet Cyberattack on Iran," *Yahoo* News, September 2, 2019, https://news.yahoo.com/revealed-how-a-secret-dutch-mole-aided-the-us-israeli-stuxnet-cyber-attack-on-iran-160026018.html?guccounter=1&guce_referrer=aHR0cHM6Ly93d3cuZ29vZ2xlLmNvbS8&guce_referrer_sig=AQAAAAxabN_isGTd6gcEqrids6nvCIkWs70xcxkIi4_r6b4895LtRl7vzfaPgoy-GxiOSRXCpeJn2tXmklkfkgWCzlWElVUDvQx41g1XEkIdxa2UArR6QmK4EtH6BLpSpS25TkTtEADbnFPHdDBEovPK6B59rCIz6sq2feamBirddgEI.

42 *new types of malware:* Rory Crump, "Flame, Stuxnet and Duqu: An Abbreviated History of Cyber Attacking Iran," Patexia, May 31, 2012, https://www.patexia.com/feed/flame-stuxnet-and-duqu-an-abbreviated-history-of-cyber-attacking-iran-20120531.

42 *Olympic Games:* Zetter and Modderkolk, "How a Secret Dutch Mole Aided the U.S.-Israeli Stuxnet Cyberattack on Iran."

42 *industrial machinery:* "What Is Stuxnet?," Trellix, https://www.trellix.com/en-us/security-awareness/ransomware/what-is-stuxnet.html#:~:text=Stuxnet%20is%20a%20computer%20worm,used%20to%20automate%20machine%20processes.

43 *destroyed as many:* Yaakov Katz, "Stuxnet May Have Destroyed 1,000 Centrifuges at Natanz," *Jerusalem Post*, December 24, 2010, https://www.jpost.com/defense/stuxnet-may-have-destroyed-1000-centrifuges-at-natanz.

CHAPTER 3: TELL YOUR FRIENDS YOU CAN USE OUR AIRSPACE

Most author interviews 2018–November 2022; some 2012–2018

45 *David Meidan:* Author interview with David Meidan; "Ex-Mossad Official Opens Up About Israel's Ties with UAE and Whether Other States Will Follow Suit," *Sputnik*, August 27, 2020, https://sputniknews.com/20200827/ex-mossad-official-opens-up-about-israels-ties-with-uae-and-whether-other-states-will

-follow-suit-1080289271.html; Ran Puni, "Senior Mossad Official: In 2005, I Visited the Emirates. That Was When Secret Ties Started" (Hebrew), *Israel Hayom*, August 20, 2020, https://www.israelhayom.co.il/article/793011.

46 *F-16 fighter jets:* Barak Ravid, "Netanyahu of Arabia" (Hebrew), Channel 13 TV, April 2, 2020, https://13tv.co.il/item/news/politics/politics/usa-israel-uea-999459/.

46 *"a connection in the UAE":* Author interview with David Meidan; "Ex-Mossad Official Opens Up About Israel's Ties with UAE and Whether Other States Will Follow Suit," *Sputnik*.

46 *After his appointment:* Author interview with David Meidan.

47 *rudimentary command:* Author interview with David Meidan.

47 *Bani Fatima Six:* "The Abu Dhabi Royal at the Nexus of UAE Business and National Security," *The Financial Times*, January 25, 2021, https://www.ft.com/content/ce09911b-041d-4651-9bbb-d2a16d39ede7.

47 *Tzipi Livni:* WikiLeaks, March 2009.

48 *Mati Kochavi:* Jonathan Ferziger and Peter Waldman, "How Do Israel's Tech Firms Do Business in Saudi Arabia? Very Quietly," Bloomberg, February 2, 2017, https://www.bloomberg.com/news/features/2017-02-02/how-do-israel-s-tech-firms-do-business-in-saudi-arabia-very-quietly?leadSource=uverify%20wall.

48 *Israel's history with Saudi Arabia:* Eli Podeh, *From Mistress to Known Partner: Israel's Secret Relations with States and Minorities in the Middle East* (Hebrew) (Tel Aviv: *Am Oved*, 2022), Chap. 11, e-vrit.

49 *"accelerate intelligence exchanges":* "A Secret Regional Alliance Against Iran," *Intelligence Online*, October 20, 2006 (subscription), https://www.intelligenceonline.com/political-intelligence/2006/10/20/a-secret-regional-alliance-against-iran,23406406-eve.

49 *Gulf Cooperation Council:* Condoleezza Rice, *No Higher Honor: A Memoir of My Years in Washington* (New York, Crown, 2011).

49 *direct channels:* Interview with Israeli intelligence official.

50 *Frances Fragos Townsend:* "US Embassy Cables: Mossad Chief Wants to 'Detach' Syria from Iran," *The Guardian*, November 28, 2010, https://www.theguardian.com/world/us-embassy-cables-documents/116742.

50 *financial sanctions:* Ibid.

50 *Robert Burns:* "US Embassy Cables: Israel Grateful for US Support," *The Guardian*, November 28, 2010, https://www.theguardian.com/world/us-embassy-cables-documents/120696.

51 *"a great chance":* Author interview with Tamir Pardo; Ilana Dayan, Interview with Tamir Pardo, *Uvda* (Hebrew), June 2, 2018, https://www.mako.co.il/tv-ilana_dayan/2017/Article-9c72d3416a0c361006.htm.

52 *"undermine the regime":* Author interview with Ehud Olmert.

52 *"operative plans":* Ilan Kfir, *"Storm" Toward Iran* (Hebrew) (Tel Aviv: Yedioth Books, 2019), Chap. 17, e-vrit.

52 *a one-on-one meeting:* Author interview with Ehud Olmert.

53 *building capabilities:* Ehud Barak, *My Country, My Life: Fighting for Israel, Searching for Peace* (New York: St. Martin's Press, 2018), 423–28; Kfir, *"Storm" Toward Iran,* Chap. 17, e-vrit; Aluf Benn, "Netanyahu, Barak Spent NIS 11 Bil. On Preparations for Iran Strike That Never Happened," *Haaretz,* January 2013, https://www.haaretz.com/2013-01-12/ty-article/.premium/aluf-benn-olmerts-money-shot/0000017f-f034-dc28-a17f-fc3728980000.

53 *"stupidest idea":* "The Spymaster: Meir Dagan on Iran's Threat," *60 Minutes,* CBS, March 12, 2012.

53 *"heat of the moment":* Author interview with Meir Dagan; Ilan Evyatar, "The Art of Espionage: Former Mossad Head Meir Dagan Discusses How Israel Should Respond to the Iranian Nuclear Threat," *Jerusalem Post,* April 5, 2012, https://www.jpost.com/features/magazine-features/the-art-of-espionage-265000.

53 *"another two billion":* Author interview with former deputy prime minister Haim Ramon.

53 *"if the sword":* Author interview with Meir Dagan; Evyatar, "The Art of Espionage."

54 *"Iran is Germany":* "Former Israeli PM Benjamin Netanyahu: 'It's 1938 and Iran Is Germany,'" YouTube, January 1, 2009, https://www.youtube.com/watch?v=cFTzYQoEgt8.

54 *new intelligence:* White House, "Statements by President Obama, French President Sarkozy, and British Prime Minister Brown on Iranian Nuclear Facility," September 25, 2009.

54 *no military purpose:* "Iran Enriching Uranium at Fordo Plant Near Qom," BBC News, January 10, 2012, https://www.bbc.com/news/world-middle-east-16470100.

54 *Dagan paid a visit:* Anshel Pfeffer, "Mossad Chief Reportedly Visited Saudi Arabia for Talks on Iran," *Haaretz,* July 26, 2010.

55 *unconfirmed reports:* Podeh, *From Mistress to Known Partner,* Chap. 11, e-vrit.

55 *expressed a willingness:* Ibid.

55 *gave him a message:* Henrique Cymerman, "Formalizing Israeli-Saudi Relations: A Question of When Not If," MirYam Institute, February 5, 2021, https://www.miryaminstitute.org/commentary-blog/formalizing-israeli-saudi-relations-a-question-of-when-not-if.

55 *thirty-day countdown:* "The Iranian Issue," *Uvda,* 2013 Season, Episode 1, November 5, 2011 (Hebrew), https://www.mako.co.il/mako-vod-keshet/uvda-2013/VOD-4023c925131da31006.htm; Kfir, *"Storm" Toward Iran,* Chap. 17, e-vrit.

55 *this order prompted opposition:* "The Iranian Issue," *Uvda*; Kfir, *"Storm" Toward Iran,* Chap. 17, e-vrit.

56 *we wouldn't have won:* Asher Zeiger, "Netanyahu, Barak Raised Idea of Iran Attack Years Ago, 'But Security Chiefs Shot Them Down,'" *Times of Israel,* August 12, 2012, https://www.timesofisrael.com/netanyahu-and-barak-reportedly-raised-idea-of-iran-attack-two-years-ago-but-security-chiefs-shot-them-down/.

56 *Admiral Mike Mullen:* Kfir, *"Storm" Toward Iran,* Chap. 17, e-vrit.

CHAPTER 4: CHANGING CIRCUMSTANCES

Most author interviews 2018–November 2022; some 2012–2018

57 *a far wider audience:* J. J. Goldberg, "Israel's Mr. Security Goes Rogue," *Forward,* June 8, 2011, https://forward.com/opinion/138492/israel-s-mr-security-goes-rogue/.

58 *a family of Holocaust survivors:* Michael Morell interview with Tamir Pardo, *Intelligence Matters,* https://www.cbsnews.com/news/transcript-tamir-pardo-talks-with-michael-morell-on-intelligence-matters/.

58 *joined the Mossad:* Yossi Melman, "Who Is New Mossad Chief Tamir Pardo?," *Haaretz,* November 29, 2010, https://www.haaretz.com/2010-11-29/ty-article/who-is-new-mossad-chief-tamir-pardo/0000017f-dbc1-d3a5-af7f-fbef8f890000; Tamir Pardo Mossad website bio (Hebrew), https://www.mossad.gov.il/heb/history/Pages/Tamir.aspx.

58 *adviser to the IDF:* Tamir Pardo Mossad website biography (Hebrew), https://www.mossad.gov.il/heb/history/Pages/Tamir.aspx.

58 *was opposed:* Ilan Kfir, *"Storm" Toward Iran* (Hebrew) (Tel Aviv: Yedioth Books, 2019), Chap. 18, e-vrit.

59 *there was a catch:* Author interviews with Israeli intelligence officials.

59 *devised the program:* Ronen Bergman, "When Israel Hatched a Secret Plan to Assassinate Iranian Scientists," *Politico,* March 5, 2018, https://www.politico.com/magazine/story/2018/03/05/israel-assassination-iranian-scientists-217223/.

59 *Darioush Rezaeinejad*: Scott Shane, "Iranian Scientist Gunned Down at Home," *New York Times,* July 24, 2011, https://www.nytimes.com/2011/07/24/world/middleeast/24iran.html; Ulrike Putz, "Mossad Behind Tehran Assassinations, Says Source," *Der Spiegel,* https://www.spiegel.de/international/world/sabotaging-iran-s-nuclear-program-mossad-behind-tehran-assassinations-says-source-a-777899.html; George Jahn, "Shot Iranian Said to Be Nuke Expert," Associated Press, July 29, 2011.

59 *mysterious explosion:* Julian Borger and Saeed Kamali Dehghan, "Iranian Missile Architect Dies in Blast. But Was Explosion a Mossad Mission?.," *The Guardian,* November 14, 2011, https://www.theguardian.com/world/2011/nov/14/iran-missile-death-mossad-mission; Karl Vick, "Intel Source: Israel Behind Deadly Explosion at Iran Missile Base," November 13, 2011, https://content.time.com/time/world/article/0,8599,2099376,00.html.

60 *"May there be more like it":* Yaakov Katz, "Barak Hopes There Will Be More Explosions in Iran," *Jerusalem Post,* November 14, 2011, https://www.jpost.com/Iranian-Threat/News/Barak-hopes-there-will-be-more-explosions-in-Iran.

60 *"God bless those who were behind it":* Phoebe Greenwood, "Israeli Secret Service the Mossad Linked to Iran Military Blast," *The Guardian,* November 14, 2011, https://www.theguardian.com/world/2011/nov/14/israel-mossad-iran-blast.

60 *Israel had every reason:* "Biography, Hassan Tehrani Moghaddam" (Persian), hamshahrionline, March 30, 2012, bit.ly/3W6eC1b; Ehsan Megrabi, "Hassan Tehrani Moghaddam: The Myths Behind the Father of Iran's Missile Program," IRAN-

WIRE, April 26, 2019, https://iranwire.com/en/features/65988/; Aaron Merat, "How Iran's Missile Strategy Has Rewritten the Rules of Middle Eastern Wars," *New Lines Magazine*, September 6, 2021, https://newlinesmag.com/reportage/how-irans-missile-strategy-has-rewritten-the-rules-of-middle-eastern-wars/.

60 *"filling Palestinian hands":* Merat, "How Iran's Missile Strategy Has Rewritten the Rules of Middle Eastern Wars."

60 *"Here Lies a Man Who Wanted to Destroy Israel":* Ibid.; MEMRI, November 16, 2018, https://twitter.com/memrireports/status/1063450580620898304?lang=bg.

60 *"a carefully-planned operation":* Megrabi, "Hassan Tehrani Moghaddam."

61 *"Mossad would never":* "Tamir Pardo Talks," *Uvda*, May 31, 2018 (Hebrew), https://www.mako.co.il/mako-vod-keshet/uvda-2018/VOD-d2c7779e1f5b361006.htm.

61 *"an organization for targeted killing":* Ibid.

61 *Netanyahu and Barak:* Kfir, *"Storm" Toward Iran*, Chap. 21, e-vrit.

62 *"checked with legal advisers":* Author interview with Tamir Pardo; Ilana Dayan, Interview with Tamir Pardo, *Uvda*, June 2, 2018 (Hebrew), https://www.mako.co.il/tv-ilana_dayan/2017/Article-8903ded8d32b361006.htm.

62 *to hold a vote:* Kfir, *"Storm" Toward Iran*, Chap. 17, e-vrit.

62 *fell out of favor:* Author interview with Tamir Pardo; author interview with Yoram Cohen; "Tamir Pardo Talks," *Uvda*.

63 *nuclear chemistry expert:* "Iran Nuclear Scientist Killed by Car Bomb," Al Jazeera, January 12, 2012, https://www.aljazeera.com/news/2012/1/12/iran-nuclear-scientist-killed-by-car-bomb; "Enemies Cannot Hamper Iranian Nation Progress," IRNA, January 11, 2012.

63 *"The MEK is being used":* Richard Sale, "Stuxnet Loaded by Iran Double Agents," *Industrial Safety and Security Source*, April 11, 2012, https://www.isssource.com/stuxnet-loaded-by-iran-double-agents/.

63 *wrecked vehicles:* "Wrecked Cars of Iranian Nuclear Martyrs on Show at Tehran Museum," *Tehran Times*, January 26, 2022, https://www.tehrantimes.com/news/469514/Wrecked-cars-of-Iranian-nuclear-martyrs-on-show-at-Tehran-museum.

63 *calls for revenge:* Lada Yevgrashina, "Azerbaijan Arrests Plot Suspects, Cites Iran Link," Reuters, January 25, 2012, https://www.reuters.com/article/azerbaijan-israel-plot-idUSL5E8CP3LB20120125; Yaakov Katz, "Israel Boosts Level of Alert After Embassy Attacks," February 13, 2012, https://www.jpost.com/Defense/Israel-boosts-level-of-alert-after-embassy-attacks; Dan Williams, "Israel Says Iran Behind New Delhi, Georgia Attacks," Reuters, February 13, 2012, https://www.reuters.com/article/delhi-blast-israel-embassy-car-idINDEE81C0HM20120213.

64 *a bomb went off:* "Iranian Suspect Maimed as Blasts Rattle Bangkok," Australian Broadcasting Corporation, February 14, 2012, https://www.abc.net.au/news/2012-02-14/man-injured-in-bangkok-bomb-blasts/3830190; Phil Mercer, "British-Australian Academic Accused of Spying by Iran Freed in Reported Prisoner Swap Deal," Voice of America, November 26, 2020, https://www.voanews.com/a/east-asia-pacific_british-australian-academic-accused-spying-iran

-freed-reported-prisoner-swap-deal/6198839.html; Evan Zlatkis, "Video Reveals Israeli Husband," *Australian Jewish News*, December 2, 2020, https://www.australianjewishnews.com/video-reveals-israeli-husband/.

64 *police arrested:* Joseph Akwiri, "Police Arrest Two Iranians over Explosives," Reuters, June 22, 2012, https://www.reuters.com/article/ozatp-kenya-security-20120622-idAFJOE85L09520120622; Tom Odula, "Kenyan Court Sentences 2 Iranians to Life in Jail," Associated Press, May 6, 2013, https://apnews.com/article/66422873ef1e4263a398a8e1c78e71ed.

64 *a Hezbollah suicide bomber:* Karin Bruilliard, "At Least 7 Killed in Bulgaria in Blast on Bus Carrying Israeli Tourists," *Washington Post*, July 19, 2012, https://www.washingtonpost.com/world/middle_east/at-least-6-killed-in-bulgaria-in-blast-on-bus-carrying-israeli-tourists/2012/07/18/gJQA1iUBuW_story.html; "2 Sentenced to Life in Absentia over Bulgarian Bus Bombing," Associated Press, September 21, 2020, https://apnews.com/article/bombings-archive-black-sea-bulgaria-0620d303fdc33bcff08119beba8d6084.

64 *"zone of immunity":* Yaakov Katz, "Barak: Iran's Nuclear Program Nearing 'Immunity Zone,'" *Jerusalem Post*, February 2, 2012, https://www.jpost.com/iranian-threat/news/barak-irans-nuclear-program-nearing-immunity-zone.

65 *a longtime friend:* Leon Panetta, *Worthy Fights: A Memoir of Leadership in War and Peace* (New York: Penguin, 2015), 403–6.

65 *Israel persisted:* "Joint U.S.-Israel Military Exercise Postponed," Reuters, January 15, 2012, https://www.reuters.com/article/us-israel-usa-exercise-idUSTRE80E0Q220120115; "Israel Called Off 2012 Strike on Iran Because It Coincided with Joint US Drill," *Times of Israel*, August 21, 2015, https://www.timesofisrael.com/israel-called-of-2012-strike-on-iran-because-it-coincided-with-joint-us-drill/; Kfir, *"Storm" Toward Iran*, Chap. 17, e-vrit.

65 *"in good conscience":* Panetta, *Worthy Fights*, 403–6.

66 *"waited patiently":* Jeremy Herb, "Netanyahu Says Israel Can't 'Wait Much Longer' on Iran," *The Hill*, March 3, 2012, https://thehill.com/policy/defense/107828-netanyahu-says-israel-cant-wait-much-longer-on-iran/.

66 *offered to mediate:* Jay Solomon, "Secret Dealings with Iran Led to Nuclear Talks," *Washington Post*, June 28, 2015, https://www.wsj.com/articles/iran-wish-list-led-to-u-s-talks-1435537004; Arshad Mohammed and Parisa Hafezi, "U.S., Iran Held Secret Talks on March to Nuclear Deal," Reuters, November 24, 2013, https://www.reuters.com/article/us-iran-nuclear-bilateral-idUSBRE9AN0FB20131124.

67 *Israel reportedly spied:* Samuel Gibbs, "Duqu 2.0: Computer Virus 'Linked to Israel' Found at Iran Nuclear Talks Venue," *The Guardian*, June 11, 2015, https://www.theguardian.com/technology/2015/jun/11/duqu-20-computer-virus-with-traces-of-israeli-code-was-used-to-hack-iran-talks; Adam Entous, "Israel Spied on Iran Nuclear Talks with U.S.," *Washington Post*, March 23, 2015, https://www.wsj.com/articles/israel-spied-on-iran-talks-1427164201; "New Zero-Day Used for Effective Kernel Memory Injection and Stealth," Kaspersky, June 10, 2015, https://securelist.com/the-mystery-of-duqu-2-0-a-sophisticated-cyberespionage-actor-returns/70504/.

67 *"long and boozy dinner":* Ian Black, "Why Israel Is Quietly Cosying Up to Gulf Monarchies," *The Guardian,* March 19, 2009, https://www.theguardian.com/news/2019/mar/19/why-israel-quietly-cosying-up-to-gulf-monarchies-saudi-arabia-uae; Ian Black, "Just Below the Surface: Israel, the Arab Gulf States and the Limits of Cooperation," LSE Middle East Center Report, March 2019; Leslie Susser, "Unlikely Bedfellows," *Jerusalem Report,* https://www.jpost.com/jerusalem-report/the-region/unlikely-bedfellows-337480; "Israeli Mossad Chief 'Secretly Visited Saudi Arabia' in 2014," *The New Arab,* February 13, 2019.

67 *the architect:* Author interviews with Israeli intelligence officials; Yossi Melman, "The Saudi Spy Chief Who Pioneered Secret Relations with Israel," *Haaretz,* July 12, 2022, https://www.haaretz.com/israel-news/2022-07-12/ty-article-magazine/.highlight/prince-bandar-bin-sultan-architect-of-the-relations-between-israel-and-saudi-arabia/00000181-f2fc-de0f-a58b-f3fed5b50000; Eli Podeh, *From Mistress to Known Partner: Israel's Secret Relations with States and Minorities in the Middle East* (Hebrew) (Tel Aviv: Am Oved, 2022), Chap. 11, e-vrit.

68 *"head of state":* Author interviews with Tamir Pardo.

68 *a "very bad deal":* "Netanyahu's Full Speech to Congress," *Times of Israel,* March 3, 2015, https://www.timesofisrael.com/full-text-netanyahus-speech-to-congress/.

68 *a different view:* Author interviews with Tamir Pardo.

68 *"a threat to Israel":* Barak Ravid, "Mossad Chief: Nuclear Iran Not Necessarily Existential Threat to Israel," *Haaretz,* December 29, 2011, https://www.haaretz.com/2011-12-29/ty-article/mossad-chief-nuclear-iran-not-necessarily-existential-threat-to-israel/0000017f-f114-df98-a5ff-f3bde4260000; Massimo Calabresi, "Exclusive: Netanyahu Canceled Intel Briefing for U.S. Senators on Iran Dangers," *Time,* March 14, 2015, https://time.com/3744265/benjamin-netanyahu-israel-iran-nuclear-talks-obama; author interviews with Tamir Pardo.

69 *his own demons:* Sajid Rizvi, "Today When a Bomb Planted Inside a Tape Recorder," UPI, June 27, 1981, https://www.upi.com/Archives/1981/06/27/today-whenA-bomb-planted-inside-a-tape-recorder-in/5746362462400/.

69 *anti-Iran operations:* Author interviews with Israeli intelligence officials.

70 *the deal:* "Iran's Ballistic Missile Program," United Against Iran, March 2022, https://www.unitedagainstnucleariran.com/iran-ballistic-missile-program.

CHAPTER 5: CODE NAME CALLAN

Most author interviews mid-2019–November 2022; some 2016–mid-2019

71 *intense competition for the job:* Ilana Dayan, Interview with Yossi Cohen, *Uvda,* June 10, 2021 (Hebrew), https://www.mako.co.il/mako-vod-keshet/uvda-2021/VOD-20cd4083fc4f971026.htm; author interviews with Israeli intelligence officials.

71 *$10 million:* Shuki Sadeh, "The (Mis)adventures of Mossad Chief Yossi Cohen," Haaretz, April 2, 2021, https://www.haaretz.com/israel-news/2021-04-02/ty-article-magazine/.premium/the-misadventures-of-mossad-chief-yossi-cohen/0000017f-e64b-da9b-a1ff-ee6f7b0b0000.

72 *he met Milchan independently of Netanyahu:* Dayan, Interview with Yossi Cohen; author interviews with Israeli intelligence officials.

72 *$20,000 wedding gift:* Dayan, Interview with Yossi Cohen; Gidi Weitz, "Ex-Mossad Chief Yossi Cohen Returns Cash Gift Received from Billionaire Packer," *Ha'aretz,* April 14, 2022, https://www.haaretz.com/israel-news/2022-04-14/ty-article/.premium/ex-mossad-chief-yossi-cohen-returns-cash-gift-received-from-billionaire-packer/00000180-5bc3-d615-a9bf-dfd3653b0000; author interviews with Israeli intelligence officials.

72 *no need to ask:* Dayan, Interview with Yossi Cohen; author interviews with Israeli intelligence officials.

73 *"Yossi Dossi":* Author interviews with Israeli intelligence officials.

73 *Katamon-Rehavia neighborhoods:* "The Head of the Mossad in a Recording a Year Ago," *Yedioth Ahronoth Hebrew Daily*; Benny Morris, *The Birth of the Palestinian Refugee Problem Revisited* (Cambridge: Cambridge University Press, 2004), 123.

74 *Pardo compartmentalized:* Author interviews with Israeli intelligence officials.

74 *"This Yeshiva":* "The Head of the Mossad in a Recording a Year Ago," *Yedioth Ahronoth Hebrew Daily*; author interviews with Israeli intelligence officials.

74 *unusual push:* Yonah Jeremy Bob, "Spooks with Tzizit: Mossad, Shin Bet, Cyber Haredi Agents Speak for First Time," *Jerusalem Post,* April 16, 2021, https://www.jpost.com/israel-news/spooks-with-tzizit-mossad-shin-bet-cyber-haredi-agents-speak-for-first-time-665192.

75 *fastidiousness about his appearance:* Author interviews with former Mossad officials; Ben Caspit, "New Mossad Chief Brings Touch of Bond, Lots of Reality to the Job," *Al-Monitor,* January 11, 2016, https://www.al-monitor.com/originals/2016/01/israel-mossad-yossi-cohen-new-chief-mideast-chaos-challenge.html#ixzz7osjysjWw.

75 *Israel Security Prize:* Herb Keinon, "PM Names Deputy Mossad Head as New National Security Council Chief," *Jerusalem Post,* August 21, 2013, https://www.jpost.com/Defense/PM-names-deputy-Mossad-head-as-new-National-Security-Council-chief-323829.

75 *His Mossad code name:* Ronen Bergman, "One of the World's Most Mysterious Organizations Gets a New Boss," Ynet, January 5, 2016; author interview with Israeli intelligence sources.

75 *he was considered:* Caspit, "New Mossad Chief Brings Touch of Bond, Lots of Reality to the Job"; author interviews with former Israeli Mossad chiefs Shabtai Shavit and Danny Yatom.

75 *A government report:* Yonah Jeremy Bob, "The Mossad Explodes with Growth While IDF Shrinks—Report," *Jerusalem Post,* August 3, 2020, https://www.jpost.com/israel-news/the-mossad-explodes-with-growth-while-idf-shrinks-comptroller-report-637300.

76 *venture capital fund:* Ori Lewis, "Israel's Mossad Sets Up Fund to Acquire New Spy Techniques," Reuters, June 27, 2017; Herb Keinon, "Israel's Mossad Is Looking for a Few Good Startups," *Jerusalem Post,* June 27, 2017; Libertad Ventures, https://www.libertad.gov.il/.

76 *high-level Israeli delegation:* Gil Ronen, "Top Israeli Delegation 'Visited Riyadh Secretly,'" *7 Israel National News*, March 2, 2016; Gili Cohen, "Israel: Saudi Arabia Gave Written Assurances over Freedom of Passage in Tiran Straits," *Haaretz*, April 12, 2016, https://www.haaretz.com/israel-news/2016-04-12/ty-article/israel-saudi-arabia-assured-freedom-of-passage-in-tiran-straits/0000017f-f7dd-d887-a7ff-fffd39300000.

77 *Saudi pundit:* Salman al-Ansari, "How Israel Can Contribute to Saudi's Vision 2030," *The Hill*, October 11, 2016, https://thehill.com/blogs/pundits-blog/international-affairs/300447-how-israel-can-contribute-to-saudis-vision-2030/.

77 *the mantra:* Herb Keinon, "Jones: Israeli-Palestinian Strife Still Core of ME Ills," *Jerusalem Post*, February 8, 2011, https://www.jpost.com/middle-east/jones-israeli-palestinian-strife-still-core-of-me-ills.

78 *An Israeli diplomat:* Author interviews with Israeli diplomatic sources.

78 *"The Arab states":* Author interviews with former Israeli ambassador to the U.S. Ron Dermer.

78 *a whole new level:* Author interviews with Ron Dermer; Benjamin Netanyahu, *Bibi: My Story* (New York: Threshold, 2022), 525–39; author interviews with Israeli intelligence officials.

79 *"Can you make peace?":* Author interviews with Israeli officials who requested anonymity on this issue.

79 *Netanyahu dispatched Cohen:* Yonah Jeremy Bob, "Headless Meetings: As Netanyahu, Trump Meet, Neither Has a National Security Council Chief," *Jerusalem Post*, February 15, 2017, https://www.jpost.com/israel-news/politics-and-diplomacy/headless-meetings-as-netanyahu-trump-meet-neither-has-a-national-security-council-chief-481579.

79 *the "strategic-diplomatic directorate":* Author interviews with Israeli intelligence officials.

79 *deposed his nephew:* Martin Chulov and Julian Borger, "Saudi King Ousts Nephew to Name Son as First in Line to Throne," June 21, 2017, https://www.theguardian.com/world/2017/jun/21/saudi-king-upends-tradition-by-naming-son-as-first-in-line-to-throne.

79 *MBS has been described:* Author interviews with Israeli intelligence officials; author interviews with Jason Greenblatt; author interviews with Israeli diplomatic officials.

80 *"the new Hitler":* Thomas Friedman, "Saudi Arabia's Arab Spring, at Last," *New York Times*, November 23, 2017, https://www.nytimes.com/2017/11/23/opinion/saudi-prince-mbs-arab-spring.html.

80 *Cohen met with:* Yoav Limor, "How Years of Clandestine Ties Put Jerusalem and Riyadh on a Path to Normalization," *Israel Hayom*, May 29, 2022, https://www.israelhayom.com/2022/05/29/how-years-of-clandestine-ties-put-jerusalem-and-riyadh-on-a-path-to-normalization; author interviews with Israeli intelligence officials.

80 *a brutal, ruthless streak:* Martin Chulov, "'Night of the Beating': Details Emerge of Riyadh Ritz-Carlton Purge," *The Guardian*, November 19, 2020, https://www

.theguardian.com/world/2020/nov/19/saudi-accounts-emerge-of-ritz-carlton-night-of-the-beating; Dan De Luce, Ken Dilanian, and Robert Windrem, "How a Saudi Royal Crushed His Rivals in a 'Shakedown' at the Ritz-Carlton," November 3, 2018, https://www.nbcnews.com/news/mideast/how-saudi-royal-crushed-his-rivals-shakedown-ritz-carlton-n930396.

80 *Saad Hariri:* Alex Ward, "The Mysterious Sudden Resignation of Lebanon's Prime Minister, Explained," *Vox*, November 13, 2017, https://www.vox.com/world/2017/11/13/16631534/lebanon-saudi-arabia-iran-hariri.

80 *ordered the murder:* William Roberts, "MBS Approved Operation to Capture or Kill Khashoggi: US Report," Al Jazeera, February 26, 2021, https://www.aljazeera.com/news/2021/2/26/mbs-oversaw-saudi-killers-of-khashoggi-us-intel-report.

81 *identified Bin Salman:* Author interviews with Israeli intelligence officials.

81 *before Israel could move:* Dayan, Interview with Yossi Cohen; author interviews with Israeli intelligence officials.

81 *a maid found:* Ronen Bergman, "The Dubai Job," *GQ*, January 4, 2011, https://www.gq.com/story/the-dubai-job-mossad-assassination-hamas; Ronen Bergman, *Rise and Kill First: The Secret History of Israel's Targeted Assassinations* (New York: Random House, 2018), Chap. 35, Kindle.

82 *"Did anybody get caught?":* Author interview with Meir Dagan; Ilan Evyatar, "The Art of Espionage: Former Mossad Head Meir Dagan Discusses How Israel Should Respond to the Iranian Nuclear Threat," *Jerusalem Post*, April 5, 2012, https://www.jpost.com/features/magazine-features/the-art-of-espionage-265000.

83 *Mossad's senior man:* Author interviews with Haim Tomer.

83 *Dan Shapiro:* Lawrence Rifkin, "How the UAE and Israel Navigated a Serious Speed Bump in Their Relationship," *The Media Line* (Audio), August 17, 2020, https://themedialine.org/audio/how-the-uae-and-israel-navigated-a-serious-speed-bump-in-their-relationship-audio-interview/.

83 *rebuilding trust:* Author interviews with former Mossad official Haim Tomer.

83 *build strong relations:* Author interviews with Israeli intelligence officials.

84 *Tony Blair:* Ariel Kahana, "Exclusive: Former World Leader Played Key Role in Israel-UAE Deal," *Israel Hayom*, September 11, 2020, https://www.middleeastmonitor.com/20171021-israeli-official-confirms-bin-salman-visited-tel-aviv-last-month/.

84 *paid a discreet visit:* "Israeli Official Confirms: Bin Salman Visited Tel Aviv Last Month," *Middle East Monitor*, October 21, 2017, https://www.middleeastmonitor.com/20171021-israeli-official-confirms-bin-salman-visited-tel-aviv-last-month/; Yasser Okbi, "Did the Saudi Crown Prince Make a Covert Visit to Israel?," *Jerusalem Post*, September 11, 2017, https://www.jpost.com/arab-israeli-conflict/did-the-saudi-crown-prince-make-a-covert-visit-to-israel-504777; author interviews with Israeli intelligence officials; author interviews with former U.S. deputy national security adviser Victoria Coates.

85 *gave an interview:* Amos Harel, "Israeli Military Chief Gives Unprecedented Interview to Saudi Media: 'Ready to Share Intel on Iran,'" *Haaretz*, November 17, 2017, https://www.haaretz.com/israel-news/2017-11-17/ty-article/idf-chief-gives-unprecedented-interview-to-saudi-media/0000017f-e901-d62c-a1ff-fd7bb4dd0000.

85 *Yuval Steinitz:* "Israeli Minister Reveals Covert Contacts with Saudi Arabia," Reuters/*Jerusalem Post*, November 19, 2017, https://www.jpost.com/israel-news/politics-and-diplomacy/israeli-minister-reveals-covert-contacts-with-saudi-arabia-514647.

85 *Arab League summit:* Author interviews with former Middle East negotiations envoy Jason Greenblatt.

86 *traveled to Saudi Arabia:* "Trump Arrives in Saudi Arabia in First Foreign Trip," Al Jazeera, May 20, 2017, https://www.aljazeera.com/news/2017/5/20/trump-arrives-in-saudi-arabia-in-first-foreign-trip.

86 *Trump signed:* Philip Rucker and Karen DeYoung, "Trump Signs 'Tremendous' Deals with Saudi Arabia on His First Day Overseas," *Washington Post*, May 20, 2017, https://www.washingtonpost.com/politics/trump-gets-elaborate-welcome-in-saudi-arabia-embarking-on-first-foreign-trip/2017/05/20/679f2766-3d1d-11e7-a058-ddbb23c75d82_story.html.

86 *skipped Israel:* Ilene Prusher, "Obama Visits Saudi Arabia, Cairo—Why Not Israel," *Christian Science Monitor*, June 3, 2009, https://www.csmonitor.com/World/Middle-East/2009/0603/p06s10-wome.html.

86 *where relations:* Michael D. Shear and Peter Baker, "Saudis Welcome Trump's Rebuff of Obama's Mideast Views," *New York Times*, May 20, 2017, https://www.nytimes.com/2017/05/20/world/middleeast/donald-trump-saudi-arabia.html.

87 *secret visits:* Author interviews with Israeli intelligence sources.

87 *would be ironclad:* Author interviews with Israeli intelligence sources.

87 *secret trips:* Annie Karni, "Kushner Took Unannounced Trip to Saudi Arabia," *Politico*, October 29, 2017, https://www.politico.com/story/2017/10/29/jared-kushner-saudi-arabia-244291; author interviews with Israeli intelligence officials.

88 *didn't know:* Author interviews with Israeli intelligence sources.

CHAPTER 6: THE REVEAL

Most author interviews 2018–November 2022; some 2016–2018

89 *Farsi-reading analysts:* Author interviews with Yarden Vatikai, former senior adviser to the prime minister; David Albright and Sandra Burkhard, *Iran's Perilous Pursuit of Nuclear Weapons* (Washington, D.C.: Institute for Science and International Security, 2021), 9.

89 *a top national secret:* Author interviews with Vatikai; author interviews with former IDF chief Gadi Eisenkot; Benjamin Netanyahu, *Bibi: My Story* (New York: Threshold, 2022), 598–99; author interviews with officials whose identity and background must remain anonymous.

90 *"How you use":* Author interviews with Israeli intelligence officials; Ilana Dayan, Interview with Yossi Cohen, *Uvda*, June 10, 2021 (Hebrew), https://www.mako.co.il/mako-vod-keshet/uvda-2021/VOD-20cd4083fc4f971026.htm; author interviews with Israeli intelligence officials.

90 *his first recruit:* Author interviews with Vatikai.

92 *a rundown:* Ibid.

92 *On top of that:* Author interviews with former Israeli ambassador to the U.K. Mark Regev; author interviews with Vatikai.

92 *naming these names:* Author interviews with Vatikai and Regev.

93 *in trusting them:* Author interviews with Vatikai and Regev; author interviews with officials whose identity and background must remain anonymous.

93 *copies of the originals:* Author interviews with Israeli intelligence officials; author interviews with Vatikai and Regev.

93 *when Cohen called:* Author interview with former U.S. secretary of state Mike Pompeo; author interviews with officials whose identity and background must remain anonymous.

94 *especially bowled over:* Author interviews with Israeli intelligence officials; author interviews with Pompeo and McMaster.

94 *Netanyahu and Cohen showed Trump:* Netanyahu, *Bibi, My Story*, 597–98; author interviews with Israeli intelligence officials; author interviews with former U.S. national security adviser H. R. McMaster; author interviews with Vatikai.

94 *pretty good*: Author interviews with McMaster.

94 *referring to the archive:* Ibid.

95 *a huge justification:* Author interviews with former U.S. national security adviser John Bolton.

95 *Telling the press:* Author interviews with Vatikai and Regev.

96 *setting the scene:* Ibid.

96 *"really important":* Author interview with Regev.

97 *very different thing:* Author interviews with Israeli intelligence officials; author interviews with Vatikai and Regev.

97 *given Iran a pass:* Author interviews with Israeli and U.S. intelligence officials.

98 *in the rehearsal room:* Author interviews with Vatikai.

98 *microphone didn't work:* Author interviews with Vatikai and Regev; Netanyahu press conference, April 30, 2018.

99 *in a black suit:* Netanyahu press conference, April 30, 2018.

99 *political opponents:* Gil Hoffman, "Netanyahu's Iran Presentation Damaged Israel, Says Lapid," *Jerusalem Post*, May 3, 2018, https://www.jpost.com/israel-news/netanyahus-iran-presentation-damaged-israel-says-lapid-553363; Yossi Beilin, "How Netanyahu's Nuclear 'Show' Could Harm Mossad," *Al-Monitor*, May 2, 2018, https://www.al-monitor.com/originals/2018/05/israel-netanyahu-iran-speech-mossad-nuclear-agreement.html.

99 *Some senior officials were furious:* Author interviews with former Mossad chiefs Tamir Pardo, Shabtai Shavit, Danny Yatom; former IDF chief Eisenkot; and former Military Intelligence chief Aharon Ze'evi Farkash.

99 *the operation classified:* Author interviews with Eisenkot and Regev.

100 *Place de l'Étoile:* "Tamir Pardo Talks," *Uvda*, May 31, 2018 (Hebrew), https://www.mako.co.il/mako-vod-keshet/uvda-2018/VOD-d2c7779e1f5b361006.htm.

100 *55,000 pages of documents:* Netanyahu press conference, April 30, 2018; and Albright and Burkhard, *Iran's Perilous Pursuit of Nuclear Weapons*, 9–12.

100 *to make public:* Netanyahu press conference, April 30, 2018; presentation to the

media of Israeli intelligence officials; author interviews with Israeli intelligence officials; author interviews with Vatikai and Regev.

101 *was a map:* Author interviews with Israeli intelligence officials; Netanyahu press conference, April 30, 2018; presentation to the media of Israeli intelligence officials; Albright and Burkhard, *Iran's Perilous Pursuit of Nuclear Weapons*, 9–15 and other sections. The "map" here does not necessarily refer to one single document as much as it does a series of documents which allowed the Mossad to map out a large number of nuclear facilities that it had not previously known about.

101 *a careful analysis:* Netanyahu press conference, April 30, 2018; IAEA December 2015 report on Iran; author interviews with Israeli intelligence officials; Albright and Burkhard, *Iran's Perilous Pursuit of Nuclear Weapons*, 9–15.

101 *shockwave generator:* Netanyahu press conference, April 30, 2018; IAEA December 2015 report on Iran; author interviews with Israeli intelligence officials; Albright and Burkhard, *Iran's Perilous Pursuit of Nuclear Weapons*, 44–45, 73–75, and other sections.

102 *in Semnan province:* Netanyahu press conference, April 30, 2018; Albright and Burkhard, *Iran's Perilous Pursuit of Nuclear Weapons*, 258, 265–68, and other sections.

102 *who warmly welcomed:* U.S. president Donald Trump press conference, May 8, 2018.

103 *"Iran is closer":* Joseph Biden, op-ed, CNN, September 13, 2020, https://edition.cnn.com/2020/09/13/opinions/smarter-way-to-be-tough-on-iran-joe-biden/index.html.

103 *treasure trove:* Author interviews with Israeli intelligence officials.

104 *avoiding conflict:* Based on numerous articles. See, e.g., *The Wall Street Journal Europe*, June 23, 2008, https://www.wsj.com/articles/SB121417304343295263; Julian Borger, "Nuclear WikiLeaks: Cables Show Cosy US Relationship with IAEA Chief," *The Guardian*, November 30, 2010, https://www.theguardian.com/world/julian-borger-global-security-blog/2010/nov/30/iaea-wikileaks.

104 *was viewed initially:* Borger, "Nuclear WikiLeaks."

104 *to be tough:* Julian Borger, "Nuclear Watchdog Chief Accused of Pro-Western Bias over Iran," *The Guardian*, March 22, 2012, https://www.theguardian.com/world/2012/mar/22/nuclear-watchdog-iran-iaea.

104 *closed issue:* IAEA December 2015 report on Iran.

105 *find a way:* Based on numerous articles. See, e.g.: Tzvi Kahn, "Politics v. Protocol: Iran's Nuclear Archive and the IAEA's Responsibilities," Foundation for the Defense of Democracies, August 2019, https://www.fdd.org/wp-content/uploads/2019/08/politics-vs-protocol-irans-nuclear-archive-and-the-iaeas-responsibilities.pdf; Yonah Jeremy Bob, "The IAEA, Mossad, Iran Dance—Analysis," *Jerusalem Post*, March 9, 2021, https://www.jpost.com/israel-news/the-iaea-mossad-iran-dance-analysis-661468.

105 *"It has not demanded":* "Full Text: Prime Minister Benjamin Netanyahu's 2018 U.N. General Assembly Speech," *Haaretz*, September 27, 2018, https://www.haaretz.com/israel-news/2018-09-27/ty-article/full-text-benjamin-netanyahus-2018-un-general-assembly-speech/0000017f-e80f-d97e-a37f-ff6f084a0000.

105 *defiantly defensive speech:* Press Conference of IAEA director general Yukiya Amano, January 30, 2019, https://www.iaea.org/newscenter/statements/remarks-by-director-general-yukiya-amano-at-new-year-reception-30-january-2019.

106 *withholding of those results:* Ongoing communications between the authors and the IAEA; David Albright and Andrea Sticker, "IAEA Visits Turquz-Abad: Too Little, Too Late? The IAEA Has Many More Sites to Inspect Associated with the Iranian Nuclear Archive," Institute for Science and International Security, April 4, 2019, https://isis-online.org/isis-reports/detail/iaea-visits-turquz-abad-too-little-too-late/; François Murphy, "Exclusive: U.N. Nuclear Watchdog Inspects Iran 'Warehouse' Netanyahu Pointed to—Sources," Reuters, April 4, 2019, https://www.reuters.com/article/us-iran-nuclear-inspection-exclusive/exclusive-un-nuclear-watchdog-inspects-iran-warehouse-netanyahu-pointed-to-sources-idUSKCN1RG2B9.

106 *ended those waivers:* Nicole Gaouette and Kylie Atwood, "US Braced for Iranian Response as Oil Crackdown Starts," CNN, May 3, 2019, https://edition.cnn.com/2019/05/02/politics/us-iran-oil-waivers/index.html.

106 *in constant touch:* Author interviews with Israeli intelligence officials.

106 *cross a red line:* Julia Masterson and Kelsey Davenport, "The IAEA's March Reports on Iran's Nuclear Activities Raise Questions," Arms Control Association, March 16, 2020, https://www.armscontrol.org/blog/2020-03-16/iaea-march-reports-iran-nuclear-activities-raise-questions; Iran Watch, "Iran Nuclear Milestones: 1967–2022," May 26, 2022, https://www.iranwatch.org/our-publications/weapon-program-background-report/iran-nuclear-milestones-1967-2022.

CHAPTER 7: AN ALLIANCE EMERGES

Author interviews 2018–November 2022

107 *impressed with the heist:* Author interviews with senior Israeli officials.

107 *"The Arab states":* Author interviews with Jason Greenblatt.

107 *gathering of spy chiefs:* "In Aqaba, Palestine Spymaster Plays Trump Card," *Intelligence Online*, June 27, 2018, (subscription), https://www.intelligenceonline.com/government-intelligence/2018/06/27/in-aqaba-palestine-spymaster-plays-trump-card,108314911-art; "Arab-Israeli Intelligence Meeting in Aqaba to Discuss the Deal of the Century," *Middle East Monitor*, June 29, 2018, https://www.middleeastmonitor.com/20180629-arab-israeli-intelligence-meeting-in-aqaba-to-discuss-the-deal-of-the-century/.

108 *Netanyahu flew to Amman:* Jonathan Lis, "Netanyahu Meets King Abdullah in Amman in First Public Meeting Since 2014," *Haaretz*, June 18, 2018, https://www.haaretz.com/israel-news/2018-06-18/ty-article/netanyahu-met-king-abdullah-in-jordan-for-talks-about-peace/0000017f-e741-df2c-a1ff-ff51eaff0000.

108 *met with MBZ:* Yossi Yehoshua, "Netanyahu Secretly Visited UAE in 2018 to Kick Start Peace Deal," *Yedioth Ahronoth*, January 9, 2020, https://www.ynetnews.com/article/rJUMmuoQP.

108 *infected the phone:* Dana Priest, "A UAE Agency Put Pegasus Spyware on Phone of Jamal Khashoggi's Wife Months Before His Murder, New Forensics Show,"

Washington Post, December 21, 2021, https://www.washingtonpost.com/nation/interactive/2021/hanan-elatr-phone-pegasus/; Suresh Matthew, "NSO and Pegasus' Role in the Killing of Journalist Jamal Khashoggi," *Quint*, July 22, 2021, https://www.thequint.com/entertainment/hot-on-web/nso-pegasus-israeli-spyware-jamal-khashoggi-killing-saudi-arabia#read-more.

108 *a sweetener:* Ronen Bergman and Marc Mazzetti, "Israeli Companies Aided Saudi Spying Despite Khashoggi Killing," *New York Times*, July 17, 2021, https://www.nytimes.com/2021/07/17/world/middleeast/israel-saudi-khashoggi-hacking-nso.html; author interviews with Israeli intelligence sources.

108 *Netanyahu and Cohen intervened:* Ronen Bergman and Marc Mazzetti, Battle for the World's Most Powerful Cyberweapon," *New York Times*, January 28, 2022, https://www.nytimes.com/2022/01/28/magazine/nso-group-israel-spyware.html;author interviews with Israeli intelligence officials.

108 *"strategic ally":* John Hudson, "Saudi Crown Prince Described Journalist as a Dangerous Islamist in Call with White House, Officials Say," *Washington Post*, November 1, 2018, https://www.washingtonpost.com/world/national-security/saudi-crown-prince-described-slain-journalist-as-a-dangerous-islamist-in-call-with-white-house/2018/11/01/b4513e05-2d8e-4533-9cc8-2cabf8bb2d0a_story.html; author interviews with Israeli intelligence sources.

108 *involved in the murder:* "How the Man Behind Khashoggi Murder Ran the Killing via Skype," Reuters, October 23, 2018, https://www.reuters.com/article/us-saudi-khashoggi-adviser-insight/how-the-man-behind-khashoggi-murder-ran-the-killing-via-skype-idUSKCN1MW2HA; Can Erözden, Sena Güler, and Ahmet Salih Alacacı, "Saudi Crown Prince's Men in Khashoggi Killing," Andolu Agency, October 25, 2018, https://www.aa.com.tr/en/middle-east/-saudi-crown-princes-men-in-khashoggi-killing/1293021.

109 *Saudi point man:* David Ignatius, "How a Chilling Saudi Cyberwar Ensnared Jamal Khashoggi," *Washington Post*, December 7, 2018, https://www.washingtonpost.com/opinions/global-opinions/how-a-chilling-saudi-cyberwar-ensnared-jamal-khashoggi/2018/12/07/f5f048fe-f975-11e8-8c9a-860ce2a8148f_story.html?noredirect=on; Amos Harel, Chaim Levinson, and Yaniv Kubovich, "Israeli Cyber Firm Negotiated Advanced Attack Capabilities Sale with Saudis, Haaretz Reveals," *Haaretz*, November 25, 2018, https://www.haaretz.com/israel-news/2018-11-25/ty-article/.premium/israeli-company-negotiated-to-sell-advanced-cybertech-to-the-saudis/0000017f-e184-d568-ad7f-f3effda20000.

109 *traveled to Israel:* Felicia Schwartz, Margherita Stancati, and Summer Said, "Covert Saudi Outreach to Israel Sputters After Journalist's Murder," *Wall Street Journal*, December 18, 2018, https://www.wsj.com/articles/covert-saudi-outreach-to-israel-sputters-after-journalists-murder-11545129001.

109 *an embarrassing breach:* Barak Ravid, "What Really Happened on Netanyahu's Landmark Visit to Oman," *Axios*, February 26, 2020.

109 *"You should not underestimate":* Simeon Kerr and Mehul Srivastava, "Netanyahu in First Israeli State Visit to Oman Since 1996," *The Financial Times*, October 26, 2018.

109 *if Qaboos:* Author interviews with Yossi Cohen and Israeli officials.

109 *Miri Regev:* Aya Batrawy and Josef Federman, "Secret No More: Israel's Outreach to Gulf States Emerges into the Open," *Times of Israel*/Associated Press, October 31, 2018.

110 *"all breaking bread together":* "US Vice President Hails Sight of Netanyahu 'Breaking Bread' with Bahrain, Saudi & Emirati Leaders in Warsaw Conference," *Bahrain Mirror*, February 15, 2019.

110 *posted a tweet:* Josh Lederman, "Netanyahu Appears to Say War with Iran Is Common Goal," NBC News, February 14, 2019, https://www.nbcnews.com/news/world/netanyahu-appears-say-war-iran-common-goal-n971266; "Israeli Leader Hopes to Rally Arabs Against Iran," Associated Press, February 13, 2019, https://apnews.com/article/a7e6e80946024e2db2802e2d1948a2ed.

110 *leak-and-delete diplomacy:* "Bahrain FM: Confronting Iran Is More Important than Palestine," *Middle East Monitor*, February 15, 2019, https://www.middleeastmonitor.com/20190215-bahrain-fm-confronting-iran-is-more-important-than-palestine/.

110 *"in the same room":* Rich Lowry, "How Trump Defied the Experts and Forged a Breakthrough in the Middle East," *National Review*, September 15, 2020, https://www.nationalreview.com/2020/09/how-trump-defied-the-experts-and-forged-a-breakthrough-in-the-middle-east/.

111 *Prince Turki Bin Faisal:* Barak Ravid, "Turki bin Faisal Interview for Israeli Channel 13," YouTube, https://www.youtube.com/watch?v=gWV-6MprsHw.

111 *hinted broadly:* "UAE Official Urges Arab Openness to Israel: Paper," Reuters, March 28, 2019, https://www.reuters.com/article/cnews-us-israel-palestinians-emirates-idCAKCN1R916W-OCATP.

111 *rapidly emerging:* Author interviews with Israeli intelligence officials; David Kirkpatrick, "The Most Powerful Arab Ruler Isn't M.B.S. It's M.B.Z.," *New York Times*, June 2, 2019, https://www.nytimes.com/2019/06/02/world/middleeast/crown-prince-mohammed-bin-zayed.html; David Kirkpatrick, "What to Know About Prince Mohammed bin Zayed, the Arab Ruler Swaying Trump," *New York Times*, June 2, 2019, https://www.nytimes.com/2019/06/02/world/middleeast/prince-mohammed-bin-zayed.html; Robert F. Worth, "Mohammed bin Zayed's Dark Vision of the Middle East's Future," *New York Times*, January 9, 2020, https://www.nytimes.com/2020/01/09/magazine/united-arab-emirates-mohammed-bin-zayed.html.

112 *privately told Jared Kushner:* Jared Kushner, *Breaking History: A White House Memoir* (New York: Broadside, 2022), 251–52.

112 *Kushner then flew:* Ibid., 256–60.

113 *"dead on arrival":* Daniel Estrin, "U.S. Mideast Plan Rejected by Palestinian Leaders, Panned by Former U.S. Envoys," June 24, 2019, https://www.npr.org/2019/06/24/735410331/u-s-mideast-plan-rejected-by-palestinian-leaders-panned-by-former-u-s-envoys; Stephen Kalin, Suleiman Al-Khalidi, and Mohamed Abdellah, "Kushner's Economic Plan for Mideast Peace Faces Broad Arab Rejection," June 23, 2019, https://www.reuters.com/article/us-israel-palestinians-plan-arabs-idUSKCN1TN0RW.

113 *on-the-record interviews:* "Bahrain Foreign Minister: Palestinians Made a Mistake by Boycotting Peace Conference," *Axios*, June 26, 2019, https://www.axios.com/2019/06/26/bahrain-peace-conference-foreign-minister-israel-palestine; Raphael Ahren, "Bahrain FM to Times of Israel: Israel Is Here to Stay, and We Want Peace with It," *Times of Israel*, June 26, 2019, https://www.timesofisrael.com/bahrain-fm-to-times-of-israel-israel-is-here-to-stay-and-we-want-peace-with-it/.

114 *prayed in the Bahrain Synagogue:* Herb Keinon, "A Synagogue in Bahrain? Not Your Average Prayer in the Persian Gulf," *Jerusalem Post*, June 26, 2019, https://www.jpost.com/international/a-synagogue-in-bahrain-not-your-average-prayer-in-the-persian-gulf-593740; author interviews with Jason Greenblatt.

114 *post a military liaison:* https://www.atlanticcouncil.org/wp-content/uploads/2023/03/ImprovingGulfSec_031023_444-Final.pdf.

114 *Introducing Cohen:* "Yossi Cohen, Director of the Mossad, Herzliya Conference, 2019," YouTube, https://www.youtube.com/watch?v=wJvHuyAA1Jw.

114 *"awarded to the Mossad team":* Ibid.

115 *"identifies a rare opportunity":* Ibid.

115 *knew they were ready*: Author interviews with Israeli intelligence officials.

116 *a massive strike:* Ben Hubbard, "Missile Attack in Syria Reportedly Kills at Least 16, Raising Regional Tensions," *New York Times*, April 30, 2018, https://www.nytimes.com/2018/04/30/world/middleeast/strikes-syria-iran-israel.html; Louisa Loveluck and Loveday Morris, "Suspected Israeli Strikes Hit Iran-Linked Targets in Syria, Escalating Regional Tensions," *Washington Post*, April 30, 2018, https://www.washingtonpost.com/world/middle_east/suspected-israeli-strikes-hit-iran-linked-targets-in-syria-escalate-regional-tensions/2018/04/30/8fe7437c-4c5b-11e8-b966-bfb0da2dad62_story.html.

CHAPTER 8: DEATH OF THE SHADOW COMMANDER

Most author interviews early 2020–November 2022; some 2016–early 2020

117 *often hint:* Author interviews with Israeli intelligence officials and other government officials; Netanyahu press conference April 30, 2018; presentation to the media of Israeli intelligence officials; Ilana Dayan, Interview with Yossi Cohen, *Uvda*, June 10, 2021 (Hebrew), https://www.mako.co.il/mako-vod-keshet/uvda-2021/VOD-20cd4083fc4f971026.htm.

117 *took place on January 3, 2020:* "Iran's Soleimani and Iraq's Muhandis Killed in Air Strike: Militia Spokesman," Reuters, January 3, 2020, https://www.reuters.com/article/us-iraq-security-blast-soleimani-idUSKBN1Z201C.

117 *blood of hundreds:* Prince Michael of Liechtenstein, *GIS Reports Online*, January 7, 2020, https://www.gisreportsonline.com/r/soleimani-killing/.

117 *the "Shadow Commander":* Dexter Filkins, "The Shadow Commander: Qassem Suleimani Is the Iranian Operative Who Has Been Reshaping the Middle East. Now He's Directing Assad's War in Syria," *The New Yorker*, September 23, 2013, https://www.newyorker.com/magazine/2013/09/30/the-shadow-commander.

118 *designated terror entities:* "Designation of Iranian Entities and Individuals for Proliferation Activities and Support for Terrorism," U.S. Department of State, January 20, 2007, https://2001-2009.state.gov/r/pa/prs/ps/2007/oct/94193.htm.

118 *in its crosshairs:* Gen. Stanley McChrystal, "Iran's Deadly Puppet Master," *Foreign Policy Magazine*, Winter 2019, https://foreignpolicy.com/gt-essay/irans-deadly-puppet-master-qassem-suleimani/.

118 *ruled against:* Christopher Dickey, Noga Tarnopolsky, Erin Banco, and Betsy Swan, "Why Obama, Bush, and Bibi All Passed on Killing Soleimani," *Daily Beast*, January 3, 2020, https://www.thedailybeast.com/why-obama-bush-and-bibi-all-passed-on-killing-qassem-soleimani; Reis Thebault, "Iranian Agents Once Plotted to Kill the Saudi Ambassador in D.C. The Case Reads Like a Spy Thriller," *Washington Post*, January 4, 2020, https://www.washingtonpost.com/history/2020/01/04/iran-agents-once-plotted-kill-saudi-ambassador-dc-case-reads-like-spy-thriller/.

119 *packed the boulevards:* "Millions Turn Out in Iran for General Soleimani's Funeral," BBC New, January 7, 2020, https://www.youtube.com/watch?v=1ndfa37Y4-0; "Dozens Killed in Stampede at Qassem Soleimani's Funeral in Iran," Al Jazeera, January 8, 2020, https://www.aljazeera.com/news/2020/1/8/dozens-killed-in-stampede-at-qassem-soleimanis-funeral-in-iran; Parisa Hafezi and Babak Dehghanpisheh, "Iran's Leader Khamenei Weeps at General's Funeral as Nation Grieves," Reuters, January 6, 2020, https://www.reuters.com/article/us-iraq-security-iran-khamenei-idUSKBN1Z50IU.

119 *went so far:* Melissa Quin, "David Petraeus: 'Impossible to Overstate' Significance of Soleimani Strike," CBS News, January 5, 2020, https://www.cbsnews.com/news/general-david-petraeus-impossible-to-overstate-the-significance-of-soleimani-strike-face-the-nation/.

119 *a major obsession:* Author interviews with Israeli intelligence officials; Mark T. Esper, *A Sacred Oath: Memoirs of a Secretary of Defense During Extraordinary Times* (New York: William Morrow, 2022), 124.

119 *"ring of fire":* Author interviews with many Israeli intelligence and other government officials; Barbara Plett Usher, "Qassem Soleimani: Crisis Puts Mid-East Friends and Foes on Edge," BBC News, January 11, 2020, https://www.bbc.com/news/world-middle-east-51048117.

120 *founded Hezbollah:* Kali Robinson, "What Is Hezbollah," Council on Foreign Relation, updated May 25, 2022, https://www.cfr.org/backgrounder/what-hezbollah; "About Hezbollah," Hezbollah.org, https://hezbollah.org/about-hezbollah.

120 *plan to smuggle:* Amos Gilboa, edited by Yonah Jeremy Bob, *A Raid on the Red Sea* (Sterling, VA: Potomac Books, 2021), 14–19.

120 *seemingly nonmilitary aircraft:* Yaghoub Fazeli, "Iran's Mahan Air Took 'Illicit Cargo' to Syria with Soleimani: Pilot," deleted report, Al Arabiya, https://english.alarabiya.net/News/middle-east/2020/06/19/Iran-s-Mahan-Air-took-illicit-cargo-to-Syria-with-Soleimani-Pilot-deleted-report; Tal Beeri, "Mahan Air—Smuggling Weapons into Syria and Lebanon in Service of the Iranian Quds Force," Alma Center, December 2022, https://israel-alma.org/2022/12/14/mahan

-air-smuggling-weapons-into-syria-and-lebanon-in-service-of-the-iranian-quds-force/.

120 *played a major role:* Adil al-Salmi, "Soleimani Reveals Details of Role He Played in the 2006 Israel-Hezbollah War," *Asharq al-Awsat,* October 3, 2019, https://english.aawsat.com//home/article/1929396/soleimani-reveals-details-role-he-played-2006-israel-hezbollah-war; Raphael Ofek and Pesach Malovany, "Iran Behind the Scenes During the Second Israel-Lebanon War," Begin-Sadat Center for Strategic Studies; Bar-Ilan University Mideast Security and Policy Studies No. 182, https://besacenter.org/wp-content/uploads/2020/11/182-Ofek-ENGLISH-FINAL.pdf.

121 *interview with Iranian media:* "General Soleimani Reveals Untold Facts of 2006 Lebanon War," *Tehran Times,* October 2, 2019, https://www.tehrantimes.com/news/440726/General-Soleimani-Reveals-Untold-Facts-of-2006-Lebanon-War.

121 *systematic campaign:* Amos Harel, "Smuggled in Suitcases: Iran's Covert Scheme to Upgrade Hezbollah's Rocket Arsenal Revealed," *Haaretz,* February 28, 2019, https://www.haaretz.com/middle-east-news/iran/2019-02-28/ty-article/.premium/irans-covert-scheme-to-upgrade-hezbollahs-rocket-arsenal-revealed/0000017f-efdb-d8a1-a5ff-ffdbef9f0000.

121 *one incident*: Ronen Bergman, *Rise and Kill First: The Secret History of Israel's Targeted Assassinations* (New York: Random House, 2018), Chap 34, Kindle; Adam Entous and Evan Osnos, "Qassem Suleimani and How Nations Decide to Kill," February 3, 2020, https://www.newyorker.com/magazine/2020/02/10/qassem-suleimani-and-how-nations-decide-to-kill.

122 *in the spare tire:* Bergman, *Rise and Kill First,* Chap 34, Kindle.

122 *was thrilled:* Author interviews with Israeli intelligence officials.

123 *to briefly take over:* "Hezbollah's Threat to the Israeli Home Front," IDF, January 2018, https://www.idf.il/en/mini-sites/hezbollah/hezbollah-s-threat-to-the-israeli-home-front/; Avi Issacharoff, "Hezbollah's Secret, Grandiose Plan to Invade Israel in the Post-Tunnel Era," *Times of Israel,* June 30, 2019, https://www.timesofisrael.com/hezbollahs-secret-grandiose-plan-to-invade-israel-in-the-post-tunnel-era.

123 *missed opportunity:* Ben Caspit, "Former IDF Chief Says Israel Came Close to Killing Soleimani Before US," January 28, 2020, https://www.al-monitor.com/originals/2022/01/former-idf-chief-says-israel-came-close-killing-soleimani-us#ixzz7p4vWOGpu.

124 *regularly pressing the issue:* Esper, *A Sacred Oath,* 124; author interviews with Bolton and Coates; author interviews with Israeli intelligence officials; David Kirkpatrick, Ronen Bergman, and Farnaz Fassihi, "Brazen Killings Expose Iran's Vulnerabilities as It Struggles to Respond," *New York Times,* April 13, 2021, https://www.nytimes.com/2020/11/28/world/middleeast/iran-assassinations-nuclear-israel.html; Jack Murphy and Zach Dorfman, "'Conspiracy Is Hard': Inside the Trump Administration's Secret Plan to Kill Qassem Soleimani," *Yahoo News,* May 8, 2021, https://news.yahoo.com/conspiracy-is-hard-inside-the-trump-administrations-secret-plan-to-kill-qassem-soleimani-090058817.html;

Carol E. Lee and Courtney Kube, "Trump Authorized Soleimani's Killing 7 Months Ago, with Conditions," NBC News, January 13, 2020, https://www.nbcnews.com/politics/national-security/trump-authorized-soleimani-s-killing-7-months-ago-conditions-n1113271; author interviews with officials whose identity and background must remain anonymous.

124 *constantly updated information:* Author interviews with former IDF intelligence chief Hayman and other Israeli intelligence officials.

124 *Perhaps in response:* Author interviews with multiple Israeli intelligence officials.

124 *"question for the lawyers":* Murphy and Dorfman, "'Conspiracy Is Hard.'"

124 *things changed:* Author interviews with Bolton, McMaster, and Deputy National Security Adviser Victoria Coates; author interviews with Israeli intelligence officials; Murphy and Dorfman, "'Conspiracy Is Hard'"; Lee and Kube, "Trump Authorized Soleimani's Killing 7 Months Ago, with Conditions"; author interviews with former secretary of defense Mark Esper.

124 *"watered down":* Murphy and Dorfman, "'Conspiracy Is Hard,'" and confirmed by author interview with Coates.

124 *"a bigger scale":* Murphy and Dorfman, "'Conspiracy Is Hard.'"; author interviews with Israeli intelligence officials.

125 *could get Iran:* Author interviews with Coates, McMaster, and Bolton.

125 *"extremely provocative":* Author interviews with Coates, Bolton, and Murphy; Dorfman, "'Conspiracy Is Hard'"; Lee and Kube, "Trump Authorized Soleimani's Killing 7 Months Ago, with Conditions"; Esper, *A Sacred Oath*, 128, 133–36; author interviews with Israeli intelligence officials.

125 *ultimately behind:* Author interviews with Coates, McMaster, and Bolton; Lee and Kube, Trump Authorized Soleimani's Killing 7 Months Ago, with Conditions"; Esper, *A Sacred Oath*, 128, 133–36; author interviews with Israeli intelligence officials.

125 *urging Trump to kill:* Author interviews with Esper, Bolton, and Coates; Esper, *A Sacred Oath*, 70–75, 119–22.

126 *"there was Abqaiq":* Author interviews with Coates, Esper, and Bolton.

126 *Trump's handling:* Author interviews with Bolton.

126 *presented with four options:* Murphy and Dorfman, "'Conspiracy Is Hard'"; author interviews with U.S. national security officials.

127 *only shortly before:* "IRGC Foils Plots to Assassinate General Soleimani," Iranian Tasnim News Agency, October 3, 2019, https://www.tasnimnews.com/en/news/2019/10/03/2110588/irgc-foils-plot-to-assassinate-general-soleimani.

128 *a conference call:* Author interview with Esper; Esper, *A Sacred Oath*, 146–49.

128 *Opponents of an assassination:* Author interviews with Pompeo, Esper, and Coates; Esper, *A Sacred Oath*, 133–36, 146–49.

129 *Esper recounted it:* Author interviews with Esper and Coates; Esper, *A Sacred Oath*, 146–49.

129 *"had been pressing":* Author interviews with Esper; Esper, *A Sacred Oath*, 124, 133–36, 146–49.

130 "the decisive moment"*:* Author interviews with Esper, Coates, and Bolton; Esper, *A Sacred Oath*, 146–49.

130 *"really thought":* Author interview with Coates.

131 *Israeli intelligence had provided:* Murphy and Dorfman, "'Conspiracy Is Hard.'"

131 *at least three times:* Ibid.

131 *taking their places:* Ibid.; author interviews with Coates.

132 *emerged at the top:* Murphy and Dorfman, "'Conspiracy Is Hard'"; Ken Dilanian and Courtney Kube, "Airport Informants, Overhead Drones: How the U.S. Killed Soleimani," NBC News, January 10, 2020, https://www.nbcnews.com/news/mideast/airport-informants-overhead-drones-how-u-s-killed-soleimani-n1113726.

132 *using data provided:* Murphy and Dorfman, "'Conspiracy Is Hard'"; author interviews with Coates.

132 *told the story:* Numerous reports: see, e.g., "Trump Gives Dramatic Account of Soleimani's Last Minutes Before Death," Reuters/CNN, January 18, 2020, https://www.reuters.com/article/us-usa-trump-iran-idUSKBN1ZH0G3.

133 *the three teams:* Murphy and Dorfman, "'Conspiracy Is Hard'"; author interviews with U.S. national security officials.

133 *a huge barrage:* "Iran Launches Missile Attacks on US Facilities in Iraq," Al Jazeera, January 8, 2020, https://www.aljazeera.com/news/2020/1/8/iran-launches-missile-attacks-on-us-facilities-in-iraq.

133 *Soleimani was replaced:* Numerous interviews with Israeli and U.S. intelligence officials.

134 *steadfast in its wish:* Esper, *A Sacred Oath*, 128; author interviews with Bolton, Coates, and Israeli intelligence officials.

CHAPTER 9: CYBER WINTER IS HERE

Most author interviews 2018–November 2022; some 2016–2018

135 *a water network:* "Critical-Infrastructure Attack Attempted Against Israeli Water Supply," Team 82 blog, April 27, 2020, https://claroty.com/team82/blog/critical-infrastructure-attack-attempted-against-israeli-water-supply; Joby Warrick and Ellen Nakashima, "Foreign Intelligence Officials Say Attempted Cyberattack on Israeli Water Utilities Linked to Iran," *Washington Post*, May 8, 2020, https://www.washingtonpost.com/national-security/intelligence-officials-say-attempted-cyberattack-on-israeli-water-utilities-linked-to-iran/2020/05/08/f9ab0d78-9157-11ea-9e23-6914ee410a5f_story.html; Aron Heller, "Israeli Cyber Chief: Major Attack on Water Systems Thwarted," Associated Press, May 28, 2020, https://apnews.com/article/63c081ec091f4c1e3f438ee35243efe0; author interviews with Israeli water industry officials.

136 *"very big damage":* Yonah Jeremy Bob, "Israeli Cyber Czar Warns of More Attacks from Iran," *Jerusalem Post*, May 28, 2020, https://www.jpost.com/israel-news/israeli-cyber-czar-warns-of-more-attacks-from-iran-629577.

136 *"even in war":* "Iran Cyberattack on Israel's Water Supply Could Have Sickened Hundreds—Report," *Times of Israel*/Channel 13, June 1, 2020, https://www.timesofisrael.com/iran-cyberattack-on-israels-water-supply-could-have-sickened-hundreds-report/.

136 *political officials' phones:* Gil Hoffman, "Iranian Intelligence Hacked Benny Gantz's phone—Report," *Jerusalem Post,* March 14, 2019, https://www.jpost.com/breaking-news/iranian-intelligence-hacks-benny-gantzs-phone-583453.

137 *"these air gaps":* Yonah Jeremy Bob, "Ex-Cyber Officials: Iran May Change Aggressive Policies Until Licks Wounds," *Jerusalem Post,* July 11, 2020, https://www.jpost.com/middle-east/a-one-two-or-six-punch-634593.

137 *Israel's response:* David Siman Tov and Shmuel Even, "A New Level in the Cyber War Between Israel and Iran," *INSS Insight,* June 3, 2020, https://www.inss.org.il/publication/iran-israel-cyber-war/; Bennett as defense minister: author interviews with Israeli intelligence officials.

138 *a sudden halt:* Joby Warrick and Ellen Nakashima, "Officials: Israel Linked to a Disruptive Cyberattack on Iranian Port Facility," *Washington Post,* May 18, 2020, https://www.washingtonpost.com/national-security/officials-israel-linked-to-a-disruptive-cyberattack-on-iranian-port-facility/2020/05/18/9d1da866-9942-11ea-89fd-28fb313d1886_story.html; Tov and Even, "A New Level in the Cyber War Between Israel and Iran"; Bob, "Israeli Cyber Czar Warns of More Attacks from Iran."

138 *"a long path":* Anna Ahronheim, "IDF Honors Troops for Successful Operation After Iran Cyberattack," *Jerusalem Post,* June 25, 2020, https://www.jpost.com/israel-news/following-iran-cyberattack-idf-honors-troops-for-successful-operation-632728.

139 *would not be tolerated:* Author interviews with Israeli intelligence officials; Tov and Even, "A New Level in the Cyber War Between Israel and Iran"; author interviews with Israeli intelligence officials.

139 *employing offensive cyber:* Author interview with former senior IDF official; Yoav Zitun, "Israeli Officer Reveals Intricate Details of IDF's First Ever Cyber Attack," Ynet, October 16, 2022, https://www.ynetnews.com/magazine/article/sja8fftqi.

139 *knowledge transfer:* "Threat Profile Israel," Hunt & Hackett, https://www.huntandhackett.com/threats/israel.

139 *one of the first:* Author interviews with Israeli cyber initiative founder Yitzhak Ben Israel and with former Israeli cyber chief Buky Carmeli; Netanyahu speech at Cybertech Conference in Tel Aviv, March 3, 2022.

139 *was testing:* Author interviews with Carmeli.

140 *cyberespionage operation:* "The Iran Primer, Israel-Iran Cyber War, Gas Station Attack," United States Institute for Peace, updated: February 24, 2022; original: November 2, 2021, https://iranprimer.usip.org/blog/2021/nov/02/israel-iran-cyber-war-gas-station-attack#:~:text=Iran%20blamed%20Israel%20and%20the,fuel%20at%20a%20subsidized%20price.

140 *most advanced cyber campaigns:* Ibid.

140 *launched by MuddyWater:* Ibid.

140 *"cyber winter":* Author interviews with former Israeli cyber chief Yigal Unna.

140 *given a tour:* Authors' tour of Israeli cyber authority command center, December 2020.

141 *"among the two strongest":* Author interviews with Unna.

141 *provides insurance:* Yonah Jeremy Bob, "Cyber Authority to Victims Post-Shirbit Hack: Get New Identity Cards," *Jerusalem Post*, December 6, 2020, https://www.jpost.com/breaking-news/shirbit-hackers-to-leak-more-documents-by-9-am-if-money-not-received-651276.

141 *"a massive attack":* Ibid.

142 *could sometimes be accessed:* Ibid.

143 *use of social media:* Gabi Siboni and Sami Kronenfeld, "Iran and Cyberspace Warfare," *INSS Journal*, December 2012, https://www.inss.org.il/wp-content/uploads/systemfiles/MASA4-3Engd_Siboni%20and%20Kronenfeld.pdf.

143 *fourteen Iranian facilities:* Paulius Ilevičius, "Stuxnet Explained—The Worm That Went Nuclear," Nord VPN Cybersecurity Blog, March 10, 2022, https://nordvpn.com/blog/stuxnet-virus/#:~:text=The%20worm%20managed%20to%20infect,various%0ifrastructure%20and%20nation%2Dstates; David Kushner, "The Real Story of Stuxnet: How Kaspersky Lab Tracked Down the Malware That Stymied Iran's Nuclear-Fuel Enrichment Program," February 28, 2013, https://spectrum.ieee.org/the-real-story-of-stuxnet.

144 *security budget by 1,200 percent:* Natasha Bertrand, "Iran Is Building a Non-nuclear Threat Faster than Experts 'Would Have Ever Imagined,'" *Business Insider*, March 27, 2015, https://www.businessinsider.com/irans-cyber-army-2015-3; Yonah Jeremy Bob, "How the IRGC Overtook Iran's Intelligence Ministry," *Jerusalem Post*, November 9, 2020, https://www.jpost.com/middle-east/how-the-irgc-overtook-irans-intelligence-ministry-648542, quoting Raz Zimmt, "The Intelligence Organization of the IRGC: A Major Iranian Intelligence Apparatus," Meir Amit Intelligence and Terrorism Information Center, November 5, 2020, https://www.terrorism-info.org.il/app/uploads/2020/11/E_269_20.pdf.

144 *"integrating cyber operations":* Eric Auchard, "Once 'Kittens' in Cyber Spy World, Iran Gains Prowess: Security Experts," Reuters, September 20, 2017, https://www.reuters.com/article/us-iran-cyber-idUKKCN1BV1VA.

144 *more than two hundred companies:* See, e.g., Duncan Riley, "Microsoft: Iranian Hackers Have Caused Hundreds of Millions of Dollars in Damage," *Silicon Angle*, March 6, 2019, https://siliconangle.com/2019/03/06/microsoft-claims-iranian-hackers-caused-hundreds-millions-damage/.

145 *elected Iran's president:* Yonah Jeremy Bob, "Ebrahim Raisi Takes Over as Iran's New President," *Jerusalem Post*, August 3, 2021, https://www.jpost.com/middle-east/iran-news/khamenei-to-endorse-raisi-today-as-new-iranian-president-675695.

145 *phishing emails to medical researchers:* Joshua Miller, "Bad Blood: TA453 Targets US and Israeli Medical Research Personnel in Credential Phishing Campaigns," *Proofpoint*, March 30, 2021, https://www.proofpoint.com/uk/blog/threat-insight/badblood-ta453-targets-us-and-israeli-medical-research-personnel-credential.

145 *another series of hacks:* "The Iran Primer, Israel-Iran Cyber War, Gas Station Attack," United States Institute for Peace.

145 *Israel Aerospace Industries:* Yonah Jeremy Bob, "Suspected Iranian Cyberattack

Targets Israel Aerospace Industries," *Jerusalem Post*, December 20, 2020, https://www.jpost.com/breaking-news/suspected-iranian-cyberattack-targets-israel-aerospace-industries-652731.

145 *into disarray:* "The Iran Primer, Israel-Iran Cyber War, Gas Station Attack," United States Institute for Peace; "Hackers Breach Iran Rail Network, Disrupt Service," Reuters/*Jerusalem Post*, July 9, 2021, https://www.jpost.com/breaking-news/severe-disruptions-in-irans-railway-network-cyber-attacks-suspected-673376.

146 *4,300 gas stations:* "The Iran Primer, Israel-Iran Cyber War, Gas Station Attack," United States Institute for Peace; Farnaz Fassihi and Ronen Bergman, "Israel and Iran Broaden Cyberwar to Attack Civilian Targets," *New York Times*, November 27, 2021, https://www.nytimes.com/2021/11/27/world/middleeast/iran-israel-cyber-hack.html; assorted Iranian media.

146 *Khamenei's home neighborhood:*, "The Iran Primer, Israel-Iran Cyber War, Gas Station Attack", United States Institute for Peace; Fassihi and Bergman, "Israel and Iran Broaden Cyberwar to Attack Civilian Targets"; assorted Iranian media.

146 *a plot:* "The Iran Primer, Israel-Iran Cyber War, Gas Station Attack," United States Institute for Peace; assorted Iranian media.

147 *had been reconnected:* "The Iran Primer, Israel-Iran Cyber War, Gas Station Attack," United States Institute for Peace; assorted Iranian media.

147 *got the blame:* "Iran Blames Foreign Country for Cyberattack on Petrol Stations," BBC News, October 27, 2021, https://www.bbc.com/news/world-middle-east-59062907.

147 *international oil sales:* Fassihi and Bergman, "Israel and Iran Broaden Cyberwar to Attack Civilian Targets"; assorted Iranian media.

148 *threatened to leak:* Yonah Jeremy Bob, "LGBT Dating Site Permanently Removed from Internet in Fight Against Black Shadow," *Jerusalem Post*, November 11, 2021, https://www.jpost.com/israel-news/atraf-website-permanently-removed-from-internet-in-fight-against-black-shadow-684665.

148 *Israeli bus companies:* Ben Zion Gad, "'Black Shadow' Hackers Leak Data from Israeli LGBT App," *Jerusalem Post*, October 31, 2022, https://www.jpost.com/israel-news/iranian-hackers-breach-israeli-company-cyberserve-683529; *Times of Israel* staff and Associated Press, "Israel Cyber Authority Says It Warned Hosting Company It Was Vulnerable to Hack," *Times of Israel*, October 21, 2021, https://www.timesofisrael.com/israel-cyber-authority-says-it-warned-hosting-company-it-was-vulnerable-to-hack/.

149 *were compromised:* Tzvi Joffre, "Israeli Hospital Targeted by Ransomware Attack," *Jerusalem Post*, October 13, 2021, https://www.jpost.com/breaking-news/hillel-yaffe-hospital-targeted-by-ransomware-attack-681842. Although ultimately the hackers of the hospital were determined to be Chinese criminals, even the fear of Iran having hacked medical infrastructure altered the playing field for Israel.

149 *warned the company:* Author interviews with Unna; Ronen Bergman, "The Outgoing National Cyber Chief: 'You Don't See It, There Are No Tanks in the Streets—But We Are at War'" (Hebrew), *Yediot Ahronot*, January 14, 2022, https://www.ynet.co.il/news/article/ry0xndphy.

149 *but not private sector:* Author interviews with Unna and with Israeli chief cyber legal adviser Amit Ashkenazi.

150 *there's an asymmetry:* "Transcript: Kevin Mandia on *Face the Nation*," CBS News, December 20, 2020, https://www.cbsnews.com/news/transcript-kevin-mandia-on-face-the-nation-december-20-2020/; Yonah Jeremy Bob, "Cyber Warfare 2022 Will Be 2021 on Steroids—Analysis," *Jerusalem Post,* January 3, 2022, https://www.jpost.com/cybertech/article-691438.

150 *old cell phone:* Yonah Jeremy Bob, "Iran's info. on Mossad Chief Barnea Is Old—Ex-Mossad Chief Yatom," *Jerusalem Post,* March 17, 2022, https://www.jpost.com/middle-east/iran-news/article-701594.

CHAPTER 10: OPPORTUNITY FROM STRANGE QUARTERS

Author interviews early 2020–November 2022

151 *"extensive and intensive contacts":* "Netanyahu Says Israel, UAE to Cooperate in Fight Against Coronavirus," Reuters, June 25, 2020, https://www.reuters.com/article/health-coronavirus-israel-gulf-idUSL8N2E25L0.

151 *"creates opportunities":* Ronen Bergman and Ben Hubbard, "Israel Announces Partnership with U.A.E., Which Throws Cold Water on It," *New York Times,* June 25, 2020, updated June 26, 2020, https://www.nytimes.com/2020/06/25/world/middleeast/israel-united-arab-emirates-coronavirus.html.

151 *muted tone:* Ibid.

152 *the Mossad was drafted:* "Mossad Agents Help to Strengthen Israel's Fight Against Covid-19," Sheba Medical Center, https://www.shebaonline.org/mossad-agents-help-to-strengthen-israels-fight-against-covid-19/; author interviews with Israeli officials; Yonah Jeremy Bob, "Exclusive: As Trump Exits, the Full Mossad Story on Normalization into Focus," *Jerusalem Post,* January 20, 2021, https://www.jpost.com/middle-east/exclusive-as-trump-exits-the-full-mossad-story-on-normalization-into-focus-656108; Yonah Jeremy Bob, "Mossad's Yossi Cohen Goes to War with Coronavirus and Iran," *Jerusalem Post,* March 26, 2020, https://www.jpost.com/israel-news/mossads-yossi-cohen-goes-to-war-with-coronavirus-and-iran-622517; Yonah Jeremy Bob, "Mossad Obtains 10 Million More Protective Masks for Israel," *Jerusalem Post,* March 30, 2020, https://www.jpost.com/israel-news/mossad-bought-10-million-coronavirus-masks-last-week-622890; Maayan Jaffe-Hoffman and Yonah Jeremy Bob, "Mossad Brings 100,000 Incomplete Coronavirus Test Kits to Israel," *Jerusalem Post,* March 21, 2020, https://www.jpost.com/health-science/mossad-brought-100000-coronavirus-tests-to-israel-report-621532.

152 *to acquire 10 million surgical masks:* "Mossad Agents Help to Strengthen Israel's Fight Against Covid-19," Sheba Medical Center; author interviews with Israeli officials; Bob, "Exclusive: As Trump Exits, the Full Mossad Story on Normalization into Focus"; Bob, "Mossad's Yossi Cohen Goes to War with Coronavirus and Iran"; Bob, "Mossad Obtains 10 Million More Protective Masks for Israel"; Jaffe-Hoffman and Bob, "Mossad Brings 100,000 Incomplete Coronavirus Test Kits to Israel."

153 *had written Netanyahu's speech:* Author interviews with Israeli intelligence officials.

153 *Netanyahu had been promising:* Oliver Holmes, "Netanyahu Vows to Annex Large Parts of Occupied West Bank," *The Guardian*, https://www.theguardian.com/world/2019/sep/10/netanyahu-vows-annex-large-parts-occupied-west-bank-trump.

154 *the political portion:* Ben Gittleson, "President Trump Unveils Middle East Peace Plan Embraced by Israel, Rejected by Palestinians," ABC News, January 28, 2020, https://abcnews.go.com/Politics/president-trump-unveils-middle-east-peace-plan-embraced/story?id=68586820.

154 *the West Bank annexation:* Dany Tirza, "Among the Maps: President Trump's Vision vs. an Israeli Proposal," Fikra Forum, https://www.washingtoninstitute.org/policy-analysis/among-maps-president-trumps-vision-vs-israeli-proposal.

154 *ran into stiff opposition:* "King Abdullah of Jordan Warns of 'Massive Conflict' if Israel Proceeds with Annexation," *Arab Weekly*, May 16, 2020, https://thearabweekly.com/king-abdullah-jordan-warns-massive-conflict-if-israel-proceeds-annexation; Michael Safi and Oliver Holmes, "Arab Leaders Denounce Netanyahu's Plan to Annex Palestinian Territories," *The Guardian*, September 11, 2019, https://www.theguardian.com/world/2019/sep/11/arab-leaders-denounce-netanyahu-plan-annex-palestinian-territories-israel; Guy Faulconbridge and Jeffrey Heller, "UK PM Tells Israel: Do Not Annex Parts of the Occupied West Bank," Reuters, July 1, 2020, https://www.reuters.com/article/israel-palestinians-annexation-britain-idINKBN2424XL.

154 *settlers were opposed:* David M. Halbfinger and Adam Rasgon, "Netanyahu's Annexation Plans Meet Surprise Opponent: Israeli Settlers," *New York Times*, June 1, 2020, https://www.nytimes.com/2020/06/01/world/middleeast/israel-annex-netanyahu-westbank.html.

154 *"President Trump's vision":* Barak Ravid, "West Bank Annexations Must Come in Context of Palestinian State, White House Tells Israel," *Axios*, https://www.axios.com/2020/04/30/israel-west-bank-annexation-netanyahu-trump-plan; author interviews with Jason Greenblatt.

154 *"The U.S. wants":* Ravid, "West Bank Annexations Must Come in Context of Palestinian State, White House Tells Israel."

154 *using its veto:* Lahav Harkov, "Kushner: Trump Admin Threatened to Allow Sanctions if Israel Annexed Parts of West Bank," *Jerusalem Post*, August 2, 2022, https://www.jpost.com/arab-israeli-conflict/article-713731.

155 *"really dangerous":* Sam Zieve Cohen, "UAE's Al Otaiba Goes Behind the Scenes of the Abraham Accords," *Jewish Insider*, September 30, 2020, https://jewishinsider.com/2020/09/uae-ambassador-al-otaiba-details-the-behind-the-scenes-on-the-uae-deal/.

155 *"understands Washington":* Omri Nahmias, "Ambassador Yousef Al Otaiba, the Man Behind the UAE-Israel Deal," *Jerusalem Post*, September 11, 2020, https://www.jpost.com/arab-israeli-conflict/ambassador-yousef-al-otaiba-the-man-behind-the-uae-israel-deal-641873.

155 *flair for the theatrical:* Michael Martinez, "Netanyahu Asks U.N. to Draw 'Red Line' on Iran's Nuclear Plans," September 28, 2012, https://edition.cnn.com/2012/09/27/world/new-york-unga/index.html.

155 *"before Iran completes":* "PM Netanyahu Addresses UN General Assembly," Israeli Foreign Ministry, September 27, 2012, https://embassies.gov.il/MFA/PressRoom/Pages/PM-Netanyahu-addresses-UN-General-Assembly.aspx.

155 *the Loews Regency:* Barak Ravid, "Exclusive: Netanyahu Secretly Met with UAE Foreign Minister in 2012 in New York," *Haaretz*, July 25, 2017, https://www.haaretz.com/israel-news/2017-07-25/ty-article/netanyahu-secretly-met-with-uae-foreign-minister-in-2012-in-new-york/0000017f-f5d4-d47e-a37f-fdfce3a30000.

155 *a kosher dinner:* Amir Tibon, "Israel's U.S. Envoy Shares Dinner Table with UAE Counterpart in Rare Sign of Warming Ties," *Haaretz*, October 11, 2018, https://www.haaretz.com/israel-news/2018-10-11/ty-article/.premium/israels-u-s-envoy-shares-table-with-uae-counterpart-in-sign-of-warming-ties/0000017f-e5fb-df2c-a1ff-fffb81880000.

156 *"All the things":* Cohen, "UAE's Al Otaiba Goes Behind the Scenes of the Abraham Accords."

156 *"If you really want":* Ibid.

156 *an open letter:* Yousef Al Otaiba, "Annexation Will Be a Serious Setback for Better Relations with the Arab World," *Yedioth Ahronoth*/Ynet, June 12, 2020, https://www.ynetnews.com/article/H1Gu1ceTL.

157 *Berkowitz met:* Author interviews with American and Israeli diplomatic sources.

157 *The Americans felt:* Author interviews with American diplomatic sources.

157 *To break the impasse:* Ibid.

157 *His instructions to Dermer:* Author interviews with Israeli diplomatic sources.

157 *the first call he received:* Author interviews with American diplomatic sources.

158 *"a very similar thought":* Barak Ravid, "Netanyahu's Cold Feet Almost Killed the Abraham Accords," *Axios*, December 13, 2021, https://www.ynetnews.com/article/H1Gu1ceTL.

158 *to brief Kushner:* Author interviews with American diplomatic sources.

158 *diplomacy moved into high gear:* Ibid.

158 *report back:* Author interviews with Israeli diplomatic sources.

158 *Kushner spoke:* Author interviews with American diplomatic sources.

158 *in frequent contact:* Author interviews with Pompeo and with Israeli intelligence officials.

158 *crucial trips*: Author interviews with Israeli intelligence officials.

158 *Group 42:* Andrew England and Simeon Kerr, "The Abu Dhabi Royal at the Nexus of UAE Business and National Security," *The Financial Times*, January 25, 2021, https://www.ft.com/content/ce09911b-041d-4651-9bbb-d2a16d39ede7; "Israeli Defense Contractors Partner with UAE Tech Firm to Fight Coronavirus," Reuters, July 3, 2020.

158 *had met many times:* Author interviews with Israeli intelligence officials and Israeli diplomatic officials.

159 *needed reinforcing:* Author interviews with U.S. and Israeli diplomatic officials; author interviews with Israeli intelligence officials.

160 *130 versions:* Author interviews with senior US diplomatic source.

160 *given their name:* Gabby Deutch, "The General Who Coined the Abraham Accords," *Jewish Insider*, January 10, 2022, https://jewishinsider.com/2022/01/general-miguel-correa-abraham-accords/.

161 *a three-way conference call:* "Netanyahu Hails 'New Era' in Israel's Relations with Arab World," Ynet/Associated Press, August 13, 2020, https://www.ynetnews.com/article/r140wx7Mv; Barak Ravid, "Behind the Scenes: How the Israel-UAE Deal Came Together," *Axios*, August 14, 2020, https://www.axios.com/2020/08/13/how-the-israel-uae-recognition-deal-came-together.

161 *The final wording:* "Joint Statement of the United States, the State of Israel, and the United Arab Emirates," U.S. Embassy in Israel, August 13, 2020.

161 *The Mossad had maintained:* "Bahrain's Secret Mossad Ties Revealed?," Ynet, April 8, 2011, https://www.ynetnews.com/articles/0,7340,L-4053981,00.html; Yossi Melman, "Haaretz WikiLeaks Exclusive: Bahrain King Boasted of Intelligence Ties with Israel," April 8, 2011, *Haaretz*, https://www.haaretz.com/2011-04-08/ty-article/haaretz-wikileaks-exclusive-bahrain-king-boasted-of-intelligence-ties-with-israel/0000017f-dc64-df62-a9ff-dcf7fe2d0000?lts=1671434079213.

161 *secret diplomatic presence:* Barak Ravid, "Israel's Secret Embassy in Bahrain," *Axios*, October 21, 2020, https://www.axios.com/2020/10/21/israel-secret-embassy-bahrain.

161 *"change the sign":* Ibid.

162 *his early meetings:* Author interviews with Israeli intelligence officials.

163 *in book form:* Kushner, *Breaking History*.

163 *the sale of F-35s:* Ben Samuels, "Two Years After Abraham Accords, Why the UAE F-35 Deal Remains Grounded," *Haaretz*, September 13, 2022, https://www.haaretz.com/israel-news/security-aviation/2022-09-13/ty-article/.premium/two-years-after-abraham-accords-why-the-uae-f-35-deal-remains-grounded/00000183-3743-d070-abef-f7d755450000.

163 *Netanyahu specifically noted:* Yonah Jeremy Bob, "Barnea Takes Over Mossad; Cohen: Mossad Struck Deep into Iran's Heart," *Jerusalem Post*, June 1, 2021, https://www.jpost.com/israel-news/mossad-cohen-out-barnea-in-incoming-chief-starts-on-tuesday-669757.

163 *below the radar:* Author interviews with Ron Dermer.

163 *As for Cohen:* Author interviews with Israeli intelligence officials.

164 *worked for many years:* Ilana Dayan, Interview with Yossi Cohen, *Uvda*, June 10, 2021 (Hebrew), https://www.mako.co.il/mako-vod-keshet/uvda-2021/VOD-20cd4083fc4f971026.htm.

164 *"layer on layer":* Author interviews with Israeli diplomatic sources.

164 *watching the news:* Author interviews with Ehud Olmert and Mossad source.

165 *"strategic thinking":* Author interview with Ehud Olmert.

165 *a Rubik's Cube:* Author interview with Jason Greenblatt.

165 *a public interview:* Author interview with Yossi Cohen at *Jerusalem Post* conference, October 14, 2021 (Cohen's first English interview), https://www.youtube.com/watch?v=2Otw0fQ7Gf8.

165 *Sudan followed:* Felicia Schwartz and Nicholas Bariyo, "Israel, Sudan Agree to Normalize Ties in U.S.-Brokered Deal," *Washington Post*, October 23, 2020, https://www.wsj.com/articles/israel-sudan-agree-to-normalize-ties-in-u-s-brokered-deal-11603469178.

165 *way station:* Amos Gilboa, edited by Yonah Jeremy Bob, *A Raid on the Red Sea* (Sterling, VA: Potomac Books, 2021), 33–38, 265, and other mentions; "Smuggling Weapons from Iran into the Gaza Strip Through Sudan and Sinai," Shin Bet, https://www.shabak.gov.il/english/publications/Pages/SmugglingWeapons.aspx; author interviews with Israeli intelligence officials.

165 *Sudan paid:* Jennifer Hansler, "US Receives $335M from Sudan for Victims of Terrorist Attacks," CNN, March 31, 2021, https://edition.cnn.com/2021/03/31/politics/sudan-settlement-received/index.html.

165 *debt relief:* Nabeel Biajo, "IMF Approves $50B in Debt Relief, $2.4 Billion Funding to Sudan," *VoA*, July 1, 2021, https://www.voaafrica.com/a/africa_south-sudan-focus_imf-approves-50b-debt-relief-24-billion-funding-sudan/6207697.html; "Paris Club Suspends Sudan's Debt Relief Process as Khartoum Seeks Arab Funds," *Sudan Tribune*, June 27, 2022, https://sudantribune.com/article260341/.

166 *Sudan's intelligence chief:* David Hearst, Simon Hooper, and Mustafa Abu Sneineh, "Exclusive: Sudanese Spy Chief Met Head of Mossad to Discuss Bashir Succession Plan," https://www.middleeasteye.net/news/exclusive-sudanese-spy-chief-met-head-mossad-discuss-bashir-succession-plan; "America's Plan B if Bashir Is Toppled," *Africa Intelligence*, February 8, 2019, https://www.africaintelligence.com/eastern-africa-and-the-horn/2019/02/08/america-s-plan-b-if-bashir-is-toppled,108343807-art.

166 *code name Maoz:* Gili Cohen, "The Secrets of Peace" (Hebrew), Kan 11 TV, August 27, 2021, https://www.kan.org.il/item/?itemid=112225; Barak Ravid, *Trump's Peace* (Hebrew) (Tel Aviv: Yedioth Books, 2021), Chap 12, e-vrit.

166 *opened up a channel:* Barak Ravid, Twitter, November 25, 2018, https://twitter.com/barakravid/status/1066640483181625344; Ravid, *Trump's Peace*, Chap 12, e-vrit.

166 *open war:* Ravid, *Trump's Peace*, Chap 12, e-vrit; author interviews with Israeli intelligence officials.

166 *threatened to cut off:* Ravid, *Trump's Peace*, Chap 12, e-vrit; author interviews with Israeli officials.

166 *a compromise was hammered out:* Author interviews with Israeli officials; Ravid, *Trump's Peace*, Chap. 12, e-vrit.

167 *Bashir was ousted:* Sarah El Sirgany, Nima Elbagir, and Yasir Abdullah, "Sudan's President Bashir Forced Out in Military Coup," CNN, April 11, 2019, https://edition.cnn.com/2019/04/11/africa/sudan-unrest-intl/index.html.

167 *Nick Kaufman:* Author interview; Ravid, *Trump's Peace*, Chap 12, e-vrit.

167 *contacts in the NSC:* Author interview with Nick Kaufman.

167 *delivered the letter:* Ibid.

168 *a meeting in Uganda:* Barak Ravid, "Netanyahu Holds Landmark Meeting with Sudan Leader," *Axios*, February 3, 2020, https://www.axios.com/2020/02/03/israel-sudan-meeting-netanyahu-normalize-relations.

168 *a third key player:* "Sudanese Government Was Not Informed About Netanyahu's Meeting," *Sudan Tribune*, February 3, 2020, https://sudantribune.com/article67048/; Arwa Ibrahim, "Netanyahu-Burhan Meeting Slammed in Sudan, Exposes Divides," Al Jazeera, February 5, 2020, https://www.aljazeera.com/news/2020/2/5/netanyahu-burhan-meeting-slammed-in-sudan-exposes-divides; author interviews with Israeli intelligence officials.

168 *Cohen had played a role:* Author interviews with Israeli intelligence officials; Ravid, *Trump's Peace*, Chap 12, e-vrit.

168 *the real power:* Author interviews with Israeli intelligence officials; Yonah Jeremy Bob, "The Wild World of the Mossad in Sudan—Analysis," *Jerusalem Post*, June 28, 2021, https://www.jpost.com/international/the-wild-world-of-the-mossad-in-sudan-analysis-672293.

168 *an illiterate former camel trader:* Jérôme Tubiana, "The Man Who Terrorized Darfur Is Leading Sudan's Supposed Transition," *Foreign Policy*, May 14, 2019, https://foreignpolicy.com/2019/05/14/man-who-terrorized-darfur-is-leading-sudans-supposed-transition-hemeti-rsf-janjaweed-bashir-khartoum/.

168 *Gadaheldam died of Covid:* Author interview with Nick Kaufman; Ravid, "Scoop: Secret Israel-Sudan Contacts Enabled Deal Sealed by Trump"; Ravid, *Trump's Peace*, Chap. 12, e-vrit.

169 *another domino fell:* Steve Holland, "Morocco Joins Other Arab Nations Agreeing to Normalize Israel Ties," Reuters, December 10, 2020, https://www.reuters.com/article/us-israel-usa-morocco-idUSKBN28K2CN.

169 *Burhan toppled:* Zeinab Mohammed Salih and Peter Beaumont, "Sudan's Army Seizes Power in Coup and Detains Prime Minister," *The Guardian*, October 25, 2021, https://www.theguardian.com/world/2021/oct/25/sudan-coup-fears-amid-claims-military-have-arrested-senior-government-officials.

169 *quiet ties:* Yonah Jeremy Bob, "Why Was Mossad Meeting in Sudan with Coup Leaders?," *Jerusalem Post*, November 2, 2021, https://www.jpost.com/international/why-was-mossad-meeting-in-sudan-with-coup-leaders-analysis-683825; Bob, "The Wild World of the Mossad in Sudan—Analysis."

169 *glimmers of this future:* "Sudan to Move Forward with Israel on Normalising Relations," Al Jazeera, February 2, 2023, https://www.aljazeera.com/news/2023/2/2/israeli-fm-heads-delegation-to-discuss-sudan-normalisation.

CHAPTER 11: THE MOSSAD SENDS A MESSAGE

Author interviews 2019–November 2022

171 *an unspecified illness:* "International Atomic Energy Agency Head Yukiya Amano Passes Away," Reuters/*Jerusalem Post*, July 22, 2019, https://www.jpost.com

/breaking-news/international-atomic-energy-agency-head-yukiya-amano-dies-596424.

171 *Grossi was loquacious:* Yonah Jeremy Bob, "Meet IAEA Chief Rafael Grossi: The Man Central to the Iran Nuclear Issue," *Jerusalem Post,* January 27, 2022, https://www.jpost.com/middle-east/article-694781; Yonah Jeremy Bob, "How Mossad Turned the IAEA Around on Iran with Evidence—Analysis," *Jerusalem Post,* March 9, 2021, https://www.jpost.com/israel-news/the-iaea-mossad-iran-dance-analysis-661468.

172 *again pressed Iran:* Live IAEA Press Conference February 10, 2020, https://www.youtube.com/watch?v=w1FLjicNG9Y; "Atomic Agency Cites Concerns over Iran Testing Sites, Offers COVID-19 Assistance," *UN News,* March 9, 2020, https://news.un.org/en/story/2020/03/1059001; Bob, "Meet IAEA Chief Rafael Grossi"; "Joint Statement by the Vice-President of the Islamic Republic of Iran and Head of the AEOI and the Director General of the IAEA," February 21, 2021, https://www.iaea.org/newscenter/pressreleases/joint-statement-by-the-vice-president-of-the-islamic-republic-of-iran-and-head-of-the-aeoi-and-the-director-general-of-the-iaea.

172 *tripled its stockpile:* IAEA March 2020 report, https://www.iaea.org/sites/default/files/20/03/gov2020-5.pdf; Nicole Gaouette, "UN Nuclear Watchdog Finds Iran Has Nearly Tripled Its Uranium Stockpile," CNN, March 4, 2020, https://edition.cnn.com/2020/03/04/middleeast/un-nuclear-report-iran-intl-hnk/index.html; IAEA statement, March 9, 2020, https://www.iaea.org/newscenter/news/iaea-director-general-calls-on-iran-to-cooperate-immediately-and-fully; Bob, "Meet IAEA Chief Rafael Grossi."

173 *his last warning:* IAEA Report June 2020, https://www.iaea.org/sites/default/files/20/06/gov2020-26.pdf; IAEA statement June 15, 2020, https://www.iaea.org/newscenter/statements/iaea-director-generals-introductory-statement-to-the-board-of-governors-15-june-2020; Yonah Jeremy Bob, "Does Russia Want Tehran to Get Nukes?—Analysis," *Jerusalem Post,* June 7, 2020, https://www.jpost.com/middle-east/does-russia-want-tehran-to-get-nukes-analysis-630582.

173 *tough with the Iranians:* Author interviews with Israeli intelligence minister Eli Cohen and former Mossad chief Yossi Cohen.

173 *condemned Iran:* IAEA Board of Governors Resolution of June 19, 2020, https://www.iaea.org/sites/default/files/20/06/gov2020-34.pdf.

173 *start of a race:* Author interviews with officials whose identity and background must remain anonymous; Yonah Jeremy Bob, "Did Mossad's 2018 Iran Operation Pave Way for 2020 Explosions?—Analysis," *Jerusalem Post,* July 23, 2020, https://www.jpost.com/middle-east/iran-news/did-mossads-2018-iran-operation-pave-way-for-2020-explosions-analysis-636027.

174 *Khojir missile production facility:* Fabian Hinz, "What Iranian Authorities Hid About the Big Explosion in East Tehran," Radio Farda, June 27, 2020, https://en.radiofarda.com/a/what-iranian-authorities-hid-about-the-big-explosion-in-east-tehran/30693889.html; assorted Iranian media.

174 *identified on the map:* Author interviews with former U.S. cyber intelligence official Jeff Bardin; author interviews with officials whose identity and background must remain anonymous.

175 *satellite images:* Hinz, "What Iranian Authorities Hid About the Big Explosion in East Tehran."

175 *"to disrupt":* Christopher Hamill-Stewart, "Explosions in Iran: Isolated Incidents or Acts of Sabotage?," *Arab News*, July 13, 2020, https://www.arabnews.com/node/1702866/middle-east.

175 *"feel considerable stress":* Author interviews with Israeli intelligence officials.

175 *killed nineteen people:* "At Least 17 Dead in Explosion in Medical Center in Tehran," Reuters/*Jerusalem Post*, June 30, 2020, https://www.jpost.com/breaking-news/explosion-fills-the-skies-of-northern-tehran-with-smoke-report-633338; "19 Killed in Gas Explosion at Clinic in Iranian Capital," AFP/Voice of America, June 30, 2020, https://www.voanews.com/a/middle-east_19-killed-gas-explosion-clinic-iranian-capital/6192021.html; assorted Iranian media.

176 *struck Iranian proxies:* Anna Ahronheim, "At least Nine Pro-Iranian Fighters Killed in Alleged Israeli Airstrike," *Jerusalem Post*, June 28, 2020, https://www.jpost.com/breaking-news/unidentified-aircraft-target-pro-iranian-militias-in-syria-report-633021.

176 *annex the West Bank:* Gabe Friedman, "Four Reasons Why Israeli Annexation Is Not Happening July 1," *Jerusalem Post*/JTA, July 1, 2020, https://www.jpost.com/arab-israeli-conflict/four-reasons-why-israels-annexation-plans-arent-happening-july-1-633389.

176 *Initial reports:* Jon Gambrell, "Analysts: Fire at Iran Nuclear Site Hit Centrifuge Facility," Associated Press, July 2, 2020, https://apnews.com/article/50c3e7f6445ae99def6bdc65fbce6c42; David Sanger, William Broad, Ronen Bergman, and Farnaz Fassihi, "Mysterious Explosion and Fire Damage Iranian Nuclear Facility," *New York Times*, July 3, 2020, https://www.nytimes.com/2020/07/02/us/politics/iran-explosion-nuclear-centrifuges.html; Seth Frantzman, "What Took Place at the Iranian Natanz Nuclear Facility?," *Jerusalem Post*, July 5, 2020, https://www.jpost.com/middle-east/what-happened-during-the-iranian-natanz-nuclear-facility-incident-633701.

177 *had deployed:* IAEA June 2020 report, https://www.iaea.org/sites/default/files/20/06/gov2020-26.pdf.

178 *claiming responsibility:* "Iran Nuclear: 'Incident' at Natanz Uranium Enrichment Facility," BBC News, July 2, 2020, https://www.bbc.com/news/world-middle-east-53265023; Jiyar Gol, "Iran Blasts: What Is Behind Mysterious Fires at Key Sites?," BBC News, July 6, 2020, https://www.bbc.com/news/world-middle-east-53305940; Sanger, Broad, Bergman, and Fassihi, "Mysterious Explosion and Fire Damage Iranian Nuclear Facility."

178 *"flammable liquids":* Author interviews with Albright; Albright interview with Israel Channel 11, July 2, 2020; Sanger, Broad, Bergman, and Fassihi, "Mysterious Explosion and Fire Damage Iranian Nuclear Facility."

178 *NASA satellite images:* Gol, "Iran Blasts."

178 *would have required hours:* Author interviews with Israeli and U.S. intelligence officials.

179 *from start to finish:* Ilana Dayan, Interview with Yossi Cohen, *Uvda*, June 10, 2021 (Hebrew), https://www.mako.co.il/mako-vod-keshet/uvda-2021/VOD-20cd4083fc4f971026.htm.; author interviews with Israeli intelligence officials.

179 *convincing some scientists:* Dayan, Interview with Yossi Cohen; Jake Wallis Simons, "Exclusive: Mossad Recruited Top Iranian Scientists to Blow Up Key Nuclear Facility," *Jewish Chronicle*, December 2, 2021, https://www.thejc.com/news/world/exclusive-mossad-recruited-top-iranian-scientists-to-blow-up-key-nuclear-facility-1.523163; Nadav Eyal, "Interview of Former Deputy Mossad Chief Ehud Lavi," *Yediot Ahronot*, March 4, 2021; author interviews with Israeli intelligence officials.

179 *spirit any scientists:* Simons, "Exclusive: Mossad Recruited Top Iranian Scientists to Blow Up Key Nuclear Facility"; author interviews with Israeli intelligence officials.

179 *to infiltrate:* Farnaz Fassihi, "Major Explosion Rocks Iran Again, the 3rd Blast in 3 Weeks," *New York Times*, July 9, 2020, https://www.nytimes.com/2020/07/09/world/middleeast/iran-explosion.html; Simons, "Exclusive: Mossad Recruited Top Iranian Scientists to Blow Up Key Nuclear Facility"; author interviews with intelligence sources.

179 *many times before:* Fassihi, "Major Explosion Rocks Iran Again, the 3rd Blast in 3 Weeks"; Simons, "Exclusive: Mossad Recruited Top Iranian Scientists to Blow Up Key Nuclear Facility"; author interviews with intelligence sources.

180 *Iranian-made parts:* Author interviews with Albright.

180 *had been a fire:* "Iran Nuclear: Natanz Fire Caused 'Significant' Damage,'" BBC News, July 5, 2020, https://www.bbc.com/news/world-middle-east-53300579; assorted Iranian media.

180 *"powerful bomb":* Yonah Jeremy Bob, "Three-Quarters of Natanz Centrifuge Assembly Hall Destroyed—Nuke Experts," *Jerusalem Post*, July 10, 2020, https://www.jpost.com/middle-east/iran-news/three-quarters-of-natanz-centrifuge-assembly-hall-destroyed-nuke-experts-634444; Fassihi, "Major Explosion Rocks Iran Again, the 3rd Blast in 3 Weeks"; Simons, "Exclusive: Mossad Recruited Top Iranian Scientists to Blow Up Key Nuclear Facility"; author interviews with Middle East intelligence officials.

180 *new sabotage:* Lahav Harkov, "Ashkenazi on Iran Explosions: Our Actions Are Better Left Unsaid," *Jerusalem Post*, July 5, 2020, https://www.jpost.com/israel-news/ashkenazi-on-natanz-explosion-our-actions-in-iran-better-left-unsaid-633923.

181 *three quarters:* Author interviews with Albright; Bob, "Three-Quarters of Natanz Centrifuge Assembly Hall Destroyed—Nuke Experts."

181 *"future capabilities":* Author interviews with Sima Shine.

182 *end his term:* Israeli Prime Minister's Office statement, July 5, 2020; Yonah Jeremy Bob, "PM Extends Mossad Chief Tenure by 6 Months," *Jerusalem Post*, July 5, 2020, https://www.jpost.com/breaking-news/netanyahu-asks-mossad-chief-to-extend-time-in-office-633955; Yonah Jeremy Bob, "Mossad Head's Short-Term

Extension Points to Politics, not Iran," *Jerusalem Post*, July 6, 2020, https://www.jpost.com/israel-news/mossad-heads-short-term-extension-points-to-politics-not-iran-634075.

182 *in southwest Tehran:* Babak Dehghanpisheh, "Explosion Reported in West Tehran, Denied by Officials," Reuters, July 10, 2020, https://www.reuters.com/article/us-iran-security-blast/explosion-heard-in-western-tehran-iran-state-media-idUSKBN24A3F9; Fassihi, "Major Explosion Rocks Iran Again, the 3rd Blast in 3 Weeks"; assorted Iran media.

183 *eight different days/total intelligence breakdown:* Yonah Jeremy Bob, "How Have Iran's Intelligence Forces Broken Down in Face of Explosions?," *Jerusalem Post*, July 11, 2020, https://www.jpost.com/middle-east/total-iranian-intelligence-breakdown-analysis-634605; Dehghanpisheh, "Explosion Reported in West Tehran, Denied by Officials"; Fassihi, "Major Explosion Rocks Iran Again, the 3rd Blast in 3 Weeks"; assorted Iranian media.

184 *"what don't you understand":* Dayan, Interview with Yossi Cohen.

184 *completely eclipsed:* Raz Zimmt, "The Intelligence Organization of the IRGC: A Major Iranian Intelligence Apparatus," Meir Amit Intelligence and Terrorism Information Center, November 5, 2020, https://www.terrorism-info.org.il/app/uploads/2020/11/E_269_20.pdf.

184 *dismantled five teams:* "Five Spy Teams Dismantled by Iran's Intelligence Ministry," Islamic Republic News Agency, August 11, 2020, https://en.irna.ir/news/83904285/Five-spy-teams-dismantled-by-Iran-s-intelligence-ministry; Zimmt, "The Intelligence Organization of the IRGC."

185 *the different focuses:* James Risen, Tim Arango, Farnaz Fassihi, Murtaza Hussain, and Ronen Bergman, "A Spy Complex Revealed," *The Intercept*, November 18, 2019, https://theintercept.com/2019/11/18/iran-iraq-spy-cables/.

185 *disastrously harmful:* Ibid.

186 *purposely pitted:* Zimmt, "The Intelligence Organization of the IRGC."

186 *remains resilient:* INSS Virtual Conference July 22, 2020; "Explosions in Iran Not Toppling Ayatollahs—Experts," *Jerusalem Post*, https://www.jpost.com/middle-east/iran-news/explosions-in-iran-not-toppling-ayatollahs-experts-635969; assorted Iranian media.

187 *sabotage operation:* INSS Virtual Conference July 22, 2020; "Explosions in Iran Not Toppling Ayatollahs—Experts," *Jerusalem Post*; assorted Iranian media.

187 *"not up in arms":* Ibid.

187 *off the table:* Author interviews with Israeli intelligence officials and Albright.

CHAPTER 12: THE FATHER OF THE BOMB IS NO MORE

Author interviews 2018–November 2022

189 *Ministry of Defense:* Dr. Ardavan Khoshnood, "The Assassination of Mohsen Fakhrizadeh: What Are the Iranian Regime's Options?," BESA Center, November 30, 2020, https://besacenter.org/iran-fakhrizadeh-assassination/.

189 *a kind of pilgrimage:* "Funeral of Mohsen Fakhrizadeh Conducted at Imam Reza Holy Shrine," Iran Students News Agency, November 29, https://en.isna.ir/photo/99090906803/Funeral-of-Mohsen-Fakhrizadeh-conducted-at-Imam-Reza-Holy-Shrine; "Martyr Fakhrizadeh Laid to Rest," Iran Press News Agency, November 30, 2020, https://iranpress.com/content/30454/martyr-fakhrizadeh-laid-rest; Maziar Motamedi, "Iran Buries Slain Nuclear Scientist, Promises Retaliation," Al Jazeera, November 30, 2020, https://www.aljazeera.com/news/2020/11/30/iran-buries-assassinated-scientist-amid-promises-of-retaliation.

189 *attended only by family:* Motamedi, "Iran Buries Slain Nuclear Scientist, Promises Retaliation"; "Iran Begins Funeral for Slain Military Nuclear Scientist Mohsen Fakhrizadeh," Al Arabiya, November 30, 2020, https://english.alarabiya.net/News/middle-east/2020/11/30/Iran-begins-funeral-for-slain-military-nuclear-scientist-Mohsen-Fakhrizadeh.

190 *read a eulogy:* Motamedi, "Iran Buries Slain Nuclear Scientist, Promises Retaliation."

190 *promised revenge:* "At Nuke Chief's Funeral, Iran Defense Minister Vows Vengeance, Nuclear Progress," *Times of Israel,* November 30, 2020, https://www.timesofisrael.com/at-nuke-chiefs-funeral-iran-defense-minister-vows-response-to-killing/; Patrick Wintour and Oliver Holmes, "Iranian Nuclear Scientist Mohsen Fakhrizadeh Given Martyr Status," November 30, 2020, https://www.theguardian.com/world/2020/nov/30/iranian-nuclear-scientist-mohsen-fakhrizadeh-given-martyr-status.

190 *A rare image:* "Factbox: Who Is the Iranian Scientist Killed in Tehran?," Reuters, November 27, 2020, https://www.reuters.com/article/uk-iran-nuclear-scientist-fakhrizadeh-idUKKBN2871XJ; Adam Taylor, "Who Is Mohsen Fakhrizadeh, the Iranian Nuclear Scientist Killed in Attack Outside Tehran?," November 27, 2020, https://www.washingtonpost.com/world/iran-fakhrizadeh-who-is-nuclear/2020/11/27/cffdb6a8-30ce-11eb-9dd6-2d0179981719_story.html; "Leading Iranian Nuclear Scientist Killed," *The Iran Primer,* November 30, 2020, updated December 1, 2020, https://iranprimer.usip.org/blog/2020/nov/30/part-1-leading-iran-nuclear-scientist-killed.

190 *physics and philosophy:* "What Traits in Fakhrizadeh Intimidated the Enemy?," Khamenei.IR, December 6, 2020, https://english.khamenei.ir/news/8156/What-traits-in-Martyr-Fakhrizadeh-intimidated-the-enemy; "Former Head of Iran's Atomic Energy Organization Abbasi-Davani Hints That Iranian Nuclear Chief Mohsen Fakhrizadeh Was Working on Nuclear Weapons and That Is Why He Was Assassinated—Part II: The Full Interview," MEMRI, December 3, 2021, https://www.memri.org/reports/former-head-irans-atomic-energy-organization-abbasi-davani-hints-iranian-nuclear-chief.

190 *only after his death:* "Iran's Khamenei Awards Military Medal to Slain Nuclear Scientist," *The New Arab,* December 13, 2020, https://www.newarab.com/news/irans-khamenei-awards-military-medal-slain-nuclear-scientist; "Fakhrizadeh Received Order of Service for Role in 2015 Deal," *Iran Front Page,* December 1, 2020; author interviews with former Israeli military intelligence

research and analysis chief Yossi Kupperwasser; photographic evidence provided by the Jerusalem Center for Public Affairs.

191 *Fakhrizadeh was well known:* "Security Council Toughens Sanctions Against Iran, Adds Arms Embargo, with Unanimous Adoption of Resolution 1747 (2007)," UN Security Council, March 24, 2007, https://press.un.org/en/2007/sc8980.doc.htm.

191 Der Spiegel: Von Erich Follath und Holger Stark, "A History of Iran's Nuclear Ambitions," *Der Spiegel*, June 17, 2010, https://www.spiegel.de/international/world/the-birth-of-a-bomb-a-history-of-iran-s-nuclear-ambitions-a-701109.html.

191 *Reuters report:* Fredrik Dahl, "Enigmatic Iranian Military Man at Center of U.N. Nuclear Investigation," Reuters, June 19, 2014, https://www.reuters.com/article/us-iran-nuclear-fakhrizadeh-idUSKBN0EU18H20140619.

191 *instrumental:* Follath und Stark, "A History of Iran's Nuclear Ambitions"; "Factbox: Who Is the Iranian Scientist Killed in Tehran?"; Dahl, "Enigmatic Iranian Military Man at Center of U.N. Nuclear Investigation."

192 *more professional body:* Author interviews with former Israeli Military Intelligence chief Aharon Ze'evi Farkash.

192 *One of his sons:* Ronen Bergman and Farnaz Fassihi, "The Scientist and the A.I.-Assisted, Remote-Control Killer Robot," *New York Times*, September 18, 2021, https://www.nytimes.com/2021/09/18/world/middleeast/iran-nuclear-fakhrizadeh-assassination-israel.html.

193 *a platoon-size hit team:* Harriet Alexander and Jemma Carr, "How Mossad Executed Iran's Nuclear Chief: Power to the Entire Region Was Cut as Gun and Bomb Attack Blasted His Convoy Before He Was Dragged from Car and Finished Off . . . Then the 12 Assassins Melted Away," *Daily Mail/Mail Online*, November 29/30, https://www.dailymail.co.uk/news/article-8997575/Assassination-Irans-nuclear-scientist-involved-62-people-including-12-gunmen.html.

193 *satellite-linked machine gun:* "Security Official: Fakhrizadeh Assassinated in Unmanned Operation," Tasnim News Agency, November 30, 2020, https://www.tasnimnews.com/en/news/2020/11/30/2400675/security-official-fakhrizadeh-assassinated-in-unmanned-operation.

193 *was not science fiction:* Author interviews with Israeli intelligence officials; Jake Wallis Simons, "Exclusive: Truth Behind Killing of Iran Scientist," *Jewish Chronicle*, February 10, 2021, https://www.thejc.com/news/world/world-exclusive-truth-behind-killing-of-iran-nuclear-scientist-mohsen-fakhrizadeh-revealed-1.511653; Bergman and Fassihi, "The Scientist and the A.I.-Assisted, Remote-Control Killer Robot.

193 *smuggled into Iran:* Simons, "Exclusive: Truth Behind Killing of Iran Scientist."

193 *"breathed with the guy":* Ibid.

193 *Rear Admiral Ali Fadavi:* "AI-Powered Weapon Used in Assassination of Iranian Scientist," Tasnim News Agency, December 7, https://www.tasnimnews.com/en/news/2020/12/07/2404916/ai-powered-weapon-used-in-assassination-of-iranian-scientist.

193 *M240C machine gun:* "Regarding the Act of State Terrorism of Assassination of Dr. Mohsen Fakhrizadeh," Letter from the Permanent Mission of the Islamic Re-

public of Iran to the United Nations, Office of the United Nations High Commissioner for Human Rights, June 28, 2021, https://spcommreports.ohchr.org/TMResultsBase/DownLoadFile?gId=36401.

193 *facial recognition technology:* "Iran Says 'Smart Satellite-Controlled Machine Gun' Killed Top Nuclear Scientist," Reuters, December 7, 2020, https://www.reuters.com/article/uk-iran-nuclear-scientist-idUKKBN28H13L.

193 *the front car:* Alon Ben David, "Targeted Assassination in Iran" (Hebrew), Channel 13 TV, December 15, 2020, https://13tv.co.il/item/documentary/hit-list/season-01/episodes/s1quj-2098948/.

193 *thirteen rounds:* Wallis Simons's article was important because even though Iran had already put out most of what he wrote, virtually no Israeli experts took the Iranian remote gun theory seriously until Wallis Simons reported it based on Mossad sources. However, due to some sources casting doubt on other details reported by Wallis Simons, the theory was still not widely accepted until reported by Bergman and confirmed by the authors. "Security Official: Fakhrizadeh Assassinated in Unmanned Operation," Tasnim News Agency.

194 *focused only:* "Mohsen Fakhrizadeh: 'Machine-gun with AI Used to Kill Iran Scientist," BBC, December 7, 2020, https://www.bbc.com/news/world-middle-east-55214359.

194 *a major consideration:* Author interviews with intelligence officials.

194 *Fakhrizadeh's personal bodyguard:* David D. Kirkpatrick, Farnaz Fassihi, and Ronen Bergman, "Killer Robot? Assassination of Iranian Scientist Feeds Conflicting Accounts," *New York Times*, December 2, 2020, https://www.nytimes.com/2020/12/02/world/middleeast/iran-assassination-nuclear-scientist.html; "Exclusive: Mass Interrogations of Assassinated Scientist's Bodyguards, Colleagues and Neighbors," IranWire, November 29, 2021, https://iranwire.com/en/features/68163/; "Exclusive: Chief Bodyguard One of 80 Interrogated on Mohsen Fakhrizadeh Killing," IranWire, December 15, 2021, https://iranwire.com/en/politics/70968/.

194 *twelve years earlier:* Ronen Bergman, "Fakhrizadeh's Secrets: New Revelations About Assassinated Nuclear Scientist" (Hebrew), *Yedioth Ahronoth*, December 4, 2020 (Hebrew), https://www.ynet.co.il/articles/0,7340,L-5854571,00.html; "Israel Has Tape of Slain Iran Nuke Chief Talking About Building Five Warheads," *Times of Israel*, December 4, 2020, https://www.timesofisrael.com/israel-has-tape-of-slain-iran-nuke-chief-talking-about-building-five-warheads/; author interviews with Ehud Olmert.

195 *"Mossad has been closely monitoring":* Ilana Dayan, Interview with Yossi Cohen, *Uvda*, June 10, 2021 (Hebrew), https://www.mako.co.il/mako-vod-keshet/uvda-2021/VOD-20cd4083fc4f971026.htm; "In Stunning, Revelatory Interview, Ex-Mossad Chief Warns Iran, Defends Netanyahu," *Times of Israel*, June 11, 2021, https://www.timesofisrael.com/in-stunning-revelatory-interview-mossad-chief-warns-iran-defends-netanyahu/.

195 *"We knew everything":* "Tamir Pardo Talks," *Uvda*, May 31, 2018 (Hebrew), https://www.mako.co.il/mako-vod-keshet/uvda-2018/VOD-d2c7779e1f5b361006.htm.

195 *"keep an eye on him":* Author interview with Shaul Mofaz.

195 *opposition to that idea:* Author interviews with Tamir Pardo.

196 *In the end:* Bergman and Fassihi, "The Scientist and the A.I.-Assisted, Remote-Control Killer Robot"; author interviews with Ehud Olmert.

197 *technical expertise:* Author interviews with former Israeli Military Intelligence chief Aharon Ze'evi Farkash.

197 *"a network of scientists":* François Murphy and Parisa Hafezi, "Iran's Top Nuclear Scientist Stayed in Shadows but His Work Was Uncovered," Reuters, November 28, 2020, https://www.reuters.com/article/uk-iran-nuclear-scientist-work-idUKKBN2880MP.

197 *"Fakhrizadeh—Remember that name":* "Netanyahu Reveals Iran Files," i24News, April 30, 2018, https://www.youtube.com/watch?v=C4zar3AuRv0.

197 *the damage caused:* "The Assassination of Fakhrizadeh: Considerations and Consequences," Institute for National Security Studies, December 2, 2020, https://www.inss.org.il/publication/fakhrizadeh/.

198 *keep talented scientists:* Author interviews with former Mossad Iran research and analysis chief Sima Shine.

198 *"a uniquely experienced manager":* Author interviews with former CIA Iran desk chief Norman T. Roule; "The Cipher Brief: 'Iran, Assassination and Retaliation' Briefing with Norman T. Roule," December 4, 2020, https://www.thecipherbrief.com/iran-assassination-and-retaliation.

198 *Israeli intelligence estimated:* Author interviews with Israeli intelligence officials.

CHAPTER 13: A BEAUTIFUL ATTACK

Author interviews late 2020–November 2022

201 *"credible path":* Joe Biden, "There's a Smarter Way to Be Tough on Iran," op-ed, CNN, September 13, 2020, https://edition.cnn.com/2020/09/13/opinions/smarter-way-to-be-tough-on-iran-joe-biden/index.html.

201 *positives and negatives:* Analysis of Israeli claims against nuclear deal.

202 *high status:* Yonah Jeremy Bob, "As Biden Enters White House, Did Israel's Mossad Win War with Iran?," *Jerusalem Post*, January 7, 2021, https://www.jpost.com/middle-east/as-biden-enters-white-house-did-israels-mossad-win-war-with-iran-654674; David Albright, "Iran Building Nuclear Weapons," Institute for Science and International Security, December 5, 2022, https://isis-online.org/isis-reports/detail/iran-building-nuclear-weapons; author interviews with Israeli intelligence officials.

202 *Israel had other criticisms:* Analysis of Israeli claims against nuclear deal.

203 *give secondary importance:* Thomas Friedman, "Joe Biden Interview: 'We're Going to Fight like Hell,'" *New York Times*, December 2, 2020, https://www.nytimes.com/2020/12/02/opinion/biden-interview-mcconnell-china-iran.html.

204 *they were nervous:* Author interviews with former Israeli national security council chief Meir Ben Shabbat, former Israeli prime minister Naftali Bennett, former Israeli Military Intelligence chiefs Amos Yadlin, Tamir Heyman, and Aharon

Ze'evi Farkash, and other Israeli intelligence officials; assorted speeches by Israeli prime minister Benjamin Netanyahu.

204 *almost identical language:* Yonah Jeremy Bob, "Biden 'Long Way' from Rejoining Iran Nuke Deal, Incoming Intel Chief Says," *Jerusalem Post,* January 19, 2021, https://www.jpost.com/american-politics/incoming-us-intel-chief-a-long-ways-from-rejoin-iran-nuke-deal-655972; Yonah Jeremy Bob, "Top Incoming Biden Aides Say No Quick Iran Deal—Analysis," *Jerusalem Post,* January 20, 2021, https://www.jpost.com/middle-east/iran-news/top-incoming-biden-aides-say-no-quick-iran-deal-analysis-656059; testimony of incoming director of national intelligence Avril Haines and incoming secretary of state Antony Blinken to the U.S. Senate Intelligence Committee, January 19, 2021.

205 *intended to stop:* Blinken testimony.

205 *Biden would return:* Ibid.

205 *could take months:* Author interviews with Aharon Ze'evi Farkash.

206 *had achieved access:* Joint Statement by the Director General of the IAEA and the Vice President of the Islamic Republic of Iran and Head of the AEOI, August 26, 2020, https://www.iaea.org/newscenter/pressreleases/joint-statement-by-the-director-general-of-the-iaea-and-the-vice-president-of-the-islamic-republic-of-iran-and-head-of-the-aeoi.

206 *almost exuberant:* Kelsey Davenport, "Iran, IAEA Reach Monitoring Agreement," Arms Control Association, March 2021, https://www.armscontrol.org/act/2021-03/news/iran-iaea-reach-monitoring-agreement.

207 *"urban myth":* Yonah Jeremy Bob, "How Mossad Turned the IAEA Around on Iran with Evidence—Analysis," *Jerusalem Post,* March 9, 2021, https://www.jpost.com/israel-news/the-iaea-mossad-iran-dance-analysis-661468.

208 *"at this point":* Yonah Jeremy Bob, "Four Wild Iran Nuclear Standoff Developments," *Jerusalem Post,* June 16, 2021, https://www.jpost.com/middle-east/iran-news/four-wild-iran-nuclear-standoff-developments-671224.

208 *Amano had broken*: Author interviews with Israeli intelligence officials.

209 *new underground plant:* IAEA Board of Governors Report, March 15, 2021 (leaked to public March 17, 2021), https://www.iaea.org/sites/default/files/22/07/govinf2021-19.pdf.

209 *did not feel:* Yonah Jeremy Bob, "Iran Has Not Yet Recovered from Natanz Explosion Hit—Exclusive," *Jerusalem Post,* March 18, 2021, https://www.jpost.com/middle-east/iran-has-not-yet-recovered-from-nanatz-explosion-hit-exclusive-662493.

210 *an "accident" had occurred:* "'Accident' Strikes Iran's Natanz Nuclear Facility: Official," Associated Press/Al Arabiya, April 11, 2021, https://english.alarabiya.net/News/middle-east/2021/04/11/-Accident-strikes-Iran-s-Natanz-nuclear-facility-Official.

210 *only hours later:* Yonah Jeremy Bob, "Incident Reported in Iranian Natanz Nuclear Facility Much Graver than Iran Reports," *Jerusalem Post* (filed 11:30 a.m., April 11, 2011, delayed by censor and posted around 12:30 p.m., overwritten April 13, 2021), https://www.jpost.com/middle-east/incident-reported-in-iranian-natanz-nuclear-facility-664792.

210 *fell down:* Parisa Hafezi, "Iran Says Natanz Nuclear Site Hit by Terrorism—

TV," Reuters, April 11, 2021, https://www.reuters.com/world/middle-east/iran-reports-incident-natanz-nuclear-site-no-casualties-press-tv-2021-04-11/.

211 *"very safe":* Kim Zetter, Israel May Have Destroyed Iranian Centrifuges Simply by Cutting Power, *The Intercept,* April 13, 2021, https://theintercept.com/2021/04/13/iran-nuclear-natanz-israel/.

211 *destroyed:* Ronen Bergman, Rick Gladstone, and Farnaz Fassihi, "Blackout Hits Iran Nuclear Site in What Appears to Be Israeli Sabotage," *New York Times,* April 13, 2021, https://www.nytimes.com/2021/04/11/world/middleeast/iran-nuclear-natanz.html; Tzvi Joffre and Yonah Jeremy Bob, "Natanz Attack Hit 50 Meters Underground, Destroyed Most of the Facility," *Jerusalem Post,* April 13, 2021, https://www.jpost.com/middle-east/natanz-attack-destroyed-facility-50-meters-underground-664979.

211 *blamed Israel:* "Zionists Want to Take Revenge on Iranians for Successful Lifting Sanctions: Zarif," Islamic Republic News Agency, April 12, 2021, https://en.irna.ir/news/84292637/Zionists-want-to-take-revenge-on-Iranians-for-successful-lifting.

211 *"very beautiful":* Joffre and Bob, Natanz Attack Hit 50 Meters Underground, Destroyed Most of the Facility."

212 *boots on the ground*: Author interview with intelligence official.

212 *in a desk:* "Iran Natanz Nuclear Site Suffered Major Damage, Official Says," BBC News, April 13, 2021, https://www.bbc.com/news/world-middle-east-56734657; Joffre and Bob, "Natanz Attack Hit 50 Meters Underground, Destroyed Most of the Facility"; assorted Iranian media.

212 *three hundred pounds:* Joffre and Bob, "Natanz Attack Hit 50 Meters Underground, Destroyed Most of the Facility"; assorted Iranian media.

212 *many years before:* Attila Somfalvi, "Olmert: Netanyahu Willing to Sell Out Israel's Security. Natanz Wasn't Broken into the Day Before Yesterday," *Yedioth Ahronoth,* April 13, 2021, https://www.ynet.co.il/news/article/Hy140aGLd; "Olmert Says Iran Natanz Bomb Could Have Been Planted 10–15 Years Ago," *Times of Israel,* April 14, 2021, https://www.timesofisrael.com/olmert-says-iran-natanz-bomb-could-have-been-planted-10-15-years-ago/; author interviews with former Israeli prime minister Ehud Olmert.

213 *the CIA concealed:* Merritt Kennedy, "The CIA 'Inadvertently Left' Explosive Material in School Bus After K-9 Drill," NPR, April 1, 2016, https://www.npr.org/sections/thetwo-way/2016/04/01/472673185/the-cia-inadvertently-left-explosives-in-virginia-school-bus-after-k-9-drill.

213 *Reza Karimi:* "Iran Names Suspect in Natanz Nuclear Site Attack, Says He Fled Country," Associated Press/*Arab News,* April 17, 2021, https://www.arabnews.com/node/1844331/middle-east; assorted Iranian media.

214 *IAEA released a report:* IAEA Report to Board of Governors, May 31, 2021, released publicly June 1, 2021, https://www.iaea.org/sites/default/files/21/06/gov2021-28.pdf.

215 *only hundreds:* Author interviews with Albright; Yonah Jeremy Bob, "The Truth About the Natanz Explosion Impact Revealed," *Jerusalem Post,* June 1, 2021,

https://www.jpost.com/middle-east/the-truth-about-the-natanz-explosion-impact-revealed-669824.

216 *outflank Israel:* Yonah Jeremy Bob, "Mossad's Cohen Doctrine on Iran: Never Stop—Analysis," *Jerusalem Post,* April 13, 2021, https://www.jpost.com/middle-east/iran-news/mossads-cohen-doctrine-on-iran-never-stop-analysis-664960; author interviews with Israeli intelligence officials.

216 *brush off:* Bob, "Mossad's Cohen Doctrine on Iran: Never Stop—Analysis"; author interviews with Israeli intelligence officials.

CHAPTER 14: DEATH BY A THOUSAND CUTS

Author interviews late 2020–April 2023

217 *operating at Natanz:* IAEA report, April 31, 2021, https://www.iaea.org/sites/default/files/22/07/govinf2021-28.pdf.

217 *Israeli delegation included:* John Hannah, "The Countdown to an Israeli War with Iran Has Begun," *Foreign Policy,* May 6, 2021, https://foreignpolicy.com/2021/05/06/iran-nuclear-deal-jcpoa-biden-israel-talks-washington-war; author interviews with Israeli officials.

218 *would alter:* Hannah, "The Countdown to an Israeli War with Iran Has Begun"; IAEA report, April 31, 2021; author interviews with Israeli officials.

219 *by his critics:* Herb Keinon, "Growing Concern in Israel over Appointment of Malley as US Rep. to Iran," *Jerusalem Post,* January 27, 2021, https://www.jpost.com/international/rob-malley-appointment-to-us-special-rep-to-iran-is-bad-news-for-israel-656812.

219 *face-to-face:* Yonah Jeremy Bob, "Mossad Chief Discussed Iran with Biden in Hour-Long Meeting," *Jerusalem Post,* May 3, 2021, https://www.jpost.com/international/how-did-mossad-chief-get-the-podium-back-with-one-hour-biden-meeting-667001.

219 *the U.S. surprised:* Yonah Jeremy Bob, "Sticking Points in the Iran Nuclear Deal—Analysis," *Jerusalem Post,* June 7, 2021, https://www.jpost.com/middle-east/iran-news/sticking-points-in-the-iran-nuclear-deal-analysis-670353; Yonah Jeremy Bob, "Khamenei Wants New Deal to Wait Until After June 18 Election—Analysis," *Jerusalem Post,* May 25, 2021, https://www.jpost.com/middle-east/iran-news/khamenei-wants-new-deal-to-wait-until-after-june-18-election-analysis-669155.

220 *retirement ceremony:* Yonah Jeremy Bob, "Pompeo to 'Post': Iran Unwound Nuclear Deal in a Matter of Months," *Jerusalem Post,* June 24, 2021, https://www.jpost.com/middle-east/iran-news/pompeo-to-post-iran-unwound-nuclear-deal-in-a-matter-of-months-671928.

220 *"penetrated into the heart":* "We Penetrated 'Heart of Hearts' of Iran, Outgoing Mossad Head Exults at Farewell," *Times of Israel,* June 1, 2021, https://www.timesofisrael.com/we-penetrated-heart-of-iran-outgoing-mossad-chief-crows-at-farewell/.

220 *began his career:* Yossi Melman, "Incoming Mossad Chief Revealed as David Barnea. Here's Where He Came From," *Haaretz,* May 24, 2021, https://www.haaretz

.com/israel-news/2021-05-24/ty-article/.premium/incoming-mossad-chief-revealed-as-david-barnea-heres-where-he-came-from/0000017f-e9ed-d62c-a1ff-fdff03d70000; Yonah Jeremy Bob, "Passing The Mossad Torch: Can David Barnea Fill Yossi Cohen's Shoes?," *Jerusalem Post*, May 27, 202, https://www.jpost.com/israel-news/passing-the-mossad-torch-can-david-barnea-fill-yossi-cohens-shoes-669428; Yonah Jeremy Bob, "Barnea Takes Over Mossad; Cohen: Mossad Struck Deep into Iran's Heart," *Jerusalem Post*, June 1, 2021, https://www.jpost.com/israel-news/mossad-cohen-out-barnea-in-incoming-chief-starts-on-tuesday-669757; Yonah Jeremy Bob, "David Barnea Appointed as New Mossad Head, Replaces Cohen Next Week," *Jerusalem Post*, May 24, 2021, https://www.jpost.com/breaking-news/david-barnea-appointed-as-new-mossad-head-to-replace-cohen-next-week-669008.

220 *newly elected:* "Netanyahu Out as New Israeli Government Approved," BBC, June 13, 2021, https://www.bbc.com/news/world-middle-east-57462470.

221 *His experiences:* Author interview with former Israeli prime minister Naftali Bennett.

221 *"We've been suckers":* Author interview with former Israeli prime minister Naftali Bennett.

222 *manufacturing parts:* Yonah Jeremy Bob, "Iran Nuclear Centrifuge Facility Substantially Damaged in Attack—Sources," *Jerusalem Post*, June 23, 2021, updated June 24, 2021, https://www.jpost.com/middle-east/drone-attack-targets-irans-atomic-energy-organization-671834.

222 *caused significant damage:* Yonah Jeremy Bob, "What Might Be the Real Target of the Sabotage in Iran?—Analysis," *Jerusalem Post*, June 23, 2021, https://www.jpost.com/middle-east/iran-news/what-might-be-the-real-target-of-the-sabotage-in-iran-analysis-671864; Bob, "Iran Nuclear Centrifuge Facility Substantially Damaged in Attack—Sources."

222 *launched the drone:* Farnaz Fassihi and Ronen Bergman, "Iran Atomic Agency Says It Thwarted Attack on a Facility," *New York Times*, June 23, 2021, https://www.nytimes.com/2021/06/23/world/middleeast/iran-atomic-agency-attack.html; Jake Wallis Simons, "Mossad Recruited Top Iranian Scientists to Blow Up Key Nuclear Facility," *Jewish Chronicle*, December 2, 2021, https://www.thejc.com/news/world/exclusive-mossad-recruited-top-iranian-scientists-to-blow-up-key-nuclear-facility-1.523163; Bob, "What Might Be the Real Target of the Sabotage in Iran?—Analysis."

222 *bogus Iranian claims:* Yonah Jeremy Bob, "IAEA Chief Shows Off Iran-Style Nuke Monitoring Camera," *Jerusalem Post*, December 17, 2021, https://www.jpost.com/middle-east/iran-news/iaea-chief-shows-off-iran-style-nuke-monitoring-camera-689060.

223 *most intense:* Author interview with former Israeli prime minister Naftali Bennett; author interviews with Israeli intelligence officials.

223 *Iran will come:* Author interviews with intelligence sources.

223 *"eye to eye":* Author interview with former Israeli prime minister Naftali Bennett; author interviews with Biden administration officials; author interviews with Is-

raeli intelligence officials; Aaron David Miller, "Analysis: Why Biden Is Trying to Keep Naftali Bennett Afloat," *Foreign Policy*, June 15, 2021, https://foreignpolicy.com/2022/06/15/biden-middle-east-trip-israel-naftali-bennett-netanyahu/.

224 *the Cold War:* Author interviews with Biden administration officials; author interview with former Israeli prime minister Naftali Bennett; author interviews with Israeli intelligence officials; Barak Ravid, "Israeli PM Presented Biden with 'Death by a Thousand Cuts' Iran Strategy," *Axios*, August 28, 2021, https://www.axios.com/2021/08/27/naftali-bennett-joe-biden-meeting-iran-strategy; Lahav Harkov, "Biden: If Diplomacy Fails with Iran, We Have Other Options," *Jerusalem Post*, August 28, 2021, https://www.jpost.com/international/bennett-and-biden-meet-in-white-house-677908. Curiously, this whole strategy was influenced in no small part by a book that the Foundation for Defense of Democracies chief executive, Mark Dubowitz, gave to Israeli intelligence officials. At some point, Barnea gave the book to Bennett, who then told the entire Israeli intelligence establishment, including the Israeli military intelligence chief, the IDF chief of staff, and the entire National Security Council, that it should be required reading. The book: Peter Schweizer, *Victory: The Reagan Administration's Secret Strategy That Hastened the Collapse of the Soviet Union* (New York: Atlantic Monthly Press), written all the way back in 1994. But Barnea and Bennett are men of history who carefully unite lessons from the past with confronting challenges in the future.

224 *the 84 percent level:* Yonah Jeremy Bob, "IAEA Chief Doubles Down Against Potential Pre-emptive Israeli Strikes on Iran," *Jerusalem Post*, March 6, 2013, https://www.jpost.com/middle-east/article-733496.

224 *90 percent enriched uranium:* Author interviews with Biden administration officials; Harkov, "Biden: If Diplomacy Fails with Iran, We Have Other Options"; Kelsey Davenport, "The Nonproliferation Consequences of Biden's Inaction on the Iran Nuclear Deal," *Just Security*, June 23, 2022, https://www.justsecurity.org/82038/the-nonproliferation-consequences-of-bidens-inaction-on-the-iran-nuclear-deal/; author interviews with former Israeli prime minister Naftali Bennett; author interviews with Israeli intelligence officials.

225 *ballistic missile program:* Julian E. Barnes, Ronen Bergman, and David E. Sanger, "Iran's Nuclear Program Ignites New Tension Between U.S. and Israel," *New York Times*, December 10, 2021, https://www.nytimes.com/2021/12/10/us/politics/iran-nuclear-us-israel-biden-bennett.html; author interviews with Israeli officials.

225 *satellite imagery:* "Satellite Images Show Damage at Iran Missile Factory After Possible Attack," *Iran International*, October 1, 2021, https://www.iranintl.com/en/20211001127160.

226 *tore up:* Patrick Wintour, "Iran Nuclear Talks Pulled Back from Brink as Tehran Shifts Stance," *The Guardian*, December 9, 2021, https://www.theguardian.com/world/2021/dec/09/iran-nuclear-deal-pulled-back-from-brink-of-collapse-as-talks-resume-in-vienna; Yonah Jeremy Bob, "Will the Iranian Nuclear Talks Ever End?," *Jerusalem Post*, July 1, 2022, https://www.jpost.com/middle-east/iran-news/article-710904.

226 *had one concession:* Arshad Mohammed and Parisa Hafezi, "U.S. Weighs Dropping Iran's IRGC from Terrorism List—Source," Reuters, March 16, 2022, https://www.reuters.com/world/us-weighs-dropping-irans-irgc-terrorism-list-source-2022-03-16/; Lahav Harkov, "Did Jerusalem Win the Fight to Keep IRGC Designated, or Is Washington Playing Games?—Analysis," *Jerusalem Post*, April 10, 2022, https://www.jpost.com/middle-east/iran-news/article-703792.

226 *ready to do this:* Alexander Ward and Nahal Toosi, "Biden Made Final Decision to Keep Iran's IRGC on Terrorist List," *Politico*, May 24, 2022, https://www.politico.com/news/2022/05/24/biden-final-decision-iran-revolutionary-guard-terrorist-00034789; Pieter Haeck, "Iran Drops 'Red Line' IRGC Demand for Nuclear Deal: Report," *Politico*, August 20, 2022, https://www.politico.eu/article/iran-drops-red-line-demand-for-a-nuclear-deal-report/; author interviews with former Israeli prime minister Naftali Bennett and Israeli intelligence officials.

227 *"more for more":* Ward and Toosi, "Biden Made Final Decision to Keep Iran's IRGC on Terrorist List"; Haeck, "Iran Drops 'Red Line' IRGC Demand for Nuclear Deal: Report"; author interviews with former Israeli prime minister Naftali Bennett and Israeli intelligence officials.

227 *central pillars:* Author interviews with U.S. Iran chief negotiator Rob Malley.

227 *it was doubtful:* Author interviews with former Israeli prime minister Naftali Bennett, senior Biden administration officials, and Israeli intelligence officials.

227 *125 Iranian drones:* Amos Harel, "Hundreds of Iranian Drones Destroyed in Israel-Attributed Attack Last Month," *Haaretz*, March 15, 2022, https://www.haaretz.com/israel-news/2022-03-15/ty-article/.highlight/israel-destroyed-hundreds-of-iranian-drones-in-massive-strike/00000180-5bc8-dc1d-afc2-fbcd1b240000; anonymous officials.

228 *Israeli strategic centers:* "Irbil Attack: Iran Launches Missiles at Northern Iraqi City," BBC, March 13, 2022, https://www.bbc.com/news/world-middle-east-60725959; Mandi Kogosowski, "Iran Claims It Targeted Mossad Facility in Erbil," March 13, 2022, https://www.israeldefense.co.il/en/node/53902l; "US Base, Mossad Training Center in Erbil Targeted by Missiles," Mehr New Agency, March 13, 2022, https://en.mehrnews.com/news/184790/US-base-Mossad-training-center-in-Erbil-targeted-by-missiles.

228 *had been lax:* Yonah Jeremy Bob, "Iran's Info. on Mossad Chief Barnea Is Old—Ex-Mossad Chief Yatom," *Jerusalem Post*, March 17, 2022, https://www.jpost.com/middle-east/iran-news/article-701594.

228 *Mansour Rasouli:* Yonah Jeremy Bob, "Between Mossad Ops, Iran Satellite Launches and Camera Removal: Who Is on Top?—Analysis," *Jerusalem Post*, June 16, 2022, https://www.jpost.com/israel-news/article-709641; Yonah Jeremy Bob, "More Details Emerge About IRGC Official Interrogated by Mossad—Report," *Jerusalem Post*, May 12, 2022, https://www.jpost.com/middle-east/article-706553.

229 *Colonel Hassen Sayyad Khodaei:* Matthew Levitt, "The Backstory Behind the Killing of Qods Force Col. Khodaei," Washington Institute for Near East Policy, June 20, 2022, https://www.washingtoninstitute.org/policy-analysis/backstory

-behind-killing-qods-force-col-khodaei; "Exclusive—Slain IRGC Officer Organized Attacks Against Israel: Source," *Iran International*, May 23, 2022, https://www.iranintl.com/en/202205236140.

229 *definitely the work:* Farnaz Fassihi and Ronen Bergman, "Israel Tells U.S. It Killed Iranian Officer, Official Says," *New York Times*, May 25, 2022, https://www.nytimes.com/2022/05/25/world/middleeast/iran-israel-killing-khodayee.html.

229 *a list of five Israelis:* Mardo Soghom, "Iranian Website Publishes Profiles of Israelis as Potential Targets," *Iran International*, May 29, 2022, https://www.iranintl.com/en/202205294162.

230 *through the roof:* Farnaz Fassihi and Ronen Bergman, "Sensitive Iranian Military Site Was Targeted in Attack," *New York Times*, May 27, 2022, https://www.nytimes.com/2022/05/27/world/middleeast/iran-drone-attack.html#:~:text=A%20drone%20exploded%20at%20a,past%20Israeli%20strikes%20on%20Iran.

230 *Iran had hacked:* Lahav Harkov, "Bennett Confirms Classified IAEA Docs Were Stolen by Iran," *Jerusalem Post*, May 31, 2022, https://www.jpost.com/middle-east/article-708147.

230 *the exact timing:* Author interviews with former Israeli prime minister Naftali Bennett, Israeli intelligence officials, and former Israeli prime minister's office adviser Yarden Vatikai.

230 *possible mole:* Bob, "Between Mossad Ops, Iran Satellite Launches and Camera Removal: Who Is on Top?—Analysis"; Farnaz Fassihi and Ronen Bergman, "Senior Iranian Officer Dies Leaving Questions About His Death," *New York Times*, June 4, 2022, https://www.nytimes.com/2022/06/04/world/middleeast/iran-israel-guards-death.html.

231 *advised to evacuate:* "Mossad, Turkey Foil Iranian Plot to Kidnap Israelis," *Jerusalem Post*, June 23, 2022, https://www.jpost.com/breaking-news/article-710182; "Iranian Cell Planning Attack on Israelis Nabbed in Turkey: Report," *Daily Sabah*/Agencies, June 23, 2022, https://www.dailysabah.com/turkey/investigations/iranian-cell-planning-attack-on-israelis-nabbed-in-turkey-report.

232 *back to life:* Author interview with EU chief negotiator on Iran Enrique Mora.

232 *thought of as guidelines:* Author interviews with U.S. chief negotiator on Iran Rob Malley.

232 *Iran's steel industry:* Yonah Jeremy Bob, "Iran's Steel Industry Halted by Cyberattack," *Jerusalem Post*, June 27, 2022, https://www.jpost.com/middle-east/iran-news/article-710522.

232 *successful launch:* Bob, "Between Mossad Ops, Iran Satellite Launches and Camera Removal: Who Is on Top?—Analysis"; assorted Iranian media.

233 *nailed down:* IAEA report, April 23, 2021, https://www.iaea.org/sites/default/files/22/07/govinf2021-28.pdf.

233 *generally not welcomed:* Author interviews with top Israeli officials and top Biden administration officials.

233 *formally condemned:* "IAEA's 35-Nation Board Passes Resolution Chiding Iran on Uranium Traces," Reuters, June 8, 2022, https://www.reuters.com/world

/middle-east/iaeas-35-nation-board-passes-resolution-chiding-iran-uranium-traces-2022-06-08/.

234 *shutting off:* Yonah Jeremy Bob and Omri Nahmias, "Fatal Blow to JCPOA if Iran Doesn't Restore Access Within 3–4 Weeks—IAEA," *Jerusalem Post,* June 9, 2022, https://www.jpost.com/breaking-news/article-708998.

234 *brush off:* Yonah Jeremy Bob, "IAEA Chief Revealed What He Wanted from Meeting with Bennett—Analysis," *Jerusalem Post,* June 6, 2022, https://www.jpost.com/middle-east/article-708687.

234 *Iranian transparency:* Author interviews with senior U.S. State Department officials.

235 *no disagreement:* Author interviews with U.S. chief negotiator on Iran Rob Malley.

CHAPTER 15: THE ABRAHAM ACCORDS, THE SAUDIS, AND THE FUTURE

Author interviews late 2020–April 2023

237 *most advanced:* Sahar Vardi, "The Real Winners in the Israel-UAE Deal? 'Arms Dealers,'" *+972 Magazine,* October 8, 2020, https://www.972mag.com/israel-uae-deal-arms-industry/; Hagai Amit, "The Real Deal for Israel and the UAE Is Weapons," *Haaretz,* August 17, 2020, https://www.haaretz.com/israel-news/business/2020-08-17/ty-article/.premium/the-real-deal-for-israel-and-the-uae-is-weapons/0000017f-f2ad-d5bd-a17f-f6bf40fc0000; Michael Peck, "Middle East Shocker: Israel May Sell Weapons to Arab Nations," *Forbes,* https://www.forbes.com/sites/michaelpeck/2020/09/03/middle-east-shocker-israel-may-sell-weapons-to-arab-nations/?sh=3aa8e4db6f86.

237 *might cooperate:* Dan Williams, "Israel Signals Openness to Future Joint Missile Defence with Gulf Partners," Reuters, December 15, 2020, https://www.reuters.com/article/us-israel-gulf-missiledefence/israel-signals-openness-to-future-joint-missile-defence-with-gulf-partners-idUSKBN28P1IL.

237 *first public appearance:* Yonah Jeremy Bob, "Ex-Mossad Chief Yossi Cohen: Potential for Israel-UAE Progress Is 'Endless,'" *Jerusalem Post,* October 17, 2021, https://www.jpost.com/middle-east/ex-mossad-chief-yossi-cohen-potential-for-israel-uae-progress-is-endless-682260; observations of the authors at the conference.

238 *had soared:* Emanuel Fabian, "Israeli Arms Sales Hit New Record of $11.3 Billion in 2021—with 7% to Gulf," *Times of Israel,* April 12, 2022, https://www.timesofisrael.com/israeli-arms-sales-hit-new-record-of-11-3-billion-in-2021/.

238 *at least three times:* Aya Batraw, "Drone Attack in Abu Dhabi Claimed by Yemen's Rebels Kills 3," Associated Press, January 17, 2022, https://apnews.com/article/business-dubai-united-arab-emirates-abu-dhabi-yemen-8bdefdf900ce46a6fd6c7bc685bf838a; "Houthi Missiles Target Saudi Arabia and UAE as Escalation Grows," Al Jazeera, January 24, 2022, https://www.aljazeera.com/news/2022/1/24/uae-says-intercepted-and-destroyed-houthi-missiles; "UAE Intercepts Houthi Missile as Israeli President Visits," Al Jazeera, January 31, 2022, https://www.aljazeera.com/news/2022/1/31/uae-intercepts-houthi-missile

-as-israeli-president-visits; "UAE Says It Destroyed Three Drones with 'Hostile' Intent," Al Jazeera, February 2, 2022, https://www.aljazeera.com/news/2022/2/2/uae-destroys-three-drones-with-hostile-intent-ministry.

238 *heavy transport planes:* Anna Ahronheim, "Eight Heavy Transport Aircraft Belonging to UAE Landed in Israel in Past Two Weeks," *Jerusalem Post*, April 30, 2022; Avi Scharf, Twitter, https://twitter.com/avischarf/status/1533783409453047810.

238 *Barak-8 aerial defense batteries:* "Israeli Barak Air Defense System Appears in UAE: Implications and Analysis," *Tactical Report*, October 28, 2022, https://www.tacticalreport.com/news/article/60738-?utm_campaign=special-report-post&utm_medium=social&utm_source=twitter; Arie Egozi, "First Israeli Barak Air Defense System Deploys to UAE, Bigger Deals Expected: Sources," *Breaking Defense*, October 19, 2022, https://breakingdefense.com/2022/10/first-israeli-barak-air-defense-system-deploys-to-uae-bigger-deals-expected-sources/.

238 *SPYDER mobile interception system:* Alexander Cornwell and John Irish, "Exclusive: Israel to Sell Air Defence System to United Arab Emirates," Reuters, October 22, 2022, https://www.reuters.com/world/middle-east/exclusive-israel-sell-air-defence-system-united-arab-emirates-sources-say-2022-09-22/.

239 *his Bahraini counterpart:* "Israel Defence Minister Signs Security Agreement with Bahrain," Reuters, February 3, 2022, https://www.reuters.com/world/middle-east/israel-defence-minister-visits-us-navy-base-bahrain-2022-02-03/.

239 *the American Fifth Fleet:* Ibid.

239 *training Bahraini intelligence officers:* Dan Nissenbaum and Dov Lieber, "Biden Presses for Israeli-Arab Security Ties to Come Out from the Shadows," *Wall Street Journal*, July 12, 2022, https://www.wsj.com/articles/biden-presses-for-israeli-arab-security-ties-to-come-out-from-the-shadows-11657650256?mod=world_major_pos10.

239 *top military officials:* Michael R. Gordon and David S. Cloud, "U.S. Held Secret Meeting with Israeli, Arab Military Chiefs to Counter Iran Air Threat," *Wall Street Journal*, June 26, 2022, https://www.wsj.com/articles/u-s-held-secret-meeting-with-israeli-arab-military-chiefs-to-counter-iran-air-threat-11656235802; author interviews with top Israeli officials.

239 *Israel had been absorbed:* Seth J. Frantzman, "US Central Command Absorbs Israel into Its Area of Responsibility," *Defense News*, September 7, 2021, https://www.defensenews.com/global/mideast-africa/2021/09/07/us-central-command-absorbs-israel-into-its-area-of-responsibility/.

239 *signed a deal:* Mike Stone, "Saudi Arabia Inks Deal for Lockheed's Missile Defense System," Reuters, November 29, 2018, https://www.reuters.com/article/us-saudi-arms-missiledefense-idUSKCN1NX2YJ.

239 *"The task in the theater":* Gordon and Cloud, "U.S. Held Secret Meeting with Israeli, Arab Military Chiefs to Counter Iran Air Threat."

240 *the "Iron Beam":* Author interviews with top Israeli officials.

240 *laser system ready:* Author interview with former Israeli prime minister Naftali Bennett.

240 *nullify Iran's ring of fire:* "Prime Minister Naftali Bennett's Remarks at the INSS

15th Annual International Conference," Israel Government Press Office, February 2, 2022, https://www.gov.il/en/departments/news/inss01022022.

240 *Middle East Air Defense Alliance:* Emanuel Fabian, "Gantz Says Regional Air Defense Alliance Has Already Thwarted Iranian Attacks," *Times of Israel*, https://www.timesofisrael.com/gantz-says-regional-air-defense-alliance-has-already-thwarted-iranian-attacks/; Aerie Egozi, "Israel Announces Regional Air Defense Network with Middle East Partners, US," *Breaking Defense*, June 20, 2022, https://breakingdefense.com/2022/06/israel-announces-regional-air-defense-network-with-middle-east-partners-us/.

240 *a March 2021 incident:* Seth J. Frantzman, "Israel Reveals First Time It Used F-35 to Shoot Down Iranian Drone," *Defense News*, March 8, 2022, https://www.defensenews.com/unmanned/2022/03/08/israel-reveals-first-time-it-used-f-35-to-shoot-down-iranian-drone/#:~:text=%E2%80%9CIn%20March%202021%2C%20the%20Iranian,world%2C%E2%80%9D%20the%20IDF%20said.

241 *the DEFEND Act:* S.4366—DEFEND Act of 2022, introduced in Congress June 9, 2022, https://www.congress.gov/bill/117th-congress/senate-bill/4366/text.

241 *convened a meeting:* Conor Finnegan, "Blinken Attends 'Historic' Israeli, Arab Summit Amid Iran Deal Tensions, Palestinian Opposition," ABC News, March 28, 2022, https://abcnews.go.com/Politics/blinken-attends-historic-israeli-arab-summit-amid-iran/story?id=83701822; author interviews with top Biden administration officials.

241 *"not just the salad":* Author interview with Biden administration Abraham Accords official Hady Amr.

242 *"There were six":* "Former Israeli prime minister Yair Lapid's September 22, 2022 speech to the UN," https://www.gov.il/en/departments/news/event-speech-un220922.

242 *the second anniversary:* Josh Block, "The Abraham Accords' Second Anniversary Defines Shared Tolerance," Hudson Institute, September 19, 2022, https://www.hudson.org/foreign-policy/the-abraham-accords-second-anniversary-defines-shared-tolerance; "UAE Foreign Minister Arrives in Israel, Marking 2 Years of Abraham Accords—WAM," Reuters, September 14, 2022, https://www.reuters.com/world/middle-east/uae-foreign-minister-arrives-israel-official-visit-state-news-agency-2022-09-14/.

242 *may share:* Yonah Jeremy Bob, "Israel May Share Nuclear Tech with Abraham Accords States—Israeli Atomic Chief," *Jerusalem Post*, September 28, 2022, https://www.jpost.com/israel-news/article-718327)\.

243 *500,000 Israelis visited:* Israeli Foreign Minister Director-General Alon Ushpiz, "Abraham Accords Is Creating New Mideast Regional Architecture—Opinion," op-ed, *Jerusalem Post*, September 19, 2022, https://www.jpost.com/opinion/article-717481.

243 *trade soared:* "UAE and Israel Sign Comprehensive Economic Partnership Agreement to Advance Bilateral Trade Beyond USD 10 Billion in 5 Years," United Arab Emirates press statement, May 31, 2022, https://www.moec.gov.ae/en/-/uae-and-israel-sign-comprehensive-economic-partnership-agreement-to-advance

-bilateral-trade-beyond-usd-10-billion-in-5-years; Ushpiz, "Abraham Accords Is Creating New Mideast Regional Architecture—Opinion."

243 *business background:* Author interviews with senior Israeli officials; Nadav Eyal, "Interview with Shimrit Meir," *Yedioth Ahronoth*, July 1, 2022, partially posted in Hebrew at: https://www.ynet.co.il/news/article/h1svwmo55.

244 *ordering the murder:* Shane Harris, Greg Miller, and Josh Dawsey, "CIA Concludes Saudi Crown Prince Ordered Jamal Khashoggi's Assassination," *Washington Post*, November 16, 2018, https://www.washingtonpost.com/world/national-security/cia-concludes-saudi-crown-prince-ordered-jamal-khashoggis-assassination/2018/11/16/98c89fe6-e9b2-11e8-a939-9469f1166f9d_story.html.

244 *giving credit:* "Joe Biden Campaign Welcomes Historic Abraham Accords," AFP/I-24 News, September 16, 2020, https://www.i24news.tv/en/news/international/americas/1600233155-joe-biden-campaign-welcomes-historic-abraham-accords; Alex Gangitano, "Biden Says He 'Strongly Supports' Trump's Abraham Accords," *The Hill*, July 14, 2022, https://thehill.com/homenews/administration/3558921-biden-says-he-strongly-supports-trumps-abraham-accords/.

244 *speaking to him:* Elise Labott, "How Biden Came Around to MBS' Plan for a New U.S.-Saudi Partnership," *Politico*, June 15, 2022, https://www.politico.com/news/2022/06/15/joe-biden-saudi-arabia-trip-bin-salman-00039679; interviews with top Israeli and U.S. officials.

244 *a rethink:* Labott, "How Biden Came Around to MBS' Plan for a New U.S.-Saudi Partnership"; author interviews with top Israeli and U.S. officials.

245 *firmly shut:* Labott, "How Biden Came Around to MBS' Plan for a New U.S.-Saudi Partnership."

245 *when he landed:* Quint Forgey and Kelly Hooper, "Biden Fist Bump with MBS Triggers Backlash," *Politico*, July 15, 2022, https://www.politico.com/news/2022/07/15/a-fist-bump-at-the-palace-biden-squares-off-with-mbs-00046106.

245 *without any promises:* Mohamad Bazzi, "Biden Decision to Grant Saudi Crown Prince Immunity Is a Profound Mistake," *The Guardian*, November 21, 2022, https://www.theguardian.com/commentisfree/2022/nov/21/bidens-decision-to-grant-mbs-immunity-is-a-profound-mistake.

246 *separating themselves:* Author interviews with top Israeli officials.

246 *deserves some credit:* Author interviews with top U.S. officials; Alexander Ward, "U.S. Announces $316M for Palestinians as Biden Visits West Bank," *Politico*, July 14, 2022, https://www.politico.com/news/2022/07/14/316m-for-palestinians-as-biden-visits-west-bank-00046014.

246 *carefully worded:* "Saudi Arabia to Open Airspace to All Airlines, Including from Israel," Reuters/CNBC, July 15, 2022, https://www.cnbc.com/2022/07/15/saudi-arabia-to-open-airspace-to-all-airlines-including-from-israel.html; "Lifting of Flight Restrictions Has Nothing to Do with Israel Ties: Saudi FM," *Daily Sabah*/Agencies, July 16, 2022, https://www.dailysabah.com/business/transportation/lifting-of-flight-restrictions-has-nothing-to-do-with-israel-ties-saudi-fm.

247 *believed that MBS:* Yonah Jeremy Bob and Aaron Reich, "Mossad Head: Saudi Normalization Ties Close; Post US Election Could See Progress," *Jerusalem*

Post, October 25, 2020, https://www.jpost.com/middle-east/mossad-head-saudi-normalization-ties-to-be-announced-after-us-election-646828; Tovah Lazaroff, "Intelligence Min: Additional Peace Deals Prior to Trump Exit Unlikely," *Jerusalem Post*, December 23, 2020, https://www.jpost.com/israel-news/intelligence-min-additional-peace-deals-prior-to-trump-exit-unlikely-653010; Yonah Jeremy Bob, "Saudi Arabia–Israel Normalization Deal Estimated Within One Year," *Jerusalem Post*, December 28, 2020, https://www.jpost.com/israel-news/saudi-arabia-israel-normalization-deal-within-one-year-653526.

247 *out of the question:* Author interview with former Israeli intelligence official.

247 *a lot of people:* Ibid.

248 *promised to make:* "Exclusive—The Netanyahu Doctrine: An In-Depth Regional Policy Interview," Al Arabiya, December 15, 2022, https://english.alarabiya.net/News/middle-east/2022/12/15/Exclusive-The-Netanyahu-Doctrine-an-in-depth-regional-policy-interview.

248 *the Saudis will not*: Author interviews with top intelligence officials.

248 *Saudi Arabia and Iran:* Parisa Hafezi, Nayera Abdallah, and Aziz El Yaakoubi, "Iran and Saudi Arabia Agree to Resume Ties in Talks Brokered by China," Reuters, March 11, 2023, https://www.reuters.com/world/middle-east/iran-saudi-arabia-agree-resume-ties-re-open-embassies-iranian-state-media-2023-03-10/; author interviews with Israeli intelligence officials; Murtaza Hussain, "The Key Factor in the Saudi-Iran Deal: Absolutely No U.S. Involvement," *The Intercept*, March 15, 2023, https://theintercept.com/2023/03/15/saudi-iran-deal/; Isaac Chotiner, "What the Saudi-Iran Deal Means for the Middle East," *The New Yorker*, March 14, 2023, https://www.newyorker.com/news/q-and-a/what-the-saudi-iran-deal-means-for-the-middle-east; Meir Ben Shabbat, "Israel's Challenge: Preserving the Abraham Accords as US Lowers Regional Profile," *Israel Hayom*, March 13, 2023, https://www.israelhayom.com/2023/03/13/israels-challenge-preserving-the-abraham-accords-as-us-lowers-regional-profile/; Yonah Jeremy Bob, "Saudi Arabia Makes Historic Purchase of Boeing Aircraft," *Jerusalem Post*, March 14, 2023, https://www.jpost.com/middle-east/article-734298; Sima Shine, Yoel Guzansky, and Eldad Shavit, "Iran and Saudi Arabia Renew Relations," INSS, March 14, 2023, https://www.inss.org.il/publication/iran-saudi-arabia-2/?utm_source=activetrail&utm_medium=email&utm_campaign=INSS%20Insight%20|%20Iran%20and%20Saudi%20Arabia%20Renew%20Relations.

249 *the day before:* Dion Nissenbaum, Dov Lieber, and Stephen Kalin, "Saudi Arabia Seeks U.S. Security Pledges, Nuclear Help for Peace with Israel," *Wall Street Journal*, March 9, 2023, https://www.wsj.com/articles/saudi-arabia-seeks-u-s-security-pledges-nuclear-help-for-peace-with-israel-cd47baaf.

249 *may ditch waiting:* Author interviews with intelligence officials.

249 *more going on*: "Abraham Accords Won't Be Harmed by Renewed Saudi-Iran Ties, Official Explains," *Jerusalem Post/Maariv Online,* March 10, 2023, https://www.jpost.com/middle-east/article-733973.

250 *Mauritania and Indonesia:* Jacob Magid, "Trump Officials: Mauritania, Indonesia Were Next to Normalize, but Time Ran Out," *Times of Israel*, January 19, 2021,

https://www.timesofisrael.com/mauritania-indonesia-were-next-in-line-to-normalize-but-trump-ran-out-of-time/; author interviews with U.S. and Israeli officials.

250 *pull out:* Author interviews with top Israeli and U.S. officials.

CONCLUSION: THE MOSSAD'S PROMISE

255 *Chariots of Fire:* Anna Ahronheim, "Israel Simulates Massive Strike Against Iran with Hundreds of IDF Aircraft," *Jerusalem Post*, June 1, 2022, https://www.jpost.com/israel-news/article-708256.

255 *veto a snapback:* "What Is 'Snapback'? US' Iran Sanctions Move Explained," AFP, August 20, 2020, https://www.france24.com/en/20200819-what-is-snapback-us-iran-sanctions-move-explained.

255 *many people believe:* Author interviews with Israeli officials and former U.S. government officials.

256 *expire in October 2025:* Author interviews with a variety of top Israeli and U.S. officials; author interview with IDF chief of staff Lieutenant General Aviv Kohavi; Kelsey Davenport, "The Joint Comprehensive Plan of Action (JCPOA) at a Glance," Arms Control Association, March 2022, https://www.armscontrol.org/factsheets/JCPOA-at-a-glance; David Albright, Sarah Burkhard, and Spencer Faragasso, "The Nuclear Deal in Charts, Assuming a Revived Nuclear Deal," Institute for Science and International Security, October 20, 2022, https://isis-online.org/isis-reports/detail/the-nuclear-deal-in-charts-assuming-a-revived-nuclear-deal/8.

256 *to find out:* Author interviews with top Israeli officials and Israeli intelligence officials.

256 *still expire:* Author interviews with top Israeli and U.S. officials; Davenport, "The Joint Comprehensive Plan of Action (JCPOA) at a Glance"; Albright, Burkhard, and Faragasso, "The Nuclear Deal in Charts, Assuming a Revived Nuclear Deal."

256 *is overblown:* Author interviews with senior Biden administration officials.

257 *significant aversion:* "Time for Plan B on Iran JINSA," May 25, 2022, https://jinsa.org/jinsa_report/iran-project-report-release-may-2022/; "The Iran Nuclear Deal Is Close to Collapsing Despite Biden's Efforts, and Experts Warn 'There Is No Plan B,'" *Business Insider*, November 2, 2021, https://www.businessinsider.com/no-plan-b-biden-iran-nuclear-talks-fail-experts-warn-2021-11; author interviews with Israeli officials, former U.S. officials, and various U.S. national security experts.

258 *allocating billions:* "Israel Said to Approve $1.5 Billion Budget for Potential Strike on Iran," *Times of Israel*, October 19 2021, https://www.timesofisrael.com/israel-said-to-approve-1-5-billion-budget-for-potential-strike-on-iran/; Barak Ravid, "Israel Has the Capability to Strike Iran, Gantz Says," *Axios*, November 9, 2022, https://www.axios.com/2022/11/09/israel-capability-strike-iran-gantz.

258 *The IDF has ordered:* Dan Williams, "Eye on Iran, Israel to Buy Four Boeing Air Force Tankers For $927 Mln," Reuters, https://www.reuters.com/business

/aerospace-defense/boeing-says-israel-buy-four-air-force-refuelling-planes-927-mln-2022-09-01/; Anna Ahronheim, "Israeli Air Force to Fly New CH-53k Helicopter in 2026," July 7, 2022, https://www.jpost.com/israeli-news/article-711412; Jacob Magid and Staff, "$1 Billion in Iron Dome Funding Introduced in Congress as Separate Bill," September 23, 2021, https://www.timesofisrael.com/1-billion-in-iron-dome-funding-introduced-in-congress-as-separate-bill/.

258 *does not possess:* "Iran Military Power," Defense Intelligence Agency, 2019, https://www.dia.mil/Portals/110/Images/News/Military_Powers_Publications/Iran_Military_Power_LR.pdf.

258 *took delivery:* April Brady, "Russia Completes S-300 Delivery to Iran," Arms Control Association, https://www.armscontrol.org/act/2016-11/news-briefs/russia-completes-s-300-delivery-iran.

259 *moving forward:* "Iran to Buy Su-35 Fighter Jets from Russia—Iranian Broadcaster," Reuters, March 12, 2023, https://www.reuters.com/world/middle-east/iran-buy-su-35-fighter-jets-russia-iranian-broadcaster-2023-03-11/; Paul Iddon, "Is Iran Really About to Buy Russian Su-35 'Super Flanker' Fighter Jets?," *Forbes*, December 30, 2021, https://www.forbes.com/sites/pauliddon/2021/12/30/is-iran-really-about-to-buy-russian-su-35se-fighter-jets/?sh=a0f99ca204db.

259 *Iran is believed:* Gabriela Rosa Hernández, "Iran Supplies Arms to Russia," Arms Control Association, November 2022, https://www.armscontrol.org/act/2022-11/news/iran-supplies-arms-russia; Robble Gramer, "Iran Doubles Down on Arms for Russia," *Foreign Policy*, March 3, 2023, https://foreignpolicy.com/2023/03/03/russia-iran-drones-uav-ukraine-war-military-cooperation-sanctions/.

259 *much easier to hide:* Author interviews with former U.S. national security adviser John Bolton; former Israeli prime minister Ehud Barak, op-ed, *Yedioth Ahronoth* (Hebrew print edition), September 20, 2021.

259 *"make the assumption":* Author interviews with former Israeli military intelligence chief Amos Yadlin.

260 *would be restored:* Author interviews with Israeli and U.S. officials.

260 *important concessions:* Ibid.

261 *delaying a final agreement:* Ibid.

261 *major weapons supplier:* Patrick Wintour and Jennifer Rankin, "Iran Breaching Nuclear Deal by Providing Russia with Armed Drones, Says UK," *The Guardian*, October 17, 2022, https://www.theguardian.com/world/2022/oct/17/iran-breaching-nuclear-deal-by-providing-russia-with-armed-drones-says-uk; Yonah Jeremy Bob, "Will UN Action on Iranian Drones in Russia Kill JCPOA Negotiations?—Analysis," *Jerusalem Post*, December 20, 2022, https://www.jpost.com/middle-east/iran-news/article-725387.

261 *absolute key moment:* Author interview with Enrique Mora.

261 *a public dispute:* Author interviews with Israeli intelligence officials.

262 *"McDonald's in Iran":* Author interviews with Tamir Pardo.

262 *despite its faults:* Author interviews with former Israeli military intelligence chief Amos Yadlin.

262 *who opposed Trump's exit:* Author interviews with former U.S. national security adviser H. R. McMaster.

263 *"Mossad's promise":* B. Michael, "Opinion: What Was the Mossad Director Thinking?," *Haaretz*, December 9, 2021, https://www.haaretz.com/opinion/2021-12-09/ty-article-opinion/.premium/what-was-the-mossad-director-thinking/0000017f-e665-dea7-adff-f7ffe56e0000.

INDEX